The Pursuit
of the White House

The Pursuit
of the White House

*A Handbook of Presidential
Election Statistics and History*

G. Scott Thomas

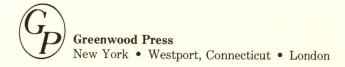

Greenwood Press
New York • Westport, Connecticut • London

Library of Congress Cataloging-in-Publication Data

Thomas, G. Scott.
 The pursuit of the White House.

 Bibliography: p.
 Includes index.
 1. Presidents—United States—Election—Statistics.
2. Presidents—United States—Election—History.
I. Title.
JK524.T44 1987   324.973'0021   87-11968
ISBN 0-313-25795-7 (lib. bdg. : alk. paper)

Library of Congress Catalog Card Number: 87-11968
ISBN: 0-313-25795-7

First published in 1987

Greenwood Press, Inc.
88 Post Road West, Westport, Connecticut 06881

Printed in the United States of America

The paper used in this book complies with the
Permanent Paper Standard issued by the National
Information Standards Organization (Z39.48-1984).

10 9 8 7 6 5 4 3 2

Contents

Preface

Thomas Dewey was a master of New York politics, but was unable to transfer his magic to the national level. His image was tarnished by three unsuccessful campaigns for the Presidency, particularly the complacent 1948 effort that resulted in his unexpected loss to Harry Truman. Dewey´s patience was strained, too. "I have learned from bitter experience," he wrote exasperatedly in 1954, "that Americans somehow regard a political campaign as a sporting event."

Presidential contests indeed contain all of the same elements that lure millions of spectators to stadiums annually. Both sports and politics offer high-stakes competition, whether in a World Series or a November election. Both rivet the national attention, as judged by the massive television audiences for championship games and election-night broadcasts alike. And both generate the lifeblood of America: statistics. Reams upon reams of statistics.

The sports fan is well served in his quest for numbers. Record books abound. But an avid spectator of Presidential campaigns, whether an historian, a political scientist, or a layman, is not as fortunate. Most reference works in this field present little more than an endless succession of charts of state-by-state and county-by-county returns from each election. Regional breakdowns for such contests cannot be found, nor the career records of Presidential candidates, nor summaries of the performances of political parties or states.

This book attempts to fill that void. The first six chapters summarize each of the fifty Presidential elections, and include tables that contain data for all major-party primaries and conventions, as well as the main contests in November. The final three chapters provide capsule profiles of the candidates, parties, and states that shaped the outcomes of those races. Each is accompanied by the relevant statistics.

How To Use This Book

This book includes statistical summaries of all fifty Presidential elections. It also presents the records of candidates, political parties, and states involved in those contests. The following definitions will help explain the charts and the terms and abbreviations used in them.

Periods. This book classes Presidential elections into six separate periods. Political parties and conditions in these eras had generally consistent characters. They are 1789-1816, 1820-1852, 1856-1900, 1904-1928, 1932-1956, and 1960-1984.

Regions. States are grouped into four regions.

East: Connecticut, Delaware, District of Columbia, Maine, Maryland, Massachusetts, New Hampshire, New Jersey, New York, Pennsylvania, Rhode Island, Vermont, West Virginia.

South: Alabama, Arkansas, Florida, Georgia, Kentucky, Louisiana, Mississippi, North Carolina, Oklahoma, South Carolina, Tennessee, Texas, Virginia.

Midwest: Illinois, Indiana, Iowa, Kansas, Michigan, Minnesota, Missouri, Nebraska, North Dakota, Ohio, South Dakota, Wisconsin.

West: Alaska, Arizona, California, Colorado, Hawaii, Idaho, Montana, Nevada, New Mexico, Oregon, Utah, Washington, Wyoming.

Some states participated in primaries and conventions while still territories and these results are included in the summaries for the appropriate regions. Territories that never attained statehood, such as Puerto Rico, are also included and their primary and convention statistics are listed in the columns under the heading "Other" in the relevant charts. For statistical purposes, the District of Columbia is considered a state.

Party abbreviations.   The following abbreviations are used to signify political parties:

AI: American Independent
AM: Anti-Masonic
A-W: American-Whig
CONST: Constitution
CU: Constitutional Union
D: Democratic
DR: Democratic-Republican
F: Federalist
F-L: Farmer-Labor
FS: Free Soil
GR: Greenback
I: Independent (When placed before a party label, it usually means the person received votes without being an announced candidate.)
LIB: Libertarian
LR: Liberal Republican
LTY: Liberty
NR: National Republican
NU: National Unity
P: Progressive
POP: Populist
PROH: Prohibition
R: Republican
SD: Southern Democratic
SOC: Socialist
SR: States´ Rights
SRD: States´ Rights Democratic
U: Union
W: Whig

Major parties.   The six political parties classified as major parties for statistical purposes are the Democratic, Democratic-Republican, Federalist, National Republican, Republican, and Whig parties.

Chapters 1-6

Each of the first six chapters tells the story of the campaigns of one of the six periods. At the end of each chapter, charts for the relevant primaries, conventions, and general elections are presented in chronological order.

Statistics for primaries and conventions are only given for major parties. For a specific year, the primary and convention charts for the party that eventually won the general election are presented first. They are followed by the primary and convention tables for the losing party, then the general election results.

Primaries.   To qualify for inclusion on a primary chart, a candidate must meet two statistical standards. He must have polled 3.95 percent or more of the popular vote cast in all of the party´s primaries that year and he must have received votes in at least two primaries. The latter provision eliminates purely "favorite son" candidacies. Candidates are listed from left to right in order of popular vote.

The following abbreviations are used in the primary charts:

W: the number of primaries won by each candidate, followed by totals in each region

W %:   the percentage of that year´s primaries won by each candidate **(Throughout this book, percentages have been figured to two decimal places, then rounded to one place for inclusion in charts.)**

PV: the total number of popular votes received by each candidate in all primaries

PV %: the percentage of the total popular vote secured by each candidate, followed by his or her percentage of the total vote in each region

Convention.   To qualify for inclusion on a convention chart, a candidate must have polled **4.00** percent or more of the total delegate vote cast on either the first ballot or, if there was more than one, on the last ballot. (A candidate whose percentage is below **4.00**, but which rounds to 4.0, is not considered to have met the necessary statistical standards.   For example, Andrew Johnson at the 1860 Democratic convention.)   The nominee is listed in the first column; the others follow from left to right in descending order of their first-ballot votes.

The abbreviations used in the convention charts are as follows:

FB: the number of delegate votes received by each candidate on the first ballot, followed by the totals in each region

FB %:   the percentage of the total vote cast for each candidate on the first ballot

LB: the results of the last ballot, if there was more than one (the number of that ballot is listed in parentheses), followed by the totals in each region

LB %:   the percentage of the total vote cast for each candidate on the last ballot

General.   To qualify for inclusion on a general-election chart, a candidate must meet either of two statistical standards. He must have received **1.95** percent or more of the total popular vote or have attracted two or more electoral votes.   (All who received one electoral vote are also included in general-election charts, but they are not considered to be "qualified" candidates for statistical purposes.)   The winner is given in the first column and the others follow from left to right in descending order of their electoral votes.

Under the double-ballot system employed from 1789 through 1800, electors cast two votes without specifying which was for President and which for Vice President. This book removes the consequent confusion by presenting the totals only for those candidates who were obviously running for the top office.

The abbreviations used on the general-election charts are as follows:

PV: the number of popular votes received by each candidate

PV %: the percentage of the total popular vote cast for each candidate, followed by his or her percentage of the total vote in each region

Counties: the number of counties in which the candidate received the largest number of popular votes

Counties %: the percentage of counties carried by each candidate

States: the number of states in which the candidate received the largest number of electoral votes (In the case of a tie in the county or state categories, neither candidate is given credit for the jurisdiction in which the tie occurred.)

States %: the percentage of states carried by each candidate

EV: the number of electoral votes received by each candidate, followed by totals in each region

EV %: the percentage of the total electoral vote cast for each candidate

Chapter 7

This chapter presents capsule profiles of all Presidential candidates, listed in alphabetical order. At the end of the chapter, each candidate's career record in pursuing the Presidency is included in chart form.

The information in parentheses following the candidate's name in the text is a listing of the years in which he reached qualification levels and the party labels he ran under. The years in parentheses next to the name in the chart section indicate that candidate's birth and death years.

To qualify for inclusion in this chapter, a person must have reached qualification levels in at least one year's primaries, convention, or general election. (Those who received one electoral vote are also listed.) Each candidate's entire record in Presidential politics is included, regardless of whether he met the qualification standards in each year.

Primaries. The party abbreviation is included next to the year. "(Q)" indicates that the candidate reached qualification levels in that year. An asterisk (*) indicates he received the highest total of popular votes of any of the contenders in his party's primaries that year.

Other abbreviations included in this section are as follows:

W: the number of primaries won in each year, with the next column to the right (%) giving the percentage of that year's primaries won by the candidate

PV: the number of popular votes received in primaries each year, with the next column to the right (%) giving the percentage of the total popular vote secured by the candidate

personal: the candidate's home state and his age (that is, the age that the candidate attained during the election year, whether before or after the election); this information is only listed once for each year

Career: the total of all lines for **W** and **PV**; the composite percentage of all years in which the candidate reached qualification levels for the two % columns (Confining percentages to "qualified" years provides a truer representation of a candidate's political strength through his career. Otherwise, his career percentages could be greatly reduced by including any years in which he received unsolicited write-ins in primaries or general elections, or a few throw-away votes at a convention, even though he was not actually a candidate that year.)

Convention. The party abbreviation is included next to the year. "(Q)" indicates the candidate reached qualification levels in that year. An asterisk (*) indicates that the candidate was the nominee.

FB: the number of delegate votes received on the first ballot at each convention, with the next column to the right (%) giving the percentage of the total first-ballot vote received by the candidate

LB: the number of delegate votes received on the last ballot at each convention, if there was more than one ballot, with the next column to the right (%) giving the percentage of the total last-ballot vote received by the candidate

Career: the total of all lines for **FB** and **LB**; the composite percentage of all years in which the candidate reached qualification levels for the two % columns

General. The party abbreviation is included next to the year. "(Q)" indicates the candidate reached qualification levels in that year. An asterisk (*) indicates that he was elected President.

PV: the number of popular votes received each year, with the next column to the right (%) giving the percentage of the total popular vote the candidate received in each year

EV: the number of electoral votes received each year, with the next column to the right (%) giving the percentage of the total electoral vote the candidate received in each year

Career: the total of <u>all</u> lines for **PV** and **EV**; the composite percentage of all years in which the candidate reached qualification levels for the two % columns

Chapter 8

This chapter profiles political parties. At the end of the chapter, statistical information about each party is included in chart form.

The years listed next to each party´s heading in the text are the first and last general elections in which its nominee reached qualification levels.

To qualify for inclusion in this chapter, a party must have had at least one nominee receive at least **1.95** percent or more of the popular vote <u>or</u> two or more electoral votes in a single election. (Parties that have received one electoral vote are also listed.) The parties are presented in alphabetical order.

The terms and abbreviations used in this section are as follows:

Elections: the total number of elections in which the party fielded a Presidential candidate

Qualified: the total number of general elections in which the party´s nominee reached qualification levels

W: the number of general elections won by the party´s nominee

PV: the number of popular votes received by all of the party´s nominees

PV % (Q):   the party´s composite percentage of the popular vote in those elections in which its nominees reached qualification levels

EV: the number of electoral votes received by all of the party´s nominees

EV % (Q):   the party´s composite percentage of the electoral vote in those elections in which its nominees reached qualification levels

Following these figures is a chart giving the party´s performance in each of the periods. **The full period is always listed on the left side, but that does not necessarily mean the party existed for the full period.** The same definitions pertain for **PV, PV % (Q), EV,** and **EV % (Q).**

Top PV, one year: the party´s nominee who received the highest number of popular votes in a single election

Top PV %, one year: the party´s nominee who received the highest percentage of the popular vote in a single election

Top EV, one year: the party´s nominee who received the highest number of electoral votes in a single election

Top EV %, one year: the party´s nominee who received the highest percentage of the electoral vote in a single election

Chapter 9

This chapter presents brief descriptions of each state´s role in Presidential politics. At the end of the chapter, each state´s voting record is presented in chart form. The states are listed in alphabetical order.

The information following the state´s heading in the text contains the region to which the state belongs and the year of the first Presidential election in which it participated.

The following terms and abbreviations also are used:

Winners: the number of Presidential elections in which each party carried all or the largest share of the state´s electoral votes

General Match: the number of times the state gave all or the largest share of its electoral votes to the candidate who won the national election, followed by the number of times it was carried by a national loser, and the state´s percentage of matching the national result

Convention Match: the state´s record in giving a plurality of its first-ballot votes at Democratic and Republican conventions to the candidates who are eventually nominated

Primary Match: the state´s record in giving the most popular votes in its Democratic and Republican primaries to the parties´ eventual nominees

County Sweeps: the number of general elections in which the nominee of one party won the largest share of popular votes in each of the state´s counties; the figures in parentheses indicate the parties of those who scored sweeps

PV %: the percentage of that state´s total popular vote in each period that was received by each major party; the abbreviation "DR/D" designates a combination of Democratic-Republican and Democratic votes during the period from 1820-1852; "NR/W" stands for the same for National Republican and Whig votes

EV: the number of that state´s electoral votes won by each major party in each period

Top PV %, one year: the candidate who received the highest percentage of the state´s popular vote in a single election

Top PV %, Democrat: the Democrat who received the highest percentage of the state´s popular vote in a single election

Top PV %, Republican: the Republican who received the highest percentage of the state´s popular vote in a single election

Top PV %, third party: the nominee of a minor or "third" party who received the highest percentage of the state´s popular vote in a single election

Home-State Candidates: the number of residents of that state who reached qualification levels in a single year´s primaries, convention, or general election, followed by the number of different years in which those persons reached that status (For example, ten different people from California have been candidates. Since some ran more than once, they reached that status 18 times.); each person´s candidacy in a given year counts for one in the "qualified" listing, regardless of whether the person met the necessary statistical levels that year in just one or all three possible categories (primaries, convention, general election)

Results: the number of times residents of a particular state won major-party nominations and general elections, followed by the total number of electoral votes received by all Presidential candidates from that state

Section 1.
The Elections

1.
All Republicans, All Federalists: 1789–1816

There were no political parties for the United States' first Presidential election in 1789. There was only one party after 1816. But the period in between was marked by some of the most vitriolic partisan debate in the nation's history. The Federalist and Democratic-Republican parties charged each other with unpatriotic alliances with foreign powers, secret designs to subvert the Constitution, and diabolical schemes for punishing their opponents.

There was no mention of parties in the Constitution. The Founding Fathers thought that a good thing. George Washington contended a party system "agitates the community with ill-founded jealousies and false alarms; kindles the animosity of one part against another; foments occasionally riot and insurrection."[1] Thomas Jefferson agreed. "If I could not go to heaven but with a party," he once said, "I would not go at all."[2] Even after factions appeared, Jefferson often tried to downplay their differences. He said all Americans should pull together: "We are all [Democratic-] Republicans, we are all Federalists."[3]

These high-minded declarations could not mask the depth of party feeling that quickly developed. It was Washington who, when asked his preference for his Vice President, said any "true Federalist" would do. Jefferson himself formed the Democratic-Republican party, once saying of the Federalists, "I wish...to see these people disarmed either of the wish or the power to injure their country."[4]

The Federalists won the first three elections of the period. But with the passing of the revered Washington, they entered a serious decline. The Democratic-Republicans took all elections from 1800 on. Their 1816 thrashing of the Federalists was so thorough that the opposition party disappeared. Jefferson's desire that all Americans be of one faction briefly came to pass.

The period of 1789-1816 allowed a testing of the

Electoral College. The original double-ballot system stipulated that each elector cast two votes without specifying which was for President and which for Vice President. The top two votegetters would be elected to the respective offices. The confused election of 1800 demonstrated the need for reform, soon provided by the 12th Amendment. In this and many other ways, the new Presidential selection process went through a shakedown during the first eight elections. Its designers were generally pleased with its performance. They even had cause to hope after 1816 that they were rid of those infernal parties.

ELECTION NO. 1:   1789

There was no need in 1789 for the trappings of Presidential elections that would become commonplace by the late 20th Century. Public opinion polls and computer projections would have been irrelevant. Even the most casual observers were certain George Washington would be sworn in as the first President.

Everyone but Washington, that is.

The man who commanded the Continental Army to triumph at Yorktown had no desire to leave semi-retirement at his beloved Mount Vernon. His mail was replete with pleas that he consent to his election. An ex-Governor of Maryland sounded a typical note, "We cannot, Sir, do without you, and I and thousands more can explain to anyone but yourself why..."[5]

Washington could not be persuaded to enthusiasm. He wrote just days before the formal counting of electoral votes, "My movements to the chair of government will be accompanied by feelings not unlike those of a culprit who is going to the place of his execution."[6] But when the time came, he went, cheered by thousands along the road from Mount Vernon to New York City.

The President-elect said his unanimous designation by the 69 electors left him no real choice other than to accept. But he harbored hopes that he wouldn't have to serve the full four-year term. He wrote one friend of his dream of "leaving to other hands the helm of the State, as soon as my services could possibly with propriety be dispensed with."[7] It would be longer than his worst fears.

ELECTION NO. 2:   1792

There was little that Alexander Hamilton and Thomas Jefferson agreed on. The Secretary of the Treasury was an economic nationalist who was the favorite of commercial interests. The Secretary of State believed in the sanctity of agrarian life, and condemned Hamilton's blueprints for a strong central government. But on one matter, the two rivals were wholeheartedly in agreement: George Washington must be convinced to accept a second term as President.

Washington was of a different mind. He argued privately

that his memory was slipping and his eyesight was deteriorating. He wanted to return to Mount Vernon while he could still enjoy it.

Hamilton and Jefferson indirectly provided a counterargument that forced Washington to spend another four years in Philadelphia. Their bickering had already produced the factionalism the President deplored, with Hamilton´s supporters becoming known as Federalists and Jefferson´s as Democratic-Republicans. Washington interceded, writing both, "How unfortunate and how much it is to be regretted...that internal dissensions should be harrowing and tearing our vitals."[8] Each man told Washington the other was to blame for the growing strife.

The President never made a public announcement, but he grudgingly decided to accept another term to protect the new government as much as possible from this political warfare. His unanimous re-election was routine.

ELECTION NO. 3:   1796

The familiar pressures were building on George Washington as the third Presidential election neared. John Jay was among those begging him to accept just one more term: "Remain with us at least while the storm lasts, and until you can retire like the sun in a calm, unclouded evening."[9]

But Washington had become a seasoned political meteorologist. He knew the skies might not clear until years past his death, a demise he did not want to face away from Mount Vernon. He felt eight years in office fulfilled any final obligation to his country, saying as much in his famous Farewell Address, "I have the consolation to believe that while choice and prudence invite me to quit the political scene, patriotism does not forbid it."[10] Thus did Washington unwittingly start the two-term tradition that would survive until America reached the dark threshold of World War II.

One New England Federalist likened publication of the Farewell Address to "a signal, like dropping a hat, for the party racers to start." The two factions were now full-fledged parties, right down to the requisite hatred of the other. The Democratic-Republicans charged that the Federalists were monarchists who planned to make political office hereditary, just as in Britain. The Federalists retorted that the Democratic-Republicans took their model from the other side of the Channel, scheming to institute an American version of the Reign of Terror that had recently rocked France.

Neither party had a formal process for nominating its candidate. Vice President John Adams was just one of a number of Federalist possibilities, but he was confident of being his party´s choice. He wrote his wife early in the year, "I am heir apparent, you know, and a succession is soon to take place."[11] He was eventually agreed upon by the party´s leaders, even though Alexander Hamilton encouraged a few Federalist electors to leave Adams off their ballots. He hoped in this manner to elevate Adams´ running mate, Thomas Pinckney, to the top job under the double-ballot system.

The Democratic-Republicans informally got behind their philosophical leader, Thomas Jefferson. But the Sage of Monticello didn´t show much enthusiasm. He wrote that his only desire was "to plant my corn, peas, etc., in hills or drills as I please...while our Eastern friends will be struggling with the storm which is gathering over us; perhaps be shipwrecked in it. This is certainly not a moment to covet the helm."[12]

Voting took place over a matter of months. It wasn´t until late December that Adams knew his Eastern base had allowed him to squeak through with a three-vote victory. But Jefferson also won office, the Vice Presidency. Hamilton´s machinations for Pinckney had triggered counter-measures by Adams´ supporters to reduce his running mate´s vote. The result was the only time in American history that members of opposing tickets were elected to the nation´s two highest offices.

ELECTION NO. 4:   1800

Perhaps the most amazing thing about the election of 1800 is that it led to the peaceful inauguration of a President on March 4, 1801. The country survived its most vituperative campaign to date, its first change in partisan control, and lengthy confusion resulting from the double-ballot system.

Thomas Jefferson, who was finally declared the winner just half-a-month before taking the oath, later fondly called the 1800 election "as real a revolution in the principles of our government as that of 1776 was in its form."[13] His overstatement was understandable after a campaign in which Federalists warned that Jefferson secretly planned to assemble an administration of atheistic "Jacobins" and the Democratic-Republicans accused President John Adams of laying the groundwork for a New World monarchy. Hyperbole was definitely in vogue in 1800.

The Federalists had no way of knowing, but their years in the American sun were ending. Thomas Jefferson had seen the approaching shadow four years earlier, predicting that the winner in 1796 would be forced to make tough, unpopular decisions. John Adams reaped the whirlwind. He reacted to growing tensions with France by bolstering the army and consenting to the Alien and Sedition Acts, designed to suppress the Democratic-Republican press. Both actions drew heavy criticism.

Adams also suffered from the growing split in his own party. Alexander Hamilton remained unenthusiastic about the Federalist Chief Executive. He wrote privately of Adams, "There are great intrinsic defects in his character, which unfit him for the office of chief magistrate."[14] The letter found its way into the newspapers late in the campaign.

This unrest among the public at large and in the

Federalist party gave Jefferson the break he needed to reverse the results of 1796. As Vice President, he presided over the official tabulation before Congress that showed him unseating the incumbent, 73-65. But Jefferson was unable to announce his own victory, since his running mate, Aaron Burr, had received 73 electoral votes, as well. The Democratic-Republican failure to properly manipulate the double-ballot system, to have one elector vote for someone other than Burr, threw the contest into the House of Representatives, where each state's delegation would have one vote.

Hamilton urged the Federalists, who held the balance of power, to vote for the leader of the opposition. "Jefferson is to be preferred," he counseled. "He is by far not so dangerous a man, and he has pretensions to character."[15] Jefferson himself saw little reason for worry after what he called Burr's "honorable and decisive" statement that he would not compete for the Presidency. But Burr didn't seem particularly displeased when Federalists ignored Hamilton and tied up the voting for a week. On roll call after roll call, eight states backed Jefferson, while six supported Burr and two abstained. Some Federalists boasted that they would prevent the Democratic-Republican succession by continuing the balloting past March 4.

This possible invitation to civil war was rebuffed only when Federalists from two states abandoned obstructionism on the thirty-sixth ballot. Jefferson was declared the winner, ten states to four. But he did not forget what a close call it had been. The 12th Amendment was put in place before the election of 1804, scrapping the double-ballot system and providing for separate voting in the Electoral College for President and Vice President.

ELECTION NO. 5:   1804

Thomas Jefferson entered 1804 a very popular President. He left it an easily reelected one.

Jefferson lowered taxes and reduced the national debt during his first term. He also fed the growing American belief in manifest destiny by arranging the Louisiana Purchase. Federalists could mount only a weak chorus of disapproval, noting sourly that the vast territory west of the Mississippi would someday yield new Democratic-Republican states. There was little Federalist sentiment west of the Appalachians.

Jefferson viewed the election of 1804 as a report card on this record. He wrote the Governor of Pennsylvania early in the year, "The abominable slanders of my political enemies have obliged me to call for that verdict from my country in the only way it can be obtained."[16]

Even the Federalists seemed to have little doubt of the outcome. The party's nominee, Charles Cotesworth Pinckney, confined himself to public condemnations of dueling, avoiding other issues. Pinckney's good friend, Alexander Hamilton, had been slain by Vice President Aaron Burr in a duel in

July.

Jefferson carried all but two states in the resulting landslide. He looked with approval on the declining fortunes of his long-time enemies, the Federalists, optimistically writing a friend in France, "The two parties which prevailed with so much violence when you were here, are almost wholly melted into one."[17]

ELECTION NO. 6:   1808

The Democratic-Republicans had long accused the Federalist party of desiring an American monarchy, planning to retire the ballot boxes that had been in use since the separation from Britain. But in 1808, the argument turned. Federalists began to moan about the "Virginia Dynasty," charging that Democratic-Republicans from the Old Dominion had worked out their own line of succession. Some suggested it was a form of electoral monarchy.

President Thomas Jefferson, a Virginian, decided not to seek a third term. He privately hoped to be succeeded by Secretary of State James Madison, also a Virginian. Madison easily won the Democratic-Republican endorsement in a caucus of the party's members of Congress. That seemed sufficient to continue the dynasty, except the caucus losers didn't agree.

Vice President George Clinton and former Minister to Britain James Monroe were angry, and each decided to stay in the race to the end. Clinton argued that his home state of New York, powerful in its own right, should not continually have to take a back seat to Virginia. Monroe felt slighted because Jefferson and Madison pigeonholed a treaty he had negotiated with England. They said it ignored the growing problem of British impressment of American seamen.

Federalists took heart from the Democratic-Republican fissures. They also expected to benefit from popular dissatisfaction with an embargo instituted in late 1807 to cut off virtually all trade with foreign nations. Designed to keep the United States safely out of the war between England and France, it also placed a heavy economic burden on shipping communities, particularly in Federalist New England.

Charles Cotesworth Pinckney was again nominated by an informal meeting of Federalist leaders. He pledged to make a stronger fight than he had in 1804, announcing his aim "to show that Federalism is not extinct, and that there is in the Union a formidable party of the old Washingtonian school."[18] It soon became evident that this resurgent Federalism was pulling support away from the dissident Democratic-Republicans. Monroe disappeared from view. Clinton was able to garner only six electoral votes.

James Madison remained at his post in the State Department through the campaign. He was helped by Congressional debate on foreign policy that led to the publication of diplomatic correspondence. Madison was shown to be taking a hard line with Britain on impressment, further increasing his popularity.

Pinckney managed to regain much of the Eastern Federalist support that had slipped away four years earlier. But the superior organization and larger base of the Democratic-Republicans were the telling factors in Madison´s 122-47 win. The dynasty lived on.

ELECTION NO. 7:   1812

James Madison was the first of three Presidents to seek reelection in wartime. He was successful, as Abraham Lincoln and Franklin Roosevelt later would be, but it was the tightest squeeze for the Democratic-Republicans since they took power in 1800.

New figures on the national scene had helped stir up the sentiment that led to declaration of the War of 1812 in June. Henry Clay and John Calhoun were among the leading "War Hawks." But not all Americans supported the war with Britain. It was particularly unpopular in the Federalist stronghold of New England.

Madison was unanimously renominated by the Democratic-Republican caucus, but party members in the New York legislature dissented. They nominated New York City Mayor DeWitt Clinton, nephew of the late Vice President George Clinton. The national Federalist party did not endorse a candidate, but some state Federalist organizations backed a coalition with Clinton.

The American surrender of Detroit in August symbolized the early failures that led to public grumbling about "Mr. Madison´s War." Clinton seized on the discontent in New England with literature that posed a simple choice: "Madison and War! or Clinton and Peace!" But he sounded a considerably different note in pro-war Southern and Midwestern states. Pamphlets distributed in those areas promised that the war "shall be prosecuted till every object shall be attained for which we fight."

This straddle allowed Clinton to mount a formidable challenge to the incumbent. Madison did nothing in response. Charles Ingersoll, who was later to take some liberty with history by dubbing the President "the father of the Constitution," noted of Madison, "While a candidate for the Presidency, no one, however intimate, ever heard him open his lips or say one word on the subject."[19]

Madison swept the South and Midwest to claim the victory. But Clinton´s strong showing in the East kept the final margin at a fairly tight 128-89. It was obvious that if the War of 1812 continued to go badly, the Federalists might enter 1816 with an excellent chance to regain the glory that had once been theirs.

ELECTION NO. 8:   1816

History played a cruel trick on the Federalist party before the election of 1816. The War of 1812, consistently marked by American reversals, ended with stunning victories on Lake Champlain and in General Andrew Jackson's famous stand at New Orleans. Although the peace treaty gave the United States none of the Canadian territory it had been seeking, it also conceded no existing American land. The popular perception was that the Democratic-Republicans had directed a successful confrontation with an Old World power.

The Federalists were also stung by their association with the Hartford Convention. Delegates from New England states met in secret to draw up a list of proposed Constitutional amendments to curtail the power of the federal government. The meeting endorsed states' rights measures that also had appeal in the South, but in the wave of post-New Orleans nationalism, it was popularly portrayed as a gathering of Federalist traitors.

The Democratic-Republican endorsement was considered in such a climate to be tantamount to election. President James Madison privately favored the elevation of a fellow Virginian, Secretary of State James Monroe. But Secretary of the Treasury William Crawford was much more popular with the rank-and-file than was the drab Monroe. And Crawford, a Georgian, knew he benefited from another factor. He confessed, "If Monroe belonged to any other state...there would be no other candidate spoken of."[20]

Crawford decided he was young enough to wait in line behind Monroe. He declined to lend his name to the battle against the "Virginia Dynasty," but his supporters offered him as a candidate, anyway. Monroe won a narrow vote in the Democratic-Republican caucus, 65-54. Crawford grumbled that the close vote might hurt his future prospects. He said he had "serious cause of complaint against my particular friends."

The Federalists put forward Senator Rufus King of New York, but he never expected to win. King said of Monroe that he "had the zealous support of nobody, and he was exempt from the hostility of everybody."[21] That was sufficient in 1816.

President-elect Monroe saw his victory as a possible end to partisan factionalism. He said privately that the "existence of parties is not necessary to free government" and he hoped they would fade to oblivion during his administration. The Federalists obliged, never again running a national campaign. Rufus King told a friend, "Federalists of our age must be content with the past."[22]

Charts for Chapter 1

1789 General Election

	George Washington (F)
PV	----
PV %	----
States	10
States %	100.0
EV	69
East	47
South	22
Midwest	----
West	----
EV %	100.0

1792 General Election

	George Washington (F)
PV	----
PV %	----
States	15
States %	100.0
EV	132
East	83
South	49
Midwest	----
West	----
EV %	100.0

1796 General Election

	John Adams (F)	Thomas Jefferson (DR)
PV	----	----
PV %	----	----
States	9	7
States %	56.3	43.8
EV	71	68
East	69	18
South	2	50
Midwest	----	----
West	----	----
EV %	51.4	49.3

Note: Under the double-ballot electoral system then used, at least one Maryland elector voted for both Adams and Jefferson. Their EV % totals consequently add to more than 100.0.

1800 General Election

	Thomas Jefferson (DR)	John Adams (F)
PV	----	----
PV %	----	----
States	8	7
States %	50.0	43.8
EV	73	65
East	25	61
South	48	4
Midwest	----	----
West	----	----
EV %	52.9	47.1

Notes: 1. Jefferson and Adams tied in one state.   2. Although Jefferson secured an electoral majority over Adams, he tied under the double-ballot system with his running mate, Aaron Burr.   The House of Representatives elected Jefferson on its 36th ballot.   Burr became Vice President.

1804 General Election

	Thomas Jefferson (DR)	Charles Cotesworth Pinckney (F)
PV	----	----
PV %	----	----
States	15	2
States %	88.2	11.8
EV	162	14
East	92	14
South	67	0
Midwest	3	0
West	----	----
EV %	92.0	8.0

1808 General Election

	James Madison (DR)	Charles Cotesworth Pinckney (F)	George Clinton (IDR)
PV	----	----	----
PV %	----	----	----
States	12	5	0
States %	70.6	29.4	0.0
EV	122	47	6
East	56	44	6
South	63	3	0
Midwest	3	0	0
West	----	----	----
EV %	69.7	26.9	3.4

1812 General Election

	James Madison (DR)	DeWitt Clinton (F-IDR)
PV	----	----
PV %	----	----
States	11	7
States %	61.1	38.9
EV	128	89
East	39	89
South	82	0
Midwest	7	0
West	----	----
EV %	59.0	41.0

1816 General Election

	James Monroe (DR)	Rufus King (F)
PV	----	----
PV %	----	----
States	16	3
States %	84.2	15.8
EV	183	34
East	90	34
South	82	0
Midwest	11	0
West	----	----
EV %	84.3	15.7

2.
The Coming of Democracy: 1820–1852

The Founding Fathers believed in letting the people rule, within reason. The Electoral College was a perfect case in point. Voters, usually white men who owned property, chose their state legislatures, which in turn picked the electors, who then designated a President. Virginia's George Mason spoke for the elite who felt a more democratic system would be dangerous, "It would be unnatural to refer the choice of a proper character for chief Magistrate to the people as it would to refer a trial of colours to a blind man."[1]

Mason's views became less popular as America expanded westward. Men helping to build a new country wanted more say in how it was run. Property qualifications for voting were dropped. Some states began allowing direct balloting for electors. The practice became sufficiently common that meaningful popular-vote totals were first tabulated in 1824.

The rise of the common man prompted a change in political tactics. Parades, barbecues, songs, and slogans became typical electioneering tools in the period of 1820-1852. The leading popular hero of the age, Andrew Jackson, swept to victory with their use in 1828. The Whigs improved his techniques with their celebrated win in 1840. The Founders would have watched the ubiquitous torchlight parades with dismay, but one observer, Michael Chevalier, found them "the episodes of a wondrous epic which will bequeath a lasting memory to posterity, that of the coming of democracy."[2]

Political parties also changed with the times. The Democratic-Republican party split into the Democratic and National Republican parties. The latter eventually dissolved into a new coalition, the Whigs. The Democrats won four of the period's nine elections, the Democratic-Republicans three, the Whigs two. Caucuses vanished in the realignment. All parties came to use conventions to choose their Presidential nominees.

Sectional questions became prominent in this period: slavery in Missouri was an issue in 1820, South Carolina and nullification were of interest in 1832, the annexation of Texas dominated the 1844 race. Compromise was the rule, with the two great Congressional agreements of 1820 and 1850 nearly bracketing the period. The Whig party did its own balancing act. It managed to survive despite containing powerful pro- and anti-slavery factions.

It was popular during the 1852 campaign to speak of the "finality" of the Compromise of 1850. The slavery question was settled. Peace was assured. But a scheme brewing in the mind of an Illinois Senator, Stephen Douglas, would unleash a firestorm. The Whigs could not survive after the resurgence of sectional feeling, nor could the spirit of compromise. America found itself on the road to civil war.

ELECTION NO. 9:   1820

It is popular to call the Monroe Administration "the Era of Good Feelings," but a more apt label might be "the Era of Apathy."

Debate over the admission of Missouri as a slave state raged into the spring of 1820. The Missouri Compromise finally deferred the thorny issue of slavery to the next generation. A national banking crisis was a more important matter to most Americans. Banks failed, land values plummeted, and thousands lost their jobs.

The surprise is that President James Monroe was elected under such volatile conditions without formal opposition. No one could mobilize against him. The Federalist party existed only on the local level in some Eastern states. Other leading Democratic-Republicans were already jockeying for position for the election of 1824.

The political apathy was best demonstrated by the caucus called to formally renominate Monroe. Not enough members of Congress even bothered to show, so no endorsement was ever given. Monroe's unanimous election was already conceded anyway, but one New Hampshire elector slightly roused the public by voting for John Quincy Adams. The myth is that William Plumer wanted to reserve the honor of unanimity for George Washington. Plumer actually disliked Monroe, contending the President suffered from "a want of foresight and economy." It was a rare strong stand in a lifeless election.

ELECTION NO. 10:   1824

William Crawford had waited eight years. James Monroe was finally leaving the White House, so it was Crawford's turn, his reward for not encouraging the opposition to Monroe in 1816.

But it didn't work that way.

Other contenders formally entered the race as early as 1821. John Quincy Adams, Henry Clay, and Andrew Jackson made it clear they would not accept the dictate of the Democratic-Republican caucus. A Baltimore newspaper ridiculed the caucus system, comparing it to a pullet, "The sickly thing is to be fed, cherished, pampered for a week, when it is fondly hoped it will be enabled to cry the name of Crawford, Crawford, Crawford."[3] The caucus did endorse Crawford, but it was an empty honor. Three-quarters of the members boycotted. "King Caucus" was, for all intents and purposes, dead.

There were serious questions about Crawford's health by the time of his formal nomination. The Secretary of the Treasury had suffered a stroke in late 1823, then was hit with a relapse in May. His supporters tried to cover up his condition, but it became known that Crawford was paralyzed and almost blind. His recovery in the fall was slow and incomplete.

The three challengers each had a base from which to frustrate Crawford's long-held hopes. Adams was Secretary of State, the position that launched Madison and Monroe. Clay was the Speaker of the House of Representatives, the favorite of trans-Appalachia for his advocacy of canal and road building. Jackson would always be the Hero of New Orleans. Although a lawyer and a slaveholder, he was gaining a reputation as a man of the people. That was an important distinction in this first election with widespread popular voting.

The biggest surprise in 1824 was Jackson's rise. The other candidates did not at first consider him a serious contender. Adams mused that he might ask the General to be his running mate, saying "it will afford an easy and dignified retirement to his old age."[4] But by fall, Jackson seemed in position to offer the same favor to Adams. Clay grumped as he saw his Southern and Midwestern support drain to Old Hickory, "I cannot believe that killing 2,500 Englishmen at New Orleans qualifies for the various, difficult, and complicated duties of the Chief Magistracy."[5]

Jackson led the popular and electoral vote counts, but was well short of a majority. It was up to the House to choose from between the top three finishers: Jackson, Adams, and Crawford. Each maneuvered to get Clay's backing. The Speaker was not fond of Adams, but thought Crawford's illness and Jackson's military background disqualified them. Clay was influential in swinging the House to the Secretary of State on its first ballot: Adams 13 states, Jackson seven, Crawford four.

What happened next changed American political history for a generation. Adams named Clay his Secretary of State; in effect, putting him first in the informal line of succession. Jackson fumed, "So you see, the Judas of the West has closed the contract and will receive the thirty pieces of silver. His end will be the same. Was there ever witnessed such a barefaced corruption in any country before?"[6] Clay denied there had been any bargain, but Martin

Van Buren astutely noted that his acceptance of a Cabinet position was "Mr. Clay´s political death warrant."[7]

Of more immediate importance, Andrew Jackson swore to pay back Adams and Clay. He immediately began plotting for revenge in 1828.

ELECTION NO. 11:   1828

The campaign of 1828 began even before John Quincy Adams recited the oath of office in 1825. Supporters of Andrew Jackson sang their refrain of "corrupt bargain" from the moment Henry Clay was named Secretary of State. Clay heatedly denied the post was a payoff for his support of Adams when the House of Representatives decided the 1824 election, but the Jacksonians would not be convinced.

The Tennessee legislature nominated Jackson in 1825 for his revenge bid; the caucus system was dead. Old Hickory spent the next four years remaking the Democratic-Republican party in his image. Vice President John Calhoun, seeing his way to the top blocked by Clay, swung his Southern supporters into Jackson´s camp. Senator Martin Van Buren of New York brought in the powerful Albany Regency, as well as others who had supported William Crawford´s 1824 bid.

The Adams-Clay coalition, believing in a strong federal government, split from this states´ rights Democratic-Republican party. Administration supporters became known as National Republicans.

The 1828 campaign was not only one of the longest in American history, it was one of the bitterest. No real issues emerged. The Democratic-Republicans persistently condemned the "theft" of their hero´s victory in 1824. They also portrayed Adams as a cold-hearted enemy of the common man. One Democratic-Republican journal sputtered, "It is rumored that it is the intention of Mr. Adams to return to England, there to purchase a PATENT OF NOBILITY."[8]

The National Republican campaign fell to Clay to coordinate. Adams sniffed, "I write no letters upon what is called politics -- that is electioneering."[9] He refused to employ patronage to generate loyalty to his administration. The Jacksonians were using parades, barbecues, and Hickory Clubs to stir up the masses. Even though all but two states now had popular voting, Adams declined to follow suit. The National Republicans were not deficient in mudslinging, however. A party paper alleged, "General Jackson spent the prime of his life in gambling, in cock-fighting, in horse racing, and has all his life been a most bloody duelist; and to cap all his frailties, he tore from a husband the wife of his bosom, to whom he had been for some years united in the holy state of matrimony."[10]

Even Adams expected Jackson´s victory, but not its depth. Old Hickory ran up the highest popular-vote percentage of the 19th Century. He swept the South and Midwest, while faring well in Adams´ native East. The crowds

that swarmed the White House on inauguration day were
testimony to a revolution in American politics. Elections
would no longer be decided solely by the elite who constituted the Electoral College. The people would henceforth
have their say.

ELECTION NO. 12: 1832

The battle lines for the 1832 election were firmly drawn on
July 10. President Andrew Jackson that day vetoed a bill to
allow the recharter of the Second Bank of the United States.
Jackson confided to his running mate, Martin Van Buren, that
the issue was simple. "The bank, Mr. Van Buren, is trying to
kill me," he declared, "but I will kill it!"[11]

The Second Bank was chartered in 1816. Government money
was deposited there and the Bank issued notes that helped
bring some organization to American currency. The National
Republican party, favored by the nation´s business interests,
called the Second Bank "this great and beneficial
institution."

But the Jacksonians, now known as Democrats, viewed the
Bank as a tool of the Eastern elite. The President thundered
in his veto message, "It is easy to conceive that great evils
to our country and its institutions might flow from such a
concentration of power in the hands of a few men
irresponsible to the people."[12] The issue, then, was not
economic. The question in the President´s mind was who
would rule: Jackson or businessmen?

Henry Clay had urged the head of the Second Bank,
Nicholas Biddle, to seek recharter four years before the 1836
expiration. He assured Biddle that Jackson would be less
likely to hand down a veto in an election year. That
miscalculation did not upset his plans. Clay decided to make
the Bank veto the cornerstone issue of his campaign to return
the National Republicans to power.

A third party complicated Clay´s task by splitting the
potential anti-Jackson vote. The Anti-Masonic party had
risen in New York in the 1820s as an opponent of privilege,
particularly Freemasonry. The party gained supporters
throughout the East. Many met in Baltimore in 1831 for the
nation´s first nominating convention. Former Attorney
General William Wirt was the unusual choice of this
gathering: unusual in that he had once been a Mason and
still called the supposedly evil organization "nothing more
than a social and charitable club."

The two major parties followed with conventions of their
own, ratifying the commonly expected choices of Clay and
Jackson. The Democrats planted a delayed-action bomb by
deciding to require a two-thirds vote for the Vice
Presidential nomination. Martin Van Buren was chosen to
replace South Carolina´s John Calhoun, who had fallen badly
out of favor with the President. Van Buren would later have
cause to regret the two-thirds rule, though it seemed
innocent at the time.

The National Republicans mounted a large-scale effort to dethrone the man they scorned as King Andrew I. Nicholas Biddle lashed at Jackson's veto as "a manifesto of anarchy." The Bank spent an estimated $100,000 to help Clay's cause. Biddle found Jackson's veto message so absurd that he paid to distribute 30,000 copies. It backfired. Average Americans actually found the President's defiance of the elite thrilling.

The opposition also underestimated the strength of Jackson's popular appeal and his political organization. Old Hickory rolled to a landslide victory in both popular and electoral votes. It was especially sweet that he had now trounced both Adams and Clay, the men he held responsible for the "corrupt bargain" that he blamed for his loss in 1824.

The opposition carried only eight of the 24 states, South Carolina supporting Virginia Governor John Floyd to dramatize its defiance of Jackson. William Wirt studied the returns, then spoke resignedly of the victor, "My opinion is that he may be President for life if he chooses."[13]

ELECTION NO. 13:   1836

Andrew Jackson willingly followed the two-term tradition, refusing to seek reelection in 1836, but he was still the leading figure in that year's campaign.

Jackson chose both members of the Democratic ticket, then brought his iron will to bear, imposing his selections on the party's convention. Not everyone was happy. Southerners suspected Presidential nominee Martin Van Buren of being a secret abolitionist. Vice Presidential candidate Richard Johnson was even worse in Southern eyes. The Congressman from Kentucky had two daughters by his late mulatto mistress.

President Jackson dismissed the critics as disunionists and tools of the Second Bank of the United States, whose federal charter expired in 1836. A grateful Van Buren promised to "endeavor to tread generally in the footsteps of President Jackson -- happy if I shall be able to perfect the work he has so gloriously begun."[14]

Such glory was scarcely evident to Jackson's large and extremely vocal group of enemies. The opposition had been divided in 1832, but its disparate elements drew together uneasily in the ensuing four years. The National Republicans, Anti-Masons, and anti-Jackson Democrats led by John Calhoun combined to form the Whig party.

The Whigs took their name from the British party that had opposed royal despotism. The parallel was hardly subtle, and its object, Jackson, charged it was badly aimed. He accused the Whigs of plotting to "build up a colossal monied power to corrupt and overshadow the government." But it was soon obvious such conniving was well beyond the Whigs. They couldn't even agree on a candidate, deciding not to hold a

convention that might split their fragile coalition. Three
Whigs eventually entered the field: former General William
Henry Harrison in the North, Massachusetts Senator Daniel
Webster in his home state, and Tennessee Senator Hugh White
in the South. A fourth party member, Senator Willie Person
Mangum of North Carolina, did not run, but received the
electoral votes of South Carolina.

The Democrats were most concerned about White, a former
friend of Jackson's who stood to benefit from Southern
antagonism toward the Democratic ticket. Van Buren wrote
exasperatedly to one Southerner, "God knows I have suffered
enough for my Southern partialities as the apologist of
Southern institutions and now forsooth you good people will
have it...that I am an abolitionist."[15] The problem turned
out to be smaller than feared, as White carried only two
Southern states.

Harrison surprised everyone with his growing
popularity. Old Tippecanoe took seven states, at least one
in each region. But Jackson's loyal supporters generally
stuck with Van Buren, and the large Democratic edge in
organization clinched his victory. His running mate was not
as lucky. Virginia withheld its electoral votes in the
interest of racial purity, thereby denying Johnson a
majority. The Vice Presidential election was thrown into the
Senate for the only time. Johnson there secured the votes to
be named Van Buren's understudy.

A Whig newspaper had complained early in the year, "We
desire a candidate who will concentrate all our suffrage and
we desire what is impossible."[16] The election returns showed
that the impossible was also the necessary. The Whigs had
demonstrated national appeal by winning eleven states but
they were split among four men. The party lacked the
cohesion that could allow it to break the Democratic
stranglehold on the White House.

ELECTION NO. 14: 1840

It became fashionable in the late 20th Century to bemoan the
deteriorating quality of Presidential campaigns: the
proliferation of meaningless slogans, staged media events,
and issue-dodging candidates. Those who considered such
problems recent developments simply didn't know their
history. The election of 1840 reached depths that perhaps
have been unplumbed by even the television generation.

The Whig party had learned from its maiden defeat in
1836. Its leaders sought to avoid any controversy that might
destroy their jury-rigged political craft holding both
Northern abolitionists and Southern slaveholders. The answer
was to nominate someone whose philosophy was unknown and then
promote him with a thoroughly cosmetic campaign.

Henry Clay was the acknowledged frontrunner for the Whig
nomination, but he definitely didn't fit the prescription.
The Senator from Kentucky was a two-time Presidential loser
who was well associated with the "corrupt bargain" of 1824

and the Bank fight of 1832, hardly noncontroversial stuff. Two military men, William Henry Harrison and Winfield Scott, seemed better bets. Harrison won on an unspecified ballot during secret voting at the Whig convention.

Clay moaned, "I am the most unfortunate man in the history of parties: always run by my friends when sure to be defeated, and now betrayed for a nomination when I, or any one, would be sure of an election."[17] Some Clay supporters took the defeat even harder. Former Senator John Tyler of Virginia was reportedly seen crying on the convention floor. The power brokers chose him as Harrison's running mate to appease the Clay forces, even though Tyler's states' rights philosophy was not shared by most Whigs.

The United States languished in a depression in 1840, boosting Whig hopes of unseating President Martin Van Buren, whom they chided as "Martin Van Ruin." But the President still held the reins of the Democratic party tightly. His renomination was unanimous.

Democratic contempt for the Whig standard-bearer was unalloyed. Asked about Harrison's ability, Missouri Senator Thomas Hart Benton said he had only one: "availability." Harrison's positions on the issues were largely unknown despite his candidacy in 1836, causing many Democrats to label him "General Mum." One Democratic paper smugly suggested that all the hero of the battle of Tippecanoe really wanted was a pension, a barrel of hard cider, and a log cabin. The delighted Whigs began distributing cider at their rallies, often held in log cabins. The Democratic jibe had played right into their efforts to portray Harrison, who lived on a massive estate in Ohio, as a man of the people.

Harrison supporters effectively turned the tables. They accused President Van Buren of living in isolation in an expensively renovated White House while thousands starved in depression-wracked America. Henry Clay, back on the Whig bandwagon, called the election a battle "between the log cabin and the palace, between hard cider and champagne."[18] Van Buren had actually spent less than $3,000 to fix up the Executive Mansion.

Perhaps the best-remembered legacies of the 1840 campaign were its slogans. Whigs chanted, "Van, Van, is a used-up man," while rolling ten-foot Whig balls through city streets. The English language thus gained the expression, "Keep the ball rolling," from the Harrisonites. Those same Whigs proclaimed undying loyalty to "Tippecanoe and Tyler, Too," while marching in a seemingly endless series of torchlight parades.

The Democrats watched the groundswell of Whig fever with a mixture of disdain and dismay. "Men whose brains are muddled at the Tippecanoe Clubs with drinking hard cider can neither reason or understand reason," complained one Democratic paper. "But they can shout, and they feel a strong propensity to lift up their voices."[19]

Those voices were solidly heard at the ballot box.

Americans reeling from economic hard times tossed Martin Van Buren out of the White House by nearly a 4-1 margin in electoral votes. Old Tippecanoe rode to Washington to rescue the country, but scarcely a month after his inauguration, he died of pneumonia. He was returned to Ohio for burial in June, while the Whigs began to discover that the tail half of "Tippecanoe and Tyler, Too," did not share most of their aims. The masterful, but vacuous, Whig campaign of 1840 had ironically ended in another defeat.

ELECTION NO. 15: 1844

Martin Van Buren and Henry Clay entered 1844 fully expecting to oppose each other for the Presidency that fall. They had met in Kentucky two years earlier, already anticipating the battle. There were rumors the two warhorses had set friendly guidelines for their contest. Neither, for example, would publicly discuss the possible annexation of Texas.

That proved an impossible promise to keep, thanks to the ambition of President John Tyler. Tyler was officially read out of the Whig party by its Congressional caucus for what it considered his political heresy. Democrats largely already committed to Van Buren showed scant interest in Tyler's future. That left the President one hope for a second term: formation of a new national party. What he needed was an issue. The best seemed to be Texas.

Tyler consequently began secret efforts to secure an annexation treaty with the Republic of Texas. He unveiled the finished product in April, deftly upsetting the calculations of politicians across the country. Clay and Van Buren hastened to condemn annexation, a classic case of misreading the national mood. No immediate damage was done to Clay's campaign. It was widely accepted that after his convention loss in 1840, he deserved the 1844 Whig nomination. He was unanimously chosen on the first ballot.

It was a different story for the New Yorker whose political skills had earned him the nickname of "The Little Magician." Van Buren's declaration that he opposed annexation as long as it might lead to war with Mexico cost him the support of his patron. Andrew Jackson said under the new circumstances, "The candidate for the first office should be an annexation man, and from the Southwest."[20] Jackson suggested one startling possibility, former Tennessee Governor and Congressman James Polk.

Van Buren complained about "the opposition and persecution to which I have been exposed" as he watched his near-certain nomination drift away.[21] Almost all of his Southern supporters defected, wishing the quick addition of Texas as a new slave state. Van Buren dueled annexation supporter Lewis Cass, a former Secretary of War, through the early convention ballots. The stampede to Polk came on the ninth ballot, when Van Buren's New York delegation gave up the fight and switched to the dark horse. Polk's platform included calls for the annexation of all of Texas and Oregon. On the latter, it raised the cry, "54° 40´ or fight!"

Nomination of a pro-annexation Democrat seemed to head off Tyler's chances, but he went forward with his planning for a fall campaign. Jackson personally handled the negotiations to secure the President's withdrawal. When Tyler complained about the insults he was receiving from Democratic newspapers, Jackson went so far as to write an editor, "I pray you to desist from the abuse of Tyler or his supporters, but treat them as brethren in democracy."[22] That was sufficient to secure a brotherly pullout in late August.

Another candidate would figure prominently in the final balloting. James Birney was again the nominee of the antislavery Liberty party. He polled only 6,797 votes in 1840, but the Texas issue had stirred up abolition sentiment. The pool of potential Liberty voters was much bigger in 1844.

The Democrats stood unambiguously for annexation through the fall, even after the Senate had defeated Tyler's first treaty. Clay sensed the political error of his original stand and began a lengthy waffle that brought scorn from both sides. He had said in April that he opposed annexation "at this time," alarming the Southern wing of the party. His July endorsement of Texas statehood "without national dishonor, without war," alienated Northern Whigs who abhorred slavery. Some decided to vote the Liberty ticket, even though Clay switched back by late September to condemning annexation.

Polk's margin in the Electoral College was substantial, 65 votes, but it was more fragile than it appeared. A turnaround of 2,554 popular votes in New York would have given the state, and the election, to Clay. Birney's Liberty ticket polled more than 16,000 votes in New York.

Polk quickly made it clear that he would not go through another such experience. He announced his "settled purpose" of serving only one term. But Henry Clay still had the bug. He soon pointed out in a letter, "I have never said that I would nor would not be a candidate at the next election."[23] From such a quadrennial campaigner, it was almost as good as an announcement.

ELECTION NO. 16: 1848

The dominant issue of the 1844 campaign was buried by the time the 1848 election rolled around. But the specter of Texas was still prominent. The Lone Star State was part of the vast territory added to the United States in the previous four years. The treaty that ended the Mexican War was signed in February, combining with the acquisition of Oregon to stretch the country to the Pacific Coast.

The Whigs, whose only electoral success came when they ran a war hero, moved quickly to cash in on the American battlefield successes. They approached the two leading generals of the Mexican campaign, Zachary Taylor and Winfield

Scott. Taylor said the idea of his running for President "never entered my head, nor is it likely to enter the head of any sane person."[24]

But Whig leaders were eminently sane. The three major contenders for their nomination had all lost previous Presidential bids. Scott, Daniel Webster, and the ever-present Henry Clay were all too well-known. All had powerful enemies within the fragile Whig coalition. Taylor was an appealing exception: popularly hailed, but still unknown. He was nominated on the convention's fourth ballot. The Louisianan's ticket was balanced with a truly obscure Vice Presidential candidate from the North, New York Comptroller Millard Fillmore.

President James Polk adhered to his pledge to refuse reelection. That opened the way for a three-way battle for the Democratic nomination. Michigan Senator Lewis Cass combined his healthy Midwestern base with strong Southern popularity. He ousted his two challengers from the East, Secretary of State James Buchanan and Supreme Court Justice Levi Woodbury, on the fourth ballot.

The seeds of Cass' eventual destruction were also scattered at that convention. New York Democrats aligned with Martin Van Buren, known as Barnburners, vented their frustration by stalking out. The Barnburners were angry that President Polk had shortchanged them on patronage. They also opposed extension of slavery to new territories, and felt Cass would allow it. The Van Buren faction marched off to Buffalo, where it formed the Free Soil party and nominated its hero for President. Most supporters of the Liberty party joined the Free Soilers.

The fire that would light the fuse at Fort Sumter in thirteen years was already aglow, fanned by the dispute over whether slaves should be allowed on former Mexican lands. Cass said the question must be decided by those living in the territories. He was the first to articulate this concept of "popular sovereignty," based on his years as Territorial Governor of Michigan. Cass said, "My doctrine is simply the doctrine of our revolutionary fathers."[25] But the Free Soilers called it immoral and many Southerners felt it was not revolutionary enough.

Taylor's position on slavery was dimly known. Southerners took hope from his ownership of a cotton plantation in Mississippi. The Democrats were dismayed at the resulting erosion of their Southern stronghold. They issued pamphlets blasting "Taylor's Two Faces" on slavery, ignoring the fact that the General's obscurity was his strength.

Some Whigs bolted their ticket. A Massachusetts delegate at the convention, Charles Allen, shouted right after Taylor's nomination, "The Whig party is here and this day dissolved. You have put one ounce too much on the strong back of Northern endurance!"[26] Webster complained that Taylor was only "an illiterate frontier colonel," but ignored the blandishments of the Free Soilers and eventually issued a lukewarm endorsement of his party´s standard-bearer.

Van Buren did not carry a single state, but he nonetheless decided the election. Massive defections of New York Democrats to the Free Soilers threw that key state to Taylor. The South gave a narrow edge to its native son, counteracting Cass´ sweep of the Midwest. The loser was surprised, but doubted the winning coalition could last. "The Whig party cannot hold together," Cass prophesied. "It contains the seeds of dissolution....For myself, my day is gone by. I think I have sense enough to know that."[27]

President Taylor´s day would also pass in short order. He died in 1850 after revealing a nationalism that surprised and alienated many Southern supporters. The Presidency fell to Millard Fillmore, who just two years earlier had been balancing the books of the state of New York.

ELECTION NO. 17: 1852

A generation was passing. One of the three giants of the Senate, John Calhoun, died in 1850. The others, Henry Clay and Daniel Webster, were failing. Each would be in his grave before the votes in the 1852 election were tallied. The men who had dominated since the War of 1812 were giving way to a movement known as "Young America."

It was a time of cautious hope. The Compromise of 1850 had lessened the tension over the vexing question of slavery. President Millard Fillmore signed all parts of the package viewed as the final solution of the nation´s thorny sectional dispute. Northern radicals heatedly condemned one provision, the Fugitive Slave Act. It required the forcible return of all escaped slaves. Abolitionists promised obstruction, but they were in a minority. Most Americans hoped for calm.

Fillmore was not enthusiastic about staying in the White House. He was dissuaded as early as 1850 from renouncing any ambitions for a full term. Southern Whigs applauded his signing of the Fugitive Slave Act and pushed his candidacy in 1852, but Easterners and Midwesterners wanted little to do with him. The President retained hopes of swinging a deal with Webster, but the Secretary of State would not release his small bloc of convention delegates. He knew his last chance at the grand prize was slipping away. When General Winfield Scott broke the deadlock on the fifty-third ballot, Webster cried to a friend, "How will this look in history?"[28]

The three men who battled for the 1848 Democratic nomination prepared for a return engagement in 1852. Lewis Cass had foreseen the end of his political career after his loss to Zachary Taylor, but the temptation of one last chance proved irresistible. Former Secretary of State James Buchanan joined the Michigan Senator in the hunt, but Justice Levi Woodbury was unable to make it a threesome. He died in 1851, forcing his New England backers to seek a new candidate.

The weakness of the Whig party was evident by 1852, making the Democratic nomination a highly esteemed prize. Others crowded the field, notably former Secretary of War William Marcy and Illinois Senator Stephen Douglas. Douglas was a young man in a hurry, only 39. His supporters belonged to the nationalistic "Young America" movement, demanding the elevation to power of the new generation and scorning experienced politicians as "old fogies."

Another young possibility was a former Senator from New Hampshire who had been a brigadier general under Scott in the Mexican War. But Franklin Pierce thought talk of making him New England´s replacement for Woodbury was ludicrous. He burned an early suggestion of his candidacy, calling it a "damned silly letter." Pierce later authorized his friends to advance his name only if the convention deadlocked.

Cass was the early frontrunner, but his opposition to the Fugitive Slave Act killed him in the South. Buchanan seized the lead as the balloting dragged on, then Douglas, then Cass again. Pierce received scattered votes, shooting through to victory after getting the backing of North Carolina. When word of his nomination on the forty-ninth ballot reached New Hampshire, Pierce just stared in amazement. His wife fainted.

A second New Hampshire resident was entered in the fall contest. Senator John Hale was the Free Soil nominee. His party was weaker than it had been in 1848. Martin Van Buren and his followers were over their pique at the Democratic party; most endorsed Pierce. The Free Soil percentage of the popular vote dropped by more than half.

Southerners suspected Scott of being controlled by Northern Whigs. Pierce, on the other hand, had always been sympathetic to the South. He lashed out at the abolitionists as "reckless fanatics." The return of the South to the Democrats restored the party´s base. "Young America" hopped on the bandwagon, finding Pierce a fresh face and Scott a "fogy." The Free Soilers drained Whig votes in the East and Midwest, clearing the way for the Democrats to carry all but four states. Pierce´s share of the electoral vote was the highest since James Monroe´s in 1820.

The calm and prosperity were short-lived. Within two years, the "finality" of the Compromise of 1850 would be disproved. Franklin Pierce would find himself fighting a desperate losing battle against the forces that would eventually unleash civil war.

Charts for Chapter 2

1820 General Election

	James Monroe (DR)	John Quincy Adams (IDR)
PV	----	----
PV %	----	----
States	24	0
States %	100.0	0.0
EV	231	1
East	128	1
South	86	0
Midwest	17	0
West	----	----
EV %	99.6	0.4

1824 General Election

	John Quincy Adams (DR)	Andrew Jackson (DR)	William Crawford (DR)	Henry Clay (DR)
PV	113,122	151,271	40,856	47,531
PV %	30.9	41.3	11.2	13.0
East	49.7	34.1	7.7	1.3
South	6.8	54.6	23.0	15.3
Midwest	23.0	38.4	1.2	37.4
West	----	----	----	----
States	7	11	3	3
States %	29.2	45.8	12.5	12.5
EV	84	99	41	37
East	81	44	8	4
South	2	48	33	14
Midwest	1	7	0	19
West	----	----	----	----
EV %	32.2	37.9	15.7	14.2

Note: No candidate secured an electoral majority, so the House of Representatives made the final decision.   It elected Adams on its first ballot.

1828 General Election

	Andrew Jackson (DR)	John Quincy Adams (NR)
PV	642,553	500,897
PV %	56.0	43.6
East	49.3	50.1
South	74.2	25.7
Midwest	54.9	45.1
West	----	----

1828 General Election
(continued)

	Andrew Jackson (DR)	John Quincy Adams (NR)
States	15	9
States %	62.5	37.5
EV	178	83
East	54	83
South	97	0
Midwest	27	0
West	----	----
EV %	68.2	31.8

1832 Democratic Convention

	Andrew Jackson (D)
FB	283
East	143
South	106
Midwest	34
West	----
FB %	100.0

1832 National Republican Convention

	Henry Clay (NR)
FB	167
East	101
South	46
Midwest	20
West	----
FB %	99.4

1832 General Election

		Andrew Jackson (D)	Henry Clay (NR)	John Floyd (ID)	William Wirt (AM)
PV		701,780	484,205	0	100,715
PV %		54.2	37.4	0.0	7.8
	East	48.8	38.1	0.0	12.2
	South	72.7	27.3	0.0	0.0
	Midwest	54.8	44.9	0.0	0.3
	West	----	----	----	----
States		16	6	1	1
States %		66.7	25.0	4.2	4.2
EV		219	49	11	7
	East	100	34	0	7
	South	80	15	11	0
	Midwest	39	0	0	0
	West	----	----	----	----
EV %		76.6	17.1	3.8	2.4

1836 Democratic Convention

		Martin Van Buren (D)
FB		265
	East	143
	South	88
	Midwest	34
	West	----
FB %		100.0

1836 General Election

	Martin Van Buren (D)	William Henry Harrison (W)	Hugh White (W)	Daniel Webster (W)	Willie Person Mangum (IW)
PV	764,176	550,816	146,107	41,201	0
PV %	50.8	36.6	9.7	2.7	0.0
East	52.0	42.7	0.0	5.1	0.0
South	50.1	10.5	39.4	0.0	0.0
Midwest	48.7	49.2	2.1	0.0	0.0
West	----	----	----	----	----
Counties	561	243	236	9	0
Counties %	53.4	23.1	22.5	0.9	0.0
States	15	7	2	1	1
States %	57.7	26.9	7.7	3.8	3.8
EV	170	73	26	14	11
East	101	28	0	14	0
South	57	15	26	0	11
Midwest	12	30	0	0	0
West	----	----	----	----	----
EV %	57.8	24.8	8.8	4.8	3.7

1840 Whig Convention

	William Henry Harrison (W)	Henry Clay (W)	Winfield Scott (W)
FB	91	103	57
East	61	25	57
South	0	69	0
Midwest	30	9	0
West	----	----	----
FB %	35.8	40.6	22.4

1840 Whig Convention (continued)

	William Henry Harrison (W)	Henry Clay (W)	Winfield Scott (W)
LB (#?)	148	90	16
East	110	17	16
South	0	69	0
Midwest	38	4	0
West	----	----	----
LB %	58.3	35.4	6.3

1840 Democratic Convention

	Martin Van Buren (D)
FB	244
East	132
South	75
Midwest	37
West	----
FB %	100.0

1840 General Election

	William Henry Harrison (W)	Martin Van Buren (D)
PV	1,275,390	1,128,854
PV %	52.9	46.8
East	52.1	47.4
South	55.0	45.0
Midwest	52.5	47.2
West	----	----

1840 General Election (continued)

	William Henry Harrison (W)	Martin Van Buren (D)
Counties	698	476
Counties %	59.3	40.4
States	19	7
States %	73.1	26.9
EV	234	60
East	136	7
South	65	44
Midwest	33	9
West	----	----
EV %	79.6	20.4

1844 Democratic Convention

	James Polk (D)	Martin Van Buren (D)	Lewis Cass (D)	Richard Johnson (D)
FB	0	146	83	24
East	0	104	11	2
South	0	3	57	20
Midwest	0	39	15	2
West	----	----	----	----
FB %	0.0	54.9	31.2	9.0
LB (#9)	231	0	29	0
East	99	0	22	0
South	86	0	0	0
Midwest	46	0	7	0
West	----	----	----	----
LB %	86.8	0.0	10.9	0.0

1844 Whig Convention

	Henry Clay (W)
FB	275
East	123
South	96
Midwest	56
West	----
FB %	100.0

1844 General Election

	James Polk (D)	Henry Clay (W)	James Birney (LTY)
PV	1,339,494	1,300,004	62,103
PV %	49.5	48.1	2.3
East	48.3	48.3	3.3
South	51.3	48.7	0.0
Midwest	50.3	47.0	2.5
West	----	----	----
Counties	709	545	0
Counties %	56.5	43.4	0.0
States	15	11	0
States %	57.7	42.3	0.0
EV	170	105	0
East	77	46	0
South	60	36	0
Midwest	33	23	0
West	----	----	----
EV %	61.8	38.2	0.0

1848 Whig Convention

		Zachary Taylor (W)	Henry Clay (W)	Winfield Scott (W)	Daniel Webster (W)
FB		111	97	43	22
	East	17	69	11	22
	South	79	15	0	0
	Midwest	15	13	32	0
	West	----	----	----	----
FB %		39.6	34.6	15.4	7.9
LB (#4)		171	32	63	14
	East	49	25	35	14
	South	89	5	0	0
	Midwest	33	2	28	0
	West	----	----	----	----
LB %		61.1	11.4	22.5	5.0

1848 Democratic Convention

		Lewis Cass (D)	James Buchanan (D)	Levi Woodbury (D)	abstention
FB		125	55	53	39
	East	14	33	40	36
	South	50	19	13	3
	Midwest	61	3	0	0
	West	----	----	----	----
FB %		43.1	19.0	18.3	13.4
LB (#4)		179	33	38	36
	East	34	26	27	36
	South	81	7	11	0
	Midwest	64	0	0	0
	West	----	----	----	----
LB %		61.7	11.4	13.1	12.4

1848 General Election

	Zachary Taylor (W)	Lewis Cass (D)	Martin Van Buren (FS)
PV	1,361,393	1,223,460	291,501
PV %	47.3	42.5	10.1
East	47.8	36.8	15.2
South	52.0	48.0	0.0
Midwest	42.4	47.5	10.1
West	----	----	----
Counties	670	747	33
Counties %	46.1	51.4	2.3
States	15	15	0
States %	50.0	50.0	0.0
EV	163	127	0
East	108	15	0
South	55	48	0
Midwest	0	64	0
West	----	----	----
EV %	56.2	43.8	0.0

1852 Democratic Convention

	Franklin Pierce (D)	Lewis Cass (D)	James Buchanan (D)	William Marcy (D)	Stephen Douglas (D)	Joseph Lane (D)
FB	0	116	93	27	20	13
East	0	57	32	27	3	0
South	0	24	61	0	2	0
Midwest	0	35	0	0	15	13
West	0	0	0	0	0	0
FB %	0.0	40.3	32.3	9.4	6.9	4.5

1852 Democratic Convention (continued)

	Frank-lin Pierce (D)	Lewis Cass (D)	James Buch-anan (D)	William Marcy (D)	Stephen Douglas (D)	Joseph Lane (D)
LB (#49)	279	2	0	0	2	0
East	118	0	0	0	0	0
South	92	0	0	0	0	0
Midwest	65	2	0	0	2	0
West	4	0	0	0	0	0
LB %	96.9	0.7	0.0	0.0	0.7	0.0

1852 Whig Convention

	Winfield Scott (W)	Millard Fillmore (W)	Daniel Webster (W)
FB	131	133	29
East	75	19	25
South	1	98	0
Midwest	53	15	3
West	2	1	1
FB %	44.3	44.9	9.8
LB (#53)	159	112	21
East	87	16	16
South	11	87	0
Midwest	58	9	4
West	3	0	1
LB %	53.7	37.8	7.1

1852 General Election

	Franklin Pierce (D)	Winfield Scott (W)	John Hale (FS)
PV	1,607,510	1,386,942	155,210
PV %	50.8	43.9	4.9
East	49.1	44.6	6.1
South	54.8	44.0	0.0
Midwest	50.6	42.4	7.0
West	53.0	46.8	0.1
Counties	1,113	432	8
Counties %	70.6	27.4	0.5
States	27	4	0
States %	87.1	12.9	0.0
EV	254	42	0
East	103	18	0
South	76	24	0
Midwest	71	0	0
West	4	0	0
EV %	85.8	14.2	0.0

3.
Waving the Bloody Shirt: 1856–1900

The Civil War lasted four years, but its impact on Presidential politics endured for decades. The sole fact that Abraham Lincoln had been a Republican provided his young party an aura of righteous immortality. Its candidates rarely failed to remind Northern audiences that the GOP had directed the successful war effort, a rhetorical practice commonly known as "waving the bloody shirt." Indiana Governor and Senator Oliver Morton was one of the foremost practitioners of the art. He blasted the Democratic party as "a common sewer and loathsome receptacle, into which is emptied every element of treason North and South, and every element of inhumanity and barbarism which has dishonored the age."[1] Such talk echoed from the stump for the rest of the 19th Century.

The Republicans made their debut in 1856, a product of the strong resurgence in sectional feeling. Lincoln scored the party's first win four years later. It took nine of the twelve elections between 1856 and 1900. James Buchanan and Grover Cleveland eked out the three Democratic triumphs.

Other issues intruded, but the big question was still North vs. South. The Grand Army of the Republic, a 19th Century version of the American Legion, became a potent supporter of Republican candidates. The 1876 nominee, Rutherford Hayes, still had the war on his mind. He wrote James Garfield, "The true issue in the minds of the masses is simply, Shall the late Rebels have the Government?"[2] A national uproar followed a Republican minister's 1884 characterization of the Democrats as advocates of "Rum, Romanism, and Rebellion," but it was the middle word that ignited the furor. Few disputed the last. The Republican candidate in 1896 and 1900, William McKinley, still liked to be called "Major." That was his brevet rank with the Ohio Volunteers more than thirty years earlier.

The Democrats paid quadrennially for their earlier miscalculations: Buchanan's failure to stop secession, the

1864 platform calling for an immediate armistice, the 1868 plank condemning Reconstruction. Some of the party's leading lights found that their lack of enthusiasm for the war shadowed the rest of their careers. Delaware Senator Thomas Bayard tried four times for the Presidency. He smashed each time into the fact that as a 33-year-old lawyer, he had endorsed peaceful secession. The South stuck with Bayard and the Democrats out of gratitude. The rest of the country was largely Republican.

The period of 1856-1900 had its share of turbulence apart from the Civil War. Three Presidents were assassinated. Scandals rocked more than one administration. The Greenbacker and Populist movements manifested agrarian discontent. But conservative Republican government, anchored firmly to the past, was the rule. It only began to change in 1901 when McKinley, the last President to serve in the war, was murdered. His successor, Theodore Roosevelt, vigorously believed in looking forward. It was little wonder that Old Guard Republicans were the ones most unhappy with his elevation.

ELECTION NO. 18: 1856

It has never been precisely determined why he did it, but Illinois Senator Stephen Douglas started a political revolution in January 1854.

Douglas introduced a bill to create two states out of Nebraska Territory, allowing the settlers to decide whether to permit slavery. This was the Kansas-Nebraska Act, one of the most potent pieces of political dynamite in American history.

Douglas' bill repudiated the 34-year restriction on slavery imposed by the Missouri Compromise on the northern portion of what had been Louisiana Territory. The bill passed in May after fiery Congressional debate. Southerners were aroused to vehement advocacy of popular sovereignty; Northerners passionately condemned the prospect of new slave lands.

Historians have advanced several possible reasons why Douglas masterminded the passage of the Kansas-Nebraska Act. He wanted to clear the way for a Western railroad from his home state. He wanted to placate the South, which was irritated by growing Northern defiance of the Fugitive Slave Act. He wanted to add Southerners to his Midwestern base for the 1856 election.

He accomplished something different: a rapid mobilization of public opinion that led to the breakup of the Whigs and the birth of the Republican party. A lawyer in Douglas' Illinois was among those who came out of political retirement to deliver speeches against the extension of slavery. Abraham Lincoln remembered later that the Kansas-Nebraska Act roused his public conscience as nothing had before.

Douglas' sponsorship and President Franklin Pierce's signing of the Kansas-Nebraska Act made both many enemies in their own Democratic party. Both were now too controversial for political power brokers. Douglas, perhaps wondering at his own miscalculation, returned to Illinois three months after his bill passed. "I could travel from Boston to Chicago by the light of my own effigy," he recalled. "I could find my effigy upon every tree we passed."[3]

James Buchanan passed the crisis out of harm's way as Minister to Great Britain, returning home in early 1856. Uncontrolled violence was now the rule in "Bleeding Kansas," where competing state governments vied for the recognition of the federal government. Pierce's support of the proslavery faction doomed his hopes for renomination. The noncontroversial Buchanan outlasted his two challengers, gaining a unanimous vote on the seventeenth convention ballot.

The Whig party had virtually dissolved by that point. Its shaky coalition of Northern opponents of slavery and Southern slaveholders could not weather the Kansas-Nebraska firestorm. Northern Whigs and Free Soilers formed the Republican party, specifically opposed to the extension of slavery in the territories, a question the Whigs had evaded. Most Southern Whigs and some of their moderate Northern counterparts drifted to another new standard, that of the American party.

Members of the American party were repelled by the escalating stream of European immigrants. They advocated requiring aliens to live twenty-one years in the United States before being eligible for citizenship. Nativism was a potent issue, but the new party couldn't ignore the one burning question. Most Northern delegates to its convention stormed out after failing to place it on record against slavery. Those who stayed nominated former President Millard Fillmore. The feeble remnants of the Whig party later endorsed the American ticket.

Republican leaders informally settled on their nominee before their convention. Noted explorer John Fremont was a popular hero. A man of antislavery views, he was not as controversial as the GOP's firebrands, such as William Seward or Salmon Chase. His selection was confirmed on the first ballot.

The fall campaign was heated. Southerners were genuinely frightened by the quickly growing strength of the Republicans, whose slogan was: "Free Soil, Free Speech, Free Men, Fremont!" Some whispered of secession if the explorer should win. Buchanan didn't blame the Southerners. He wrote, "The Black Republicans must be, as they can be with justice, boldly assailed as disunionists, and this charge must be reiterated again and again."[4] Fremont retorted that Southern Democrats were reactionaries whose support of slavery "is now directed to turn back the impulse of the Revolution and reverse its principles."[5]

The polarization of the country was plainly evident in

voters' reaction to this rhetoric. Buchanan swept the defiant South, where only Fillmore was on the ballot to challenge him. Fremont ran up electoral-vote majorities in the increasingly militant East and Midwest. Buchanan did just well enough in the latter regions to win the right to govern a nation that had truly become what Abraham Lincoln would describe in immortal words two years later: "a house divided."

ELECTION NO. 19: 1860

New York Senator William Seward was just one of millions who saw the storm clouds gathering, but he had a greater facility with words than most. "It is an irrepressible conflict between opposing and enduring forces," he declared in 1858 of the nation's sectional strife. "And it means that the United States must and will, sooner or later, become either entirely a slaveholding nation or entirely a free-labor nation."[6] The election of 1860 provided the spark that put the country on the long, bloody road to the resolution of Seward's "irrepressible conflict" at Appomattox.

President James Buchanan anxiously awaited the day when he could pass these problems to his successor. He wrote friends in 1859 of his "final and irrevocable" intent to retire. He confided a year later, "I am now in my sixty-ninth year and am heartily tired of my position as President."[7]

Buchanan was also heartily displeased that his political enemy, Stephen Douglas, appeared almost certain to be his replacement as Democratic standard-bearer. Douglas' gracious withdrawal in 1856 had won him friends for the future. He also benefited from a weak field of challengers, led by Virginia Senator Robert Hunter.

The Democratic convention was ironically held in Charleston, already a hotbed of disunion sentiment. It was the perfect setting for the split that rent the party. Southern delegates were angered by the convention's rejection of a platform plank guaranteeing federal protection for slavery in the territories. Eight state delegations immediately stalked out. The Douglas supporters who stayed were determined to push on whatever the cost to the party. A New York newspaperman wrote that he had "never heard abolitionists talk more rancorously of the people of the South than the Douglas men here."[8] The Illinois Senator led on every tally, but could not reach the magic two-thirds level. The convention was adjourned to Baltimore after fifty-seven ballots.

Dissident Democrats also headed to the Maryland city. While party regulars finally nominated Douglas by waiving the two-thirds stipulation, the Southern Democrats chose Vice President John Breckinridge. President Buchanan and former President Franklin Pierce snubbed Douglas and endorsed the rump ticket. "Breckinridge may not be for disunion," Douglas sniffed. "But all the disunionists are for Breckinridge."[9]

A new entry worked to stir up Union spirit. The Constitutional Union party consisted mainly of members of the late Whig and American parties. Former Senator John Bell of Tennessee was its nominee. He rejected secession "both as a Constitutional right and as a remedy for existing evils."[10]

The fragmented opposition opened the door for the Republicans, still a Northern sectional party. Seward was the frontrunner, but he had made strong enemies in his long career. Many delegates were attracted to the party's quickly rising star, an Illinois lawyer named Abraham Lincoln. He won national renown for the tough challenge he posed to Douglas' 1858 Senate reelection, particularly in their famous debates. An Eastern speaking tour in early 1860 added to his reputation. Lincoln received a rousing ovation at New York's Cooper Union when he defended the Republican cause, "Let us have faith that right makes might, and in that faith let us, to the end, dare to do our duty as we understand it."[11]

His managers did their duties at the GOP convention, fortuitously held on Lincoln's home ground, Chicago. They packed the galleries with supporters of Honest Abe, then swung a deal with Pennsylvania Senator Simon Cameron. Cameron got a Cabinet post, Lincoln the nomination on the third ballot.

Douglas was the only candidate to speak publicly in the fall. He traveled the nation, the first Presidential nominee ever to do so. An Illinois newspaper looked askance at the spectacle, "Douglas is going about peddling his opinions as a tin man peddles his wares. The only excuse for him is that since he is a small man, he has a right to be engaged in small business."[12] The Democrat first hoped for victory, but eventually turned his tour into a crusade for Union, foreseeing his inevitable defeat.

There was only one issue: slavery in the territories. The candidates' stands were well-known. Lincoln was opposed to any extension. Douglas peddled popular sovereignty. Breckinridge insisted slaves were property, and people had the right to take their possessions anywhere in the territories. Bell hid behind ambiguous pleas for Union.

The extremists did best in the Electoral College: Lincoln polling 180 votes to win, Breckinridge second with 72. Moderates Bell and Douglas only won four states between them.

Lincoln quickly pledged that the South had nothing to fear from him, but the region decided not to wait to find out. South Carolina took the first step toward secession just days after his election. By December 20, it could declare, "The union now subsisting between South Carolina and other States, under the name of the 'United States of America,' is hereby dissolved."[13] Others followed.

The President-elect continued to hope publicly for compromise, but he was not totally displeased. Lincoln wrote a friend, "The tug has to come, and better now than later."[14]

ELECTION NO. 20: 1864

Perhaps the most significant thing about the election of 1864 is that it occurred. It was the fourth summer of a Civil War that had been met by the Lincoln Administration with strict, some said dictatorial, measures at home. But the President drew the line when it came to disturbing the ballot box. "We cannot have free government without elections," he said. "If the rebellion could force us to forgo, or postpone a national election, it might fairly claim to have already conquered and ruined us."[15]

His intention to proceed with the voting was no indication of Lincoln's confidence. He wrote privately in August, "This morning, as for some days past, it seems exceedingly probable that the Administration will not be reelected."[16] It was a commonly held opinion. Horace Greeley editorialized that summer, "Mr. Lincoln is already beaten. He cannot be elected."[17] John Fremont toyed with a general-election challenge on a Radical Republican ticket, asserting that the President was "politically, militarily, and financially a failure."

The Democrats anticipated success with a potent combination: General George McClellan as their popular nominee, coupled with a peace platform to appeal to a war-weary nation. McClellan had been an overly cautious commander, but was loved by his troops. He was the over-whelming choice of the party's convention on its first ballot. The delegates had already approved a resolution endorsing an immediate armistice on the well-worn battle-fields of Virginia.

Lincoln maneuvered skillfully to avoid a challenge to his renomination. Fremont and Secretary of the Treasury Salmon Chase both abandoned their efforts. Missouri gave its Republican convention votes to General Ulysses Grant, who had endorsed Lincoln. The President received all other tallies.

The Republicans faced the country that fall with a temporary name change. It was thought War Democrats would find backing Lincoln more palatable if he were the standard-bearer of the Union party. The Democratic Military Governor of Tennessee, Andrew Johnson, was slated as the President's running mate as an added inducement.

The Democrats still had cause to feel they had the upper hand. McClellan posters were plastered across the North, decrying "four years of failure to restore the Union by the experiment of war." They were unfaded when word came in August of the capture of the Port of Mobile, and in September, when Union forces seized Atlanta.

A wave of nationalism swept the North, buoying Lincoln's reelection effort. McClellan moved quickly to disassociate himself from his peace platform: "I could not look in the face my gallant comrades of the army and navy, who have survived so many bloody battles, and tell them that their labor and the sacrifice of so many of our slain and wounded brethren had been in vain."[18] It was not enough. Lincoln carried 91 percent of the electoral votes and all but three states. His fears of August seemed ridiculously distant in those glory days of November.

The President now turned his attention to postwar America. He declared in his famous second inaugural address, "With malice toward none; with charity for all...let us strive on to finish the work we are in; to bind up the nation's wounds."[19] Thirty-six days later, the shooting stopped at Appomattox Courthouse.

Lincoln did not live to institute his reconstruction plans. His assassination within a week after the surrender left the unhappy task to Andrew Johnson, whose stormy administration made some forget peace had ever come.

ELECTION NO. 21: 1868

Ulysses Grant was a wanted man in 1868.

Both the Democrats and the Republicans sought the hero of Appomattox to head their national tickets. Never mind that the General had no government experience and indeed had only voted once in his life. It was generally accepted that he had just to say the word, and the White House was his.

The Democrats had cause to feel they were on the inside track. Grant's lone vote was for James Buchanan in 1856. He considered himself a Douglas Democrat at the outbreak of the war. His opinions after that were not well-known, except for his endorsement of his Commander-in-Chief, Abraham Lincoln, in 1864.

President Andrew Johnson inadvertently resolved the situation. His feuds with the Radical Republicans in Congress over Reconstruction were legendary, leading to his impeachment in 1868. Johnson escaped eviction from the Executive Mansion by only one vote in the Senate. The trial resulted in large part from Johnson's replacement of a Radical favorite, Secretary of War Edwin Stanton, with Grant. It was a test of the Tenure of Office Act, passed by the Radicals to prevent exactly such a move. The Senate invoked the act and Grant relinquished his office, even though Johnson implored him to stay on. The General had added to his stature in Republican eyes.

Grant's nomination by the GOP was now taken as an accomplished fact, but his path to avowed Republicanism was tortuous. A New York newspaper found Grant "at first shy; he then wavered; then enveloped himself in a thick mystery; and at last he has changed his politics."[20] The vote on the first convention ballot was unanimous.

Democrats yearned for such simplicity. They had the most crowded convention field in American history. Eight candidates got at least four percent of the vote on the first ballot. The frontrunner was former Ohio Congressman George Pendleton, the party's 1864 Vice Presidential nominee.

Pendleton was the favorite of the Midwest, but was an anathema to the East because of his support for soft money. President Johnson, the winning Vice President in 1864 on the Republican ticket, now declared, "I was born a states´ rights Democrat and I shall die one!"[21] He was in second place on the first ballot, largely through the support of Southerners grateful for his lenient Reconstruction proposals. The rest of the party wanted nothing to do with such a controversial and nationally reviled figure.

Pendleton led for fifteen ballots, then was passed by a war hero, General Winfield Hancock. Supporters of Chief Justice Salmon Chase prepared to offer the name of the former Republican into the confusion. Chase´s home state made it unnecessary. Ohio switched its votes from Pendleton to the chairman of the convention, former New York Governor Horatio Seymour. Seymour tried to stop the stampede, but found himself the recipient of a unanimous nomination on the twenty-second ballot. He later called his acceptance "the mistake of my life."

The Democratic platform set Reconstruction as the key issue. It blasted the Radical Republicans for having "subjected ten States, in time of profound peace, to military despotism and negro supremacy."[22] Republicans campaigned as the party that had won the war, led by the man who had done it. Grant himself said little, but received widespread acclaim for a simple sentence ending his letter accepting the GOP nomination: "Let us have peace."[23]

Seymour became the second nominee in history to undertake a national campaign tour, considered his only hope of counteracting Grant´s immense popularity in the North. Republicans added to their base by controlling most Reconstruction governments in the South. The result was a landslide of almost 3-1 in the Electoral College.

It was surprisingly close in the popular count. Grant´s margin was slightly more than 300,000 votes. It was estimated that 500,000 blacks exercised their new voting rights. Most certainly went for Grant, meaning it was likely Seymour had actually secured a majority of the nation´s white vote. That had once been enough. No longer.

ELECTION NO. 22: 1872

Roscoe Conkling was a proud, irascible man. The New York Senator was boss of his state´s massive Republican machine, a lofty perch from which he looked down on almost everyone and everything. But he professed to an exception. Conkling insisted he was genuinely impressed with the performance of Ulysses Grant, who had "made a better President than...we...had any right to expect, and he is a better President every day than he was the day before."[24]

Conkling viewed the Grant Administration through partisanly colored glasses, but not all of his fellow Republicans did the same. They lambasted the President as a poor executive who was allowing the government to be torn by scandal.   "That...a man like Grant should be called...the highest product of the most advanced evolution, made evolution ludicrous," scoffed Henry Adams.   "One must be as commonplace as Grant's own commonplaces to maintain such an absurdity."[25]

Republican critics decided to form their own party, based on the Liberal movement that had begun in Missouri in 1870.   That state's Governor, Gratz Brown, was a leading contender for the nomination of the national Liberal Republican party.   So was Supreme Court Justice David Davis. But the eccentric editor of the New York Tribune, Horace Greeley, worked behind the scenes for more than a year to line up support.   His nomination on the sixth ballot at the Liberal Republican convention was a shock even to many of the delegates.   The famed political tactician, Thurlow Weed, voiced a common sentiment, "Six weeks ago, I did not suppose that any considerable number of men, outside of a lunatic asylum, would nominate Greeley for President."[26]   Democrats didn't enjoy the joke.   They had already virtually committed themselves to a coalition with the Republican dissidents.   At a short and gloomy convention, delegates endorsed the man who not so long ago had written, "All Democrats may not be rascals, but all rascals are Democrats."[27]

The Grand Army of the Republic and the nation's business leaders quickly lined up behind Grant, who contemptuously dismissed the Liberal Republicans as "soreheads."   Many Democrats decided to ignore the campaign.   Greeley did his best to accelerate his adopted party's decline.   He said in speeches that he could conceive of circumstances under which he would accept secession.   He later admitted his prewar opposition to slavery "might have been a mistake!"   His running mate, Brown, was drunk when he gave a speech at his alma mater's graduation exercises.   The Missouri Governor confessed he really didn't think very highly of Yale, and didn't know why he had gone there.

Grant was destined for a mammoth victory almost by default.   Among the amazed was Ohio Congressman James Garfield, who had written earlier in the year that Grant was "the second choice of most of our people, and they are not agreed on a first."[28]   He was the choice of 55.6 percent of the voters in November, sweeping more than four-fifths of the electoral votes.

Greeley was shocked by the condemnation his candidacy provoked.   He complained, "I have been assailed so bitterly that I hardly knew whether I was running for the Presidency or the penitentiary."[29]   He faced other heartbreaks.   His wife died just before the election.   His efforts to regain the editorship of his beloved Tribune were rebuffed.   Greeley died in despair just twenty-four days after the balloting. His Democratic and Liberal Republican electors scattered their votes among four men: former Indiana Senator Thomas Hendricks, Brown, former Georgia Governor Charles Jenkins, and Davis.   Then came a second death, as the Liberal Republican party ended its short life.   There were few mourners.

ELECTION NO. 23:   1876

America's centennial year seemed indisputably destined to be
one of Democratic triumph. The economy was in a shambles in
the wake of the devastating Panic of 1873. Newspapers
headlined scandal after scandal in the Grant Administration
and Congress: indictments of hundreds of government agents
and distillers for conspiring to divert taxes, the impeachment of the Secretary of War for receiving bribes,
revelations of widespread influence buying by the giant
railroads. The Republicans were also losing their grasp on
the South. As Reconstruction governments fell, the bitter
Southern elite turned to the Democratic party as its agent
for a return to white supremacy.

      Ulysses Grant was no longer a national hero. Even
leading Republicans discouraged talk of a third term. The
House of Representatives passed a resolution condemning any
departure from the two-term tradition as "unwise,
unpatriotic, and fraught with peril to our free
institutions." Grant was compelled to announce in May that
he would not accept a nomination "unless it should come under
such circumstances as to make it an imperative duty,
circumstances not likely to arise."[30] His wife was greatly
upset to be leaving the White House.

      The President's withdrawal signaled a free-for-all for
the Republican nomination. Maine's charismatic Congressman,
James Blaine, was the favorite of the rank-and-file. But he
had not escaped the taint of corruption. Testimony before a
House committee in May indicated Blaine had received favors
from the Little Rock and Fort Smith Railroad after he saved
the line's federal land grant. Blaine skillfully defended
himself on the House floor, reading selectively from the
now-famous "Mulligan letters" that implicated him. But his
bandwagon was irretrievably slowed. Some would say derailed.

      Four opponents seemed best positioned to benefit.
Indiana Senator Oliver Morton gathered the support of soft
money advocates. Secretary of the Treasury Benjamin Bristow
was backed by the party's reform elements, including those
who had launched the Liberal Republican crusade in 1872.
Bristow had exposed the Whiskey Ring, securing 253 indictments. New York Senator Roscoe Conkling held the remaining
Grant loyalists. Ohio Governor Rutherford Hayes was the dark
horse of the group, but had busily gathered commitments for
late-ballot switches. He hoped for a deadlock.

      Congressman James Garfield saw it in advance. He wrote
Hayes, "We should give you the solid vote of the Ohio
delegation, and await the breakup which must come when the
weaker candidates drop out."[31] Bristow, Morton, and Conkling
followed the scenario by withdrawing during the seventh
ballot. Both Hayes and Blaine gained support in a mad dash
to the finish, the Ohioan winning by just 33 votes.

      The Republican nominee was little-known. Some also
thought him little qualified. The New York World moaned that
honesty seemed to be his only virtue, "Hayes has never

stolen. Good God, has it come to this?"[32]

The Democrats intended to do their share of harping on honesty. Their nominee was New York Governor Samuel Tilden, not seriously challenged on his way to a second-ballot victory. Tilden was the mastermind of successful efforts to smash the corrupt Tweed and Canal Rings. He pledged to turn his skills toward the fetid atmosphere of Washington.

Hayes and Tilden agreed on much more than the need for ethical standards. Each endorsed hard money and civil-service legislation. It was not surprising that their race became a close one. Tilden grabbed an early lead in the popular count, widening it to a margin of more than 250,000 votes. He was also just one electoral vote short of winning as tallying continued on the morning after the election. The New York Tribune headlined Tilden's victory.

Rutherford Hayes wrote his son that he had lost "and I bow cheerfully to the result." Republican strategists were in a less resigned mood. They sent telegrams to their agents in Florida, Louisiana, and South Carolina, ordering that those states be "held." A single elector in Oregon was also questioned. All four states soon sent multiple sets of returns to Congress, reporting both Democratic and Republican victories. Hayes needed all twenty disputed electors to eke out a one-vote win. Tilden remained a single vote short of the magic 185.

There was no established procedure for resolving such confusion, so Congress created a 15-member Electoral Commission to settle the controversy. Seven commissioners were Democrats, seven Republicans. The final member would hold the swing vote. He was expected to be Supreme Court Justice David Davis, Lincoln's 1860 convention manager who had since drifted to Democratic ideals. But the Illinois legislature showed a disastrous sense of timing for Tilden's chances. It elected Davis to the Senate. His commission seat went to a Republican, Justice Joseph Bradley.

Congress began the official state-by-state count of electoral votes on February 1, 1877. Each time a disputed state was reached, the roll call stopped and the Electoral Commission began its deliberations. Democratic anger rose with the successive 8-7 decisions for Hayes. There were cries of "Tilden or blood!" and vague threats of a resumed Civil War.

The Republicans were worried about violence or at least a Democratic effort to filibuster the vote count past inauguration day, March 4. So they initiated quiet negotiations with Southern Democrats to gain their cooperation. The price was a Southern Cabinet member and withdrawal of the remaining military Reconstruction governments. Hayes agreed. The deal was struck.

It was not until 4:10 a.m. on March 2 that Hayes' one-vote victory was officially announced before Congress. Tilden urged cooperation with the new administration, but Democrats needed to vent their extreme frustration at losing in a year where it appeared everything was going their way. The Democratic-controlled House passed a nonbinding resolution just before the inaugural, declaring Tilden the real winner. The New Yorker himself always felt that way. He mused, "I think I can retire to private life with the consciousness that I shall receive from posterity the credit of having been elected to the highest position in the gift of the people without any of the cares and responsibilities of the office."[33]

Those cares belonged to President Hayes, already being ridiculed as "Rutherfraud" and "Old Eight-to-Seven." He could at least take comfort that he would not have to go through another such grind. Hayes confirmed his "inflexible purpose" to return to his quiet Ohio home when his four years were up.

ELECTION NO. 24: 1880

An election as close as the one in 1876 would seem to set the stage for a rematch. But neither Rutherford Hayes nor Samuel Tilden had the stomach for a second campaign. The Republican President adhered to his one-term pledge. Party leaders angered by his commitment to civil-service reform were ready to force his retirement had he changed his mind. Tilden was ill and showed little enthusiasm for another race. When a reporter mentioned he had heard that Thomas Hendricks wanted to run again as the second man on a Tilden ticket, the 1876 nominee joked, "I do not wonder, considering my weakness!"[34]

There nonetheless was no shortage of old faces in the running. The most prominent on the Republican side was former President Ulysses Grant. His two-year world tour was an overwhelming success, with the old General being acclaimed a hero by kings and the masses. Grant's welcome to the United States in late 1879 was a triumphal series of parades.

James Blaine was another former candidate gearing up for a repeat chance. He was the favorite of Easterners and Midwesterners, noting sourly that "wherever Republican success is most hopeless, there Grant enthusiasm runs highest."[35] It was true that Grant was most popular in the region he had conquered, the solidly Democratic South. Reformers and those who opposed a third term shared Blaine's wish to keep the former President in retirement.

Grant held a 20-vote lead on the first ballot and the convention quickly settled into deadlock. Marshaling the coalition of anti-Grant candidates on the floor was Ohio Congressman James Garfield, a supporter of the colorless Secretary of the Treasury, John Sherman. Garfield was receiving a few token votes himself on early ballots, but no one took him seriously as a candidate. No one, that is, but Wharton Barker. The Philadelphia banker had written Garfield, "All anti-machine Republicans...see that the only safety for the Republican party is in making some man such as yourself our candidate."[36] Barker worked behind the scenes before the convention, lining up switches for the Ohioan. It paid off on the thirty-fourth ballot, when Wisconsin shifted. Two roll calls later, one of the darkest horses ever had a nomination.

Garfield moved quickly to appease the Grant forces, led by New York´s Roscoe Conkling. He offered the Vice Presidential nomination to another New Yorker, Levi Morton. But Conkling imperiously insisted that Morton decline. Next to be summoned was the former Collector of the Port of New York, Chester Arthur. Conkling gave the same order, but Arthur replied, "The office of the Vice Presidency is a greater honor than I ever dreamed. A barren nomination would be a great honor."[37] He took it. Conkling spun on his heel in disgust.

The Democrats settled their ticket more quickly. The two frontrunners were General Winfield Hancock and Delaware Senator Thomas Bayard. Hancock was a Civil War hero who was hailed in his nominating speech as "the soldier statesman with a record as stainless as his sword." Bayard was best remembered by many for his 1861 speech calling on the North to allow its "erring sisters" to secede in peace. A stampede toward the safe and quiet Hancock gave him the nod on the second ballot.

The fall campaign was enlivened by Congressman James Weaver of the Greenback party. He amused the major parties with his advocacy of such heresies as an eight-hour workday and women´s suffrage. They dismissed him as a crackpot.

Few issues surfaced as the public struggled to learn something about the two virtually anonymous contenders. Republicans chortled as Hancock answered an inquiry on the tariff, "The tariff question is a local question."[38] Democrats reminded voters that Garfield had been suspected of receiving a $329 bribe in the Credit Mobilier scandal. They chalked the number, "329," on buildings all over the country.

The election was one of the closest in history. Garfield´s popular-vote margin was less than 2,000. A reversal in New York would have given Hancock an electoral-vote majority. Garfield had temporarily patched up his differences with Conkling, but Hancock suffered from intra-party squabbling between Tilden supporters and Tammany Hall in New York City. The Republican squeaked through in the Empire State by 21,000 votes.

But the brief harmony among GOP elements did not last. Garfield was assassinated the following year by a crank who insisted he was a supporter of Conkling´s Stalwart faction. "I did it and I want to be arrested," Charles Guiteau told police. "I am a Stalwart and Arthur is President now."[39]

ELECTION NO. 25: 1884

Grover Cleveland expected a nice, clean campaign in 1884. The reform Governor of New York was the obvious frontrunner for the Democratic nomination. He fully anticipated his Republican opponent in the fall to be a man of rectitude, Vermont Senator George Edmunds.

The year fell short of Cleveland's expectations. The campaign of 1884 is now remembered as perhaps the most vicious in American history. It became, as one contemporary observer noted, a contest over "the copulative habits of one and the prevaricative habits of the other."[40]

Cleveland's road to the Democratic endorsement was smooth. Delaware Senator Thomas Bayard posed the only serious threat, but his support was concentrated in the South, which still remembered his 1861 defense of peaceful secession. Cleveland's backing was more broadly based. He had received extensive publicity for his battles with Tammany Hall. One of the speakers seconding his nomination at the convention declared of Cleveland's supporters, "They love Cleveland for his character, but they love him also for the enemies he has made!"[41] Victory came easily on the second ballot.

The Republicans were in control of the White House, and President Chester Arthur was interested in winning a term in his own right. His problem was lack of a base. Former Senator Roscoe Conkling, head of the Stalwart faction that had provided Arthur's path to power, remained estranged from his protege. Reformers had warned shrilly in 1880 that Arthur was a spoilsman itching to get his hands on federal patronage. They were pleasantly surprised by the President's support of reform legislation, particularly his signing of the bill creating the Civil Service Commission. But their hearts remained primarily with Edmunds.

The "Magnetic Man," former Secretary of State James Blaine, was again on the scene. He had lost two tough battles for the nomination in the previous eight years. Even former Senator Thomas Platt of New York, a lieutenant of Blaine's archrival, voted for the man from Maine, "believing as I do that his turn has come." Platt confessed that Roscoe Conkling had been speechless when warned in advance of his intentions. Conkling's white-hot hatred of Blaine would not allow a similar shift. When later asked to assist in Blaine's fall campaign, he thundered, "No, thank you, I don't engage in criminal practice."[42]

The tensions in New York would hurt in the fall, but they were no barrier to the nomination. Blaine led from the beginning, winning on the fourth ballot. President Arthur did well only among Southern delegates, most of whom feared alienating an administration that provided them federal jobs.

The Blaine-Cleveland contest was unprecedented. The Nation complained that fall, "Party contests have never before reached so low a depth of degradation in this...country."[43] The Republican was bedeviled by the publication of more of the "Mulligan letters" that had linked him to a railroad scandal in 1876. Blaine's protestations of innocence seemed less convincing in light of his correspondence. He advised the recipient of some of his instructions, "Burn this letter!" Democrats took up the phrase as a taunt. They also chanted, "Blaine, Blaine, James G. Blaine. The continental liar from the state of Maine!"

Republicans responded with, "Ma! Ma! Where´s my pa?" A Buffalo newspaper revealed that Cleveland, a bachelor, had fathered a child in 1874. There was some doubt about his paternity, but Cleveland provided for the boy´s support. The GOP considered it a sign of guilt.

George William Curtis, a leader of reform Republicans, was among those exasperated by the quality of the campaign. He finally decided to shift allegiances, "We are told that Mr. Blaine has been delinquent in office but blameless in private life, while Mr. Cleveland has been a model of official integrity, but culpable in his personal relations. We should therefore elect Mr. Cleveland to the public office which he is so well qualified to fill, and remand Mr. Blaine to the private station which he is admirably fitted to adorn."[44]

The contest was tight to the wire, but a late October day in New York City provided the difference. Blaine was present at a meeting of Protestant clergymen, where the welcoming address was delivered by the Rev. Samuel Burchard. "We are Republicans," Burchard declared, "and don´t propose to leave our party and identify ourselves with the party whose antecedents have been Rum, Romanism, and Rebellion."[45] Blaine did not repudiate the remarks until a public furor was in full flame. The Democrats made certain that Catholic voters were aware.

Blaine concluded his fateful day by attending a lavish dinner with millionaires and important financiers. The press ridiculed the gathering in the next morning´s editions. It was labeled "Belshazzar´s Feast" and "The Boodle Banquet."

Cleveland won the popular vote by slightly more than 25,000, but the important margin was in New York. The defections of Catholics and irate laborers to the Democratic cause provided the Governor a win of 1,047 votes in his home state. A reversal in New York would have put Blaine in the White House. The loser knew fully well where to place the blame. He later wrote, "I should have carried New York by 10,000 if the weather had been clear on election day and Dr. Burchard had been doing missionary work in Asia Minor or Cochin China."[46]

ELECTION NO. 26: 1888

The Democrats found themselves in an unusual position in 1888. For the first time since Franklin Pierce in 1856, a man elected President as a Democrat was seeking a second term. Grover Cleveland succeeded where Pierce had failed; his renomination was the first for a Democratic President since Martin Van Buren in 1840.

Cleveland was essentially conservative, but had secured the passage of some reform legislation, such as the creation of the Interstate Commerce Commission. His control of the party was challenged only by New York Governor David Hill, who engaged in patronage disputes with the President. Cleveland made certain Hill wasn´t even chosen as a delegate to the convention. His renomination came off without a hitch.

The Republicans put on a better show. Ohio Senator John Sherman was the frontrunner in a crowded field. Seven contenders polled at least four percent of the vote on the first ballot. James Blaine was among them, even though he denied any interest in another race. Blaine´s charisma remained a powerful attraction to delegates disillusioned with the stodgy Sherman. If they couldn´t have the "Magnetic Man," they wanted an acceptable substitute.

Steps toward breaking the deadlock were initiated by one of the candidates. The president of the New York Central Railroad, Chauncey Depew, doubted a man of his position could be elected in the dawn of the Populist era. He told his key backers he had "been very much impressed by General Harrison." Benjamin Harrison was a former Senator from Indiana, the grandson of William Henry Harrison. Depew threw his support to the new Tippecanoe on the fourth ballot. Harrison took the lead on the seventh and won on the eighth. His campaign manager wired the nominee, "You are put in command."

The Republicans knew their new commander faced the most formidable obstacles besetting the choice of their party in decades. Cleveland was a rare bird, a Democratic incumbent. He was guaranteed the votes of a solid South, which had not awarded a single electoral vote to a Republican since the end of military Reconstruction in 1877. A young party also posed a threat. The Prohibition party, which had nominated former General Clinton Fisk, was riding the crest of dry sentiment in the Midwest. Most of its support came from renegade Republicans.

President Cleveland had determined the key campaign issue in 1887. He harangued Congress to lower "our present tariff laws, the vicious, inequitable, and illogical sources of unnecessary taxation."[47] That struck at the heart of the Republican gospel that a protective tariff was the best guarantee of prosperity. Harrison ridiculed Cleveland´s desire to lower trade barriers. "We have men who boast that they are cosmopolitans, citizens of the world," said the Republican. "I prefer to say that I am an American citizen, and I freely confess that American interests have first place in my regard."[48]

Democratic strategists pleaded with Cleveland to wage an educational campaign on the tariff, but the President did nothing at all to help the reelection effort. He said he was too busy. The Republicans were not similarly reticent. The chairman of the party´s National Committee, Matthew Quay, assembled a massive war chest of $3,000,000. His army of stump speakers was deployed across the country. Harrison himself delivered more than eighty speeches from his front porch in Indianapolis.

The Republican assault pulled the race even by October. It went over the top with an assist from an unlikely quarter. The British minister to Washington, Lord

Sackville-West, answered a letter from a California fruit grower who posed as a former British citizen seeking advice on how to vote. Sackville-West implied that Cleveland would be the best selection because he "will manifest a spirit of conciliation." Publication of the letter inflamed the passions of Irish-Americans, many of whom wanted anything but conciliation with England. Cleveland quickly ordered Sackville-West out of the country, but the damage was done.

New York, with its heavy Irish population, was again the key. Harrison won the state by only 14,373 votes. Without its electors, he would have lost the White House. The President-elect exclaimed to Matthew Quay, "Providence has given us the victory!" Quay, who once said Harrison would never know how close some people came to going to prison in order to win certain key states, could only scoff, "Think of the man! He ought to know that Providence hadn´t a damn thing to do with it!"[49]

ELECTION NO. 27: 1892

The men who directed Benjamin Harrison´s march to the front door of the White House in 1888 were ready to push him out the back door by 1892. Matthew Quay, Thomas Platt, and former Speaker of the House Thomas Reed were irritated at what they saw as the President´s lack of appreciation. The trio particularly disliked Harrison´s reserved manner and stinginess with patronage. When asked if he planned to eventually board Harrison´s bandwagon, Reed snapped, "I never ride in an ice-cart."[50]

Harrison was uncertain about seeking reelection, but confessed to intimates that the criticism from within his party drove him to it. The Republican bosses searched for an alternative, but never agreed on one. The two most prominent possibilities were Secretary of State James Blaine and Ohio Governor William McKinley. Blaine was indecisive and ill. A Wisconsin Congressman was shocked at his appearance, "His countenance is that of a man standing in the shadow of death."[51] McKinley was contrastingly vigorous, but eager to stay away from a nomination in what promised to be an unhappy year for Republicans.

Blaine´s friends opened a national headquarters and began rounding up delegates. The Secretary of State was once again unable to shake his lifelong Presidential fever. On the eve of the convention, he resigned from the Cabinet. The New York Herald was not alone in believing the "Plumed Knight" deserved the nomination as a last hurrah. It editorialized that "if health is restored to him, James G. Blaine and no other, must head the ticket." His supporters were so unrestrained in their demonstrations at the convention that they became known as "Blainiacs." But noise does not equal votes. Harrison used the power of incumbency to sew up a first-ballot renomination. McKinley was shocked at the strength of his own showing, more than 20 percent of the vote. His attempt to withdraw was ruled out-of-order. Industrialist Mark Hanna worried that his friend might stampede the convention. As the two left the hall, Hanna turned to a relieved McKinley, "My God, William, that was a damned close squeak!"[52]

The Democratic contest also appeared to be headed to the wire. New York Senator David Hill demonstrated early strength in gathering delegates. His victory at the New York state convention in February seemed to dash the hopes of former President Grover Cleveland. But Cleveland detested Hill and would not quit. He warned, "Forces are at work which certainly mean the complete turning back of the hands on the dial of Democracy and the destruction of party hopes."[53] His May win at the Georgia convention, supposedly ready to go for Hill, put Cleveland back in the role of frontrunner. He steamrolled to an easy first-ballot triumph that summer.

Both parties kept nervous eyes on rural America while completing their nomination rituals. That sector provided the strongest support for two minor parties at their heights of influence. Former Congressmen headed their tickets: James Weaver of the Populist party and John Bidwell of the Prohibition party. The Populists had special appeal in the grain belt, where farmers were struggling through hard times that they blamed on the callousness of Eastern financiers. Weaver's platform embraced an astounding number of reforms, including direct election of Senators, an income tax, and tough antitrust legislation.

The fall campaign was surprisingly uninspired. Cleveland again refused to speak in public. Harrison, worried by his wife's illness, gave his campaign virtually no assistance. He took no active role after her death in October. The major contenders clashed on only a few issues, chief among them the tariff. Cleveland wrote that dropping trade barriers was "a question of morals as well as a question of markets."[54] Harrison condemned free trade as "a mad crusade against American shops and...manufacturers."[55] But Americans were less inclined to believe the President. The high McKinley Tariff of 1890 was blamed by many for the agricultural depression.

The Democrats were in the rare position of being better organized than the divided Republicans. Even Senator Hill finally endorsed Cleveland, but the fractious GOP bosses never professed much enthusiasm for Harrison. Discontent in the Midwest was the key. Cleveland, who received 16 electoral votes from the region four years earlier, took 75 this time. He also benefited from an increased share of the labor vote, partly a reaction to the bloody attempt by management to suppress the strike at a Carnegie Steel Company plant in Homestead, Pennsylvania, earlier in the year. Cleveland scathingly referred to the effort to bring in armed strikebreakers as "the tender mercy the workingman receives from those made selfish and sordid by unjust governmental favoritism."[56]

Cleveland won his rematch with Harrison by a margin of nearly 2-1 in the Electoral College, but the outgoing President was almost relieved at the thought of going home to Indiana. "For me, there is no sting in it," Harrison told a friend. "Indeed, after the heavy blow the death of my wife dealt me, I do not think I could have stood the strain a reelection would have brought."[57]

ELECTION NO. 28: 1896

Perhaps no other campaign has stirred the passions of Americans as the contest of 1896 did. The quadrennial struggle between Democrats and Republicans was rhetorically elevated to class warfare. Journalist William Allen White was still amazed years later at the depth of feeling that was aroused. He remembered, "It was a fanaticism like the Crusades."[58]

The depression that gripped the farm country in 1892 now choked the entire nation. The Panic of 1893 forced the closing of thousands of businesses. The national unemployment rate settled above 20 percent by 1894. Farm foreclosures were a common occurrence. Farmers and laborers became increasingly convinced that their problems were the result of tight money policies dictated by the elite East. Support for an increase in the money supply through the free coinage of silver reached epidemic proportions west of the Appalachians.

President Grover Cleveland stood steadfastly against silver. He predicted early in 1896 that abandoning the gold standard would devastate the Democratic party. "If we should be forced away from our traditional doctrine of sound and safe money, our old antagonist will take the field on the platform which we abandon, and neither the votes of reckless Democrats nor reckless Republicans will avail to stay their easy march to power."[59] But the unemployed and the starving were not interested. Cleveland´s public standing was as low as Herbert Hoover´s would be thirty-five years later. A former Nebraska Congressman, William Jennings Bryan, said his fellow Democrats should have the same feeling for Cleveland as "toward the trainman who has opened a switch and precipitated a wreck."[60]

Silver sentiment existed in both parties, but it was much stronger among the Democrats. The Republicans followed Cleveland´s scenario, putting an ever-tighter embrace on the gold standard. Former Ohio Governor William McKinley easily clinched his party´s nomination, thanks largely to the organizational skills of Mark Hanna. McKinley had voted for silver legislation in Congress, but he now okayed a platform standing solidly behind gold. A small group of silver Republicans dramatically walked out of the convention. Hanna was among those angrily shouting, "Go! Go! Go!" as the tiny band departed.

The tables were turned when the Democrats met. The silver element had toiled for more than a year to seize the party machinery. It was solidly in control before the first gavel fell. The sole question was the nominee. Former Missouri Congressman Richard Bland was the acknowledged leader of the silverites. But critics said Bland´s surname was cruelly accurate. They also whispered that his wife was

Catholic. Pamphlets warned, "If you want to see a con-
fessional box in the White House, vote for Bland."[61] Other
silverites crowded the contest. Former Pennsylvania Governor
Robert Pattison was the only conservative.

William Jennings Bryan harbored hopes of emerging the
choice of a deadlocked convention. He wrote hundreds of
letters seeking delegate support, mentioning his tireless
work on the stump for the holy cause of silver. But at 36,
he was the youngest Presidential candidate ever. Few took
his candidacy seriously, at least until he spoke. The
Nebraskan´s voice boomed out to all corners of the convention
hall at the finish of the emotional debate over the monetary
plank of the platform. Bryan closed dramatically, "You shall
not press down upon the brow of labor this crown of thorns!
You shall not crucify mankind upon a cross of gold!"[62] The
roar from the delegates was deafening. Bryan was nominated
the next day on the fifth ballot. Most Eastern delegates
either voted for Pattison or abstained. New York Senator
David Hill joked with reporters as he headed home, "I am a
Democrat still. Very still."[63]

The two major-party nominees did more than take opposite
sides on the monetary question. They presented sharply
contrasting styles. Bryan traveled more than 18,000 miles
during the fall, delivering more than 600 speeches with an
evangelical fervor. He lashed out bitterly at "the money
power." McKinley´s slogan promised that the Republican was
the "advance agent of prosperity." He stayed at home in
Ohio, speaking from his front porch. McKinley told Hanna to
resist all pressure for a campaign tour, "I might just as
well put up a trapeze on my front lawn and compete with some
professional athlete as go out speaking against Bryan. I
have to think when I speak."[64]

Party distinctions were blurred in the fall. The
Populist party endorsed the Democratic ticket, as did silver
Republicans. Gold Democrats tried to draft President
Cleveland. Failing that, many joined the McKinley camp. A
few supported an independent Democratic ticket headed by
Illinois Senator John Palmer.

The rhetoric sharpened once these lines were drawn.
Republicans labeled Bryan an anarchist and a Socialist.
Employers warned workers they would be laid off if the
Democrat won. Bryan lashed back at the Republican, branding
McKinley a tool of Wall Street. Worn nearly to exhaustion by
his extensive tour, the Democratic nominee closed his
campaign, "My hand has been used until it is sore, but it can
handle a pen to sign a free-coinage bill, if I am elected. I
have been wearied with work, but I still have the strength to
stand between the people, if they elect me, and the Wall
Street syndicates which have been bleeding this country."[65]

The returns showed the polarization of the country.
McKinley won by carrying the two most-populous regions, the
East and the Midwest. Bryan was the first Democratic nominee
to fail to win a single Eastern electoral vote. His fortunes
were substantially better in the South and West. He polled
more than 60 percent of the popular vote in each. The nation

had chosen the conservative route to escape from its economic despair, but Bryan retained hope for the future. He soon wrote a book on the 1896 campaign. Its title: <u>The First Battle</u>.

ELECTION NO. 29: 1900

The candidates were the same, but the election of 1900 took place in a much different world than its predecessor did. William McKinley and William Jennings Bryan were not preoccupied with monetary policy in their second battle. Prosperity had returned and the gold supply was greatly increased. America's silver fever had cooled.

The significant event of the first McKinley Administration was the Spanish-American War. The fighting lasted only three months in 1898, but put Cuba on the road to independence and led to the annexation of the Philippines and Puerto Rico. This expansion seemed popular with most Americans, but there was an influential anti-imperialism movement centered in the East.

Few popular heroes emerged from the short war. The most significant was Admiral George Dewey, who directed the destruction of Spain's Far Eastern fleet in Manila Bay. There was talk of a Dewey candidacy in 1900. Bryan himself was concerned for awhile, but Dewey's fortunes sank as soon as he began talking politics. "I do not know on what ticket I will be nominated," announced the Admiral. "I have no politics. I am the people's candidate."[66] Democrats lost interest in the Hero of Manila, leaving the way open for Bryan's unanimous nomination. Grocer Cleveland groaned that his party's conservative faction failed to find an alternative, "Hundreds of thousands of our prominent Democrats are convinced that Bryan's nomination means defeat, and yet they are silent....What a sad condition!"[67]

The Republican renomination of McKinley was a foregone conclusion. At question was a running mate to replace the late Garret Hobart. McKinley exasperated his chief political operative, Mark Hanna, by insisting it was a question for the convention to settle. Hanna knew the Republican bosses of New York wanted to get outspoken Governor Theodore Roosevelt out of their hair. He feared they would shove the famed Rough Rider into the Vice Presidency, which is precisely what happened. Hanna lectured McKinley, "Your <u>duty</u> to the country is to <u>live</u> for <u>four</u> years from next March."[68]

The Republicans ran as the party of prosperity and territorial expansion. The popular Roosevelt handled the load of campaigning. McKinley's slogan neatly summed up the Republican strategy: "Let well enough alone." That advice was contrary to Bryan's nature. He attacked the Republicans for their annexation of foreign lands. The Democratic platform called imperialism "the paramount issue," but it rang hollow. Bryan himself had worked for Senate approval of the treaty that made the Philippines and Puerto Rico American possessions. He explained that he wanted the treaty in place to end the state of war, hoping to later rescind the annexation provisions. The public seemed to believe the treaty had settled the matter.

The failure of anti-imperialism as an issue caused Bryan to fall back on his 1896 favorite, silver. He declared he would "stand just where I stood" on the subject, but the country was no longer interested. The New York <u>Press</u> heckled, "Sit down, Mr. Bryan. You must be awfully tired, too." Former Speaker of the House Thomas Reed, noting that the economy seemed to be robust under the gold standard, put a twist on Henry Clay´s famous declaration. "Mr. Bryan," observed Reed, "had rather be wrong than be President."[69]

The Populists again endorsed Bryan, but a faction of the party nominated its own candidate. The improvement in the economy dampened the agrarian revolt. The Populists were firmly on the road to political oblivion.

The results in 1900 were not much different from the 1896 figures. McKinley´s share of the popular vote jumped just seven-tenths of a percentage point; his margin increased by approximately 263,000 votes. Bryan was again shut out of electoral votes in the East, but his share of the region´s popular vote increased. It dropped in the other three sections.

William McKinley had the endorsement he wanted for his mission of letting well enough alone. Vice President-elect Theodore Roosevelt groused to friends that he doubted he would have much work in such a placid administration. He expected to be a "dignified nonentity for four years." But less than seven months after Roosevelt was sworn in, McKinley was assassinated. The man Mark Hanna called "that damned cowboy" was now President.

Charts for Chapter 3

1856 Democratic Convention

		James Buchanan (D)	Franklin Pierce (D)	Stephen Douglas (D)
FB		135½	122½	33
	East	75	46	0
	South	25	72	3
	Midwest	35½	4½	30
	West	0	0	0
FB %		45.8	41.4	11.1
LB	(#17)	296	0	0
	East	121	0	0
	South	100	0	0
	Midwest	71	0	0
	West	4	0	0
LB %		100.0	0.0	0.0

1856 Republican Convention

	John Fremont (R)	John McLean (R)
FB	520	37
East	322	23
South	5	0
Midwest	181	14
West	12	0
FB %	91.7	6.5

1856 General Election

	James Buchanan (D)	John Fremont (R)	Millard Fillmore (A-W)
PV	1,836,072	1,342,345	873,053
PV %	45.3	33.1	21.5
East	38.9	43.2	17.8
South	57.3	0.0	42.7
Midwest	45.6	43.0	11.4
West	48.4	18.8	32.8
Counties	1,067	362	269
Counties %	62.8	21.3	15.8
States	19	11	1
States %	61.3	35.5	3.2
EV	174	114	8
East	37	76	8
South	100	0	0
Midwest	33	38	0
West	4	0	0
EV %	58.8	38.5	2.7

1860 Republican Convention

		Abraham Lincoln (R)	William Seward (R)	Simon Cameron (R)	Salmon Chase (R)	Edward Bates (R)
FB		102	173½	50½	49	48
	East	23	108½	47½	4	22
	South	20	17	1	8	2
	Midwest	59	40	2	37	19
	West	0	8	0	0	5
FB	%	21.9	37.2	10.8	10.5	10.3
LB	(#3)	350	111½	0	2	0
	East	148	86½	0	2	0
	South	52	0	0	0	0
	Midwest	140	22	0	0	0
	West	10	3	0	0	0
LB	%	75.1	23.9	0.0	0.4	0.0

1860 Democratic Convention

		Stephen Douglas (D)	abstention	Robert Hunter (D)	James Guthrie (D)
FB		145½	50	42	35½
	East	74	1	16	19
	South	1	49	26	12
	Midwest	70½	0	0	4½
	West	0	0	0	0
FB	%	48.0	16.5	13.9	11.7
LB	(#59)	190½	99½	0	5½
	East	93½	17½	0	2½
	South	26½	72	0	1½
	Midwest	70½	3	0	1½
	West	0	7	0	0
LB	%	62.9	32.8	0.0	1.8

1860 General Election

	Abraham Lincoln (R)	John Breckin- ridge (SD)	John Bell (CU)	Stephen Douglas (D)
PV	1,865,908	848,019	590,901	1,380,202
PV %	39.8	18.1	12.6	29.5
East	53.4	13.9	4.7	28.0
South	0.3	48.9	41.1	9.7
Midwest	48.9	3.6	4.9	42.6
West	32.7	29.0	6.9	31.3
Counties	556	672	359	276
Counties %	29.8	36.0	19.2	14.8
States	18	11	3	1
States %	54.5	33.3	9.1	3.0
EV	180	72	39	12
East	107	11	0	3
South	0	61	39	0
Midwest	66	0	0	9
West	7	0	0	0
EV %	59.4	23.8	12.9	4.0

1864 Republican Convention

	Abraham Lincoln (R)	Ulysses Grant (R)
FB	494	22
East	240	0
South	61	0
Midwest	168	22
West	25	0
FB %	95.2	4.2

1864 Democratic Convention

	George McClellan (D)	Thomas Seymour (D)	Horatio Seymour (D)
FB	174	38	12
East	100	14	½
South	5½	5½	0
Midwest	64	15	11½
West	4½	3½	0
FB %	77.0	16.8	5.3

1864 General Election

	Abraham Lincoln (R)	George McClellan (D)
PV	2,218,388	1,812,807
PV %	55.0	45.0
East	54.3	45.7
South	30.2	69.8
Midwest	57.0	42.9
West	58.1	41.9
Counties	719	393
Counties %	64.6	35.3
States	22	3
States %	88.0	12.0
EV	212	21
East	110	10
South	0	11
Midwest	92	0
West	10	0
EV %	91.0	9.0

1868
Republican Convention

	Ulysses Grant (R)
FB	650
East	242
South	184
Midwest	192
West	32
FB %	100.0

1868 Democratic Convention
(first of two charts)

	Horatio Seymour (D)	George Pendle-ton (D)	Andrew Johnson (D)	Sanford Church (D)	Winfield Hancock (D)
FB	0	105	65	34	33½
East	0	17	3½	33	17½
South	0	11	61	0	14
Midwest	0	72	½	1	2
West	0	5	0	0	0
FB %	0.0	33.1	20.5	10.7	10.6
LB (#22)	317	0	0	0	0
East	120	0	0	0	0
South	91	0	0	0	0
Midwest	95	0	0	0	0
West	11	0	0	0	0
LB %	100.0	0.0	0.0	0.0	0.0

1868 Democratic Convention
(second of two charts)

		Asa Packer (D)	James English (D)	Joel Parker (D)	James Doo-little (D)
FB		26	16	13	13
	East	26	11	7	5
	South	0	5	0	0
	Midwest	0	0	0	8
	West	0	0	6	0
FB %		8.2	5.0	4.1	4.1
LB (#22)		0	0	0	0
	East	0	0	0	0
	South	0	0	0	0
	Midwest	0	0	0	0
	West	0	0	0	0
LB %		0.0	0.0	0.0	0.0

1868 General Election

		Ulysses Grant (R)	Horatio Seymour (D)
PV		3,013,650	2,708,744
PV %		52.7	47.3
	East	53.0	47.0
	South	44.8	55.2
	Midwest	55.9	44.1
	West	50.6	49.4
Counties		991	712
Counties %		58.1	41.7
States		26	8
States %		76.5	23.5

1868 General Election
(continued)

	Ulysses Grant (R)	Horatio Seymour (D)
EV	214	80
East	70	50
South	41	27
Midwest	95	0
West	8	3
EV %	72.8	27.2

1872
Republican Convention

	Ulysses Grant (R)
FB	752
East	260
South	214
Midwest	238
West	40
FB %	100.0

1872
Democratic Convention

	Horace Greeley (D)
FB	686
East	218
South	208
Midwest	236
West	24
FB %	93.7

1872 General Election

	Ulysses Grant (R)	Horace Greeley (D-LR)	Thomas Hendricks (D)	Gratz Brown (D-LR)	Charles Jenkins (D)	David Davis (D-LR)
PV	3,598,235	2,834,761	----	----	----	----
PV %	55.6	43.8	----	----	----	----
East	57.9	42.0	----	----	----	----
South	52.7	47.1	----	----	----	----
Midwest	55.4	43.5	----	----	----	----
West	56.9	41.9	----	----	----	----
Counties	1,340	836	----	----	----	----
Counties %	61.5	38.3	----	----	----	----
States	29	----	4	2	0	0
States %	82.9	----	11.4	5.7	0.0	0.0
EV	286	----	42	18	2	1
East	121	----	8	0	0	0
South	50	----	28	10	2	0
Midwest	103	----	6	8	0	1
West	12	----	0	0	0	0
EV %	81.9	----	12.0	5.2	0.6	0.3

1876 Republican Convention

	Rutherford Hayes (R)	James Blaine (R)	Oliver Morton (R)	Benjamin Bristow (R)	Roscoe Conkling (R)	John Hartranft (R)
FB	61	285	124	113	99	58
East	8	73	2	37	69	58
South	2	49	80	55	25	0
Midwest	50	130	42	14	2	0
West	1	33	0	7	3	0
FB %	8.1	37.7	16.4	14.9	13.1	7.7

1876 Republican Convention (continued)

		Rutherford Hayes (R)	James Blaine (R)	Oliver Morton (R)	Benjamin Bristow (R)	Roscoe Conkling (R)	John Hartranft (R)
LB	(#7)	384	351	0	21	0	0
	East	142	111	0	7	0	0
	South	118	92	0	4	0	0
	Midwest	108	120	0	10	0	0
	West	16	28	0	0	0	0
LB	%	50.8	46.4	0.0	2.8	0.0	0.0

1876 Democratic Convention

		Samuel Tilden (D)	Thomas Hendricks (D)	Winfield Hancock (D)	William Allen (D)	Thomas Bayard (D)
FB		401½	140½	75	54	33
	East	161	3	58	10	8
	South	137½	36½	15	0	25
	Midwest	82	92	2	44	0
	West	21	9	0	0	0
FB	%	54.4	19.0	10.2	7.3	4.5
LB	(#2)	535	85	58	54	4
	East	188	2	58	10	0
	South	185	25	0	0	4
	Midwest	134	58	0	44	0
	West	28	0	0	0	0
LB	%	72.5	11.5	7.9	7.3	0.5

1876 General Election

	Rutherford Hayes (R)	Samuel Tilden (D)
PV	4,034,311	4,288,546
PV %	48.0	51.0
East	50.1	49.3
South	40.0	59.9
Midwest	51.0	46.8
West	51.1	48.7
Counties	948	1,299
Counties %	42.2	57.8
States	21	17
States %	55.3	44.7
EV	185	184
East	63	66
South	19	88
Midwest	88	30
West	15	0
EV %	50.1	49.9

1880 Republican Convention

	James Garfield (R)	Ulysses Grant (R)	James Blaine (R)	John Sherman (R)	George Edmunds (R)
FB	0	304	284	93	34
East	0	95	113	9	32
South	0	140	27	45	1
Midwest	0	61	108	39	1
West	0	8	36	0	0
FB %	0.0	40.2	37.6	12.3	4.5

1880 Republican Convention (continued)

	James Garfield (R)	Ulysses Grant (R)	James Blaine (R)	John Sherman (R)	George Edmunds (R)
LB (#36)	399	306	42	3	0
East	155	98	7	0	0
South	56	139	16	3	0
Midwest	165	61	6	0	0
West	23	8	13	0	0
LB %	52.8	40.5	5.6	0.4	0.0

1880 Democratic Convention (first of two charts)

	Winfield Hancock (D)	Thomas Bayard (D)	Henry Payne (D)	Allen Thurman (D)
FB	171	153½	81	68½
East	67	59½	72	11½
South	69	79	0	10
Midwest	35	15	9	44
West	0	0	0	3
FB %	23.2	20.8	11.0	9.3
LB (#2)	705	2	0	0
East	256	2	0	0
South	214	0	0	0
Midwest	205	0	0	0
West	30	0	0	0
LB %	95.5	0.3	0.0	0.0

1880 Democratic Convention
(second of two charts)

	Stephen Field (D)	William Morrison (D)	Thomas Hendricks (D)	Samuel Tilden (D)
FB	65	62	49½	38
East	5	0	8½	18
South	40	0	5	7
Midwest	6	62	35	8
West	14	0	1	5
FB %	8.8	8.4	6.7	5.1
LB (#2)	0	0	30	1
East	0	0	0	0
South	0	0	0	0
Midwest	0	0	30	1
West	0	0	0	0
LB %	0.0	0.0	4.1	0.1

1880 General Election

	James Garfield (R)	Winfield Hancock (D)	James Weaver (GR)
PV	4,446,158	4,444,260	305,997
PV %	48.3	48.3	3.3
East	51.1	47.0	1.7
South	37.5	59.4	3.0
Midwest	51.8	43.0	5.1
West	49.5	48.6	1.8
Counties	1,055	1,253	7
Counties %	45.6	54.1	0.3
States	19	19	0
States %	50.0	50.0	0.0

1880 General Election (continued)

		James Garfield (R)	Winfield Hancock (D)	James Weaver (GR)
EV		214	155	0
	East	104	25	0
	South	0	107	0
	Midwest	103	15	0
	West	7	8	0
EV %		58.0	42.0	0.0

1884 Democratic Convention

		Grover Cleveland (D)	Thomas Bayard (D)	Allen Thurman (D)	Samuel Randall (D)	Joseph McDonald (D)	Thomas Hendricks (D)
FB		392	170	88	78	56	1
	East	147	44	4	69	0	0
	South	84	101	17	4	6	0
	Midwest	148	21	44	4	45	1
	West	13	4	23	1	5	0
FB %		47.8	20.7	10.7	9.5	6.8	0.1
LB (#2)		683	81½	4	4	2	45½
	East	202	20½	1	4	0	34½
	South	175	59	2	0	1	3
	Midwest	264	2	0	0	1	3
	West	42	0	1	0	0	5
LB %		83.3	9.9	0.5	0.5	0.2	5.5

1884 Republican Convention

		James Blaine (R)	Chester Arthur (R)	George Edmunds (R)	John Logan (R)
FB		334½	278	93	63½
	East	125	56	64	1
	South	43½	179	2	11½
	Midwest	127	35	26	51
	West	39	8	1	0
FB %		40.8	33.9	11.3	7.7
LB (#4)		541	207	41	7
	East	155	51	40	0
	South	82	149	1	1
	Midwest	258	5	0	6
	West	46	2	0	0
LB %		66.0	25.2	5.0	0.9

1884 General Election

		Grover Cleveland (D)	James Blaine (R)
PV		4,874,621	4,848,936
PV %		48.5	48.2
	East	46.1	49.8
	South	58.7	40.5
	Midwest	45.3	50.8
	West	44.7	52.4
Counties		1,276	1,098
Counties %		53.7	46.2
States		20	18
States %		52.6	47.4

1884 General Election
       (continued)

		Grover Cleveland (D)	James Blaine (R)
EV		219	182
	East	68	62
	South	120	0
	Midwest	31	103
	West	0	17
EV %		54.6	45.4

1888 Republican Convention
    (first of two charts)

		Benjamin Harrison (R)	John Sherman (R)	Walter Gresham (R)	Chauncey Depew (R)
FB		85	229	107	99
	East	31	50	6	85
	South	17	123	20	8
	Midwest	33	56	69	6
	West	4	0	12	0
FB %		10.2	27.5	12.9	11.9
LB (#8)		544	118	59	0
	East	246	10	1	0
	South	116	61	6	0
	Midwest	133	47	52	0
	West	49	0	0	0
LB %		65.4	14.2	7.1	0.0

1888 Republican Convention
(second of two charts)

		Russell Alger (R)	William Boyd Allison (R)	James Blaine (R)
FB		84	72	35
	East	11	14	11
	South	31	14	5
	Midwest	36	33	2
	West	6	11	17
FB %		10.1	8.7	4.2
LB (#8)		100	0	5
	East	1	0	1
	South	52	0	3
	Midwest	45	0	0
	West	2	0	1
LB %		12.0	0.0	0.6

1888
Democratic Convention

		Grover Cleveland (D)
FB		822
	East	262
	South	240
	Midwest	270
	West	50
FB %		100.0

1888 General Election

	Benjamin Harrison (R)	Grover Cleveland (D)	Clinton Fisk (PROH)
PV	5,443,892	5,534,488	249,819
PV %	47.8	48.6	2.2
East	50.9	46.6	2.2
South	37.9	59.5	1.0
Midwest	50.1	45.0	2.8
West	51.7	44.8	2.3
Counties	1,157	1,290	0
Counties %	47.2	52.6	0.0
States	20	18	0
States %	52.6	47.4	0.0
EV	233	168	0
East	98	32	0
South	0	120	0
Midwest	118	16	0
West	17	0	0
EV %	58.1	41.9	0.0

1892 Democratic Convention

	Grover Cleveland (D)	David Hill (D)	Horace Boies (D)	Arthur Gorman (D)
FB	$617\frac{1}{3}$	114	103	$36\frac{1}{2}$
East	174	78	1	$13\frac{1}{2}$
South	$149\frac{1}{3}$	26	37	11
Midwest	244	6	43	6
West	50	4	22	6
FB %	67.8	12.5	11.3	4.0

1892 Republican Convention

		Benjamin Harrison (R)	James Blaine (R)	William McKinley (R)
FB		$535\frac{1}{6}$	$182\frac{1}{6}$	182
	East	133	59	75
	South	$189\frac{1}{6}$	$44\frac{1}{6}$	17
	Midwest	183	40	81
	West	30	39	9
FB %		59.1	20.1	20.1

1892 General Election

		Grover Cleveland (D)	Benjamin Harrison (R)	James Weaver (POP)	John Bidwell (PROH)
PV		5,551,883	5,179,244	1,024,280	270,770
PV %		46.1	43.0	8.5	2.2
	East	47.5	48.5	1.0	2.5
	South	57.3	27.0	14.5	0.9
	Midwest	41.5	46.4	9.4	2.7
	West	29.1	43.0	25.4	2.6
Counties		1,390	1,017	276	0
Counties %		51.8	37.9	10.3	0.0
States		23	16	4	0
States %		52.3	36.4	9.1	0.0
EV		277	145	22	0
	East	69	65	0	0
	South	125	0	0	0
	Midwest	75	66	11	0
	West	8	14	11	0
EV %		62.4	32.7	5.0	0.0

Note: Cleveland, Harrison, and Weaver also tied in one state.

1896 Republican Convention

	William McKinley (R)	Thomas Reed (R)	Matthew Quay (R)	Levi Morton (R)
FB	661½	84½	61½	58
East	91	65	58	55
South	232½	17½	3½	3
Midwest	276	2	0	0
West	62	0	0	0
FB %	71.6	9.1	6.7	6.3

1896 Democratic Convention
(first of two charts)

	William Jennings Bryan (D)	Richard Bland (D)	abstention	Robert Pattison (D)
FB	137	235	178	97
East	12	4	139	93
South	83	84	1	1
Midwest	37	106	38	3
West	5	41	0	0
FB %	14.7	25.3	19.1	10.4
LB (#5)	652	11	162	95
East	28	7	138	95
South	262	0	0	0
Midwest	276	0	24	0
West	86	4	0	0
LB %	70.1	1.2	17.4	10.2

1896 Democratic Convention
(second of two charts)

	Joseph Blackburn (D)	Horace Boies (D)	John McLean (D)
FB	82	67	54
East	12	1	5
South	51	23	0
Midwest	2	41	46
West	17	2	3
FB %	8.8	7.2	5.8
LB (#5)	0	0	0
East	0	0	0
South	0	0	0
Midwest	0	0	0
West	0	0	0
LB %	0.0	0.0	0.0

1896 General Election

	William McKinley (R)	William Jennings Bryan (D-POP)
PV	7,108,480	6,511,495
PV %	51.0	46.7
East	60.5	36.0
South	37.5	60.6
Midwest	52.6	45.8
West	34.8	63.7
Counties	1,168	1,554
Counties %	42.8	57.0
States	23	22
States %	51.1	48.9

1896 General Election
(continued)

	William McKinley (R)	William Jennings Bryan (D-POP)
EV	271	176
East	134	0
South	12	113
Midwest	113	39
West	12	24
EV %	60.6	39.4

1900
Republican Convention

	William McKinley (R)
FB	926
East	270
South	262
Midwest	304
West	90
FB %	100.0

1900
Democratic Convention

	William Jennings Bryan (D)
FB	936
East	274
South	262
Midwest	304
West	96
FB %	100.0

1900 General Election

	William McKinley (R)	William Jennings Bryan (D)
PV	7,218,039	6,358,345
PV %	51.7	45.5
East	56.5	40.5
South	38.1	59.3
Midwest	53.6	43.7
West	49.7	47.1
Counties	1,385	1,342
Counties %	50.8	49.2
States	28	17
States %	62.2	37.8
EV	292	155
East	134	0
South	0	125
Midwest	135	17
West	23	13
EV %	65.3	34.7

4.
The Road to Normalcy: 1904-1928

Ohio Senator Warren Harding prided himself on his podium style and mellifluous voice. But his knowledge of the English language was another matter. A speech during his 1920 Presidential campaign included the word, "normality." Harding came as close as he could, pronouncing it "normalcy." Reporters found it funny, but the new word caught on as code for Republican prosperity. It remains in the dictionary today.

The period of 1904-1928 was largely one of such normalcy. Republicans won five of the seven elections, all by lopsided margins. The two Democratic victories belonged to Woodrow Wilson, neither with a majority of the popular vote. Wilson first reached the White House because of a serious but temporary split in Republican ranks.

The dominant figure of the period was the charismatic, some said hyperactive, Theodore Roosevelt. He succeeded to the White House in 1901, won his own term by a landslide in 1904, then dictated the choice of his successor four years later. The president of Columbia College, Nicholas Murray Butler, knew the still youthful Roosevelt was in a fix. "The real problem that confronts you is whether you can be a sage at fifty," Butler told him. "If you can, your permanent reputation seems to me certain. If you cannot, then the outlook is different."[1] It was too much to expect Roosevelt to fidget on the sidelines. He returned to play crucially destructive roles in the Republican defeats of 1912 and 1916. The 1920 nomination was conceded to be his for the asking. It fell to Harding after Roosevelt's death.

Republican dominance was aided by Democratic discord. The period commenced with battles between William Jennings Bryan and his conservative enemies, each wishing more to beat the other than win in the fall. After the Wilson interlude and the disillusionment that followed World War I, the party endured an amazing series of campaigns in the 1920s. It crashed in 1920 by embracing the vilified League of Nations, self-destructed in 1924 by requiring 103 ballots to find a nominee, and broke wide open in 1928 over the nomination of a Catholic. Will Rogers joked, "I don´t belong to an organized political party. I´m a Democrat."

The Republican coalition seemed airtight. It included farmers, labor, blacks, and the urban East. They strayed during the Wilson elections, but were generally loyal. It would take startling news from that bastion of normalcy, Wall Street, to do the unthinkable: smash the Republican stranglehold on the Presidency.

ELECTION NO. 30:   1904

Grover Cleveland loved to beat the Republicans. He did it twice himself in Presidential elections. But he was more concerned in 1904 about enemies within, musing, "What an inspiration it would be to hear Democratic leadership proclaim, `Bryanism is not Democracy.´"[2] William Jennings Bryan encouraged the former President by forswearing a third straight candidacy. But Bryan made it clear he would not willingly concede power. He chided Cleveland and his fellow conservatives, "They demand the leadership and say to the party, ´Did we not hold office in thy name, and in thy name draw large salaries?´"[3]

While the Democrats concentrated on fighting each other, President Theodore Roosevelt was laying the groundwork for a landslide victory in the fall. Roosevelt seized control of the Republican machinery soon after assuming the Presidency in 1901. Only one man caused him worry by 1904, "Senator Hanna...has been intoxicated by the thought that perhaps he could be nominated himself, or at least dictate the nomination."[4] Roosevelt´s concern was misplaced. Mark Hanna had already concluded there was no way he could prevent the President´s nomination. The Ohio Senator´s death in February settled the matter.

The Republican Old Guard was not enamored of its busy young President with his talk of "the strenuous life." Roosevelt didn´t fit the image of a safe and sane Republican leader. His advocacy of conservation and antitrust prosecution were contrary to party policy. But without Hanna, the Republican right had no choice other than to acquiesce in the President´s candidacy. Roosevelt was the first man to become Chief Executive upon his predecessor´s death and subsequently be nominated himself.

Conservatives were faring better in the Democratic camp. They managed to regain the upper hand they lost in 1896. What they lacked was a candidate. Cleveland refused to run again. Maryland Senator Arthur Gorman was interested, but failed to stir up any enthusiasm. He dropped out in February. Former New York Senator David Hill introduced another name into this vacuum: Alton Parker, the Chief Justice of the New York Court of Appeals. Bryanites laughed that no one knew who Parker was; they called him "the enigma from New York." But Cleveland knew Parker was a conservative and a strong votegetter in his home state. The former

President soon tendered his endorsement.

Bryan had trouble of his own in locating a champion. He shared many of the views of publisher William Randolph Hearst, who had already entered the contest. But Bryan, the religious, anti-imperialist Nebraskan, was uncomfortable with the flamboyant Hearst, who liked to boast that his papers had triggered the Spanish-American War. Bryan eventually gave lukewarm support to Missouri Senator Francis Cockrell. Both challengers were swamped by Parker, the conservatives' darling, on the first ballot at the convention.

The Populist party again fielded a ticket, but its impact was negligible. Prominence on the left passed to the Socialist party, which nominated a former Populist from Indiana, Eugene Debs. Debs was a famous firebrand by World War I, but his 1904 campaign was decidedly low-key.

Theodore Roosevelt was also playing it safe that fall. His fundraisers pulled in the then-astonishing sum of $2.2 million in contributions, three-quarters of it from cor- porations. The New York World dispelled the overwhelming boredom of the campaign in October by suggesting that Roosevelt was playing at conservatism to raise funds. It asked if the corporations "that are pouring money into your campaign chests assume that they are buying protection?"[5] Parker, who had been unable to find a potent issue, gleefully called the contributions "blackmail." Roosevelt angrily labeled the charge "a wicked falsehood." That by-play completed, the dullness descended again.

Roosevelt's victory was one of the most convincing in history. He carried all but seven electoral votes in the East, and swept the Midwest and the West. Parker announced he would never run again, fleeing to the obscurity from which he had emerged just months earlier. Conservatives settled down for a restful four years, but soon watched in dismay as Roosevelt returned to his interests in regulatory legislation and antitrust cases. "We bought the son of a bitch," Henry Clay Frick complained, "and then he did not stay bought."[6]

ELECTION NO. 31: 1908

The campaign of 1904 was so dull that some people couldn't wait for 1908. Even as he spoke on the stump for Alton Parker, William Jennings Bryan was preparing for a third try at the Presidency. Reporters noted that his 1904 addresses seemed more like advance declarations of candidacy than pleas for the current Democratic nominee. Bryan reinforced that impression as soon as Parker was trounced by Theodore Roosevelt. He blamed the Democratic defeat on abandonment of "the fixed principle -- equal rights to all and special privileges to none."[7]

Roosevelt did his part to set the stage early. On election night in 1904, he went down to meet White House reporters. The press corps got more than it bargained for. The President went beyond the usual victory statement to drop a blockbuster, "Under no circumstances will I be a candidate for or accept another nomination."[8]   It was a declaration he would regret even before departing the White House. Roosevelt confided to Bryan in early 1908 that he still liked the Presidency too much to leave.

By then, it was too late. Roosevelt had typically taken it on himself to select his successor. His first choice was Secretary of State Elihu Root, who did not share the President's enthusiasm. Roosevelt wanted Root to run for Governor of New York in 1906 to establish a political base, but Root insisted on staying in Washington. The candidate hunt moved on, with Roosevelt writing his Secretary of War, William Howard Taft, in 1906 that he was, "I think the best man to receive it." Taft wasn't much more excited than Root had been. His goal was the Supreme Court, not the White House. "Politics," he once said, "when I am in it, makes me sick."[9] His wife and family were instrumental in convincing Taft to reluctantly accept the Roosevelt anointment.

The word from the White House was sufficient to lock up Taft's first-ballot Republican nomination. Roosevelt worried to the end, "If Taft's foolish opponents...are able to hold up the nomination until after the first ballot, there is a chance of a stampede for me, and if it really gets under way, nothing that I could do would stop it."[10] Not that Roosevelt would have minded a draft, but he feared the two-term tradition was so entrenched that he would soil his image with certain defeat in the fall. It was better to dictate the choice of Taft.

William Jennings Bryan had few worries on the Democratic side. His trip around the world after the 1904 campaign increased his stature, while Roosevelt's progressive program gave Bryan's ideas new respectability. The Wall Street Journal marveled at the Great Commoner's continuing appeal, "He has built up a personal following unparalleled for one with a record of nothing but defeat, and with no patronage to strengthen his control."[11] His two opponents, Circuit Court Judge George Gray and Minnesota Governor John Johnson, were not well-known. Bryan defeated them with ease on the first convention ballot.

Eugene Debs was back literally to add color to the fall campaign. The Socialist nominee traveled the country on a train dubbed the Red Special. He delivered more than 300 speeches, but saw his share of the popular vote decline slightly from 1904.

Bryan also set a wearying pace, giving as many as thirty speeches a day. He conceded the death of silver as an issue and now advocated a general package of reform legislation. His slogan was a throwback to his Populist roots: "Shall the people rule?" Bryan declared the alternative was to allow Roosevelt to get away with his plot for "a forced succession to the Presidency."

Taft based his campaign on his experience in government. He reminded his audiences that Bryan could boast only of four years in Congress, while Taft had been a judge, territorial governor, and Cabinet member. Roosevelt played

an active behind-the-scenes role in directing Taft´s
strategy, dispatching a seemingly endless series of
suggestions. One was that the nominee stop playing golf
until election day.

The outcome in the Electoral College rivaled Roosevelt´s
1904 triumph. Taft defeated Bryan by a margin of almost 2-1,
holding the Democrat to just 22 electoral votes outside of
the Solid South. Taft knew his personal performance was not
the real cause of his victory. He wrote his good friend,
Theodore Roosevelt, as soon as the returns were in, "You have
always been the chief agent in working out the present status
of affairs, and my selection and election are chiefly your
work."[12] Roosevelt now faced a greater challenge. The most
active of Presidents was entering retirement at the tender
age of 50.

ELECTION NO. 32: 1912

Theodore Roosevelt and William Howard Taft were good friends
in 1909 when Roosevelt departed for Africa and Taft settled
down in the White House. They were bitter enemies by 1912.
Roosevelt ridiculed his chosen successor as a "fathead" and a
"puzzlewit." Taft more elegantly blasted his benefactor as a
"dangerous egotist" and "a demagogue." All signs pointed to
a campaign that would be unusually dominated by personality.

The Roosevelt-Taft split had its base in issues, but ego
seemed to play a larger role. Although Taft had pledged to
follow his predecessor´s policies, he was by nature more
conservative than Roosevelt, making it increasingly difficult
to keep his word. The vocal group of progressive Republicans
in Congress turned against the President. Roosevelt returned
from Africa to be greeted by pleas that he break with Taft
and join the fight.

The old Rough Rider was irritated by what he saw as
Taft´s ungrateful independence. He was also frankly bored
with life away from the political arena. In a speech in
Kansas, Roosevelt unveiled a new program, "The New
Nationalism." Taft and the Old Guard were shocked at its
more radical provisions, including a proposal that voters be
allowed to challenge judicial decisions in referendums.

Wisconsin Senator Robert La Follette launched a
challenge to Taft. La Follette´s state had pioneered in use
of the primary election, which now burst on the national
scene. He hoped to stop the President by demonstrating
Taft´s unpopularity with the Republican rank-and-file. La
Follette´s miscalculation was in assuming Roosevelt would
suppress his smoldering resentment and stay on the sidelines. But Roosevelt joined the race early in 1912, leaving
La Follette to complain bitterly of "the studied undermining"
of his candidacy as his progressive supporters defected to
the former President.

Roosevelt won nine of the twelve primaries, but unlike
in later years, their results were not binding. Taft held
the levers of Republican power and secured a majority of the

convention delegates. He confided to a visitor that he felt
himself to have an important mission, "Whether I win or lose
is not the important thing. But I am in this fight to
perform a great public duty -- the duty of keeping Theodore
Roosevelt out of the White House."[13] Roosevelt challenged
the credentials of many Taft delegates, including some he
knew were valid. His supporters derisively chanted
"choo-choo" at the convention as challenge after challenge
was rejected. Thousands in the galleries rubbed sandpaper
together to add to the steamroller sound effect aimed at
Taft's managers. Roosevelt denounced the "naked robbery" and
asked his delegates to abstain from voting. Taft won on the
first ballot.

It would have been unlike Theodore Roosevelt to accept
defeat, particularly under such circumstances. He trooped
his delegates to a nearby convention hall, where he
harangued, "We stand at Armageddon and we battle for the
Lord!"[14] The Progressive party was created to continue the
Roosevelt campaign into the fall. Taft dismissed the instant
third party's supporters as being of the "labor, socialistic,
discontented, ragtag, and bobtail variety."

The Democrats could not match the Republican drama, but
they also had a spirited two-man race. Speaker of the House
Champ Clark and New Jersey Governor Woodrow Wilson each won
five primaries, with Clark more successful in lining up
delegates. The Missourian had been a faithful supporter of
William Jennings Bryan, while Wilson had a more conservative
past. He had once expressed a desire to knock Bryan "into a
cocked hat."

The Great Commoner was on hand as a convention delegate
from Nebraska, having renounced a fourth candidacy. Skeptics
thought Bryan's secret hope was for a deadlock that would
lead to his nomination. Such a tie-up seemed unlikely by the
tenth ballot, when New York shifted its votes to Clark,
giving him a majority. The Speaker prepared his telegram of
acceptance, figuring the two-thirds barrier would soon be
broken. Bryan, who had been voting for Clark, rose on the
fourteenth ballot to prevent the inevitable. He announced
that he was switching to Wilson because New York's backing
showed the frontrunner to be under the influence of Tammany
Hall. Clark furiously blasted the "outrageous aspersion,"
but his support inexorably eroded. Wilson passed him on the
thirtieth ballot and won on the forty-sixth.

There was a fourth entry in the crowded autumn field.
Eugene Debs was now well-known as the leading spokesman for
American Socialism. He confidently told his supporters,
"This is our year." Debs won no electoral votes, but he was
right in one respect. His popular-vote percentage proved to
be the high-water mark for the Socialist party, 6 percent.

Although Roosevelt was running on a third-party ticket,
he was the dominant personality that fall. He declared,
"I've been growing more radical instead of less radical."[15]
He savaged both Taft and Wilson in his speeches. The New
York _Times_ thought the Progressive machine was fueled not by
idealism, but by its standard-bearer's massive ego. The

Times speculated that if Roosevelt somehow won, he would then seek in order a fourth term, a dictatorship, and monarchy. Everything about the Rough Rider seemed larger than life. When he was wounded by an assassin in Milwaukee in October, the nation thrilled to his insistence, "I will make this speech or die. It is one thing or the other."[16] He lived.

Taft and Wilson seemed dull by comparison. The President conceded his impending defeat, a result of the Republican split. His only hope was to prepare his party for its future comeback. Wilson looked with awe at Roosevelt, "He is a real, vivid person, whom they have seen and shouted themselves hoarse over and voted for, millions strong; I am a vague, conjectural personality, more made up of opinions and academic prepossessions than of human traits and red corpuscles."[17] But Wilson's style was better suited to the campaign of 1912. He had only to keep the Democratic party together while the Republican chieftains carried on their feud. The result was inevitable: Wilson carried 40 states, 81.9 percent of the electoral votes. The new President had once incorrectly written, "I am _not_ conservative. I am a radical." But such a landslide win by a Democrat was radical in itself.

ELECTION NO. 33:   1916

The Republican calculus added to victory in 1916. The party had won four of the five previous elections. It viewed Woodrow Wilson's Democratic triumph in 1912 as a fluke resulting from a divided opposition. Reconcile the Republican and Progressive parties, went the GOP's reasoning, and Wilson could pack his bags and return to New Jersey.

It didn't seem a bad idea to Theodore Roosevelt. His Progressives were virtually annihilated in the 1914 Congressional elections. He concluded, "The people as a whole are heartily tired of me and of my views."[18] Roosevelt began to consider a party merger that would rehabilitate his image and position him for the Republican nomination.

Old Guard Republicans willingly worked for reconciliation, but they had no intention of suffering the indignity of again marching behind the man who had excoriated them from coast to coast four years earlier. A crowded field of candidates struggled for position, but no one made headway. Unpledged slates won twice as many votes as any of the contenders in the primaries. It was the kind of situation where a charismatic leader such as Roosevelt could galvanize the convention.

William Howard Taft thought he had the alternative: Supreme Court Justice Charles Evans Hughes, once the progressive Governor of New York. Hughes ran unsuccessfully in 1908, but refused to assist any new efforts in 1916, writing, "It seems to me very clear that, as a member of the Supreme Court, I have no right to be a candidate, either openly or passively."[19] Taft continued his efforts, even bringing in members of his old campaign staff to start lining up delegate support for the non-candidate.

The Republican and Progressive conventions met simultaneously. Leaders dickered to arrive at a joint ticket. The Progressives insisted on Roosevelt; the Republicans demanded anyone but Roosevelt. The former President's name was entered for both nominations, triggering the longest demonstration at the GOP gathering. But reporters also noted cries of "Throw him out!" Roosevelt got less than seven percent of the Republican first-ballot vote. Hughes had the lead despite, or perhaps because of his silence. He won on the third ballot. Roosevelt was nominated by the Progressives. His heart was not into another quixotic crusade. He declined, and the party dissolved.

Events had taken an unusual course, but Republicans had the harmony they wanted. The Democrats were also united. There were scattered rumblings of challenges to President Wilson by former Secretary of State William Jennings Bryan or Speaker of the House Champ Clark. Both men quickly ended the rumors by endorsing the President, who was renominated by acclamation.

World War I dominated the headlines during the fall campaign. Wilson and Hughes both advocated American pre- paredness, but the Democrats took a softer line. Wilson's amazingly effective slogan was: "He kept us out of war." Hughes was associated in the public mind with Roosevelt's bellicose declarations. A Democratic pamphlet reinforced the connection: "The Lesson is Plain: If You Want WAR, vote for HUGHES! If You Want Peace With Honor, VOTE FOR WILSON!"[20]

The war issue also bedeviled the Socialist party. Journalist Allan Benson was running in place of Eugene Debs, a fixture on previous tickets. Benson was not as well-known, and he found Socialism tougher to sell in an era of growing nationalism. The party's share of the popular vote was almost cut in half from 1912.

Wilson was active in the fall: signing social legis- lation, preventing a national railroad strike, stressing peace. Hughes had trouble finding an issue to use against the administration, leading the President to scoff that he had no need to attack the Republican nominee, "I am inclined to follow the course suggested by a friend of mine who says...never to murder a man who is committing suicide."[21] Farm states that were traditionally isolationist were switching to the Democrats on the peace issue. They were further lured by the administration's new farm-loan system. Many bitter Progressives were also spurning the GOP.

Republicans tried to remain hopeful. Hughes was doing poorly, but the nation was still traditionally Republican. The election would be close. One key state was California, where insurgent Republican Governor Hiram Johnson was running for the Senate. Hughes and Johnson stayed in the same Long Beach hotel one day by coincidence. The Governor waited for a call from his party's nominee, but Hughes' traveling party was dominated by Republican regulars who detested Johnson. They never told Hughes of the Governor's presence. The nominee later insisted, "If I had known that Johnson was in the hotel, I would have seen him if I had been obliged to kick the door down."[22]   But he didn´t. Johnson, sensing a snub, told his highly effective organization not to bother working for Hughes. Wilson carried California by 3,420 votes.

It appeared Hughes would weather the Long Beach fiasco. Early returns on election night showed him with a large lead. The New York _Times_ declared a Republican victory by 10 p.m. Reporters badgered Hughes for a victory statement. "Wait till the Democrats concede my election," he said carefully. "The newspapers might take it back."[23] That they did, as the Democratic tide rolled in from the Midwest and West. Final figures on Thursday from a Western state clinched Wilson´s 23-vote win in the Electoral College. The state was California.

ELECTION NO. 34:   1920

America was in a sour mood in 1920. The country had sacrificed to win World War I to secure what President Woodrow Wilson promised would be "open covenants of peace, openly arrived at." What the public got was a long, acrimonious Senate debate on the League of Nations, and a world that didn´t seem considerably different. There was a growing desire for what Warren Harding would soon mistakenly call "normalcy." Idealism and progressivism were decidedly on the wane.

The Democrats had long assumed Wilson would defy tradition in 1920, seeking a third term. He gave signs of such an intention in 1919, but his physical collapse later that year made renomination unthinkable. The President was secluded in the White House, unavailable even to his own Cabinet. But he continued to hope for a draft, and expressed his wish that the election be made a "solemn referendum" on the Senate´s rejection of his cherished dream of League membership.

The Republicans also had been waiting for an old standby. The wounds of the 1912 split had healed. Theodore Roosevelt was virtually conceded the nomination. His death in 1919 propelled his old friend, General Leonard Wood, into leadership of the Roosevelt forces. Wood was a hardliner, declaring of Communism, "Kill it as you would a rattlesnake and smash those who follow it, speak for it, or support it."[24] Wood´s rhetoric was too extreme for many Republicans. Illinois Governor Frank Lowden, also in the contest, liked to compare the General´s positions to his as "the goose step vs. the forward step." The third major contender was California Senator Hiram Johnson, who received the most popular votes in the primaries. The Old Guard was in no mood to accept Johnson, no matter how many votes. He was held partly responsible for the last two GOP defeats: serving as Roosevelt´s Progressive running mate in 1912, giving the cold shoulder to Charles Evans Hughes in 1916.

There was an ample supply of dark horses waiting for an

opportunity. The best-known was Herbert Hoover, who had distinguished himself in handling war-relief efforts. Ohio Senator Warren Harding also entered the primaries, but tried to withdraw after an embarrassing loss in Indiana. His wife stopped him. Harding nonetheless had no illusions about his chances or his abilities. He wrote a friend, "I have such a sure understanding of my own inefficiency that I should really be ashamed to presume myself fitted to reach out for a place of such responsibility."[25]

Events and the maneuverings of Harding's manager, Harry Daugherty, expanded the Senator's reach. Wood, Lowden, and Johnson deadlocked at the convention. None would defer, so party leaders met in the infamous "smoke-filled room" to find an alternative. They reached informal agreement on Harding, who was nominated the next day on the tenth ballot. "There ain't any first-raters this year," explained Connecticut Senator Frank Brandegee. "We got a lot of second-raters and Warren Harding is the best of the second-raters."[26] The delegates accepted that rationale, but rebelled at the leadership's Vice Presidential choice, instead drafting Massachusetts Governor Calvin Coolidge.

The Democrats likewise had to reach a compromise choice. Wilson's refusal to withdraw despite his obvious infirmity forced other candidates to tread lightly. The softest step belonged to former Secretary of the Treasury William Gibbs McAdoo, who was also the President's son-in-law. McAdoo refused even to allow his name to be formally entered at the convention. He still led the first ballot. Right behind him was Attorney General Mitchell Palmer, famous to all and reviled by many for his direction of the mass arrests and deportations of political agitators during the "Red Scare." The convention droned through forty-four ballots before rejecting both men, each so closely associated with Wilson. It finally nominated Ohio Governor James Cox. He selected his running mate largely for his name: Assistant Secretary of the Navy Franklin Roosevelt.

Cox quickly sealed the Democratic doom during a July meeting with Wilson. "Mr. President," he pledged, "we are going to be a million percent with you, and your administration, and that means the League of Nations."[27] It was exactly what a strife-weary nation did not want to hear. Cox spread the message during a frenzied nationwide tour. Harding largely spoke from his front porch. The Socialist nominee, Eugene Debs, was even more confined in his movements. He was in prison for violating the Espionage Act during the war. The authorities let him issue weekly statements.

Cox's steadfast support of American membership in the League contrasted with Harding's extended waffle during the fall. "The issue, therefore, is clear," the Republican once said about Cox and himself. "In simple words, it is that he favors going into the Paris League and I favor staying out."[28] But in other speeches, Harding alluded vaguely to an "Association of Nations" that would be an acceptable improvement upon the League. He never said how.

The candidates faced a greatly expanded electorate. The Nineteenth Amendment was ratified in August, giving women the right to vote. They proved to be as eager as men to punish the Democrats. As election day neared, Hiram Johnson mused, "If it were a prize fight, the police would interfere on the ground of brutality."[29] Harding scored a clean knockout of Wilson's "solemn referendum." He swept all electoral votes in the East, Midwest, and West. His popular-vote percentage was the first ever recorded above 60 percent. But it was a transitory vote of confidence in the new President. His administration was soon mired in scandal. Harding's death in 1923 saved him from further embarrassment, but not from the judgment of history. Frank Brandegee turned out to be right: 1920 just wasn't the year for first-raters.

ELECTION NO. 35: 1924

It might have been a minority opinion when he expressed it, but Calvin Coolidge was good to his boast. Coolidge once said his first thought upon being elevated to the Presidency by the death of Warren Harding in 1923 was, "I believe I can swing it."[30] Democrats scoffed. They were certain 1924 would be their year because of the administration scandals known collectively as Teapot Dome. Progressive Republicans viewed Coolidge as an ineffectual standpatter. Hiram Johnson and Robert La Follette prepared to challenge his drive for the nomination. Even conservative Republicans were far from overjoyed. It wasn't too long ago that Senator Henry Cabot Lodge had laughed at the idea of the middle-class Coolidge ever being President. "Nominate a man who lives in a two-family home?" he bellowed. "Never! Massachusetts is not for him!"[31]

Coolidge soon proved he _could_ swing it. He moved quickly after Harding's death to take control of the national Republican machinery. Johnson announced he would oppose the President in the primaries, but the matter seemed settled even before the first ballot was marked. Coolidge won fifteen primaries, including the contest in Johnson's California. The challenger carried only South Dakota. The Old Guard, always impressed by power, fell quickly in line behind the President. He was nominated with token opposition.

Coolidge handled Teapot Dome with what one journalist called "alert inactivity." Cabinet members suspected of illegal activity were quietly eased out. Special prosecutors were handed the job of initiating legal action that would drag on for years. The nation gave Coolidge credit for sweeping corruption from his own party's administration! It was an ironic bonus that the Democratic frontrunner, William Gibbs McAdoo, was spattered by the mud from Teapot Dome that missed the President. Wealthy oilman Edward Doheny revealed during hearings on the scandal that he had McAdoo on retainer. The former Secretary of the Treasury had not been involved in the questionable diversion of federal oil reserves, but his name was now vaguely linked in the public mind to Teapot Dome. The chairman of the Senate investigating committee, Thomas Walsh, was an ardent McAdoo

backer, but he now wrote his man, "You are no longer available as a candidate."[32]

McAdoo was the only major Democratic contender to go the
primary route. He lured enough delegates to enter the
convention as the frontrunner, but further gains were stymied
by his deteriorating image. New York Governor Alfred Smith
was running second, but many delegates doubted he had the
ability to beat Coolidge in the fall. McAdoo was Protestant,
a supporter of Prohibition, and a man who called New York
City "wanting in national ideals, devoid of conscience."
Smith was Catholic, an opponent of Prohibition, and a
resident of New York City. There seemed little common ground
for reconciliation.

Balloting continued for nine days. A cartoon in a
Portland, Oregon, newspaper showed the Democrats´ dilemma. A
donkey on a highwire found himself poised over two large
vats: "McAdoo Oil" and "Smith Beer." A fall either way would
be messy. The stalemate dragged on to the ninety-ninth
ballot, when both antagonists withdrew. Former Ambassador to
Great Britain John Davis, who had been in third place,
crawled to victory on the 103rd. Friends congratulated
Davis on winning the nomination of the longest convention
ever. "Thanks," he replied. "But you know what it´s
worth."[33]

The Republican slogan in the fall was, "Keep Cool With
Coolidge." The President was an unexciting speaker, as was
Davis. The only fire was supplied by Robert La Follette, who
campaigned under the banner of a new Progressive party. His
opponents depicted La Follette as a radical for trying to
fashion a coalition of the factory and the farm. "I´m
radical, but not too darned radical," he retorted. "Just
enough to make the farmers and the laborers high-paid
people."[34] La Follette´s appeal in the Midwest and West drew
a flood of votes primarily from the already crippled
Democratic ticket.

The final results demonstrated that Coolidge´s early
confidence was not misplaced. He nearly doubled Davis´s
popular vote. The Democrat did not receive an electoral vote
outside of the Solid South. A year that began with
Republican scandal ended gloriously in Republican triumph.

Calvin Coolidge had looked forward to his vindication
for a long time, but found it meant little. His 14-year-old
son, Calvin, died of blood poisoning in the summer of 1924.
"When he went, the power and glory of the Presidency went
with him," Coolidge later wrote. "I don´t know why such a
price was exacted for occupying the White House."[35]

ELECTION NO. 36: 1928

Calvin Coolidge remained an enigma to the end. The President
was so popular that his reelection in 1928 was considered a
strong likelihood. His supporters opened a headquarters in
Boston during the summer of 1927. Reporters filing into a
small office in South Dakota that August were aware of all

this, and hardly expected any blockbusting news from the vacationing Coolidge. The silent President handed each journalist a small piece of paper. It said, "I do not choose to run for President in 1928."[36] He had not even discussed the decision with his wife. All questions were turned aside.

The terse announcement caused consternation in Washington. Commerce Secretary Herbert Hoover wanted to chase the suddenly available Republican nomination, but he wasn't certain how available it really was. He wrote, "The word 'choose' has various connotations in its New England usage."[37] Efforts to smoke out the President's true intentions were predictably fruitless. Hoover asked Coolidge if he should enter the Ohio primary. The President responded, "Why not?" The Secretary lined up 400 convention delegates by May, but confessed to Coolidge in another meeting that they still probably preferred the President's reelection, if he would accede to a draft. Coolidge said only, "If you have 400 delegates, you better keep them."[38]

Hoover continued along his uncertain path, still half-expecting to be ambushed by a sudden surge for the President at the convention. The Commerce Secretary won almost half of the primaries, based largely on his still-gleaming reputation as a relief administrator during World War I and an efficient defender of the interests of postwar big business. The Old Guard advanced Kansas Senator Charles Curtis. Farmers who were already suffering from a depression were attracted to the economic plans of former Illinois Governor Frank Lowden. Neither was able to stop the Hoover steamroller from a first-ballot win. Coolidge received only 17 delegate votes.

The Democrats, who struggled through 103 ballots four years earlier, faced a remarkably uncomplicated decision in 1928. Everyone expected a return grudge match between Alfred Smith and William Gibbs McAdoo, but McAdoo announced in 1927 that he was pulling out "in the interest of party unity." Smith, who had been organizing since the gavel fell on the nomination of John Davis, suddenly had a free ride. His first-ballot nomination was strongly backed by all regions except the South.

One of the key issues that fall was spoken, the other was largely whispered. The Republicans loudly took credit for the prosperity that bathed most of the nation but the farm belt. Hoover pamphlets predicted, "A Chicken in Every Pot." Many Americans found a more compelling issue in quiet talk about Smith's religion. He was the first Catholic ever nominated by a major party. The Ku Klux Klan warned that the Pope was trying to seize control of the White House. Smith's campaign train passed burning crosses more than once.

The Democratic candidate had long ago stressed his belief in the separation of church and state, but there was ample proof he was not believed. The problem was particularly serious in the South, where Democrats defected to Hoover by the thousands. Smith decided to meet the whispering campaign head-on in Oklahoma City, after his train passed a line of fiery crosses near the railroad station. "Nothing could be so out of line with the spirit of America," he thundered. "Nothing could be so contradictory to our whole history."[39] The next night, a large anti-Catholic rally was held on the same spot.

Smith had other problems. His opposition to Prohibition was unpopular in the heartland, as were his connections with Tammany Hall and his New York accent. "He did not sound like a man who knew pigs and chickens," sighed one of his supporters, Frances Perkins.[40]

The public's association of the Republicans with prosperity was probably enough to defeat Smith, even without the concerns about his Catholicism. Hoover insisted the religious issue "had no weight in the final result," pointing out correctly that while it helped him win several Southern states, it cost him the Republican strongholds of Massachusetts and Rhode Island, both heavily Catholic. The tradeoff was still in his favor. Hoover was the first Republican since Ulysses Grant to win a majority of the South's electoral votes.

It was another Republican landslide, the third in a row. Prosperity was an unbeatable recipe for electoral success, and both seemed endless. So thought Herbert Hoover, who had confidently predicted earlier in the year, "We in America today are nearer to the final triumph over poverty than ever before in the history of any land."[41] Few raised voices in dissent.

Charts for Chapter 4

1904
Republican Convention

	Theodore Roosevelt (R)
FB	994
East	290
South	278
Midwest	320
West	102
Other	4
FB %	100.0

1904 Democratic Convention

	Alton Parker (D)	William Randolph Hearst (D)	Francis Cockrell (D)
FB	679	181	42
East	244	8	0
South	269	7	0
Midwest	120	111	42
West	44	55	0
Other	2	0	0
FB %	67.9	18.1	4.2

1904 General Election

	Theodore Roosevelt (R)	Alton Parker (D)	Eugene Debs (SOC)
PV	7,626,593	5,082,898	402,489
PV %	56.4	37.6	3.0
East	58.7	37.0	2.0
South	33.4	62.3	0.8
Midwest	60.7	32.0	3.8
West	61.7	29.5	6.4
Counties	1,608	1,107	0
Counties %	59.0	40.6	0.0
States	32	13	0
States %	71.1	28.9	0.0
EV	336	140	0
East	137	7	0
South	0	133	0
Midwest	160	0	0
West	39	0	0
EV %	70.6	29.4	0.0

1908 Republican Convention

		William Howard Taft (R)	Phil- ander Knox (R)	Charles Evans Hughes (R)	Joseph Cannon (R)	Charles Fair- banks (R)
FB		702	68	67	58	40
	East	142	68	65	6	5
	South	261	0	2	0	5
	Midwest	209	0	0	52	30
	West	86	0	0	0	0
	Other	4	0	0	0	0
FB %		71.6	6.9	6.8	5.9	4.1

1908 Democratic Convention

		William Jennings Bryan (D)	George Gray (D)	John Johnson (D)
FB		888½	59½	46
	East	224½	39½	22
	South	258	20	2
	Midwest	298	0	22
	West	102	0	0
	Other	6	0	0
FB %		88.7	5.9	4.6

1908 General Election

	William Howard Taft (R)	William Jennings Bryan (D)	Eugene Debs (SOC)
PV	7,676,258	6,406,801	420,380
PV %	51.6	43.0	2.8
East	56.1	38.4	2.2
South	36.4	59.6	2.2
Midwest	53.3	41.6	2.8
West	53.4	37.8	6.2
Counties	1,494	1,354	0
Counties %	52.3	47.4	0.0
States	29	17	0
States %	63.0	37.0	0.0
EV	321	162	0
East	138	6	0
South	0	140	0
Midwest	152	8	0
West	31	8	0
EV %	66.5	33.5	0.0

1912 Democratic Primaries

	Woodrow Wilson (D)	Champ Clark (D)	Judson Harmon (D)
W	5	5	1
East	2	2	0
South	----	----	----
Midwest	2	2	1
West	1	1	0
W %	41.7	41.7	8.3

1912 Democratic Primaries (continued)

	Woodrow Wilson (D)	Champ Clark (D)	Judson Harmon (D)
PV	435,169	405,537	116,294
PV %	44.6	41.6	11.9
East	70.4	26.6	2.7
South	----	----	----
Midwest	35.4	44.8	17.1
West	34.2	65.0	0.8

1912 Democratic Convention

	Woodrow Wilson (D)	Champ Clark (D)	Judson Harmon (D)	Oscar Underwood (D)
FB	324	440½	148	117½
East	110	95	95	4
South	109	71	6½	111½
Midwest	83	171	46	0
West	19	101½	½	1
Other	3	2	0	1
FB %	29.6	40.3	13.5	10.7
LB (#46)	990	84	12	0
East	316	4	0	0
South	291	7	0	0
Midwest	283	37	12	0
West	94	30	0	0
Other	6	6	0	0
LB %	90.5	7.7	1.1	0.0

1912 Republican Primaries

	Theodore Roosevelt (R)	William Howard Taft (R)	Robert La Follette (R)
W	9	1	2
East	3	1	0
South	----	----	----
Midwest	4	0	2
West	2	0	0
W %	75.0	8.3	16.7
PV	1,164,765	766,326	327,357
PV %	51.5	33.9	14.5
East	56.3	43.0	0.7
South	----	----	----
Midwest	48.1	29.2	22.5
West	51.4	27.6	21.0

1912 Republican Convention

	William Howard Taft (R)	abstention	Theodore Roosevelt (R)
FB	556	348	107
East	147	150	21
South	237	53	5
Midwest	90	119	72
West	78	26	9
Other	4	0	0
FB %	51.6	32.3	9.9

1912 General Election

	Woodrow Wilson (D)	Theodore Roosevelt (P)	William Howard Taft (R)	Eugene Debs (SOC)
PV	6,293,152	4,119,207	3,486,333	900,369
PV %	41.8	27.4	23.2	6.0
East	38.5	29.2	26.5	4.4
South	61.0	15.9	17.7	4.8
Midwest	38.8	28.4	24.6	6.3
West	37.2	33.2	16.3	10.5
Counties	2,204	486	277	4
Counties %	74.2	16.4	9.3	0.1
States	40	6	2	0
States %	83.3	12.5	4.2	0.0
EV	435	88	8	0
East	118	38	4	0
South	149	0	0	0
Midwest	135	32	0	0
West	33	18	4	0
EV %	81.9	16.6	1.5	0.0

1916
Democratic Primaries

	Woodrow Wilson (D)
W	20
East	7
South	----
Midwest	10
West	3
W %	100.0

1916
Democratic Primaries
(continued)

	Woodrow Wilson (D)
PV	1,173,220
PV %	98.8
East	99.4
South	----
Midwest	98.3
West	100.0

1916
Democratic Convention

	Woodrow Wilson (D)
FB	1,092
East	326
South	298
Midwest	334
West	122
Other	12
FB %	100.0

1916 Republican Primaries
(first of two charts)

	unpledged	Albert Cummins (R)	Robert La Follette (R)	Henry Ford (R)
W	4	5	2	1
East	3	0	0	0
South	----	----	----	----
Midwest	0	4	2	1
West	1	1	0	0
W %	20.0	25.0	10.0	5.0
PV	453,464	191,950	133,426	131,889
PV %	23.6	10.0	6.9	6.9
East	40.1	0.0	0.0	3.7
South	----	----	----	----
Midwest	0.0	14.8	12.8	10.7
West	68.9	11.1	0.0	0.0

1916 Republican Primaries
(second of two charts)

	Theodore Burton (R)	Charles Evans Hughes (R)	Theodore Roosevelt (R)
W	2	2	1
East	1	1	1
South	----	----	----
Midwest	1	0	0
West	0	1	0
W %	10.0	10.0	5.0

1916 Republican Primaries
(second of two charts, continued)

	Theodore Burton (R)	Charles Evans Hughes (R)	Theodore Roosevelt (R)
PV	122,165	80,737	80,019
PV %	6.4	4.2	4.2
East	[?]	1.4	11.2
South	----	----	----
Midwest	11.8	1.6	1.9
West	0.0	16.6	0.0

Note: Burton won the West Virginia primary, the only Eastern primary in which he competed. The vote totals for that election are unavailable.

1916 Republican Convention
(first of two charts)

	Charles Evans Hughes (R)	John Weeks (R)	Elihu Root (R)	Albert Cummins (R)
FB	253½	105	103	85
East	97	51	62	0
South	68½	36	12	3
Midwest	39	11	2	74
West	49	7	26	8
Other	0	0	1	0
FB %	25.7	10.6	10.4	8.6

1916 Republican Convention
(first of two charts, continued)

		Charles Evans Hughes (R)	John Weeks (R)	Elihu Root (R)	Albert Cummins (R)
LB	(#3)	949½	3	0	0
	East	307	1	0	0
	South	200½	0	0	0
	Midwest	329	2	0	0
	West	111	0	0	0
	Other	2	0	0	0
LB	%	96.2	0.3	0.0	0.0

1916 Republican Convention
(second of two charts)

		Theodore Burton (R)	Charles Fairbanks (R)	Lawrence Sherman (R)	Theodore Roosevelt (R)
FB		77½	74½	66	65
	East	9	3	0	22
	South	16½	28½	6	26
	Midwest	49	38	58	2
	West	3	4	2	15
	Other	0	1	0	0
FB	%	7.9	7.5	6.7	6.6
LB	(#3)	0	0	0	18½
	East	0	0	0	8
	South	0	0	0	7½
	Midwest	0	0	0	0
	West	0	0	0	3
	Other	0	0	0	0
LB	%	0.0	0.0	0.0	1.9

1916 General Election

	Woodrow Wilson (D)	Charles Evans Hughes (R)	Allan Benson (SOC)
PV	9,126,300	8,546,789	589,924
PV %	49.2	46.1	3.2
East	44.3	51.9	2.5
South	65.0	30.0	3.4
Midwest	46.7	48.7	3.1
West	50.6	43.1	4.5
Counties	2,039	976	0
Counties %	67.5	32.3	0.0
States	30	18	0
States %	62.5	37.5	0.0
EV	277	254	0
East	13	147	0
South	149	0	0
Midwest	65	102	0
West	50	5	0
EV %	52.2	47.8	0.0

1920 Republican Primaries

	Hiram Johnson (R)	Leonard Wood (R)	Frank Lowden (R)	Herbert Hoover (R)	un-pledged	Warren Harding (R)
W	7	8	1	0	2	1
East	0	5	0	0	2	0
South	1	0	0	0	0	0
Midwest	3	3	1	0	0	1
West	3	0	0	0	0	0
W %	35.0	40.0	5.0	0.0	10.0	5.0

1920 Republican Primaries (continued)

	Hiram Johnson (R)	Leonard Wood (R)	Frank Lowden (R)	Herbert Hoover (R)	un-pledged	Warren Harding (R)
PV	965,651	710,863	389,127	303,212	298,109	144,762
PV %	30.3	22.3	12.2	9.5	9.4	4.5
East	9.3	14.3	0.0	0.5	38.0	0.0
South	73.3	26.7	0.0	0.0	0.0	0.0
Midwest	26.8	33.0	22.3	4.3	0.0	8.8
West	59.1	6.8	3.0	30.9	0.0	0.1

1920 Republican Convention

	Warren Harding (R)	Leonard Wood (R)	Frank Lowden (R)	Hiram Johnson (R)	William Sproul (R)	Nicholas Murray Butler (R)
FB	$65\frac{1}{2}$	$287\frac{1}{2}$	$211\frac{1}{2}$	$133\frac{1}{2}$	84	$69\frac{1}{2}$
East	2	89	16	11	76	68
South	$14\frac{1}{2}$	63	92	$9\frac{1}{2}$	$4\frac{1}{2}$	$1\frac{1}{2}$
Midwest	44	$98\frac{1}{2}$	94	67	$3\frac{1}{2}$	0
West	5	34	$8\frac{1}{2}$	46	0	0
Other	0	3	1	0	0	0
FB %	6.7	29.2	21.5	13.6	8.5	7.1
LB (#10)	$644\frac{7}{10}$	$181\frac{1}{2}$	28	$80\frac{4}{5}$	0	2
East	202	90	3	9	0	2
South	192	$16\frac{1}{2}$	3	0	0	0
Midwest	$215\frac{1}{5}$	43	17	$30\frac{4}{5}$	0	0
West	$33\frac{1}{2}$	30	5	41	0	0
Other	2	2	0	0	0	0
LB %	65.5	18.4	2.8	8.2	0.0	0.2

1920 Democratic Primaries

	un-pledged	Mitchell Palmer (D)	James Cox (D)	William Gibbs McAdoo (D)	Edward Edwards (D)
W	4	1	1	2	2
East	3	1	0	1	1
South	----	----	----	----	----
Midwest	0	0	1	0	1
West	1	0	0	1	0
W %	25.0	6.3	6.3	12.5	12.5
PV	165,460	91,543	86,194	74,987	28,470
PV %	28.9	16.0	15.1	13.1	5.0
East	55.4	31.4	0.0	10.6	1.9
South	----	----	----	----	----
Midwest	0.0	4.2	32.7	8.7	8.9
West	45.7	0.0	0.0	47.9	0.0

1920 Democratic Convention

	James Cox (D)	William Gibbs McAdoo (D)	Mitchell Palmer (D)	Alfred Smith (D)	John Davis (D)
FB	134	266	254	109	32
East	11½	ù0½	108	100	20
South	43	81	55	2	7
Midwest	67½	86½	69	6	1
West	12	66	19	1	3
Other	0	2	3	0	1
FB %	12.2	24.3	23.2	10.0	2.9

1920 Democratic Convention (continued)

	James Cox (D)	William Gibbs McAdoo (D)	Mitchell Palmer (D)	Alfred Smith (D)	John Davis (D)
LB (#44)	699½	270	1	0	52
East	259½	41	1	0	20½
South	155½	92½	0	0	29½
Midwest	209	77	0	0	1
West	66½	54½	0	0	1
Other	9	5	0	0	0
LB %	63.9	24.7	0.1	0.0	4.8

1920 General Election

	Warren Harding (R)	James Cox (D)	Eugene Debs (SOC)
PV	16,133,314	9,140,884	913,664
PV %	60.3	34.2	3.4
East	64.4	29.8	4.2
South	40.1	56.3	1.4
Midwest	64.1	30.6	3.4
West	61.5	29.5	3.7
Counties	1,944	1,102	0
Counties %	63.6	36.1	0.0
States	37	11	0
States %	77.1	22.9	0.0
EV	404	127	0
East	160	0	0
South	22	127	0
Midwest	167	0	0
West	55	0	0
EV %	76.1	23.9	0.0

1924 Republican Primaries

		Calvin Coolidge (R)	Hiram Johnson (R)
W		15	1
	East	6	0
	South	----	----
	Midwest	6	1
	West	3	0
W %		88.2	5.9
PV		2,410,363	1,007,833
PV %		68.4	28.6
	East	94.3	3.3
	South	----	----
	Midwest	65.0	30.9
	West	59.5	40.5

1924
Republican Convention

		Calvin Coolidge (R)
FB		1,065
	East	356
	South	232
	Midwest	326
	West	147
	Other	4
FB %		96.0

1924 Democratic Primaries

	William Gibbs McAdoo (D)	unpledged
W	9	2
East	1	2
South	----	----
Midwest	5	0
West	3	0
W %	64.3	14.3
PV	456,733	57,654
PV %	59.8	7.5
East	10.7	38.1
South	----	----
Midwest	59.2	0.4
West	89.2	10.8

1924 Democratic Convention

	John Davis (D)	William Gibbs McAdoo (D)	Alfred Smith (D)	James Cox (D)	Oscar Underwood (D)	Thomas Walsh (D)
FB	31	431½	241	59	42½	0
East	20	36	185	0	10	0
South	0	192	0	0	24	0
Midwest	5	103	48	59	2	0
West	1	91½	5	0	5½	0
Other	5	9	3	0	1	0
FB %	2.8	39.3	21.9	5.4	3.9	0.0

1924 Democratic Convention (continued)

	John Davis (D)	William Gibbs McAdoo (D)	Alfred Smith (D)	James Cox (D)	Oscar Underwood (D)	Thomas Walsh (D)
LB (#103)	844	11½	7½	0	102½	58
East	208½	0	5½	0	61½	34½
South	268	3	0	0	0	0
Midwest	266½	3	1	0	27	13½
West	86	5½	1	0	12	9
Other	15	0	0	0	2	1
LB %	76.9	1.0	0.7	0.0	9.3	5.3

1924 General Election

	Calvin Coolidge (R)	John Davis (D)	Robert La Follette (P)
PV	15,717,553	8,386,169	4,814,050
PV %	54.1	28.8	16.6
East	59.5	27.5	12.3
South	34.2	60.1	5.1
Midwest	56.1	23.3	20.2
West	53.6	15.9	29.7
Counties	1,567	1,282	234
Counties %	50.8	41.6	7.6
States	35	12	1
States %	72.9	25.0	2.1
EV	382	136	13
East	160	0	0
South	13	136	0
Midwest	154	0	13
West	55	0	0
EV %	71.9	25.6	2.4

1928 Republican Primaries

		Herbert Hoover (R)	Frank Lowden (R)	George Norris (R)
W		7	2	2
	East	3	0	0
	South	----	----	----
	Midwest	2	2	2
	West	2	0	0
W %		46.7	13.3	13.3
PV		2,020,325	1,283,535	259,548
PV %		49.2	31.2	6.3
	East	77.8	0.1	0.0
	South	----	----	----
	Midwest	27.7	48.5	9.8
	West	99.8	0.2	0.0

1928 Republican Convention

		Herbert Hoover (R)	Frank Lowden (R)	Charles Curtis (R)	James Watson (R)
FB		837	74	64	45
	East	336	0	1	0
	South	190	3	23	0
	Midwest	165	71	38	42
	West	142	0	2	3
	Other	4	0	0	0
FB %		76.9	6.8	5.9	4.1

1928 Democratic Primaries

	Alfred Smith (D)	unpledged	James Reed (D)	Thomas Walsh (D)
W	9	4	1	0
East	3	1	0	0
South	0	2	0	0
Midwest	4	1	1	0
West	2	0	0	0
W %	56.3	25.0	6.3	0.0
PV	499,452	263,061	207,367	59,871
PV %	39.5	20.8	16.4	4.7
East	61.7	4.0	31.5	0.1
South	0.0	100.0	0.0	0.0
Midwest	40.5	1.3	13.2	0.3
West	53.4	0.0	23.3	20.4

1928 Democratic Convention

	Alfred Smith (D)	Walter George (D)	James Reed (D)	Cordell Hull (D)
FB	$849\frac{2}{3}$	$52\frac{1}{2}$	52	$50\frac{5}{6}$
East	315	$4\frac{1}{2}$	1	$2\frac{1}{2}$
South	$117\frac{1}{6}$	48	9	$46\frac{1}{3}$
Midwest	$275\frac{1}{2}$	0	42	2
West	122	0	0	0
Other	20	0	0	0
FB %	77.2	4.8	4.7	4.6

1928 General Election

	Herbert Hoover (R)	Alfred Smith (D)
PV	21,411,991	15,000,185
PV %	58.2	40.8
East	56.2	42.5
South	51.8	47.8
Midwest	60.8	38.3
West	63.3	35.2
Counties	2,203	894
Counties %	71.1	28.9
States	40	8
States %	83.3	16.7
EV	444	87
East	137	23
South	85	64
Midwest	167	0
West	55	0
EV %	83.6	16.4

5.
Rendezvous With Destiny: 1932–1956

Few Americans willingly gave Herbert Hoover credit for anything in the dark autumn of 1932, but he deserved acknowledgement for a flash of prescience. "This election is not a mere shift from the ins to the outs," he warned of his impending defeat. "It means deciding the direction our nation will take over a century to come."[1] Franklin Roosevelt soon set the country on an erratic course that changed the American conception of government and its powers. It confirmed the worst fears of Hoover, whose engineering background fed his love of consistency and precision. Roosevelt´s experience was in politics. "Take a method and try it," he told the men and women implementing his New Deal. "If it fails, try another. But above all, try something."[2]

Roosevelt restored public confidence. He also elevated the Democratic party to dominance. It won five of the seven Presidential elections in the period of 1932-1956. That equaled the total of Democratic victories between 1856 and 1928. Republican orators tried vainly to arouse discontent. Alfred Landon warned in 1936, "He threatens to destroy the one classless nation in the world."[3] Wendell Willkie broadcast a dire message four years later, "If you return this administration to office, you will be serving under an American totalitarian government before the long third term is up."[4] The New Deal withstood the verbal assaults. Roosevelt won a record four elections.

The President showed a gift for occasional prophecy comparable to Hoover´s. He declared in 1936, "This generation of Americans has a rendezvous with destiny."[5] The elections from 1932 to 1956 were conducted in a turbulent time, as the country confronted successively the Great Depression, World War II, and the Cold War. Government met the challenges with unprecedented expansion. An isolationist nation was transformed into the world´s policeman. The atomic bomb´s debut in 1945 guaranteed that Warren Harding´s beloved "normalcy" would never return.

The Republicans could rationalize their four defeats to the charismatic Roosevelt, but their big shock came in 1948. Harry Truman´s victory demonstrated the serious erosion of public confidence in the GOP. The new minority party restored its popularity only by taking counsel from the Whigs of a century earlier. It nominated a popular war hero, Dwight Eisenhower, in 1952. The Republicans also admitted, at least temporarily, defeat in the long battle commenced by Herbert Hoover. Eisenhower was asked about the hundreds of New Deal programs that still angered so many conservatives in his party. The General answered quickly, "They are rights, not issues."[6] The stormy debate seemed closed.

ELECTION NO. 37: 1932

President Herbert Hoover entered the 1932 campaign with few illusions. "I had little hope of reelection in 1932," he later wrote, "but it was incumbent on me to fight it out to the end."[7] Millions of Americans were fighting their own battles, trying to survive in the depths of the Great Depression. Shantytowns of the unemployed were now bitterly called "Hoovervilles." A nation waited eagerly to repudiate the austere President whose conservative philosophy led him to approve federal aid to save the livestock of Arkansas farmers, but turn down extra money to feed the farmers´ families. Hoover piously insisted an outright gift of money "would have injured the spiritual responses of the American people."

No serious opposition to Hoover emerged in the Republican camp. The party´s nomination was considered virtually worthless. Former Maryland Senator Joseph France ran as a protest candidate in the primaries, winning seven of the fourteen. "Mine is not a personal candidacy. I represent a principle," he told reporters at the convention. "I cannot tell you who the candidate will be, but it will not be Hoover."[8] France hoped to trigger a draft of former President Calvin Coolidge, but Hoover held the party reins tightly. He received 97.6 percent of the first-ballot vote.

The competition was stiffer on the Democratic side, where nomination was deemed tantamount to a four-year lease on the White House. New York Governor Franklin Roosevelt was the frontrunner, thanks to strong political field work by James Farley and Louis Howe. Former Governor Alfred Smith, once Roosevelt´s mentor, now aimed to stop a man he believed was drifting toward radicalism. The increasingly conservative Smith declared he was in the battle to the finish, "I will take off my coat and vest and fight to the end against any candidate who persists in any demagogic appeal to the masses of the working people of this country to destroy themselves by setting class against class and rich against poor."[9] The balance of power fell to Speaker of the House John Nance Garner, who was supported by powerful publisher William Randolph Hearst. Garner controlled the California and Texas delegations to the convention.

Roosevelt´s strong performance in the primaries helped him to secure a majority of delegates on the first ballot, but he landed short of the two-thirds barrier. Deadlock threatened. Roosevelt's agents pleaded with Garner and Hearst to swing the needed votes. Texas leaders were agreeable, but said they would only switch to Roosevelt if Garner were his running mate. The Speaker barked, "Hell, I'll do anything to see the Democrats win one more national election."[10] It fell to California's William Gibbs McAdoo to announce the change on the convention floor, sinking the last hopes of his longtime archrival, Smith. Roosevelt won on the fourth ballot.

The New York Governor dramatically flew to the convention, becoming the first to directly address the gathering that nominated him. He pledged "a new deal for the American people." Some doubted he was capable of it. Journalist Walter Lippmann gave his famous assessment of Roosevelt, "He is a pleasant man who, without any important qualifications for the office, would very much like to be President."[11] Lippmann complained the Democratic nominee would certainly not propose innovative measures to restore the people's confidence. The party's platform, with its guarantee of a balanced budget, was little different from its Republican counterpart.

The economic and political situations seemed tailor-made for the Socialist party, which nominated a former Presbyterian minister, Norman Thomas. But the Socialists had never recovered their prewar strength, now spending much of their energy in intraparty battles. Thomas polled only 2.2 percent of the popular vote in November.

Roosevelt's strength was that he was not Hoover. He declared his real opponents were "the 'Four Horsemen' of the present Republican leadership: the Horsemen of Destruction, Delay, Deceit, Despair."[12] Some of his speeches contained hints of the startling policy shifts that would mark the New Deal. Hoover desperately painted his opponent as a closet Socialist, "Indeed, this is the same philosophy of government which has poisoned all Europe. They have been the fumes of the witch's cauldron which boiled in Russia."[13] Such dire warnings could not stem massive defections from the Republican party, led by Senators George Norris and Robert La Follette Jr. Roosevelt carried all but six states, trouncing the President by an 8-1 margin in the Electoral College.

Herbert Hoover knew his political fates had been dictated by economics. He wrote in military terms, "General Prosperity had been a great ally in the election of 1928. General Depression was a major enemy in 1932."[14] The public had vested its confidence in the mythic figure Roosevelt called "Dr. New Deal." It was the beginning of a streak that would see the once-minority Democratic party win seven of nine Presidential elections.

ELECTION NO. 38: 1936

"There's one issue in this campaign," President Franklin Roosevelt told an adviser in 1936. "It's myself, and people must be either for me or against me."[15] The Republicans were

only too glad to oblige. Buoyed by surveys that showed
Roosevelt in a precarious position, they directed a fusillade
of partisan abuse on the man they considered a virtual
dictator. That suited the President´s purposes just fine.
He confided to his Cabinet, "We will win easily...but we are
going to make it a crusade."[16]

The Republicans, stung by massive Congressional and
state election defeats in 1932 and 1934, had a small pool of
possible nominees. The irascible Senator from Idaho, William
Borah, was the favorite in early polls. He entered the
primaries to defend "liberal principles," drawing twice as
many popular votes as any other candidate. But the Old Guard
and big business had no intention of allowing his
nomination. Borah reveled in their opposition, "One of the
DuPonts...said the other day that I am a dangerous man. He
said he´d take anybody but me for President. Thank God, I
haven´t lived in vain!"[17] Republican leaders found a more
congenial choice in Kansas Governor Alfred Landon, the only
Republican state executive reelected in 1934. He piled up so
many delegates that all other candidates, including Borah,
withdrew before the convention roll call.

The Democrats renominated Roosevelt by acclamation. The
President was in total control of his convention. He
directed the scuttling of the century-old two-thirds rule
that almost prevented his nomination four years earlier.
After his name was formally entered for the 1936 prize,
Roosevelt coordinated a massive self-tribute. Delegates were
forced to endure a record fifty-six seconding speeches!

The chairman of the Democratic National Committee, James
Farley, had long been worried about a challenge from other
than the Republicans. Louisiana Senator Huey Long organized
thousands of clubs across the country, coordinated by his
Share Our Wealth Society. It seemed in 1935 the beginning of
a third party that Farley warned could draw millions of
votes. Roosevelt veered his policies leftward to
short-circuit a danger Farley contended "could easily mean
the difference between victory or defeat." Long´s
assassination in September 1935 removed the threat, but famed
radio priest Charles Coughlin went ahead with formation of
the Union party. Coughlin´s harsh rhetoric, blasting
Roosevelt as "a scab President," heavily burdened his
nominee. North Dakota Congressman William Lemke failed to
get even 900,000 votes.

The burden of the challenge to the New Deal thus fell on
Landon, who had pledged in 1933 to "enlist for the duration
of the war in this campaign of President Roosevelt´s to get
America on its feet."[18] The Kansas Governor now mustered
himself out, ridiculing the new Social Security program as
"unjust, unworkable, stupidly drafted, and wastefully
financed."[19] Former Democratic nominees John Davis and
Alfred Smith, alarmed at the rapid proliferation of
government agencies under Roosevelt, endorsed the Republican
challenger. Landon gained momentum in October, demanding
that Roosevelt say "whether he intends to change the form of
our government -- whether labor, agriculture, and business
are to be directed and managed by government."[20]

The focus was where the President wanted it: on himself. The economy had been on the upswing since 1935, bringing him the backing of millions of farmers and laborers. Roosevelt labeled his opponents "economic royalists" and declared defiantly, "They are unanimous in their hate for me -- and I welcome their hatred!"[21] Organized labor threw its resources behind a Democratic nominee for the first time, fired by Roosevelt's insistence that the Republicans felt "that government is best which is most indifferent to mankind."

A leading national magazine predicted that despite the bold Presidential phrases, the GOP was on the verge of victory. The Literary Digest had been correct in every election since 1920. Its survey showed Landon sweeping the Electoral College, 370-161. Roosevelt expected to win, but gloomed that his opponent would carry as many as 171 electors. Farley tried to cheer the President by forecasting a 523-8 triumph. It seemed in the realm of fantasy, but proved to be right on the mark. Roosevelt won his personal referendum in smashing style, breaking Warren Harding's record for highest popular-vote percentage. Just two states separated the President from the first unanimous victory since George Washington's. "I knew I should have gone to Maine and Vermont," he laughed, gesturing at Farley. "But Jim wouldn't let me."[22]

ELECTION NO. 39: 1940

The tradition was clear. Presidents did not serve more than two terms. Franklin Roosevelt would be packing for home in early 1941. He privately spoke often of how much he would enjoy his return to the idyll of Hyde Park. Several Cabinet members, Senators, and judges received Presidential assurance that the Democratic nomination was available. Two took Roosevelt at his word. Vice President John Nance Garner announced his candidacy in late 1939. Democratic National Committee Chairman James Farley followed suit in early 1940.

Roosevelt's real intentions remain shrouded in secrecy and confusion even decades later. He evaded reporters' questions about a possible third term and pretended ignorance of endorsements proffered by leading Democrats. His name was placed on several primary ballots without his public direction. He smashed Garner in every contest.

If Roosevelt was maneuvering to receive a third term, events were playing into his hands. The Nazis ended their "phony war" in April by launching a blitzkrieg against Scandinavia. Belgium and the Netherlands fell in May, France in June. Public-opinion polls charted a dramatic rise in the number of Americans who wanted a seasoned President in such times of trial. Roosevelt released a statement to the Democratic convention that he had "no desire or purpose to continue in the office," but a stage-managed demonstration of support showed the fine hand of the White House. Renomination over Farley and Garner came easily.

Two new faces dominated the early phase of the

Republican search for a contender to succeed where Herbert Hoover and Alfred Landon had failed. Manhattan District Attorney Thomas Dewey was only 38, but was already nationally known as the "Gangbuster" for his flamboyantly successful prosecution of organized crime figures. Ohio Senator Robert Taft, the son of William Howard Taft, was an icy but articulate spokesman for isolationism.

Dewey won six of the thirteen primaries and took a dramatic lead over other Republicans in the polls. But the reheating of the European war hurt the District Attorney as much as it aided Roosevelt. Americans began to remember Interior Secretary Harold Ickes´ jibe that Dewey had "thrown his diaper into the ring" in announcing his candidacy. The isolationist view was also quickly falling from vogue, as did Taft´s chances.

Into the void shuffled a very unlikely candidate. Wendell Willkie was a folksy Indiana native who headed a New York-based utility. He was seasoned and an internationalist. His pungent criticism of the New Deal spurred mention of Willkie as a Presidential dark horse as early as 1937. He bragged, "All the headquarters I have are under my hat," but it wasn´t true.[23] Powerful businessmen and several leading Republicans fanned the flames. Dewey led on the first ballot at the convention, but the packed galleries chanted, "We want Willkie!" Their hero seized the lead on the third. Willkie won three roll calls later, then shouted to reporters, "Bring on the champ!"

The champion´s attention was engaged elsewhere in the fall. Franklin Roosevelt was arranging the Lend-Lease program with Britain and gearing up the nation´s first peacetime draft in September. Willkie agreed Lend-Lease was a fine idea, but he took exception to Democratic assertions that such programs would founder if the nation decided to change horses in treacherous waters. "There comes a time when it is very wise to get off that horse in midstream," the Republican insisted, "because if we don´t, both you and the horse will sink."[24] The Democrats continued to call Roosevelt´s experience the key issue. Willkie made little headway against it.

The first draft numbers were selected in October. Roosevelt had joined Willkie in active campaigning by then. The President declared in Boston, "I have said this before, but I shall say it again and again and again: Your boys are not going to be sent into any foreign wars."[25] He blamed isolationist Republicans for slowing American preparedness. Willkie countered that Roosevelt was going beyond defense planning to all-out scheming for American intervention. The Republican bitterly assailed the President, "If his promise to keep our boys out of foreign wars is not better than his promise to balance the budget, they´re almost on the transports!"[26]

It was too much to expect a newcomer to upset a two-term President during a crisis. Roosevelt scored another lopsided victory. His only weakness was in the remaining hotbed of isolationism, the Midwest. Roosevelt and Willkie were almost neck-and-neck in that region's popular voting, but the President was triumphant elsewhere. Little more than a year later, 1940's heated debate about "foreign wars" would instantly become irrelevant as Japanese bombers dived toward Pearl Harbor.

ELECTION NO. 40:   1944

The election of 1944 was the first to be conducted during wartime since Abraham Lincoln's vindication in 1864. Lincoln was hounded by tales of his desire to cancel the voting, and a reporter told Franklin Roosevelt he had heard similar rumors about him and wanted to know if they were true. "You have come to the wrong place," the President replied. "Gosh, all these people around town haven't read the Constitution. Unfortunately, I have."[27]

Roosevelt employed tricky footwork to win a third term, but none was necessary for a fourth. Polls showed Americans felt he should stay on the job until the war was won. The President said he would be a "good soldier" and accepted his fourth Democratic nomination. Virginia Senator Harry Byrd offered token opposition, backed by Southerners who could no longer stomach Roosevelt's beliefs in strong government and racial equality.

Southerners were also annoyed by Vice President Henry Wallace, who said in a speech the year before, "Those who fan the fires of racial clashes for the purpose of political capital here at home are taking the first step toward Nazism."[28] Bosses of urban Democratic machines considered Wallace to be naive and visionary, not the kind of man with whom they were comfortable. Rumors that Roosevelt was dying were in wide circulation, lending a special urgency to the search for a new running mate.

The President handled the problem in a way that confused even those who knew him best. He publicly said of Wallace, "I personally would vote for his renomination if I were a delegate to the convention."[29] Roosevelt also began to line up opposition to Wallace. The head of the Office of Economic Stabilization, James Byrnes, got the distinct impression he was the President's real choice. He asked his old friend, Missouri Senator Harry Truman, to place his name before the convention. Truman himself was then approached by party leaders. He put them off until he heard Roosevelt lecture a Democratic chieftain on the phone, "Well, you tell him if he wants to break up the Democratic party in the middle of a war, that's his responsibility."[30] Truman ousted Wallace on the second ballot.

The Republican race was much simpler. The 1940 nominee, Wendell Willkie, was again a strong contender, as was General Douglas MacArthur. Willkie destroyed his chances by alienating the backers who had made his first race possible. "I don't know whether you are going to support me or not, and I don't give a damn," he snapped at a meeting with business leaders. "You're a bunch of political liabilities, anyway."[31] A poor showing in the Wisconsin primary forced

Willkie´s withdrawal. MacArthur, preparing for his triumphant recapture of the Philippines, won two primaries, but soon joined Willkie on the political sidelines. His unannounced candidacy was destroyed by the publication of his letters critical of the administration he was still serving. MacArthur stated in May he would not accept the nomination.

That left a clear road for New York Governor Thomas Dewey. He denied all the way to the convention that he was a candidate, but his operatives had been working for a year to line up delegates. Dewey´s nomination was virtually unanimous.

The former District Attorney was in full prosecutorial form in the fall. Governor Dewey ripped an administration that he said consisted of "quarrelsome, tired old men" who were inattentive to a growing problem. "Now the Communists are seizing control of the New Deal," he accused. "Through [this] they aim to control the government of the United States."[32]

Roosevelt muttered that he failed to see how he could be both a monarchist and a Communist, two charges favored by the Republicans. The President endured a severe angina attack during one speech, but maintained a heavy campaign schedule in late October to demonstrate his vigor to a skeptical public. He also presented one last famous display of his sense of humor, responding to Republican accusations that a destroyer had been dispatched to retrieve his dog from the Aleutian Islands. "These Republican leaders have not been content with attacks on me, or my wife, or on my sons," he declared with mock indignation. "No, not content with that, they now include my little dog, Fala."[33]

American troops landed in the Philippines and advanced into Germany in October, adding to Roosevelt´s stature as a war leader. He eliminated Dewey almost as easily as his three previous opponents, but this unprecedented fourth victory meant more to him. The President told an aide on election night that 1944 had been the meanest campaign of his life. Dewey soon dispatched a telegram of congratulations, but Roosevelt´s opinion didn´t change. He turned to his adviser and said of the man he had just trounced, "I still think he is a son of a bitch."[34]

ELECTION NO. 41: 1948

The death of Franklin Roosevelt in April 1945 was perhaps the ultimately traumatic event for a generation becoming accustomed to trauma. Millions of Americans found it impossible to imagine a world without the man they credited with smashing the Depression and leading the country to the verge of victory in World War II. Cabell Phillips of the New York _Times_ later remembered the White House press corps had a second reason for shock: "`Good God,´ we said, `Truman will be President!´"[35] It was difficult to view the short, bespectacled Missourian as the heir to the patrician of Hyde Park. The new President´s popularity ratings dived to unplumbed depths by early 1948, as the nation joked, "To err is Truman."

The Republicans were poised to return to the White House after four consecutive thrashings at the hands of Roosevelt. There seemed no shortage of fresh, attractive contenders for the party's nomination. Former Minnesota Governor Harold Stassen scored early impressive primary wins in Wisconsin and Nebraska, becoming the frontrunner. California Governor Earl Warren led all candidates in primary popular votes, largely from his home state. Ohio Senator Robert Taft remained the darling of conservatives, lining up substantial support in state conventions.

The 1944 nominee, New York Governor Thomas Dewey, had joked in 1945 that he was now above the fray, an elder statesman. "The serenity of this position," he said, "is copper-riveted by the fact that in selecting nominees for President, my party has an unbroken tradition of never having made the same mistake twice in a row."[36] Dewey privately cared little for the precedent. His victory in the Oregon primary derailed Stassen. Taft and Stassen then failed to coordinate their opposition at the convention, both being forced to withdraw after the second ballot. Dewey won unanimously on the third.

The Republican unity was in sharp contrast to apparently fatal Democratic schisms. Former Vice President Henry Wallace was appalled by Harry Truman's hard line with America's wartime allies, the Soviets. He threatened early in 1947, "If the Democratic party departs from the ideals of Franklin Roosevelt, I shall desert altogether from that party."[37] He made good his threat by the end of that year, leading yet another incarnation of the Progressive party. The Democratic right was also in revolt, although not yet defecting. South Carolina Governor Strom Thurmond was among those who withdrew their endorsements of the President after he unveiled a civil-rights package in February 1948.

Even Democrats remaining in the fold were skeptical that Truman could stay close to Dewey under such conditions. Liberals and big-city bosses united in a drive to draft General Dwight Eisenhower, whose party affiliation was unknown. Ike killed the movement just before the convention by expressing his belief that "life-long professional soldiers [should] abstain from seeking high political office."[38] Most delegates were forced to vote unenthusiastically for Truman. The South got behind Georgia Senator Richard Russell in symbolic protest.

The President had entered the convention hoping to placate the South by offering a mild civil-rights platform plank. Liberals led by Minneapolis Mayor Hubert Humphrey insisted on stronger language. Humphrey declared, "The time has arrived for the Democratic party to get out of the shadow of states' rights and walk forthrightly into the bright sunshine of human rights."[39] Some Southern delegates found the glare uncomfortable after the liberals won. They stalked out of the convention, soon to create the States' Rights Democratic party, with Thurmond its nominee.

Pollsters saw no possible hope for Truman, whose party was split three ways. Dewey held an eleven-point lead near Labor Day. Elmo Roper announced "no amount of electioneering" could change the result, so he wouldn't waste his money conducting any more surveys. Dewey promised to run a safe campaign befitting a President-to-be. "I will not get down into the gutter with that fellow," he said, making obvious his distaste for Truman.[40]

The President had different plans. He shouted at the convention, "I will win this election and make these Republicans like it, don't you forget that!"[41] He dramatically called a special session of Congress, daring the Republicans to enact their platform before the election. Senator Taft sourly called it a political gimmick and refused Dewey's pleas to pass something, anything. Truman now had the ammunition for a nationwide whistlestop tour to lambaste the "do-nothing Congress."

The two minor-party candidates saw their support erode during autumn. Wallace's refusal to repudiate the Communist party's endorsement of his Progressive ticket dogged him across the country. His explanation that "the Communists are the closest things to the early Christian martyrs" hardly helped.[42] The former Vice President often faced hostile crowds, some of which threw eggs and rotten vegetables. Thurmond stuck to congenial territory, but found Southern backing more difficult to obtain than he had expected. Regional hearts thrilled to his characterization of Truman's civil rights program as a sop for "the parlor pinks and the subversives." But most Southerners stuck with the Democratic party that had become their way of life, and that still controlled patronage.

President Truman energetically covered more than 20,000 miles by rail as his party slowly drew back together. He blasted the Republicans as "bloodsuckers with offices in Wall Street" and charged their farm policies with sticking "a pitchfork in the farmer's back." Dewey was ready to take the gloves off by late October, but was dissuaded by his confident advisers.

The Chicago *Tribune* reported early election-night returns with its famous headline, "DEWEY DEFEATS TRUMAN." But it was the other way around. Americans rewarded the Democrats for postwar prosperity, with Truman confounding all the experts by leading the popular vote in all four regions and running up a 114-vote margin in the Electoral College. The pollsters were embarrassed. "I don't want to seem malicious," said Wilfred Funk, editor of the late *Literary Digest*. "But I can't help but get a good chuckle out of this."[43] Harry Truman was laughing, too.

ELECTION NO. 42: 1952

South Dakota Senator Karl Mundt said the Republican formula for victory in 1952 was best expressed in chemical notation: K_1C_3. The mixture of Korea, crime, Communism, and corruption was a potent blend of issues with which to confront the Truman Administration. America seemed to believe twenty years of Democratic rule were enough.

The Republican search for a nominee to unseat President Harry Truman followed the familiar pattern. It pitted Thomas Dewey´s wing of Eastern moderates against Robert Taft´s Midwestern conservatives. Dewey refused to run again. He proposed a draft of General Dwight Eisenhower, "a man who really understands the problems of the world." Taft again entered to defend his conservative gospel. He ridiculed the Eisenhower movement as an unprincipled coalition of "international bankers, the Dewey organization allied with them, Republican New Dealers."[44]

Eisenhower remained on duty in Europe while his self-appointed campaigners won the New Hampshire primary for him. His interest grew and he soon agreed to return to the United States. Taft won six primaries to Ike´s five, and the Ohio Senator entered the Republican convention with a slight lead in delegates. Tensions between the two sides were high. Illinois Senator Everett Dirksen, a Taft backer, pointed at Dewey from the podium and shouted, "We followed you before and you took us down the path to defeat!"[45] Dirksen´s man was already losing momentum. Taft yielded on some disputed delegates and was stripped of others by the convention. Eisenhower grabbed a 95-vote lead on the first ballot. An avalanche of switches quickly gave the General the nomination. California Senator Richard Nixon was tapped for Vice President to add a conservative Western element to the ticket.

The Republicans had hoped to run against President Truman. The nation was frustrated by the stalemate in the Korean War. House Minority Leader Joseph Martin said, "If we are not in Korea to win, then this administration should be indicted for the murder of thousands of American boys."[46] The GOP also planned to rip the President for revelations of corruption among his aides and for his antipathy to Wisconsin Senator Joseph McCarthy, then in the glory days of his anti-Communist crusade. But Truman, who insisted he had reached the decision in 1951, pulled out in March 1952.

The President was actually pushed a bit by his loss of the New Hampshire primary to Tennessee Senator Estes Kefauver, an unlikely challenger whose symbol was a coonskin cap. Kefauver was well-known for his recent chairmanship of televised hearings on organized crime, but he was not loved by the party bosses. "The boys in the smoke-filled rooms have never taken very well to me," he said in classic understatement.[47] Kefauver had the field virtually to himself, winning twelve of sixteen primaries. Truman searched for an alternative, failing to snag Illinois Governor Adlai Stevenson, finally settling on Vice President Alben Barkley. The South again gathered behind Georgia Senator Richard Russell.

Stevenson waffled under growing pressure from party leaders. He doubted Eisenhower could be beaten, but also had a hard time saying "no" to a nomination. His welcoming speech to the Chicago convention showed how close he was to

entering the field after months of indecision. Before taking
the podium, Stevenson eliminated the last two sentences:
"And, in any case, come back in 1956. If you do, I hope to
have the privilege of welcoming you again -- as Governor of
Illinois."[48] He soon consented to run, defeating the dreaded
Kefauver on the third ballot.

Republicans grandiloquently labeled their campaign "The
Great Crusade." But Eisenhower proved to be no match on the
stump to the witty Stevenson. One newspaper complained, "Ike
is running like a dry creek." He was also hurt by charges
that his running mate had a secret slush fund. Nixon went on
national television to defend the fund as legitimate in his
famous "Checkers" speech. Ike had considered dropping Nixon,
but told him the next night, "You´re my boy."

Stevenson accused Eisenhower of bowing to McCarthyism.
"My opponent has been worrying about my funnybone," he said.
"I´m worrying about his backbone." But the Democratic legacy
of K_1C_3 was dragging the Governor down. Even Stevenson
talked openly of "the mess in Washington," greatly annoying
Truman. When Eisenhower announced he would travel to Korea
if elected, it was all over but the counting. Farmers
returned to the party they had scorned four years earlier,
the South continued its slide from the Democrats, and the
whole nation seemed to agree a military man could best handle
the Korean problem. Ike won in a landslide. One supporter
told Stevenson on election night he still had consolation,
"Governor, you educated the country with your great
campaign." Stevenson couldn´t resist one last
witticism: "But a lot of people flunked the course."[49]

ELECTION NO. 43: 1956

Dwight Eisenhower remained immensely popular as his first
term in the White House wrapped up, but it was uncertain
whether he would run again. The President suffered a serious
heart attack in September 1955. His recovery was lengthy.
Democrats, doubting a man in his condition could undertake a
strenuous national campaign, looked gleefully at the lack of
depth on the Republican bench behind Eisenhower. Vice
President Richard Nixon and the other possible replacements
all appeared to be easy pickings.

The Democratic nomination seemed a glittering prize in
early 1956. Two contestants from 1952 were back to try to
claim it. Former Illinois Governor Adlai Stevenson was the
frontrunner in the polls, but he suffered a shocking loss in
the Minnesota primary to Tennessee Senator Estes Kefauver.
Columnists speculated that Stevenson was through. Kefauver
predicted the California primary would confirm it, but he
warned that "one of the great dangers of the present campaign
is that the Old Guard politicians are using the campaign of
Mr. Stevenson to climb back into power." Stevenson snapped
back, "You can´t teach an underdog new tricks."[50] The former
nominee swamped Kefauver by a 2-1 margin in California. The
Tennessean had won two more primaries than Stevenson, but
knew his cause was now hopeless. He withdrew. New York
Governor Averell Harriman had Harry Truman´s blessing to

continue the fight, but Stevenson was easily nominated on the convention's first ballot. The nominee then left the choice of his running mate up to the delegates. They selected Kefauver by a tiny margin over a national newcomer, Massachusetts Senator John Kennedy.

Prospects for the Democrats no longer seemed bright by the time Stevenson and Kefauver accepted the cheers of their convention. Eisenhower had recovered from his heart attack. Far from whetting his appetite for retirement, the forced inactivity convinced him of the need for further challenges. Presidential press secretary James Hagerty said, "It was then that he faced the sheer, God-awful boredom of not being President."[51] Doctors cleared him in March and Ike announced for reelection. He returned to the hospital in June for removal of an intestinal obstruction, but was soon back at work.

Foreign affairs and military issues dominated the fall campaign. Stevenson advanced two controversial proposals. He said he would end the peacetime draft, and also called for a treaty to "save man from the greatest horror his ingenuity has ever devised." He wanted an agreement with the Soviets to ban all tests of hydrogen bombs. Monitoring in the Pacific showed that fallout from H-bombs spread contamination over thousands of miles.

Eisenhower was accepted by the nation as the expert on these issues, based on his experience as a general and as President. He rejected what he called Stevenson's "theatrical national gesture." The President called it a "strange new formula" for a country that wanted to keep the peace, "It is this: simultaneously to stop our military draft and to abandon our most advanced military weapons."[52] Eisenhower insisted the United States could not meet its global commitments under the Stevenson plan.

Events in late October and early November added weight to the President's depiction of a perilous world. Soviet tanks rolled into Budapest to crush the Hungarian Revolution. Israel, Britain, and France attacked Egypt to prevent that country's nationalization of the Suez Canal. Eisenhower brought pressure that led to a cease-fire on the Sinai peninsula. Polls showed voters drifting toward the safe harbor of the incumbent, so Stevenson tried a last-minute shocker, "And distasteful as this matter is, I must say bluntly that every piece of scientific evidence we have, every lesson of history and experience, indicates that a Republican victory tomorrow would mean that Richard Nixon would probably be President of this country within the next four years."[53] His own aides gasped as Stevenson predicted Eisenhower's death.

A landslide was probably inevitable, but Suez and Hungary expanded its dimensions. Eisenhower carried all four sections of the country. His electoral-vote margin was 457-73. One Stevenson elector defected to an Alabama judge, Walter Jones, as a protest against federal-court-ordered desegregation. It was entirely a personal victory for the Republican leader. The Democrats retained both houses of

Congress, making Eisenhower the first President since Zachary Taylor to begin a term at such a legislative disadvantage.

Charts for Chapter 5

1932 Democratic Primaries

		Franklin Roose-velt (D)	Alfred Smith (D)	John Nance Garner (D)	William Murray (D)	un-pledged
W		9	2	1	1	2
	East	2	2	0	0	1
	South	2	0	0	0	1
	Midwest	4	0	0	1	0
	West	1	0	1	0	0
W %		56.3	12.5	6.3	6.3	12.5
PV		1,314,366	406,162	249,816	226,392	150,182
PV %		44.5	13.8	8.5	7.7	5.1
	East	57.9	36.5	0.0	2.8	2.2
	South	60.2	0.0	0.0	5.9	31.8
	Midwest	34.8	0.4	2.3	13.9	0.0
	West	37.2	23.6	37.0	2.0	0.0

1932 Democratic Convention

		Franklin Roosevelt (D)	Alfred Smith (D)	John Nance Garner (D)
FB		$666\frac{1}{4}$	$201\frac{3}{4}$	$90\frac{1}{4}$
	East	129	189½	0
	South	218	0	46
	Midwest	$208\frac{1}{4}$	$6\frac{1}{4}$	$\frac{1}{4}$
	West	97	0	44
	Other	14	6	0
FB %		57.7	17.5	7.8
LB (#4)		945	190½	0
	East	152	171½	0
	South	310	0	0
	Midwest	321	19	0
	West	142	0	0
	Other	20	0	0
LB %		81.9	16.5	0.0

1932 Republican Primaries

		Joseph France (R)	Herbert Hoover (R)	Jacob Coxey (R)
W		7	2	1
	East	3	1	0
	South	----	----	----
	Midwest	3	0	1
	West	1	1	0
W %		50.0	14.3	7.1
PV		1,137,948	781,165	100,844
PV %		48.5	33.3	4.3
	East	80.4	7.8	0.0
	South	----	----	----
	Midwest	55.6	3.9	12.0
	West	9.5	90.5	0.0

1932
Republican Convention

	Herbert Hoover (R)
FB	1,126½
East	348
South	275
Midwest	337½
West	162
Other	4
FB %	97.6

1932 General Election

	Franklin Roosevelt (D)	Herbert Hoover (R)	Norman Thomas (SOC)
PV	22,825,016	15,758,397	883,990
PV %	57.4	39.6	2.2
East	50.8	45.7	2.9
South	75.9	23.4	0.4
Midwest	56.5	40.7	2.1
West	58.3	37.2	2.7
Counties	2,723	373	0
Counties %	88.0	12.0	0.0
States	42	6	0
States %	87.5	12.5	0.0
EV	472	59	0
East	100	59	0
South	146	0	0
Midwest	161	0	0
West	65	0	0
EV %	88.9	11.1	0.0

1936
Democratic Primaries

	Franklin Roosevelt (D)
W	12
East	4
South	1
Midwest	5
West	2
W %	85.7
PV	4,814,978
PV %	92.9
East	89.5
South	89.7
Midwest	98.7
West	84.0

1936
Democratic Convention

	Franklin Roosevelt (D)
FB	1,100
East	324
South	292
Midwest	322
West	142
Other	20
FB %	100.0

1936 Republican Primaries

	William Borah (R)	Alfred Landon (R)	Frank Knox (R)
W	5	2	1
East	2	2	0
South	----	----	----
Midwest	2	0	1
West	1	0	0
W %	41.7	16.7	8.3
PV	1,474,152	729,908	493,562
PV %	44.4	22.0	14.9
East	57.4	36.8	0.2
South	----	----	----
Midwest	49.5	2.8	33.8
West	12.9	37.1	0.0

1936 Republican Convention

	Alfred Landon (R)
FB	984
East	333
South	208
Midwest	303
West	136
Other	4
FB %	98.1

1936 General Election

	Franklin Roosevelt (D)	Alfred Landon (R)	William Lemke (U)
PV	27,747,636	16,679,543	892,492
PV %	60.8	36.5	2.0
East	57.0	40.4	1.5
South	75.3	24.2	0.3
Midwest	58.1	38.4	3.1
West	66.0	31.7	1.3
Counties	2,636	459	0
Counties %	85.2	14.8	0.0
States	46	2	0
States %	95.8	4.2	0.0
EV	523	8	0
East	151	8	0
South	146	0	0
Midwest	161	0	0
West	65	0	0
EV %	98.5	1.5	0.0

1940 Democratic Primaries

	Franklin Roosevelt (D)	unpledged	John Nance Garner (D)
W	7	5	0
East	2	2	0
South	0	1	0
Midwest	3	2	0
West	2	0	0
W %	53.8	38.5	0.0

1940 Democratic Primaries (continued)

		Franklin Roosevelt (D)	unpledged	John Nance Garner (D)
PV		3,204,054	734,571	426,641
PV %		71.7	16.4	9.5
	East	80.0	9.2	0.0
	South	0.0	100.0	0.0
	Midwest	72.6	14.0	13.4
	West	75.5	12.6	11.8

1940 Democratic Convention

		Franklin Roosevelt (D)	James Farley (D)	John Nance Garner (D)
FB		$946\frac{13}{30}$	$72\frac{9}{10}$	61
	East	$269\frac{1}{2}$	$41\frac{1}{2}$	0
	South	$226\frac{13}{30}$	$4\frac{2}{5}$	$55\frac{1}{2}$
	Midwest	$309\frac{1}{2}$	8	$4\frac{1}{2}$
	West	130	10	1
	Other	11	9	0
FB %		86.0	6.6	5.5

1940 Republican Primaries

	Thomas Dewey (R)	Robert Taft (R)	unpledged
W	6	1	3
East	3	0	2
South	----	----	----
Midwest	3	1	1
West	0	0	0
W %	46.2	7.7	23.1
PV	1,605,754	516,428	186,157
PV %	49.7	16.0	5.8
East	60.9	0.8	18.1
South	----	----	----
Midwest	63.5	28.1	2.9
West	0.8	0.0	0.0

1940 Republican Convention

	Wendell Willkie (R)	Thomas Dewey (R)	Robert Taft (R)	Arthur Vanden-berg (R)	Arthur James (R)	Joseph Martin (R)
FB	105	360	189	76	74	44
East	50	110	13	2	70	36
South	11	93	83	11	3	0
Midwest	26	112	69	54	1	2
West	17	44	22	9	0	6
Other	1	1	2	0	0	0
FB %	10.5	36.0	18.9	7.6	7.4	4.4
LB (#6)	655	11	318	0	0	0
East	298	6	17	0	0	0
South	94	1	115	0	0	0
Midwest	181	3	136	0	0	0
West	78	1	50	0	0	0
Other	4	0	0	0	0	0
LB %	65.5	1.1	31.8	0.0	0.0	0.0

1940 General Election

		Franklin Roosevelt (D)	Wendell Willkie (R)
PV		27,263,448	22,336,260
PV %		54.7	44.8
	East	52.8	46.8
	South	72.5	27.3
	Midwest	49.9	49.7
	West	56.7	42.4
Counties		1,950	1,144
Counties %		63.0	37.0
States		38	10
States %		79.2	20.8
EV		449	82
	East	151	8
	South	146	0
	Midwest	93	68
	West	59	6
EV %		84.6	15.4

1944 Democratic Primaries

		Franklin Roosevelt (D)	unpledged
W		7	5
	East	2	2
	South	0	2
	Midwest	3	1
	West	2	0
W %		50.0	35.7

1944 Democratic Primaries
(continued)

	Franklin Roosevelt (D)	unpledged
PV	1,324,006	464,426
PV %	70.9	24.9
East	73.2	13.8
South	0.0	100.0
Midwest	42.4	52.0
West	99.9	0.0

1944 Democratic Convention

	Franklin Roosevelt (D)	Harry Byrd (D)
FB	1,086	89
East	337½	1½
South	234½	87½
Midwest	320	0
West	174	0
Other	20	0
FB %	92.3	7.6

1944 Republican Primaries

	Douglas MacArthur (R)	unpledged	Thomas Dewey (R)
W	2	5	3
East	0	4	2
South	----	----	----
Midwest	2	1	0
West	0	0	1
W %	15.4	38.5	23.1
PV	662,127	539,575	262,746
PV %	29.1	23.8	11.6
East	2.4	47.3	43.3
South	----	----	----
Midwest	52.9	29.2	3.9
West	0.0	0.0	7.6

1944
Republican Convention

	Thomas Dewey (R)
FB	1,056
East	337
South	219
Midwest	336
West	162
Other	2
FB %	99.7

1944 General Election

	Franklin Roosevelt (D)	Thomas Dewey (R)
PV	25,611,936	22,013,372
PV %	53.4	45.9
East	51.9	47.6
South	67.4	30.1
Midwest	49.2	50.4
West	55.2	44.2
Counties	1,754	1,340
Counties %	56.7	43.3
States	36	12
States %	75.0	25.0
EV	432	99
East	149	8
South	148	0
Midwest	73	82
West	62	9
EV %	81.4	18.6

1948 Democratic Primaries

	Harry Truman (D)	unpledged
W	8	6
East	2	3
South	0	2
Midwest	4	1
West	2	0
W %	57.1	42.9

1948 Democratic Primaries (continued)

	Harry Truman (D)	unpledged
PV	1,375,452	745,678
PV %	63.9	34.7
East	59.3	38.2
South	0.0	100.0
Midwest	29.5	68.2
West	99.2	0.0

1948 Democratic Convention

	Harry Truman (D)	Richard Russell (D)
FB	926	266
East	338½	4
South	63	262
Midwest	325	0
West	189½	0
Other	10	0
FB %	75.0	21.6

1948 Republican Primaries

	Earl Warren (R)	unpledged	Harold Stassen (R)	Thomas Dewey (R)
W	1	3	4	2
East	0	2	2	1
South	----	----	----	----
Midwest	0	1	2	0
West	1	0	0	1
W %	8.3	25.0	33.3	16.7

1948 Republican Primaries (continued)

	Earl Warren (R)	unpledged	Harold Stassen (R)	Thomas Dewey (R)
PV	771,295	527,812	449,713	304,394
PV %	29.1	19.9	16.9	11.5
East	0.0	20.2	38.9	16.1
South	----	----	----	----
Midwest	0.2	36.9	12.7	9.2
West	77.2	0.0	10.8	11.8

1948 Republican Convention

	Thomas Dewey (R)	Robert Taft (R)	Harold Stassen (R)	Arthur Vandenberg (R)	Earl Warren (R)	Dwight Green (R)
FB	434	224	157	62	59	56
East	199	40	19	15	1	0
South	98	96	13	2	1	0
Midwest	66	59	105	44	2	56
West	71	27	20	1	55	0
Other	0	2	0	0	0	0
FB %	39.7	20.5	14.4	5.7	5.4	5.1
LB (#3)	1,094	0	0	0	0	0
East	341	0	0	0	0	0
South	234	0	0	0	0	0
Midwest	343	0	0	0	0	0
West	174	0	0	0	0	0
Other	2	0	0	0	0	0
LB %	100.0	0.0	0.0	0.0	0.0	0.0

1948 General Election

	Harry Truman (D)	Thomas Dewey (R)	Strom Thurmond (SRD)	Henry Wallace (P)
PV	24,105,587	21,970,017	1,169,134	1,157,057
PV %	49.5	45.1	2.4	2.4
East	47.7	47.6	0.0	3.9
South	52.2	29.6	17.5	0.5
Midwest	50.3	48.0	0.0	1.0
West	49.4	46.3	0.0	3.7
Counties	1,638	1,190	266	0
Counties %	52.9	38.4	8.6	0.0
States	28	16	4	0
States %	58.3	33.3	8.3	0.0
EV	303	189	39	0
East	28	129	0	0
South	109	0	39	0
Midwest	101	54	0	0
West	65	6	0	0
EV %	57.1	35.6	7.3	0.0

1952 Republican Primaries

	Robert Taft (R)	Dwight Eisenhower (R)	Earl Warren (R)	Harold Stassen (R)
W	6	5	1	1
East	1	4	0	0
South	----	----	----	----
Midwest	5	0	0	1
West	0	1	1	0
W %	46.2	38.5	7.7	7.7

1952 Republican Primaries (continued)

		Robert Taft (R)	Dwight Eisenhower (R)	Earl Warren (R)	Harold Stassen (R)
PV		2,794,736	2,114,588	1,349,036	881,702
PV %		35.8	27.1	17.3	11.3
	East	28.3	63.5	0.1	7.7
	South	----	----	----	----
	Midwest	59.0	10.9	7.7	19.4
	West	1.0	9.5	59.1	0.4

1952 Republican Convention

		Dwight Eisenhower (R)	Robert Taft (R)	Earl Warren (R)
FB		845	280	77
	East	357	15	0
	South	209	16	0
	Midwest	153	212	7
	West	124	35	70
	Other	2	2	0
FB %		70.1	23.2	6.4

1952 Democratic Primaries

		Estes Kefauver (D)	Richard Russell (D)	unpledged
W		12	1	1
	East	5	0	1
	South	0	1	0
	Midwest	5	0	0
	West	2	0	0
W %		75.0	6.3	6.3

1952 Democratic Primaries (continued)

	Estes Kefauver (D)	Richard Russell (D)	unpledged
PV	3,169,448	369,671	237,832
PV %	64.3	7.5	4.8
East	53.9	0.2	29.3
South	42.3	54.5	0.0
Midwest	71.6	0.0	0.0
West	70.6	0.0	0.0

1952 Democratic Convention

	Adlai Stevenson (D)	Estes Kefauver (D)	Richard Russell (D)	Averell Harriman (D)	Robert Kerr (D)	Alben Barkley (D)
FB	273	340	268	123½	65	48½
East	107½	63½	9½	98	½	7
South	6	41	220	0	24	27
Midwest	137	126½	12	4	14	12½
West	15½	108	24½	21½	26½	2
Other	7	1	2	0	0	0
FB %	22.2	27.6	21.8	10.0	5.3	3.9
LB (#3)	617½	275½	261	0	0	67½
East	277	37½	10	0	0	5
South	28½	42	219	0	0	50½
Midwest	222	93	5	0	0	12
West	80	103	27	0	0	0
Other	10	0	0	0	0	0
LB %	50.2	22.4	21.2	0.0	0.0	5.5

1952 General Election

	Dwight Eisenhower (R)	Adlai Stevenson (D)
PV	33,936,137	27,314,649
PV %	55.1	44.4
East	54.8	44.5
South	48.8	51.0
Midwest	57.6	42.0
West	57.3	41.9
Counties	2,104	995
Counties %	67.9	32.1
States	39	9
States %	81.3	18.8
EV	442	89
East	145	8
South	65	81
Midwest	153	0
West	79	0
EV %	83.2	16.8

1956 Republican Primaries

	Dwight Eisenhower (R)
W	15
East	6
South	1
Midwest	5
West	3
W %	78.9

1956
Republican Primaries
(continued)

		Dwight Eisenhower (R)
PV		5,007,970
PV %		85.9
	East	90.2
	South	92.0
	Midwest	75.3
	West	97.6

1956
Republican Convention

		Dwight Eisenhower (R)
FB		1,323
	East	378
	South	325
	Midwest	378
	West	238
	Other	4
FB %		100.0

1956 Democratic Primaries

		Adlai Stevenson (D)	Estes Kefauver (D)	Frank Lausche (D)
W		7	9	1
	East	2	3	0
	South	1	0	0
	Midwest	1	5	1
	West	3	1	0
W %		36.8	47.4	5.3

1956 Democratic Primaries (continued)

		Adlai Stevenson (D)	Estes Kefauver (D)	Frank Lausche (D)
PV		3,058,470	2,283,172	276,923
PV %		52.3	39.1	4.7
	East	56.6	25.1	0.0
	South	51.5	48.5	0.0
	Midwest	42.5	44.2	13.0
	West	60.1	39.8	0.0

1956 Democratic Convention

		Adlai Stevenson (D)	Averell Harriman (D)	Lyndon Johnson (D)
FB		905½	210	80
	East	256	112½	½
	South	159	29	78½
	Midwest	268	40	0
	West	210½	28½	1
	Other	12	0	0
FB %		66.0	15.3	5.8

1956 General Election

	Dwight Eisenhower (R)	Adlai Stevenson (D)	Walter Jones (ID)
PV	35,585,245	26,030,172	0
PV %	57.4	42.0	0.0
East	60.4	39.4	0.0
South	50.0	47.3	0.0
Midwest	58.6	41.2	0.0
West	56.3	43.3	0.0
Counties	2,143	924	0
Counties %	69.1	29.8	0.0
States	41	7	0
States %	85.4	14.6	0.0
EV	457	73	1
East	153	0	0
South	85	60	1
Midwest	140	13	0
West	79	0	0
EV %	86.1	13.7	0.2

6.
Beyond the New Frontier: 1960–1984

The political climate changed drastically in the years following the Eisenhower Presidency. John Kennedy, the first President born in the 20th Century, ushered in this period with a challenge. "And so, my fellow Americans," he implored in launching his New Frontier, "ask not what your country can do for you; ask what you can do for your country."[1] But such idealism was no match for the Vietnam War, urban riots, Watergate, and a social revolution over the next two decades. Disillusioned Americans became less interested in national issues, more concerned with themselves. Ronald Reagan accurately sensed this mood in 1980. He asked voters, "Are you better off than you were four years ago?"[2]

This growing preoccupation with self contributed to two political trends: the virtual self-destruction of the Democratic party and the rebirth of conservatism. The Democrats won the first two elections in the period of 1960-1984, but then dropped four of the remaining five. The four losers scraped up a combined total of 270 electoral votes, the bare minimum needed for a single victory. The worst defeats followed the 1972 reforms designed to "open up" the party. Actress Shirley MacLaine was a member of the California delegation at that year's convention. She joked it contained "a couple of high schools, a grape boycott, a Black Panther rally, and four or five politicians who walked in the wrong door."[3] It was hardly a group designed to appeal to mainstream America. New York City Mayor John Lindsay grumbled, "This party seems to have an instinct for suicide."[4]

The same had been said about conservatives ever since Franklin Roosevelt routed their spiritual leader, Herbert Hoover, in 1932. The Republicans nominated conservative idol Barry Goldwater in 1964, declaring in advertisements, "In Your Heart, You Know He's Right." The Democrats jeered, "In Your Guts, You Know He's Nuts." The country agreed with the latter, repudiating the threat to the New Deal tradition. But in 1980, Ronald Reagan converted the very same voters who had laughed off Goldwater. They were now tired of distant wars, political scandals, and a burgeoning bureaucracy. A former New Deal supporter himself, Reagan charged, "Government became a drug: providing temporary relief, but addiction as well."[5] His landslide reelection in 1984 was interpreted as a solid confirmation of the public´s conversion to conservatism.

The Republicans had once despaired of ever regaining their majority status. But they were entrenched by the mid-1980s. The Democrats were back where they had been in the 1920s: wandering in the political wilderness, hoping for a break to present them another opportunity for control of the White House.

ELECTION NO. 44:   1960

Franklin Roosevelt´s four-term stranglehold on the Presidency infuriated an impotent Republican party. The GOP finally won a majority of both houses of Congress in 1946. Still livid at the Roosevelt "dictatorship," its leaders pushed through the 22nd Amendment less than three months after taking power. It took effect in 1951, guaranteeing that no future President could be elected more than twice.

The first application of the new law came in 1960 with unmistakable irony. One of the most popular Republican Presidents ever, Dwight Eisenhower, was blocked from seeking a third term he easily could have won. Vice President Richard Nixon and New York Governor Nelson Rockefeller were the two obvious contenders to replace him as the party´s nominee. The Vice President had the edge, having campaigned for Republican candidates across the country for years. Rockefeller pronounced a 1959 exploratory tour "great fun," but said he would go no further. Nixon took all but ten votes at the convention.

Three Senators were most visible in the Democratic race. John Kennedy of Massachusetts and Hubert Humphrey of Minnesota lacked connections with the party´s power brokers. They had to go the primary route. Lyndon Johnson of Texas was Majority Leader. He planned to use his influence to line up support.

Each of the primary competitors came to national prominence through earlier Democratic conventions: Humphrey for his leadership of the fight for a tough civil-rights plank in 1948, Kennedy for his nearly successful Vice Presidential candidacy in 1956. Each also had liabilities: the Minnesotan was called too liberal for much of the country, his rival was Catholic and was considered too young at 43. Kennedy´s win in West Virginia knocked out Humphrey. The winner told reporters in the heavily Protestant state, "I think we have now buried the religious issue once and for all."[6] He went on to win ten of the sixteen primaries.

Kennedy emerged more quickly than his rivals expected. Johnson discovered his strategy of wheeling-and-dealing put him no better than a distant second. The stop-Kennedy drive desperately reached into the past, proposing to draft Adlai Stevenson. "Do not reject this man," Minnesota Senator Eugene McCarthy pleaded when placing Stevenson´s name before the convention. "Do not leave this prophet without honor in his own party."[7] The most enthusiastic demonstration of the convention followed, but it was all for show. Kennedy was nominated on the first ballot, then astounded his aides by choosing Johnson as his running mate. "The problems are not all solved and the battles are not all won," the nominee declared in his acceptance speech. "We stand today on the edge of a New Frontier, the frontier of the 1960s, a frontier of unknown opportunities and perils, a frontier of unfulfilled hopes and threats."[8]

Nixon was better known than Kennedy, and he planned to campaign harder. The Vice President said he would be the first candidate to reach all fifty states, a commitment he fulfilled, but with great difficulty. Nixon pledged at each stop to continue the policies of the Eisenhower Administration. When Kennedy repeatedly promised "to get this country moving again," Nixon snapped back, "I´m getting sick and tired of hearing this constant whimpering and yammering and wringing of the towel with regard to the poor United States."[9]

Polls showed Nixon in the lead in early autumn. He pressed his advantage, contending his eight years as Vice President were better preparation than Kennedy´s tenure in the Senate. Two developments destroyed that assertion. The first came when a reporter asked Eisenhower to name the major decisions Nixon had participated in. The President inexplicably responded, "If you give me a week, I might think of one."[10] More important were the four televised debates between the two contenders, the first such confrontations in history. The cool and confident Kennedy appeared every bit the equal of the Vice President. He surged ahead in the surveys after the first telecast.

Kennedy was now close to becoming the first Catholic ever elected President. The religious issue he thought he had buried in the mountains of West Virginia reemerged. It was the final dangerous obstacle, one Kennedy surmounted in a speech to a group of Protestant ministers in September. "I am not the Catholic candidate for President," Kennedy declared. "I am the Democratic party´s candidate for President who happens also to be a Catholic."[11]

It was the second-closest election ever in terms of percentage difference between the candidates. Kennedy didn´t secure the necessary total of electoral votes until the day after the election. Unpledged Democratic electors almost took the balance of power, winning two states. They later cast their ballots for Virginia Senator Harry Byrd. Kennedy knew he entered the White House with a precarious mandate. "The margin is narrow," he conceded, "but the responsibility is clear."[12]

ELECTION NO. 45:   1964

For the Republican party, 1964 was just like old times. The GOP had the first wide-open battle for its nomination in twelve years, signaling a resumption of the warfare between its moderate and conservative wings. Gone were Thomas Dewey and Robert Taft. The new ideological commanders were New York Governor Nelson Rockefeller and Arizona Senator Barry Goldwater. The stakes were the same.

     Rockefeller inherited the Eastern strength that had allowed Dewey to win two nominations and dictate a third. The New Yorker easily led all other Republican contenders by 17 percentage points in an April 1963 Gallup Poll. The next month, he triggered public outrage by remarrying, to a divorcee, no less. Goldwater soared to a five-point bulge over Rockefeller in the immediately following survey. The Arizonan was much like Taft, a frank-speaking believer in conservative principles. He once insisted, "I fear Washington and centralized government more than I do Moscow."[13]

     President John Kennedy liked Goldwater, if not his politics, and looked forward to their possible contest in 1964. But he refused to publicly comment on Goldwater´s tart tongue. Kennedy joked with reporters, "He himself has had a busy week selling TVA and giving permission or suggesting that military commanders overseas be permitted to use nuclear weapons, and attacking the President of Bolivia while he was here in the United States, and involving himself in the Greek election. So I thought it really would not be fair for me this week to reply to him."[14] That could wait for later. But Kennedy´s assassination in November 1963 drastically changed the political calculus. Goldwater considered dropping out of the race for awhile, but finally gave his supporters the go-ahead.

     Conservatives had begun work in 1961 to seize control of the party machinery. Goldwater originally offered them scant encouragement. Asked in 1963 what he thought about becoming President, the Senator replied, "Frankly, it scares the hell out of me."[15] His gradual decision to make a serious effort provided a rallying point for the conservative movement, whose power in 1964 surprised and frightened moderate leaders. Rockefeller was faltering, so they scrambled for an alternative. Richard Nixon was unthinkable after his 1962 defeat in the race for Governor of California. Ambassador to South Vietnam Henry Cabot Lodge astounded everyone by winning the New Hampshire primary on write-ins, but he showed no interest in making a commitment. After Goldwater´s win in the California primary, Pennsylvania Governor William Scranton quixotically agreed to pick up the fallen moderate banner. His poorly organized effort was smashed on the convention´s first ballot.

     The conservatives, accustomed to intraparty defeat, were suddenly on top. They celebrated with gusto. Rockefeller was roundly booed when he tried to address the convention. "This is still a free country, ladies and gentlemen," he chided.[16] Goldwater was acclaimed a hero, particularly when he declared, "Extremism in the defense of liberty is no vice! And...moderation in the pursuit of justice is no virtue!"[17]

There was no doubt that President Lyndon Johnson would be Goldwater´s opponent. He implored Congress after Kennedy´s assassination, "Let us continue." Johnson deftly assumed the Democratic party reins. He virtually ignored the primaries, where Alabama Governor George Wallace gave the first demonstration of white backlash with a surprisingly strong showing against three favorite sons in the North. The President had no cause to worry. His unanimous nomination was long assumed. The only suspense centered on his choice of a running mate. Pressure grew in favor of Attorney General Robert Kennedy, hardly a friend of the President. Johnson solved that problem by announcing he wouldn´t pick anyone from the Cabinet. Kennedy joked, "I´m sorry I took so many nice fellows over the side with me."[18] Johnson finally chose Minnesota Senator Hubert Humphrey.

Republican advertisements lauded Goldwater as "a choice, not an echo." He was the first GOP nominee in decades to truly attack the foundations of the New Deal, "We have gotten where we are not because of government, but in spite of government."[19] Johnson retorted, "Government is not an enemy of the people. It is the people."[20] His television commercials reinforced the image of Goldwater as someone who shot from the hip and would be likely to involve the United States in an atomic conflagration. The President suggested Goldwater might get entangled in the fighting in Vietnam. "We don´t want our American boys to do the fighting for Asian boys," he told voters that fall. "We don´t want to...get tied down in a land war in Asia."[21]

Johnson lusted for the biggest landslide in history. He campaigned like a dervish, shouting through bullhorns, "Come on down and hear the speakin´!" A leadership change in the Soviet Union and China´s explosion of its first atomic bomb punctuated his assertion that the world situation was too critical to change leaders. Johnson´s resulting share of the popular vote was the highest ever. Goldwater carried only Arizona and five Southern states that applauded his opposition to the 1964 Civil Rights Act. His prediction of a conservative revolution would eventually come true, but first, Lyndon Johnson would preside over the final flowering of the New Deal, known as "the Great Society," accompanied by the predicted "land war in Asia."

ELECTION NO. 46: 1968

Author William Manchester was on the mark when he christened 1968, "the year everything went wrong." The Vietnam War dragged bloodily on, two prominent Americans were assassinated, the papers were full of stories about "runaway inflation," urban riots and college demonstrations seemed epidemic, and political polarization was extreme. Lyndon Johnson´s Great Society, born in the euphoria of his 1964 landslide, was dying in an orgy of violence and disillusionment.

Republicans were not immune from the nightmare. Michigan Governor George Romney was their Presidential frontrunner. But Vietnam got him, too. Romney admitted he had originally supported Johnson´s Vietnam policy because he had been "brainwashed" by government briefing officers. Public ridicule forced Romney out by February. Richard Nixon, launching a comeback, was the unwitting beneficiary. He was suddenly the only major GOP contender, easily winning the early primaries.

Opposition was slow in forming. California Governor Ronald Reagan refused to expand his favorite-son candidacy. His New York counterpart, Nelson Rockefeller, called a March press conference, where he stunned everyone by announcing he would <u>not</u> run. Rockefeller changed his mind in April, after the assassination of Martin Luther King Jr. He cited "the new circumstances that confront the nation. I frankly find that to comment from the sidelines is not an effective way to present the alternatives."[22] His decision and Reagan´s later full-scale entry were much too late. Nixon sewed up a first-ballot convention victory.

The first entrant in the Democratic contest drew cynical laughter from party professionals. Minnesota Senator Eugene McCarthy, a searing critic of the Vietnam War, announced he would challenge President Johnson´s expected bid for reelection. McCarthy was not well-known and relied heavily on young volunteers to run his campaign. It was downplayed as a "Children´s Crusade" until the Minnesotan almost upset Johnson in the New Hampshire primary. New York Senator Robert Kennedy now saw an opportunity, entering the race four days after New Hampshire. He said of McCarthy, "My candidacy would not be in opposition to his, but in harmony."[23] Few believed it, least of all McCarthy.

An even bigger surprise waited at the end of March, just before the Wisconsin primary McCarthy expected to win. President Johnson announced on television, "I shall not seek and I will not accept the nomination of my party for another term."[24] Vice President Hubert Humphrey was informed of the bombshell just before it was exploded. He entered the contest too late to compete in the primaries, working behind the scenes for delegates while Kennedy and McCarthy locked horns in increasingly bitter public matchups. The New Yorker won head-to-head battles in Indiana and Nebraska; the Minnesotan struck back in Oregon. Kennedy´s potentially decisive win followed a week later in California. He shouted to his supporters, "On to Chicago!" An assassin fatally wounded him a few minutes afterward.

Party leaders now closed ranks behind Humphrey. McCarthy seemed to lose interest in further campaigning. In any case, bitter Kennedy supporters refused to join him. They advanced South Dakota Senator George McGovern as their new leader, while still dreaming of Massachusetts Senator Edward Kennedy, who said that summer, "Like my three brothers before me, I pick up a fallen standard."[25] But Kennedy did not want to take his banner into battle so soon after his brother´s death. He discouraged talk of a draft.

The Democratic convention was a disaster. Thousands of antiwar protestors came to Chicago. Mayor Richard Daley rasped, "No one is going to take over the streets." The resulting violence outside the convention hall mirrored the discord inside. Connecticut Senator Abraham Ribicoff condemned "Gestapo tactics on the streets of Chicago." Mayor Daley and his lieutenants angrily shouted during the rest of Ribicoff's speech. Humphrey's nomination was almost anticlimactic.

A third party wielded considerable power during the troubled autumn. Former Alabama Governor George Wallace, best known for his defiance of federal college-desegregation orders, created the American Independent party. His organizers startled the major parties by getting Wallace on the ballot in all fifty states. His attacks on "pointy-headed" bureaucrats struck home in a frustrated middle America. Wallace contended there was not "a dime's worth of difference" between the Democrats and Republicans. He hoped to win enough electoral votes to prevent an outright winner. Then he would bargain with Nixon and Humphrey.

Nixon began the fall campaign well ahead in the public-opinion surveys. He appealed for the support of "forgotten Americans" who wondered what had happened to their country. His promises to put the brakes to Democratic social programs attracted whites who believed the New Frontier and the Great Society had laid the kindling for the flames that were consuming American cities. Nixon's smooth television effort sought to link Humphrey with the national unrest. The Republican called his opponent "the most articulate and the most uncompromising defender of the Johnson Administration."[26]

Humphrey insisted, "The President has not made me his slave and I am not his humble servant."[27] His critics didn't believe it. Hecklers dogged his every step. The change came in late September when the nominee finally broke publicly with Johnson, announcing support for a Vietnam bombing halt. Signs appeared at his rallies, "If you mean it, we're with you!" McCarthy finally endorsed him. Money poured in. Humphrey neared Nixon in the polls. When Johnson announced a real cessation of bombing at the end of October, Humphrey concluded an amazing comeback by drawing even.

The popular-vote margin was just 510,645 out of more than 73,000,000 votes cast. Humphrey carried the East, but Nixon held on to the other three regions. It wasn't until the day after the election that the Republican was guaranteed a majority of the Electoral College. George Wallace came close to amassing the balance-of-power he sought. His popular-vote total was the highest of any third-party candidate in history.

Richard Nixon was now President-elect of a bitterly divided country. He pledged to wind down the Vietnam War and said his administration would take its theme from a sign he had seen during the campaign in Ohio. It echoed a plea heard from coast to coast: "Bring Us Together."

ELECTION NO. 47:   1972

Chicago Mayor Richard Daley had an unusually strong flash of prescience at the end of the 1968 Democratic convention that so severely tarnished his image. The way George McGovern remembered it, Daley walked up to him and said, "I think our Presidential nominee in ´72 will either be you or young Kennedy."[28] Daley perceived something hardly anyone else did. The little-known South Dakota Senator´s announcement of candidacy in early 1971 was generally greeted with derision. "Young Kennedy," Massachusetts Senator Edward Kennedy, had it even worse. His 1969 auto accident on Chappaquiddick Island left a woman dead and raised serious questions about his legal and moral conduct. A 1972 race for him was unthinkable.

The real frontrunners for the nomination to challenge President Richard Nixon were two other Senators, Edmund Muskie of Maine and Hubert Humphrey of Minnesota. Muskie gained a reputation for self-control as the Democratic Vice Presidential candidate in 1968, but the image masked a man-sized temper. The public saw his other side in early 1972. Muskie tearfully denounced a New Hampshire publisher for attacks on his wife. "I was just goddamned mad and choked up over my anger," he said later.[29] The outburst raised questions about Muskie, whose candidacy soon collapsed. Humphrey avoided a similar fate, but never caught fire, either. He won four primaries, but lost the key ones, Wisconsin and California, to McGovern.

The resulting void invited candidates who truly sensed the strength of public frustration in 1972. The Vietnam War continued despite Nixon´s promise to end it. Inflation remained a serious problem despite wage and price controls. McGovern and another Democratic contender, Alabama Governor George Wallace, capitalized on this discontent. The South Dakotan´s slogan was "Come Home, America." His fiery denunciations of the war formed the base of his candidacy. Wallace´s populist effort invited average citizens to "Send Them a Message." He won five primaries, but was never really an important force after being paralyzed in a May assassination attempt.

McGovern further benefited from a superior knowledge of the new rules designed to open the nominating process to everyone. He had chaired the panel that insisted on strong female and minority participation in the convention. Now many of those new delegates were for him. "The McGovern-O´Hara-Fraser commissions reformed us out of the Presidency," groused Ohio Congressman Wayne Hays, "and now they´re trying to reform us out of a party."[30] The free-spirited convention that nominated McGovern seemed an absurdity to the old-timers. The nominee added to his burden by choosing Missouri Senator Thomas Eagleton as his running mate, then dropping him after discovering Eagleton had earlier been treated for nervous exhaustion. "From that moment on, the 1972 Presidential results were determined," McGovern later wrote. "Richard Nixon and Spiro Agnew were home free."[31]

Nixon did much to help his own cause. His acclaimed trips to China in February and Moscow in May were Presidential firsts. Nixon easily dispatched a primary challenge from Ohio Congressman John Ashbrook and was renominated by a carefully stage-managed Republican convention.

The fall campaign was not much more difficult for the Republicans. McGovern campaign manager Gary Hart said the Democratic effort "lost its direction, if not its soul" after the convention. Dispirited by the Eagleton fiasco and badly outspent by the Republicans, McGovern could not capture the public´s attention. He blasted the continuation of the Vietnam War. Presidential aide Henry Kissinger countered that "peace is at hand." McGovern cited the June break-in at Democratic headquarters as proof that the Nixon Administration was "the most corrupt in history." Watergate would eventually be the downfall of twenty administration officials, imprisoned for such crimes as perjury, forgery, and bribery. But most details became public long after the election.

Nixon had little need to campaign. His foreign-policy coups provided a strong contrast to the popular perception that the disorganized McGovern campaign stood for the Three A´s: acid, amnesty, and abortion. The President carried 49 states and won by nearly 18,000,000 votes, the largest margin in history. The count in the Electoral College was 520-17. One Nixon elector defected to the nominee of the Libertarian party, John Hospers.

The Republicans celebrated their retention of power with a $4,000,000 inaugural extravaganza. But the glory steadily drained away for eighteen months after that. Vice President Agnew resigned after pleading no contest to charges of income-tax evasion. Michigan Congressman Gerald Ford replaced him. Wave after wave of Watergate revelations washed against the White House. Impeachment proceedings began in Congress. Richard Nixon declared, "I am not a crook," but his massive mandate vanished. He resigned in disgrace in August 1974.

ELECTION NO. 48:   1976

Jimmy Carter was wrapping up his final days as Governor of Georgia in 1974. He thought it was time to confide in his mother about his future plans. Lillian Carter´s reaction would soon be echoed across the country. Told that her son was going to run for President, she could only reply, "President of what?"

Democratic power brokers didn´t pay much attention to Carter. The thought that a former Governor of a Southern state could be elected President was patently ludicrous. Carter spent more than 300 days on the road in 1975, traveling in semi-anonymity. "I´ll never tell a lie," he promised Watergate-weary voters. He pledged to create an administration "as good and honest and decent and compassionate and filled with love as are the American people."[32] It was an unusual and effective message.

Carter's diligent spadework paid off spectacularly in early 1976, with his stunning victories in the Iowa caucuses and the New Hampshire primary. He suddenly vaulted from unknown to frontrunner, a status he never relinquished. Carter's wins in Florida and North Carolina dismissed his chief Southern rival, Alabama Governor George Wallace. His victory in Pennsylvania ended the hopes of Washington Senator Henry Jackson. Arizona Congressman Morris Udall ran close in several primaries, but never won a single one. California Governor Jerry Brown and Idaho Senator Frank Church entered in mid-battle, hoping to derail the Georgia express. But Carter was too far ahead by then, easily capturing a first-ballot nomination. The Democratic convention seemed unusually unified to veterans of 1968 and 1972. "When Jimmy Carter says he'll beat you, he'll beat you, and he beat us fair and square," Udall graciously told delegates as he snapped on a Carter pin. "As I leave the convention hall tonight, I'm going to have one of those green buttons that dogged me all over America."[33]

Tensions were considerably higher on the Republican side. President Gerald Ford received praise for restoring a sense of order to the government, but his pardon of Richard Nixon for possible Watergate crimes was highly controversial. Former California Governor Ronald Reagan considered Ford a typical Washington insider. He announced he would run against "evil incarnate in the buddy system in Washington."

Ford won several early primaries. His advisers prematurely began seeking a way of easing Reagan's with-drawal. Southern and Western primaries then triggered the Californian's comeback. He even took the lead in committed delegate votes. Ford regained it through heavy use of White House influence on wavering delegates. The President eventually won sixteen primaries, Reagan ten.

The Republican contest took on the vitriolic tone of a general-election campaign. Reagan contended Ford had shown "neither the vision nor the leadership necessary to halt and reverse the diplomatic and military decline of the United States."[34] He accused the President of plotting to give away the Panama Canal. Ford countered that the former Governor couldn't be trusted in the White House. He ran commercials that said, "When you vote Tuesday, remember: Governor Ronald Reagan couldn't start a war. President Ronald Reagan could."[35] The power of incumbency made the difference. Ford and his moderates edged Reagan and his conservatives at the convention by 117 votes.

The President's victory seemed hollow. He entered the fall campaign as the leader of a party associated with a recent scandal, a badly divided party that was opposed by a popular fresh face. He trailed Carter by the astounding margin of 33 percentage points in the first polls. Forced to take dramatic steps, Ford challenged Carter to televised debates. The President turned in a strong performance in the first, slicing the Democrat's lead in the surveys to single digits. But in the rematch, he declared, "There is no Soviet domination of Eastern Europe, and there never will be under a Ford Administration."[36] Critics asked if the President was living in fantasy or merely ignorant. Ford´s momentum slowed.

Carter ran into his own problems. He had carefully nurtured his image as a "born again" Christian who dwelled on the loftiest of moral planes. The facade crumbled in an interview with Playboy. "I´ve looked on a lot of women with lust," Carter admitted. "I´ve committed adultery in my heart many times."[37] The man who had campaigned all year for a higher standard now seemed to be just like everyone else.

The Democratic lead slowly eroded through October. Ford, who spent much of the campaign shut in the White House, now emerged for a frenetic conclusion. He shouted to crowds, "We´re in the last quarter and the ninth inning. That´s when you win."[38] But he couldn´t push the final run across the plate. Carter held on for a 57-vote margin in the Electoral College. (One Ford elector defected to Reagan.) "Jimmy Who?" had successfully reached the end of the long and improbable road from Plains, Georgia, to the White House.

ELECTION NO. 49: 1980

America was restless in 1979. The inflation and unemployment rates were soaring to heights few could remember. Queues of motorists waited impatiently for scarce gasoline. The country´s overseas image was already bruised, and would suffer a virtual knockout when embassy personnel in Iran were captured by militants late in the year. President Jimmy Carter surveyed the gloomy landscape that summer and announced that Americans were suffering a "crisis of confidence."

Many Democrats placed the blame squarely on the man who had engineered their return to the White House in 1976. Polls through the summer of 1979 showed Carter trailing Massachusetts Senator Edward Kennedy by a 2-1 margin among party members. Kennedy announced his challenge for the Democratic nomination in November, just three days after the Iranian hostage-taking that would cast its shadow on the entire campaign. Carter was ready. He told a group of Democratic Congressmen, "I´ll whip his ass." Kennedy, also confident of victory, said the President promised "four more years of uncertain policy and certain crisis." He accused Carter of abandoning his party´s traditional liberalism, of being "a clone of Ronald Reagan."

Kennedy´s attacks were not as effective as the polls had led him to expect. After the hostage-taking, Americans followed their nationalistic impulses and rallied to the President. Carter shrewdly played to that sentiment in December, "At the height of the Civil War, Abraham Lincoln said, `I have but one task and that is to save the Union.´ Now I must devote my considered efforts to resolving the Iranian crisis."[39] Kennedy´s lead vanished almost overnight. Carter, staying in the White House, scored a series of stunning wins in the early primaries. The challenger closed with a rush, but still managed only ten victories. Carter won twenty-four primaries, and took the nomination on the first ballot.

A large pack of Republicans started the year eager to draw the assignment to square off against Carter. Three emerged from the early skirmishing. Former California Governor Ronald Reagan was the frontrunner, the favorite of conservatives. Former United Nations Ambassador George Bush labeled himself a moderate. Blasting Reagan´s "voodoo economics," the transplanted Texan had special appeal in his native East. Illinois Congressman John Anderson was the most liberal of the three, and consequently had the least success in the primaries. Bush won the Iowa caucuses, appearing ready to give Reagan a strong fight, but the Californian scored the first of twenty-nine primary victories in New Hampshire. Bush took the other six.

Anderson gave up on the Republican battle in April, well before Reagan´s nearly unanimous convention triumph. The Illinoisan announced creation of the National Unity party, which managed to get his name on the ballot in all fifty states. He was accused of being nothing more than a spoiler, but countered, "What´s to spoil? Spoil the chances of two men at least half the country doesn´t want?"[40] Early polls showed Anderson getting more than ten percent of the general-election vote.

Reagan´s rhetoric picked up in the fall where Kennedy left off at the Democratic convention. No one needed reminding that the hostages were still being held in Iran; a raid to rescue them had ended disastrously in April. The Republican now blasted Carter for "his vacillation, his weakness, his allowing our allies throughout the world to no longer respect us." He promised to "bring our government back under control."[41]

Carter returned the favor, renewing charges made against Reagan in his bitter intraparty contest with Gerald Ford four years earlier. The President warned that Reagan was trigger-happy. His election would mean "the risk of an uncontrollable, unaffordable, and unwinnable nuclear arms race."[42] Carter envisioned racial, religious, and regional polarization under a Reagan Presidency.

Polls showed a neck-and-neck race. A televised debate in late October proved to be the difference. Reagan was in control, laughing, "There you go again!" at what he considered Carter´s wild charges. The President evoked snickers across the nation by confessing he had asked his young daughter what issue to stress. She said nuclear arms control. Reagan differed. He concluded by telling voters the big question was, "Are you better off than you were four years ago?"[43]

The answer was resoundingly negative. Reagan´s Electoral College margin was almost 10-1. He carried all four regions. Anderson´s share of the popular vote slid to less than seven percent. Jimmy Carter´s theory of 1979 seemed to have been proven.   The nation did have a "crisis of confidence."   It was in him.

ELECTION NO. 50:   1984

Walter Mondale had run for President once before.   He spent much of 1974 on the road, weighing his chances for the Democratic nomination that would eventually go to Jimmy Carter.   Mondale decided that he did not have what he considered the prime requisite for a candidate, a willingness "to go through fire."   He spoke disparagingly of having to spend the following two years sleeping in Holiday Inns. Mondale announced late in the year that he would not formally enter the 1976 race.

It was different by 1982.   "I know myself," the former Vice President said.   "I am ready.   I am ready to be President of the United States."[44]   Organized labor quickly swung its powerful muscle behind Mondale, making him the frontrunner.   The Democratic nomination indeed seemed well worth pursuing.   President Ronald Reagan's popularity had declined severely after the 1981 Congressional honeymoon that saw the enactment of his conservative economic program.   The promised recovery was uneven at best.   Reagan had no major foreign policy achievements.   His advocacy of a stronger military led to charges that the President was itching to put his finger on the nuclear trigger.

Mondale was one of eight Democrats hoping to capitalize on the slide in Republican fortunes.   Massachusetts Senator Edward Kennedy surprisingly was not among them.   His 1980 campaign seemed the basis for success in 1984, but Kennedy announced that his family responsibilities would be foremost.   Mondale, Colorado Senator Gary Hart, and civil rights activist Jesse Jackson benefited from his absence as they moved to the top of the Democratic pack.   Hart contended he spoke for a new generation, "It is time for the old order to pass, for the old establishment politicians to give way.   It is time for our voices to be heard at last."[45]   Jackson, the first black man to be considered a serious national candidate, ran a campaign with strong religious overtones. Sounding much like Hart, Jackson preached to his self-proclaimed Rainbow Coalition, "It's time for a change. Our time has come!"[46]

Mondale expected an easy path to the nomination, but it was obstructed in New Hampshire.   Hart's shocking win in that primary put the former Vice President on the defensive well into the spring.   Facing a rising chorus of voters advocating Hart's "new ideas," Mondale responded by mimicking a popular television commercial, "Where's the beef?"   Hart won sixteen of the thirty primaries, but his momentum slowed under the implication that there was little substance behind his slogans.   Mondale rebounded to win the nomination by a sizable margin on the first ballot, then made history by choosing the first female running mate for a major-party ticket, New York Congresswoman Geraldine Ferraro.

The Democrats faced a resurgent Republican party.

President Reagan´s economic recovery was late arriving, but had finally pulled into the station. The October 1983 invasion to rout the Marxist government of Grenada presented the image of a leader unafraid to act. The President´s supporters said it provided a sharp contrast to Jimmy Carter´s waffling over Iran in 1979 and 1980. Reagan was renominated without opposition.

Polls showed Mondale trailing badly at the start of the fall campaign. He decided to draw the issues sharply, beginning with his speech accepting the nomination, "Let´s tell the truth. Mr. Reagan will raise taxes, and so will I. He won´t tell you. I just did."[47] Mondale contended higher taxes were the necessary medicine to reduce an annual federal deficit approaching $200,000,000,000. Reagan swiftly denied he would raise taxes, and blamed the Democratic-controlled Congress for the deficit. "We could say they spend like drunken sailors," he said, "but that would be unfair to drunken sailors."[48]

Mondale blasted the Reagan Administration for providing "government of the rich, by the rich, and for the rich." He condemned the "utter moral bankruptcy" of the administration´s cuts in social programs. But the sharp rhetoric failed to pierce Reagan´s armor of popularity. The President ran on the theme, "Leadership That´s Working." Reagan declared it was a time for optimism, "America is coming back and is more confident than ever about the future."[49]

Republican faith flagged only once. Reagan stumbled his way through the first of two televised debates with Mondale. Rumors immediately circulated that the 73-year-old President was no longer up to his job. Voters were reassured when Reagan did well in the second confrontation. Asked about the age issue, he countered, "I want you to know that also I will not make age an issue of this campaign. I am not going to exploit for political purposes my opponent´s youth and inexperience."[50] Even Mondale laughed.

A nation in recovery gave an overwhelming endorsement to the Reagan brand of leadership. The President carried 49 states, rolling up 525 electoral votes, the largest number in history. His popular-vote total was more than 7,000,000 above the previous record. Republicans cheered when Reagan exulted, "You ain´t seen nothing yet!" Democrats just cringed.

Charts for Chapter 6

1960 Democratic Primaries

		John Kennedy (D)	Hubert Humphrey (D)	unpledged
W		10	2	1
	East	5	1	1
	South	0	0	0
	Midwest	4	1	0
	West	1	0	0
W %		62.5	12.5	6.3
PV		1,847,259	590,410	241,958
PV %		32.5	10.4	4.3
	East	57.5	13.3	18.4
	South	0.0	0.0	0.0
	Midwest	53.6	22.6	0.0
	West	6.4	0.7	0.0

1960 Democratic Convention

	John Kennedy (D)	Lyndon Johnson (D)	Stuart Symington (D)	Adlai Stevenson (D)
FB	806	409	86	79½
East	334½	24	4	14
South	13	336	4	5
Midwest	293½	3	57½	7½
West	154	42	20½	53
Other	11	4	0	0
FB %	53.0	26.9	5.7	5.2

1960 Republican Primaries

	Richard Nixon (R)	unpledged
W	11	4
East	3	3
South	1	0
Midwest	5	1
West	2	0
W %	73.3	26.7
PV	4,975,938	486,451
PV %	89.9	8.8
East	69.7	28.1
South	100.0	0.0
Midwest	96.6	2.2
West	99.1	0.0

1960
Republican Convention

	Richard Nixon (R)
FB	1,321
East	386
South	317
Midwest	372
West	242
Other	4
FB %	99.2

1960 General Election

	John Kennedy (D)	Richard Nixon (R)	Harry Byrd (ID)
PV	34,221,344	34,106,671	116,248
PV %	49.7	49.6	0.2
East	52.7	47.1	0.0
South	49.4	47.7	0.9
Midwest	47.6	52.2	0.0
West	48.5	51.1	0.0
Counties	1,202	1,856	71
Counties %	38.4	59.3	2.3
States	22	26	2
States %	44.0	52.0	4.0
EV	303	219	15
East	141	12	0
South	81	50	15
Midwest	71	82	0
West	10	75	0
EV %	56.4	40.8	2.8

1964 Democratic Primaries

		unpledged	Lyndon Johnson (D)	George Wallace (D)
W		4	8	0
	East	2	4	0
	South	0	1	0
	Midwest	1	2	0
	West	1	1	0
W %		25.0	50.0	0.0
PV		2,705,290	1,106,999	672,984
PV %		43.3	17.7	10.8
	East	17.6	29.1	21.8
	South	0.0	100.0	0.0
	Midwest	1.4	6.7	21.7
	West	90.1	9.8	0.0

1964 Democratic Convention

		Lyndon Johnson (D)
FB		2,318
	East	686
	South	587
	Midwest	621
	West	403
	Other	21
FB %		100.0

1964 Republican Primaries

	Barry Goldwater (R)	Nelson Rocke- feller (R)	Henry Cabot Lodge (R)	William Scranton (R)
W	5	2	3	1
East	0	1	3	1
South	1	0	0	0
Midwest	3	0	0	0
West	1	1	0	0
W %	31.3	12.5	18.8	6.3
PV	2,267,079	1,304,204	386,661	245,401
PV %	38.2	22.0	6.5	4.1
East	8.5	16.9	23.5	27.3
South	61.1	2.6	5.1	0.3
Midwest	37.0	0.2	3.8	0.1
West	47.6	46.6	3.2	0.2

1964 Republican Convention

	Barry Goldwater (R)	William Scranton (R)	Nelson Rocke- feller (R)
FB	883	214	114
East	71	170	92
South	314	10	1
Midwest	281	14	3
West	217	12	18
Other	0	8	0
FB %	67.5	16.4	8.7

1964 General Election

	Lyndon Johnson (D)	Barry Goldwater (R)
PV	43,126,584	27,177,838
PV %	61.1	38.5
East	68.2	31.6
South	51.0	47.4
Midwest	61.4	38.5
West	59.4	40.3
Counties	2,294	825
Counties %	73.4	26.4
States	45	6
States %	88.2	11.8
EV	486	52
East	149	0
South	98	47
Midwest	149	0
West	90	5
EV %	90.3	9.7

1968 Republican Primaries

	Ronald Reagan (R)	Richard Nixon (R)
W	1	9
East	0	3
South	0	0
Midwest	0	5
West	1	1
W %	6.7	60.0

1968 Republican Primaries
(continued)

	Ronald Reagan (R)	Richard Nixon (R)
PV	1,696,270	1,679,443
PV %	37.9	37.5
East	1.8	51.6
South	0.0	0.0
Midwest	5.0	59.1
West	86.5	11.1

1968 Republican Convention

	Richard Nixon (R)	Nelson Rockefeller (R)	Ronald Reagan (R)	James Rhodes (R)
FB	692	277	182	55
East	116	216	1	0
South	264	9	65	0
Midwest	185	35	10	55
West	125	11	106	0
Other	2	6	0	0
FB %	51.9	20.8	13.7	4.1

1968 Democratic Primaries

		Eugene McCarthy (D)	Robert Kennedy (D)	unpledged	Lyndon Johnson (D)
W		6	5	1	1
	East	3	1	1	1
	South	0	0	0	0
	Midwest	2	3	0	0
	West	1	1	0	0
W %		40.0	33.3	6.7	6.7
PV		2,914,933	2,304,542	670,328	383,048
PV %		38.7	30.6	8.9	5.1
	East	49.9	17.1	12.8	4.8
	South	28.7	0.0	25.2	0.0
	Midwest	30.0	21.4	0.5	12.3
	West	42.0	45.4	10.7	1.3

1968 Democratic Convention

		Hubert Humphrey (D)	Eugene McCarthy (D)	George McGovern (D)
FB		$1,759\frac{1}{4}$	601	$146\frac{1}{2}$
	East	$461\frac{3}{4}$	243	13
	South	$518\frac{1}{2}$	45	7
	Midwest	517	139	$56\frac{1}{2}$
	West	240	174	69
	Other	22	0	1
FB %		67.1	22.9	5.6

1968 General Election

	Richard Nixon (R)	Hubert Humphrey (D)	George Wallace (AI)
PV	31,785,148	31,274,503	9,901,151
PV %	43.4	42.7	13.5
East	42.7	50.0	6.9
South	35.9	31.4	32.5
Midwest	46.8	43.7	9.3
West	48.7	43.7	7.1
Counties	1,859	692	578
Counties %	59.4	22.1	18.5
States	32	14	5
States %	62.7	27.5	9.8
EV	301	191	46
East	27	122	0
South	74	25	46
Midwest	118	31	0
West	82	13	0
EV %	55.9	35.5	8.6

1972 Republican Primaries

	Richard Nixon (R)	unpledged	John Ashbrook (R)
W	18	2	0
East	5	2	0
South	3	0	0
Midwest	7	0	0
West	3	0	0
W %	90.0	10.0	0.0

1972 Republican Primaries (continued)

	Richard Nixon (R)	unpledged	John Ashbrook (R)
PV	5,378,704	322,398	311,543
PV %	86.9	5.2	5.0
East	51.0	36.4	2.7
South	90.3	0.0	5.6
Midwest	98.0	0.4	0.4
West	89.2	0.1	9.2

1972
Republican Convention

	Richard Nixon (R)
FB	1,347
East	351
South	342
Midwest	362
West	281
Other	11
FB %	99.9

1972 Democratic Primaries

	Hubert Humphrey (D)	George McGovern (D)	George Wallace (D)	Edmund Muskie (D)
W	4	8	5	2
East	2	2	1	1
South	0	0	3	0
Midwest	2	3	1	1
West	0	3	0	0
W %	19.0	38.1	23.8	9.5

1972 Democratic Primaries (continued)

	Hubert Humphrey (D)	George McGovern (D)	George Wallace (D)	Edmund Muskie (D)
PV	4,121,372	4,053,451	3,755,424	1,840,217
PV %	25.8	25.3	23.5	11.5
East	29.6	24.7	21.7	15.0
South	12.1	4.4	49.5	5.9
Midwest	22.9	22.0	22.8	18.3
West	35.5	43.8	9.6	2.2

1972 Democratic Convention

	George McGovern (D)	Henry Jackson (D)	George Wallace (D)	Shirley Chisholm (D)
FB	$1,728\frac{35}{100}$	525	$381\frac{7}{10}$	$151\frac{95}{100}$
East	$663\frac{15}{100}$	$154\frac{2}{5}$	41	$22\frac{15}{100}$
South	$160\frac{3}{4}$	$122\frac{1}{4}$	238	69
Midwest	$464\frac{2}{5}$	$163\frac{4}{5}$	$94\frac{7}{10}$	$48\frac{1}{5}$
West	$427\frac{55}{100}$	$81\frac{55}{100}$	8	$12\frac{1}{10}$
Other	$12\frac{1}{2}$	3	0	$\frac{1}{2}$
FB %	57.3	17.4	12.7	5.0

1972 General Election

	Richard Nixon (R)	George McGovern (D)	John Hospers (LIB)
PV	47,170,179	29,171,791	3,671
PV %	60.7	37.5	0.0
East	57.8	41.3	0.0
South	69.5	29.0	0.0
Midwest	59.1	39.4	0.0
West	57.1	39.0	0.0
Counties	2,997	133	0
Counties %	95.8	4.2	0.0
States	49	2	0
States %	96.1	3.9	0.0
EV	520	17	1
East	127	17	0
South	146	0	1
Midwest	145	0	0
West	102	0	0
EV %	96.7	3.2	0.2

1976 Democratic Primaries
(first of two charts)

	Jimmy Carter (D)	Jerry Brown (D)	George Wallace (D)	Morris Udall (D)
W	17	3	0	0
East	5	1	0	0
South	6	0	0	0
Midwest	6	0	0	0
West	0	2	0	0
W %	63.0	11.1	0.0	0.0

1976 Democratic Primaries
(first of two charts, continued)

	Jimmy Carter (D)	Jerry Brown (D)	George Wallace (D)	Morris Udall (D)
PV	6,235,609	2,449,374	1,995,388	1,611,754
PV %	38.8	15.3	12.4	10.0
East	30.4	7.8	10.3	12.3
South	54.9	0.0	23.5	3.8
Midwest	48.7	0.0	14.1	17.6
West	21.1	52.7	2.8	4.7

1976 Democratic Primaries
(second of two charts)

	Henry Jackson (D)	Frank Church (D)
W	1	4
East	1	0
South	0	0
Midwest	0	1
West	0	3
W %	3.7	14.8
PV	1,134,375	830,818
PV %	7.1	5.2
East	15.1	1.8
South	10.2	0.4
Midwest	3.6	4.7
West	1.2	12.8

1976 Democratic Convention

		Jimmy Carter (D)	Morris Udall (D)	Jerry Brown (D)
FB		2,238½	329½	300½
	East	714	137½	25½
	South	588	10	24
	Midwest	668	137	9
	West	235	45	241½
	Other	33½	0	½
FB %		74.4	11.0	10.0

1976 Republican Primaries

		Gerald Ford (R)	Ronald Reagan (R)
W		16	10
	East	8	0
	South	3	3
	Midwest	4	3
	West	1	4
W %		61.5	38.5
PV		5,529,899	4,758,325
PV %		53.3	45.9
	East	80.1	17.8
	South	47.9	51.4
	Midwest	56.6	42.8
	West	35.7	63.7

1976 Republican Convention

	Gerald Ford (R)	Ronald Reagan (R)
FB	1,187	1,070
East	514	67
South	164	442
Midwest	412	192
West	81	369
Other	16	0
FB %	52.5	47.4

1976 General Election

	Jimmy Carter (D)	Gerald Ford (R)	Ronald Reagan (IR)
PV	40,830,763	39,147,793	0
PV %	50.1	48.0	0.0
East	51.5	47.0	0.0
South	53.7	45.0	0.0
Midwest	48.3	49.7	0.0
West	45.7	51.0	0.0
Counties	1,714	1,419	0
Counties %	54.7	45.3	0.0
States	24	27	0
States %	47.1	52.9	0.0
EV	297	240	1
East	108	36	0
South	127	20	0
Midwest	58	87	0
West	4	97	1
EV %	55.2	44.6	0.2

1980 Republican Primaries

	Ronald Reagan (R)	George Bush (R)	John Anderson (R)
W	29	6	0
East	6	4	0
South	10	0	0
Midwest	7	1	0
West	6	0	0
Other	0	1	0
W %	82.9	17.1	0.0
PV	7,709,793	3,075,449	1,572,174
PV %	59.9	23.9	12.2
East	46.5	38.4	9.2
South	62.0	28.1	4.3
Midwest	56.6	23.1	18.0
West	77.7	8.0	12.6
Other	0.0	60.1	0.0

1980 Republican Convention

	Ronald Reagan (R)
FB	1,939
East	487
South	475
Midwest	510
West	445
Other	22
FB %	97.2

1980 Democratic Primaries

		Jimmy Carter (D)	Edward Kennedy (D)	unpledged
W		24	10	1
	East	4	7	0
	South	9	0	0
	Midwest	6	1	1
	West	4	2	0
	Other	1	0	0
W %		68.6	28.6	2.9
PV		10,043,016	7,381,693	1,288,423
PV %		51.2	37.6	6.6
	East	42.0	51.5	3.6
	South	64.5	19.9	11.4
	Midwest	57.4	34.5	1.7
	West	40.2	42.9	10.5
	Other	51.7	48.0	0.0

1980 Democratic Convention

		Jimmy Carter (D)	Edward Kennedy (D)
FB		2,123	1,150½
	East	438	501
	South	689	92
	Midwest	636	270
	West	325½	265½
	Other	34½	22
FB %		63.7	34.5

1980 General Election

	Ronald Reagan (R)	Jimmy Carter (D)	John Anderson (NU)
PV	43,904,153	35,483,883	5,720,060
PV %	50.7	41.0	6.6
East	47.0	42.7	8.8
South	51.8	44.2	3.0
Midwest	50.9	40.9	6.7
West	54.0	34.4	8.8
Counties	2,229	903	0
Counties %	71.1	28.8	0.0
States	44	7	0
States %	86.3	13.7	0.0
EV	489	49	0
East	121	23	0
South	135	12	0
Midwest	135	10	0
West	98	4	0
EV %	90.9	9.1	0.0

1984 Republican Primaries

	Ronald Reagan (R)
W	24
East	9
South	4
Midwest	6
West	5
W %	100.0

1984
Republican Primaries
(continued)

	Ronald Reagan (R)
PV	6,176,274
PV %	98.8
East	97.7
South	98.1
Midwest	99.3
West	99.1

1984
Republican Convention

	Ronald Reagan (R)
FB	2,233
East	542
South	622
Midwest	565
West	482
Other	22
FB %	99.9

1984 Democratic Primaries

	Walter Mondale (D)	Gary Hart (D)	Jesse Jackson (D)
W	11	16	2
East	5	5	1
South	4	1	1
Midwest	1	6	0
West	0	4	0
Other	1	0	0
W %	36.7	53.3	6.7
PV	6,943,429	6,501,612	3,281,992
PV %	38.3	35.8	18.1
East	41.6	32.5	18.7
South	33.3	30.9	21.4
Midwest	39.8	40.8	16.3
West	34.2	41.4	16.7
Other	99.2	0.5	0.0

1984 Democratic Convention

	Walter Mondale (D)	Gary Hart (D)	Jesse Jackson (D)
FB	2,191	1,200½	465½
East	676	225	117
South	575	265	199
Midwest	605	316	101
West	257	393	46
Other	78	1½	2½
FB %	55.7	30.5	11.8

1984 General Election

	Ronald Reagan (R)	Walter Mondale (D)
PV	54,451,521	37,565,334
PV %	58.8	40.5
East	54.8	44.7
South	62.5	37.0
Midwest	58.0	41.3
West	59.6	39.2
Counties	2,803	336
Counties %	89.3	10.7
States	49	2
States %	96.1	3.9
EV	525	13
East	132	3
South	155	0
Midwest	127	10
West	111	0
EV %	97.6	2.4

Section 2.
The Participants

7.
The Candidates

JOHN ADAMS (F 1796, 1800)

Adams was always an impatient man. His grandson remembered that "his anger, when thoroughly roused, was, for a time, extremely violent."[1] His contemporaries knew firsthand of his restlessness. As a member of the Continental Congress, Adams agitated for independence well before most of his colleagues could face the shocking idea. He later played a key role in securing the appointment of George Washington to lead the Continental Army.

A man of Adams´ temperament was hardly suited to the Vice Presidency, yet he was the first elected to the post. He sourly called it "the most insignificant office that ever the invention of man contrived or his imagination conceived."[2] He followed his eight years of inaction by winning election to the Presidency. Never an ardent Federalist, Adams nonetheless was heartily suspicious of the Democratic-Republicans. He was certain that Thomas Jefferson´s dislike of England was motivated by nothing more than his pocketbook. "I wish somebody would pay his debt of seven thousand pounds to Britain...," Adams wrote, "and then I believe his passions would subside, his reason return, and the whole man and his whole state become good friends of the Union and its government."[3] Adams and Jefferson later became good friends themselves.

JOHN QUINCY ADAMS (DR 1824, NR 1828)

The eldest son of John Adams grew up in the family businesses: politics and diplomacy. John Quincy traveled with his father to the latter´s assignment as commissioner to France in 1778. It was the beginning of a career that would take the son to his own ministerial posts in Russia and England, then on to be Secretary of State and President.

John Quincy Adams was like his father in other

respects. He was austere, some thought cold. John Quincy was politically independent, breaking with the Federalists, becoming a Democratic-Republican, then providing the rallying point for formation of the National Republicans. And he was similar to John Adams in refusing to politick for office. Encouraged to make a personal appearance while President, John Quincy refused. He wrote back, "See thou a man diligent in his business."[4]

The Presidency is the crowning glory for most who reach it, but John Quincy Adams had a long political career after the White House. He served seventeen years in the House of Representatives, earning the nickname of Old Man Eloquent for his impressive performance in debate. He literally died on the job, suffering a massive stroke just moments after answering a roll call.

RUSSELL ALGER (R 1888)

Alger was taken seriously as a businessman, but not as a politician. He deftly amassed a fortune in the lumber industry, but was inept at Presidential politics. The former one-term Michigan Governor wrote Ohio Governor Joseph Foraker in 1888, "I wish I had you in my office an hour. I would prove to you that I am going to be nominated." Foraker quickly buried the letter in his files, writing on it, "Sick people are always going to get well, and candidates are always going to get elected, you know."[5]

Alger, a Civil War colonel, later was given his chance on the national stage. He was Secretary of War during the Spanish-American War. The army that invaded Cuba was poorly trained and improperly equipped. Supplies and men sat idle in Florida. Alger was blamed. He resigned under pressure after the war ended.

WILLIAM ALLEN (D 1876)

Allen combined impressive public-speaking ability with an unfortunate tendency to choose the losing side in heated political arguments. His eloquence on the stump was legendary in Ohio and in the Senate, where he served two terms. The Washington Globe, admittedly pro-Democratic, once crowed after Allen took on the renowned Henry Clay in debate, "In the mere accessories of oratory -- such as voice and delivery -- Mr. Allen is far Mr. Clay´s superior....He is to Mr. Clay what the lower tier of a man of war -- the forty-two pounders -- are to the cannonades which run upon the wheels on the upper decks."[6]

But all the speaking ability in the world could not save Allen in 1849. His refusal to condemn slavery cost him his Senate seat from a state with rising free-soil sentiment. Allen later seemed to guarantee his berth in political oblivion by opposing the Civil War and backing soft money. But a Republican fissure in 1873 allowed him to make a remarkable comeback, being elected Governor of Ohio. It was short-lived. Allen was returned to retirement in 1875 by

Rutherford Hayes. Both men tried for the Presidency a year later; Hayes had better luck.

WILLIAM BOYD ALLISON (R 1888)

Allison was probably better suited for the Senate, where he served thirty-six years, than the White House. His great talent was in legislative manipulation. New York Senator Chauncey Depew once remarked of Allison, "He could grant to an adversary an amendment with such grace and deference to superior judgment that the flattered enemy accepted a few suggestions from the master as a tribute to his talents. The post-mortem revealed his mistake."[7]

Allison belonged to the so-called "School of Philosophy Club," the group of Senators who ran things behind the scenes in the late 19th Century. He was the senior Republican on the Appropriations Committee, a position that wielded substantial power in those days before creation of the Budget Bureau. Iowa voters kept returning him to Washington to accumulate greater influence. Allison was a virtual invalid by 1908, but still won a nomination for a seventh term. He died of cancer before taking the oath.

JOHN ANDERSON (R 1980, NU 1980)

Anderson, once a hero of conservative Republicans, began a leftward drift in 1968 that led to his splinter Presidential candidacy twelve years later. The Illinois Congressman was honored by a conservative organization in the late 1960s for standing "firm against the liberal pressures in Washington." But his vote for open-housing legislation signaled a break with the right. Anderson denounced the Vietnam War in 1970 and was one of the first Republicans to demand Richard Nixon's resignation after Watergate. His 1978 challenger in a Congressional primary election blasted Anderson as a turncoat who "comes back here talking like some god of the East."[8] The incumbent won by a small margin and decided he had no stomach for further local party infighting. He opted instead to run for President two years down the road, first as a Republican, then on his own National Unity ticket.

Anderson was a favorite of reporters during the 1980 campaign. Jimmy Carter ridiculed him as being "primarily a creation of the press." Anderson quipped at his next press conference: "I feel very humble. I'm standing before my creators."[9]

CHESTER ARTHUR (R 1884)

Anyone in 1878 suggesting Arthur as a potential President would have been considered a trifle crazy. The New York Republican had just been made an example by President Rutherford Hayes, dismissed as Collector of the Port of New York for his activities as a spoilsman. The case received national notoriety.

Comebacks are often swift in politics, but Arthur's return amazed even jaded observers. Republican Presidential nominee James Garfield needed a running mate from New York to guarantee party unity in 1880. After Levi Morton turned him down, Garfield asked Arthur, who in turn sought the advice of his mentor, Senator Roscoe Conkling. Refuse it, Conkling commanded. But Arthur showed unexpected backbone and accepted. A year later, he was President upon Garfield's assassination. Arthur's administration stunned both his cronies and the nation, as the President advocated civil-service reform.

Critics said Arthur's Presidency was shocking for another reason. Democrats alleged that the native Vermonter was actually born in Canada or Ireland, which would have made him ineligible to be Chief Executive. A New York lawyer was hired by the party in 1880 to find evidence. He never turned up any.

JOHN ASHBROOK (R 1972)

Ashbrook was one of the most conservative members of Congress in the 1960s and 1970s, but he argued that he was really a liberal in the classic sense. "The true liberal fought for the individual's rights against the crown," he once said. "But the modern liberal wants to give all power to the crown -- to the executive -- and that I will always fight."[10]

Ashbrook's categorization of "modern liberals" was surprisingly broad. It included Richard Nixon, whose "leftward drift" he deplored. Ashbrook's decision to challenge the leader of his own party in 1972 was in keeping with family tradition. His father was a Democratic Congressman from Ohio during Franklin Roosevelt's administration. The senior Ashbrook harassed the New Deal at every turn. His son valued such ideological obstinacy. "You cannot view with alarm under Lyndon Johnson and point with pride to the same things under Richard Nixon," he asserted. "I'm applying the same standards to all of them."[11]

ALBEN BARKLEY (D 1952)

Barkley was at his best with an audience. His florid, heavily partisan oratory was a favorite with Democrats in Congress, where the Kentuckian served for thirty-eight years. He was selected three times to deliver the keynote address at Democratic conventions, an honor traditionally given but once. His popularity with delegates at the 1948 gathering virtually forced Harry Truman to choose him as his running mate.

Barkley's tenure as Vice President was undistinguished, but did add a word to the dictionary. His grandson called him the "Veep," quickly seized upon by grateful headline writers as shorthand for all Vice Presidents. Barkley failed in his 1952 attempt to step up to the White House, then returned to the Senate. He died while delivering a speech at Washington and Lee University in 1956, just after declaring,

"I would rather be a servant in the house of the Lord than to sit in the seats of the mighty!" A friend marveled, "It is the way he would have wanted to go. He never could turn down a crowd."[12]

EDWARD BATES (R 1860)

Bates served notice early in his career that he was not going to be drawn into the torrid politics of his brawling era. He went to Washington in 1827 as a Congressman from the wide-open frontier state of Missouri and promptly pronounced Andrew Jackson's ideas to be "dangerous." It was a stand that earned him a ticket home after one term.

Bates stuck with the fence-straddling Whigs long after most party members hit the lifeboats. He was chairman of the 1856 national convention that feebly endorsed the ticket already nominated by the American party. His conversion to the Republicans didn't come until 1860, and even then, Bates rejected the party's only true issue. "Slavery is not the real question," he said calmly. "The question is only a struggle among politicians for sectional supremacy, and slavery is drawn into the contest only because it is a very exciting topic about which sensible people are more easily led to play the fool."[13] Republican delegates were hardly in the mood for such syrup in the year before the Civil War. Bates had to abandon his dreams of the Presidency and content himself with becoming Attorney General in the Lincoln Administration.

THOMAS BAYARD (D 1876, 1880, 1884)

One of the leading Democrats of his era, Bayard nonetheless had no prayer of becoming President. He inadvertently settled that question in 1861. The 33-year-old lawyer, a son of a pro-Southern Senator, delivered a speech in Dover, Delaware, saying the "erring sisters" of the South should be allowed to peacefully secede. He wrote privately, "My heart is full of abhorrence for the Northern sentiment."[14] Bayard's opponents never failed to publicize these unpopular remarks each time he made a strong run for the Democratic nomination.

Bayard served sixteen years in the Senate. He stuck to his Southern sympathies, fighting Reconstruction at every turn. "The South does not need legislation," he wrote in 1879. "The South needs sympathy and respect."[15] This concern with regional politics led some to believe Bayard had fallen behind the times, failing to recognize the drastic changes brought by the Civil War. He concluded his career as a diplomat, serving as Grover Cleveland's Secretary of State and ambassador to Great Britain.

JOHN BELL (CU 1860)

Bell was a cool man in hot times, a bit out of place as the nation surged toward civil war. He once wrote, "I am not ultraist, and favor no extreme measures."[16] It was a philosophy that led this Tennessee slaveholder to try to keep the peace by occasionally opposing bills to allow the spread of slavery in the territories. The prime example was his vote in the Senate against the Kansas-Nebraska Act. Georgia's Robert Toombs lashed out at Bell for voting to continue "this prohibition on his own section, although high-minded, noble, generous, and patriotic men of the North feel and see its injustice, and labor for its overthrow."[17] The Southern press was similarly bitter.

Bell's independence brought him powerful enemies during his fourteen years in the House of Representatives and twelve in the Senate. He broke from Andrew Jackson on the National Bank and other issues. He later defeated James Polk to become Speaker. But throughout these controversies, Bell remained cold and cautious. He was the perfect nominee for the Constitutional Union party, one last prudent effort to throw cold water on the fever of disunion.

ALLAN BENSON (SOC 1916)

Benson seemed at the turn of the century to be an unlikely candidate for conversion to Socialism. A reporter in Chicago and the West, he worked his way to become managing editor of the Detroit Times and then the Washington Times. He voted in 1900 for the prophet of conservatism, William McKinley.

An almost religious experience changed Benson's thinking in 1902. He recalled looking up Socialism in an encyclopedia. "I experienced that forenoon an internal sensation that I had never felt up to that time and never have felt since," he remembered. "All the things I had been bothering about, all the questions I could not answer, seemed nearer solution."[18] Benson, with his reporter's penchant for cold facts, became a leading Socialist writer and theorist. He was the opposite of Eugene Debs, who cared little for ideology, but brought an evangelical fervor to the stump. The two also differed in their reactions to World War I. Debs went to prison for his fiery condemnations of the war effort. Benson quit the party because he disapproved of such rhetoric. He went on to attain some fame for his writing, particularly a biography of Daniel Webster.

JOHN BIDWELL (PROH 1892)

Bidwell was the quintessential California pioneer. He arrived in 1841 with the first wagon train to successfully travel the vast distance from Missouri. He participated in the Bear Flag Revolt five years later. "We simply marched all over California from Sonoma to San Diego and raised the American flag without opposition or protest," he later laughed. "We tried to find an enemy, but could not."[19] The gold rush of 1848 found Bidwell a prospector. He later became a successful rancher and winemaker.

Bidwell was mercurial in his politics. He was a delegate to both Democratic and Republican national conventions. He served in Congress as a Republican, but later ran for Governor as an independent. His fiancee triggered his final switch. She frowned on intoxication, so Bidwell had his workers rip up his vineyard. He became interested in the Prohibition movement.

Bidwell´s sense of humor was a bit unusual in the temperance crusade. He liked to tell about a visit he paid to San Francisco while he was the Prohibition party´s candidate for President. Hit by a neuralgic attack, he sprawled on a nearby doorstep to rest, imagining he must appear to be drunk. Feeling better, he got back to his feet and noticed he had chosed the steps of a saloon for his respite.

JAMES BIRNEY (LTY 1844)

Birney was a native Kentuckian who moved easily in Southern society during his early adulthood. He served in both the Kentucky and Alabama legislatures, was Mayor of Huntsville, Alabama, and owned a plantation. He was able in 1821 to purchase nineteen slaves for $13,495. That brought his holdings to forty-three.

Events in the 1820s caused Birney to question the Southern way of life. His conversion to the Presbyterian church led him to wonder about the morality of slavery. A Northern visit in 1829 convinced him that a free-labor system was preferable to forced labor. Birney began to publicly advocate gradual emancipation. He grew more outspoken in the 1830s, moving north and becoming executive secretary of the American Anti-Slavery Society. He helped form the Liberty party to increase the political pressure for emancipation.

Birney´s Southern friends watched with dismay. "We deeply regret that he has made himself the victim of such a cause," editorialized a newspaper in his old hometown of Huntsville. "We must...sorrowfully call to mind Pope´s celebrated line, as true in this instance: `The worst of madmen is a Saint run mad!´"[20]

JOSEPH BLACKBURN (D 1896)

Blackburn was a Chicago lawyer at the dawn of the critical year of 1860. He decided to return to Kentucky to work for a fellow native son who was seeking the Presidency, John Breckinridge. It was a move that exposed him to the rising secession spirit in his divided state. Kentucky opted to remain in the Union, but Blackburn followed his hero in joining the Confederate army. His rebel background actually helped him win election to the state legislature in 1871 from a district still not reconciled to the outcome at Appomattox.

Blackburn went on to serve ten years in the House of Representatives and eighteen in the Senate. He achieved no great distinction as a lawmaker, but was a strong debater. His characteristically heated partisan feeling was demonstrated in the House after Republican Rutherford Hayes

was declared the winner of the disputed election of 1876.
Blackburn noted the decision came on a Friday, the day of
Christ´s death. He called it a fitting time for the
crucifixion of "constitutional government, justice, honesty,
fair dealings...[carried out] among a number of thieves."[21]

JAMES BLAINE (R 1876, 1880, 1884, 1888, 1892)

Blaine was a member of a Pennsylvania family of devout Whigs,
so it was natural that Henry Clay would become his hero. He
always remembered his one meeting with the Great
Compromiser. The young Blaine, then serving a brief stint as
a teacher in Kentucky, sat spellbound with "pencil and
notebook in hand" as Clay spoke. Neither could know the
parallels that would develop between their lives. Each
served in the House and Senate, being elected Speaker of the
former. Each was Secretary of State. Each surpassed
qualification levels as a Presidential candidate five times,
the only men to do so. And each was dogged by charges of
corrupt deals: Clay in helping elect John Quincy Adams, his
worshiper in selling railroad bonds.

    Blaine was also like his hero in his almost superhuman
ability to inspire loyalty. Settling in Maine to publish a
newspaper, he quickly made powerful allies. He was so
personable that he became known as the "Magnetic Man." A
friend once said, "I defy anyone, Republican or Democrat, to
be in his company half an hour and go away from him anything
less than a personal friend."[22] Blaine added to his
popularity with his powerful style at the podium. He was one
of the great orators of his era.

    But not everyone found the man from Maine to be spell-
binding. Blaine´s Half-Breed faction of the Republican party
was bitterly opposed by the Stalwarts of New York Senator
Roscoe Conkling. The rumors of Blaine´s allegedly illegal
dealings with the Little Rock and Fort Smith Railroad stirred
further criticism. Conkling alluded to those stories when
asked to campaign for Blaine in 1884. "No, thank you," he
demurred. "I don´t engage in criminal practice."[23]

RICHARD BLAND (D 1896)

Bland´s life provided the perfect preparation for a man
destined to lead the fight for the free coinage of silver.
The native Kentuckian heard the call of distant riches in his
youth. He spent a decade prospecting and mining in Colorado,
Nevada, and California. His return east landed him in the
poor Ozark country of Missouri, where he became a lawyer.
Bland thus gained intimate knowledge of the needs of miners
and farmers, two groups that constituted the backbone of the
silver movement.

    "Silver Dick" served as a Democrat in the House of
Representatives for all but two years from 1873 to his
death. He was greatly embittered when President Grover
Cleveland in 1893 secured repeal of the Sherman Silver
Purchase Act, which had provided for government issue of

silver certificates. "We have come to the parting of the ways," Bland declared in a famous speech. "I believe that I do speak for the great masses of the great Mississippi Valley when I say that we will not submit to the domination of any political party, however much we may love it, that lays the sacrificing hand upon silver and will demonetize it in this country."[24] Bland's speech served as the gospel of the silver movement until William Jennings Bryan railed against the "cross of gold" three years later.

HORACE BOIES (D 1892, 1896)

Boies' adulthood had two distinct phases. He spent the first fifteen years as a lawyer in Buffalo, serving one term as a Republican member of the New York legislature. But he always fondly remembered his teenaged years in Wisconsin Territory. The lure finally became too strong. Boies moved his practice to Iowa in his late thirties.

Prohibition was a major issue on the prairie in the years following the Civil War. Boies was a teetotaler, but he condemned forced temperance as a violation of "the largest possible liberty of the individual consistent with the welfare of the whole." Iowa Republicans supported prohibition, so Boies switched to the Democrats. He was elected Governor on the issue in 1889, quickly gaining national prominence. It was almost unheard-of for a Democrat to carry a solidly Republican state such as Iowa.

Boies' two terms occurred during the period of agrarian unrest that spawned the Populist party. But he was no radical, suggesting that free coinage of silver be "approached by degrees." Rabid silverites wanted someone with more passion, such as William Jennings Bryan.

WILLIAM BORAH (R 1936)

Borah's iron-willed independence was evident from the beginning. Journalist William Allen White was a classmate at the University of Kansas. He vividly remembered the future Idaho Senator's "obvious indifference to the opinion of others." It was a trait that later became familiar to official Washington.

Borah entered the Senate in 1907. He often bucked the Old Guard leadership of his Republican party with his support of progressive measures. He antagonized Woodrow Wilson by marshaling the "irreconcilables" who refused to accept the League of Nations under any circumstances. He annoyed hard-liners by advocating diplomatic relations with the Soviet Union a decade before they were established. And the story goes that he nonplused the unflappable Calvin Coolidge. The President asked Borah to take the open place on his 1924 ticket. "Which place, Mr. President?" was Borah's response.[25] He then turned down the Vice Presidency. Borah could never be anyone's second-hand man.

JOHN BRECKINRIDGE (SD 1860)

Breckinridge was a rising star in 1857, when he took the oath as the youngest Vice President in history. His future seemed limitless, but events would put him into permanent eclipse within five years. A former two-term Congressman from Kentucky, Breckinridge loyally battled disunionist sentiment as James Buchanan's understudy. He expressed his fervent hope that his home state would "cling to the Constitution while a shred of it remains." It did, but its favorite son didn't.

Breckinridge had already been elected to the Senate to follow his Vice Presidential term, so it was with reluctance that he accepted the 1860 Presidential nomination of the Southern Democratic party. Carrying his region's banner triggered a radical shift. He joined the Confederate Army in 1861, was indicted for treason in the United States and expelled from the Senate. Breckinridge was defiant, "I exchange with proud satisfaction a term of six years in the Senate of the United States for the musket of a soldier."[26] He served as a general and Confederate Secretary of War. Only after four years of exile in Europe and Canada was he allowed to return to Kentucky following the war, his political career but a memory.

BENJAMIN BRISTOW (R 1876)

Bristow's tenacity was the force behind his quick rise in government, but it also proved to be his undoing. The son of a Congressman from Kentucky, he demonstrated his fierce spirit by signing on with the Union army at the start of the Civil War. His wife's uncle mocked him for being "Yankee-hearted" and threatened to disinherit him. Bristow is said to have replied, "I will not sell my country for gold and silver. You may take your property and go to hell!"[27] He served as a lieutenant-colonel and was seriously wounded at Shiloh.

Bristow's Republican loyalty was repaid with a postwar appointment as U.S. Attorney for Kentucky, a job in which he aroused strong local opposition with stringent enforcement of civil-rights laws. That same vigor marked his tenure as Secretary of the Treasury. Bristow earned the nickname, "Bulldog in the Treasury," for uncovering the Whiskey Ring and obtaining 253 indictments of distillers and government agents. Reformers pushed him for President. President Ulysses Grant waited for the 1876 Republican convention to end, then shoved Bristow out of his administration. The Bulldog, his bite having become too sharp for the scandal-ridden government, moved to New York to practice law.

GRATZ BROWN (D-LR 1872)

Brown journeyed full circle in his political career in Missouri. He entered the state legislature in 1852 as a Democrat, a member of the party that favored keeping Missouri a slave state. Brown gradually became uncomfortable with his party's opposition to emancipation. He joined the Republicans by 1860.

Brown manifested the zeal of a convert during the Civil War. He accused President Lincoln of moving too slowly to free the slaves and demanded permanent disenfranchisement of all rebels. "Franchise is not for such, cannot be for such, will not be for such!" he thundered. One newspaper called him "the Prince of the Radicals."[28]

A four-year tour in the Senate changed Brown yet again. He began to worry that military Reconstruction would drive former slave states such as Missouri permanently into the arms of the Democrats. He now pleaded for universal amnesty for ex-Confederates. His support of reconciliation was a key reason for his 1870 election as Governor on the ticket of the Liberal coalition. These Missouri Liberals were the inspiration for creation of the national Liberal Republican party in 1872, which in turn chose Brown as its Vice Presidential candidate. This way station eased him back toward the party of his youth. By 1876, the trip was complete. Brown was a featured speaker at the Democratic convention.

JERRY BROWN (D 1976)

Brown's father, Pat, was the epitome of the traditional politician. He was at home glad-handing through a crowd or wheeling and dealing with power brokers. Pat Brown's two elections as Governor of California, including a smashing 1962 triumph over Richard Nixon, were testimony to his skill.

Jerry Brown scorned traditional politics. He said it was "full of free suits, free dinners, freeloaders." Elected Governor in 1974 at the age of 36, he became nationally known for refusing to use the limousine or live in the mansion that came with the job. He assembled an administration of young technocrats. His policies defied labels. "Is it a liberal program? Is it a conservative program?" he asked. "It's my program."[29]

Jerry Brown could not flout orthodoxy at every turn. In an indirect way, he owed his success to old-style politics. Both he and his father went by nicknames. Jerry was actually Edmund Brown Jr., a name that allowed him to piggyback on his father's reputation at the ballot box. "I want to thank my mother for naming me after my father," he confessed after being elected California's Secretary of State in 1970, the victory that launched his career. "I grew to like that during the campaign."[30]

WILLIAM JENNINGS BRYAN (D-POP 1896, D 1900, 1908)

Bryan was never elected President, but he was a power in the Democratic party for two decades. His followers exalted the "Boy Orator of the Platte" as if he were a permanent resident of the White House. Their adoration was a reaction to Bryan's powerful, spellbinding speeches. Josephus Daniels was present at the 1896 Democratic convention that stampeded to Bryan after his immortal "Cross of Gold" address. Daniels wrote of the mesmerized delegates, "They believed that Bryan was a young David with his sling, who had come to slay the giants that oppressed the people and they felt that a new day had come and with it, a new leader."[31] Bryan's rich voice masked a lack of profundity. Illinois Governor John Peter Altgeld turned to a companion after the same address, "I've been thinking over Bryan's speech. What did he say, anyhow?"[32]

Bryan's only stint in elective office lasted just two terms as a Congressman from Nebraska, but he managed to win three Democratic nominations for President. He was influential at other conventions. The Great Commoner always demanded that the party not stray from his populist principles. A group of Southern Democrats aroused his ire by suggesting moderation in 1908. "That's it! You want to win!" Bryan shouted. "You would sacrifice principle for success. I would not." Virginia Senator John Daniel dared to intervene, "But some of the things you have stood for in the past have proved wrong, and you may prove wrong again." The nominee fixed him with a steely glare, "I have always been right."[33] For Bryan, the crusade never ended.

JAMES BUCHANAN (D 1848, 1852, 1856)

Buchanan entered the Pennsylvania legislature at 23, but he found it unstimulating. He intended to end his brief, unrewarding political career after marrying Ann Coleman. He would devote himself to his law practice.

But Buchanan's plans were destroyed when his fiancee broke their engagement, probably because of rumors that he was marrying her for her money. She fled to stay with relatives in Philadelphia and suddenly died. The cause was never adequately determined, but residents of Buchanan's hometown of Lancaster had their own theories. One wrote, "I believe that her friends now look upon him as her murderer." A distraught Buchanan confided, "I may sustain the shock of her death, but I feel that happiness has fled from me forever."[34] He never married.

Politics was suddenly a refuge from his grief. Buchanan was elected to the House of Representatives in 1820, the year following Ann's death. He also served in the Senate, as minister to Russia and Great Britain, and as Secretary of State. He began a long quest for the Presidency in 1844, but even attaining it did not relieve him from the torment of his life. Always with Buchanan was a small packet tied with a silk ribbon. It contained every letter written him long ago by Ann Coleman.

THEODORE BURTON (R 1916)

Burton ran up an admirable record of success in Cleveland and Ohio elections, but he never much enjoyed it. A lawyer with a scholarly bent, he always seemed to want public office

handed to him without a campaign. He swallowed his disdain
for the process while being elected to the Cleveland City
Council for two years and then winning eight of nine contests
for the House of Representatives.

Burton found pleasure in his 1909 selection to the
Senate. The state legislature, not the voters, made the
choice. Then the rules were changed. Reelection in 1914
would require popular vote. Burton complained, "The thought
of making a strenuous and statewide campaign to secure the
nomination, followed by another equally severe and extensive
effort for election, is distasteful to me."[35] He declined to
run.

Other campaigns were in his future: a 1916 favorite-son
try for the Presidency, a return to the House in 1920, and
even a 1928 election to the Senate. But Burton's legacy was
the man elevated to the Senate in 1914 because of his pique.
A man named Warren Harding.

GEORGE BUSH (R 1980)

Bush handled his share of thankless tasks on the way to
becoming Ronald Reagan's Vice President. The son of a
Senator from Connecticut, Bush moved to Texas after World War
II. He started his own companies dealing in oil property and
equipment. He also joined the uphill struggle to build a
Republican party in that thoroughly Democratic state. Bush
lost two races for the Senate, but managed to win two terms
in the House of Representatives. That made him Houston's
first Republican Congressman.

Bush advanced to the national scene after his second
Senate defeat. He was Ambassador to the United Nations when
the Nixon Administration futilely tried to straddle the
controversy over the admission of China. He was handed the
chairmanship of the Republican National Committee just in
time to be slapped with the fallout from Watergate. "I'm
really glad Dad is not alive," he told friends. "It would
have killed him to see this happen. He thought we were the
party of virtue and all bosses were Democrats."[36] Later came
a stretch as director of a demoralized Central Intelligence
Agency.

Bush castigated Reagan in 1980 for advocating "voodoo
economics," but he changed his tune as Vice President. He
became a loyal team player as he maneuvered to become the
President's heir apparent in 1988.

NICHOLAS MURRAY BUTLER (R 1920)

Butler was not a professional politician, but he possessed
the vanity of one. The president of Columbia University for
forty-three years, he also rose to prominence in Republican
circles. Theodore Roosevelt called him "one of my right-hand
men" before their mammoth egos clashed fatally. Other
Presidents, particularly Warren Harding, sought his advice.

Butler wrote twenty books. Every one was listed in the biographical sketch included in Who's Who, as was almost everything else Butler could think of. He deliberately kept his listing the longest of any in the book. Some saw his enormous public-speaking schedule as a further sign of rampant egotism. Columnist Heywood Broun speculated that in Butler's house was a brass pole that he slid down immediately upon any invitation to give an address. Another joke made the rounds during Butler's Presidential campaign. In it, Sigmund Freud was arriving at the pearly gates. "Come with us quickly. We want you to see God professionally," implored the angels. "He has been acting strangely. He has hallucinations. He thinks He is Nicholas Murray Butler."[37]

HARRY BYRD (D 1944, ID 1960)

Franklin Roosevelt pulled strings to get Byrd in the Senate in 1933, an irony not lost on FDR or subsequent Democratic Presidents. Roosevelt named Virginia Senator Claude Swanson to his Cabinet. That opened the way for the Senate appointment of former Governor Byrd, then a strong New Dealer. However, he quickly soured on Roosevelt's jumble of new government agencies, emerging as the spokesman for Southern discontent. It was a role he played for three decades.

Byrd's political machine controlled Virginia's local governments with an iron fist. One lieutenant termed it "government by gentlemen," with the tacit understanding that all gentlemen were white. Byrd picked the racial issue as the one on which his region must make its stand. He coined the phrase, "massive resistance," and exhorted home crowds to ignore federal desegregation orders. "If Virginia surrenders," he cried, "if Virginia's line is broken, the rest of the South will go down, too."[38] That defiance extended to the Democratic party. Once a firm loyalist, Byrd refused to endorse the party's national candidates in the 1950s and 1960s. He confided, "I have found at times that silence is golden."[39]

SIMON CAMERON (R 1860)

"There is no rest for the wicked," Cameron once wrote, "and who is not wicked?"[40] His many enemies thought he certainly qualified. Cameron rose from being a printer's apprentice to amass a fortune in canals, railroads, banks, and insurance. He broadened his power by building the Republican machine that controlled Pennsylvania for three generations. It was said he never forgot an enemy. Most were punished through his ruthless use of patronage.

Cameron was so closely identified with the Republican party that it was commonly forgotten he had once been a close friend of James Buchanan and was first elected to the Senate as a Democrat. His independence alienated party leaders. Andrew Jackson blasted him as a "renegade politician." James Polk called him a "tricky man in whom no reliance can be placed." Only after losing Senate races on the Democratic and American party labels did Cameron join the Republicans.

His biggest service to his new party came at the 1860 convention. Cameron swung crucial votes to Abraham Lincoln in exchange for being named Secretary of War. He was overmatched in his new post and was quickly shuffled out of it. Cameron went back to the two things he knew best: the Senate and running Pennsylvania.

JOSEPH CANNON (R 1908)

Cannon's countrified ways drew ridicule from his colleagues when he arrived in Congress in 1873. Some called him "the Hayseed Member from Illinois." But Cannon lived to laugh back. He served forty-six of the next fifty years in the House of Representatives. After his election as Speaker in 1903, he exercised iron-fisted control that most of his predecessors had only dreamed about. "Cannonism" became a synonym for legislative dictatorship.

Cannon hoped for the White House, but Democrats and reform Republicans had different plans for him. Missouri Congressman David DeArmond advised a class at Yale Law School, "When the opportunity comes to you, young gentlemen, to deal with czarism, don't trouble yourselves about Russia. Direct your efforts against the czarism which flourishes in the House of Representatives of our own country."[41] The renegades finally succeeded in 1910, stripping Cannon of his control of the House Rules Committee. He lost the position of Speaker the following year, but stayed in the House until 1923, a conservative fossil from the era of one-man rule.

JIMMY CARTER (D 1976, 1980)

Carter came to national attention overnight in 1971. A peanut farmer and former career naval officer, he was elected Governor of Georgia the previous November. Carter had not been shy during the campaign to call himself a "redneck" and to praise a famous segregationist, "Lester Maddox is the embodiment of the Democratic party."[42] But what made headlines was his stunning reversal in his inaugural address. "I say to you quite frankly," he told the crowd at his swearing-in, "the time for racial discrimination is over."[43] Carter was hailed by the national press as a symbol of New South moderation.

A second part of that inaugural speech received little attention, but proved to be prophetic. Carter quoted William Jennings Bryan, "Destiny is not a thing to be waited for. It is a thing to be achieved."[44] Meetings with 1972 Presidential candidates convinced the Governor he was their equal. He set out to attain the White House with the same single-mindedness that had won him Georgia's top job.

Carter's promise never to lie, his common touch, and his obvious ambition catapulted him to his improbable victory in 1976. Those same qualities also set the stage for a national disillusionment that caused his defeat four years later, making Carter the first elected incumbent to lose since Herbert Hoover in 1932.

LEWIS CASS (D 1844, 1848, 1852)

Cass was a New Hampshire native who attended Exeter Academy with Daniel Webster. Cass moved to the Midwest, Webster stayed East, but the two old classmates had much in common. Each played a major role in appointive positions and the Senate. Neither was able to consummate a lengthy dalliance with the prize he wanted most of all, the Presidency.

Cass served as a Senator, Minister to France, Secretary of War, and Secretary of State. But the position that most shaped his thinking was his eighteen-year tenure as Territorial Governor of Michigan. He came to believe federal powers should be tightly restricted. His insistence that Congress did not have the right to allow a territory to prohibit slavery earned Cass the oft-cited label of "a Northern man with Southern principles." He earned further support below the Mason-Dixon Line by calling on fellow Northerners to stop agitating for the end of slavery, "It is a cheap way to be charitable, looking at its results upon the peace of the country."[45] Cass insisted the North had enough of its own problems to worry about, but not everyone agreed. The Free Soil party, which cost him victory in 1848, had a white-hot hatred for him. Its members chanted that fall, "And he who still for Cass can be, he is a Cass without the C..."[46]

SALMON CHASE (R 1860)

"I care nothing for names," Chase once declared on the subject of political parties. "All that I ask for is a platform and an issue, not buried out of sight, but palpable and paramount."[47] The Ohioan backed his words with deeds. He belonged to five parties during his long career: Whig, Liberty, Free Soil, Republican, and Democratic. His fluidity did not bar him from high office. Chase served as a Senator, Governor, Secretary of the Treasury, and Chief Justice. And his eye was always on the top job. Abraham Lincoln thought Chase "a little insane" on the Presidency.

A hatred for slavery provided Chase his issue for most of his public life. He was nicknamed "the Attorney General for runaway Negroes" for his willingness to defend fugitive slaves as a Cincinnati lawyer in the 1830s. He chaired the 1848 Free Soil convention. The Emancipation Proclamation was partly his work, but he typically found the final product too equivocal. He thought Lincoln should not have admitted any exceptions to the freeing of the slaves.

Emancipation was the fulfillment of Chase's life work. He felt stifled as Chief Justice after the war. "I think I have a good deal of executive faculty," he wrote. "I often wish I were in some more active employment."[48] He turned to the Democrats as a final hope, but got no support for President in 1868, relegated to work out his days on the Supreme Court.

SHIRLEY CHISHOLM (D 1972)

Five feet four inches tall and sometimes as light as ninety-six pounds, Chisholm certainly did not have a formidable presence. But the first black woman elected to Congress compensated for her tiny stature with a strong voice. She ran her 1968 race for the House of Representatives under the slogan, "Unbought and Unbossed." House leaders routinely appointed her to the Agriculture Committee, but she stunned them by refusing. She snapped, "Apparently all they know here in Washington about Brooklyn is that a tree grew there."[49] She was switched to another panel.

Chisholm's 1972 Presidential campaign did not receive the support from blacks that Jesse Jackson did twelve years later. Jackson himself worked for George McGovern. Chisholm remarked that black men were just as chauvinistic as their white counterparts. "Other kinds of people can steer the ship of state besides white men," she told audiences. "Regardless of the outcome, they will have to remember that a little hundred-pound woman, Shirley Chisholm, shook things up."[50]

FRANK CHURCH (D 1976)

Most people inherit their political beliefs from their parents. Church deliberately adopted the opposite views. The Idaho Senator said he became a Democrat in self-defense. His parents were staunch Republicans and his father "did nothing but talk politics at home." Church said he went to the library "to find out about the other side" to hold up his end of family discussions. He was transformed into an ardent New Dealer.

Church's 1956 election to the Senate was a major surprise. He was only 32. Six years later, he was the first Democratic Senator ever reelected from Idaho. Church became nationally known as one of the first critics of the Vietnam War. He later led the probe into illegal activities of the FBI and CIA. It was an unusually liberal record for someone from one of the most conservative states. "If a people believe you are serving the state, they will not demand that you agree on all issues," Church insisted.[51] He cited William Borah as proof that Idahoans were tolerant of iconoclasts. But the state's patience with Church ran out in 1980. He lost his bid for a fifth Senate term to a conservative.

SANFORD CHURCH (D 1868)

Church was as obscure to most of the delegates at the 1868 Democratic convention as he has been to historians ever since. "When nominated yesterday, the great majority of the delegates were totally ignorant of his name, his nature, and his claims to the Presidency," the New York _Times_ related at the time. "They have already learned a great deal about him. They have been furnished with his biography and his picture. They have found out his birthplace and his public services. If they have not learned his position in regard to the great questions which divide the Democratic party, it is all the better for themselves, and his chances are all the more hopeful."[52]

Church was a former New York Lieutenant Governor and Comptroller. It was commonly believed that he was a Presidential stalking horse, but observers differed on whether he was a front for Salmon Chase or Horatio Seymour. Two years after his brief fling at national publicity, Church returned to state office. He was elected Chief Judge of the New York Court of Appeals, a position he held until his death.

CHAMP CLARK (D 1912)

Most of his contemporaries would have laughed at any accusation that Clark was a tool of Wall Street. His background was purely mid-American. A native Kentuckian, he was a lawyer briefly in Kansas, then moved to Missouri. He entered Congress in 1893, serving there for all but two years of the rest of his life. His sharp wit and strong speaking skills earned him the Speaker´s post in 1911. He held it for the next eight years.

Clark polled a majority of the votes cast on the tenth ballot at the 1912 Democratic convention, but fell short of the needed two-thirds. He was the first Presidential candidate in sixty-eight years to pass 50 percent and not be nominated. Clark blamed one man for spreading the fatal rumors that he was beholden to New York interests. "I lost the nomination solely through the vile and malicious slanders of Colonel William Jennings Bryan of Nebraska," he said on the day after the convention. "True, these slanders were by innuendo and insinuation, but they were no less deadly for that reason."[53] Twenty-four years later, Clark´s son offered the resolution that finally eliminated the two-thirds rule.

HENRY CLAY (DR 1824, NR 1832, W 1840, 1844, 1848)

Clay´s most quoted remark was, "I would rather be right than be President."[54] But many of those who watched the Kentuckian´s futile quarter-century pursuit of the White House were skeptical of his sincerity. Clay himself once wrote an admirer, "I expressed that sentiment to which you refer that I would rather be right than be President, but it has been applauded beyond its merit."[55]

Something always seemed to be in his way. The field in 1824 was too crowded and Clay´s support drained to Andrew Jackson. He faced a heavily popular incumbent in 1832. The Whigs preferred to nominate military heroes in 1840 and 1848. Clay´s best chance, in 1844, slipped away because of his miscalculation of the national mood on the annexation of Texas. And always there was the specter of the "corrupt bargain," the accusation that Clay threw his support to John Quincy Adams in 1824 in exchange for being made Secretary of State. He always denied it, but admitted he had made a mistake in "underrating the power of detraction and the force of ignorance."[56]

Clay's fame remains rooted in his career in the House of Representatives and the Senate. He led the War Hawks who agitated for the War of 1812. His American System of internal improvements touched off debate on the federal government's role in aiding the development of trans-Appalachia. But most important was his key role in securing the passage of the Missouri Compromise and the Compromise of 1850, hoping to buy time to save the country from civil war. These efforts earned Clay the enduring tag of "the Great Compromiser."

GROVER CLEVELAND (D 1884, 1888, 1892)

When Woodrow Wilson was elected in 1912, it was commonly noted that he was the first Democrat to win the Presidency since Cleveland. But the President-elect maintained his party's drought really extended much further, all the way back before the Civil War. "Cleveland was a conservative Republican," Wilson insisted.[57] That was a view commonly held by progressive Democrats who bitterly remembered Cleveland's staunch defense of the gold standard and his oft-expressed desire to rid the party of the element that adored William Jennings Bryan.

It was typical of Cleveland that he aroused such condemnation. His meteoric rise to national fame was sparked by his battles with entrenched political machines when he was Mayor of Buffalo and Governor of New York. "They love Cleveland for his character," one speaker said of his supporters, "but they love him also for the enemies he has made!"[58] Cleveland seemed almost perverse in his straightforwardness. Advisers told him to go easy on controversial tariff reform. He barked back, "What is the use of being elected or reelected unless you stand for something?"[59] His stubborn insistence on generally conservative policies helped split the Democrats by 1896, but Cleveland refused to ever compromise his high personal standards. Harvard University officials were amazed when they offered the President an honorary degree, the kind of prize politicians can't refuse. Cleveland did. He said he didn't deserve it.

DeWITT CLINTON (F-IDR 1812)

Clinton had attained considerable power in New York by 1802. His uncle, George, was the long-time Governor. DeWitt had already served in both houses of the state legislature. His membership on the Council of Appointment gave him tremendous control over Democratic-Republican patronage. And the national stage beckoned. DeWitt Clinton was elevated to the Senate in 1802.

A decision in 1803 drastically changed the thrust of Clinton's career. He resigned from the Senate to become Mayor of New York City, a position he held off and on until

1815. His new job removed him from national prominence. It also brought him into close contact with the city´s commercial classes, angered by President Thomas Jefferson´s agrarian bias. The Embargo was the most obvious of many events that eroded Clinton´s once-fierce loyalty to the Democratic-Republican party. He unsuccessfully sought the Presidency in 1812 with the tacit support of the Federalists.

Clinton later served as Governor, where he launched the most ambitious project of his career, the Erie Canal. Critics laughed at "Clinton´s Ditch," but its completion guaranteed New York commercial supremacy in the nation.

GEORGE CLINTON (IDR 1808)

Clinton´s brief stint in the Continental Congress and undistinguished service in the Continental Army led his contemporaries to underestimate him. His 1777 election as Governor of New York caught them off-guard. John Jay sputtered, "Clinton´s family and connections do not entitle him to so distinguished a pre-eminence."[60] The new Governor made up for his poor bloodlines with strong leadership. He was reelected five times, serving continuously until 1795.

Clinton lost the biggest fight of his tenure. He vigorously opposed the Constitution. He warned that the President would become a monarch because "the progress of a commercial society begets luxury, the parent of inequality, the foe to virtue, and the enemy to restraint."[61] It was largely because of Clinton´s diatribes that Alexander Hamilton, James Madison, and Jay penned their famous Federalist Papers. They carried the day, but Clinton managed to prevent New York´s approval until the Constitution had already been ratified.

After a seventh term as Governor, Clinton was twice elected Vice President. One Senator charged in 1804 that he was chosen only because potential candidates for 1808 wanted "to elect an old man who is too feeble to aspire to the Presidency." Clinton had his own hopes in 1808, but was again relegated to the second spot. He died in office.

FRANCIS COCKRELL (D 1904)

Some observers thought that even if he hadn´t been qualified for the office, Cockrell would have brought an appropriate appearance to the Presidency. "His strong resemblance to the pictured representation of `Uncle Sam´ appeals irresistibly to the aspiring artist visitors who throng the galleries," noted one journalist in the 1890s. "They all want snapshots of the man who looks like the national idol."[62]

But Cockrell´s patriotic looks could not obscure the fact that he had been a brigadier general in the Confederate Army. His past was no barrier to his winning five terms as a Senator from Missouri, a state that had been seriously divided in the Civil War. He thought it would be quite a different story in a national election, expecting never to see a former rebel like himself advance to the White House.

Cockrell's 1904 Presidential candidacy largely provided refuge for Midwestern devotees of William Jennings Bryan, who was not running that year. He left the Senate the following year. President Theodore Roosevelt, who once called Cockrell one of the three finest men he had met in public life, quickly appointed him to the Interstate Commerce Commission.

ROSCOE CONKLING (R 1876)

Conkling was irascible and proud, the dictator of New York's Republican party at the height of his power. President Grant thought so highly of him that he tried to make Conkling Chief Justice, an offer that was politely turned down. Others had little use for the three-term Senator. Clarence Darrow called him "a cold, selfish man, who had no right to live except to prey upon his fellowmen."[63] Conkling's mortal enemy, James Blaine, mocked the dignified appearance of which the New Yorker was so vain. Blaine laughingly referred to Conkling's "majestic, super-eminent, overpowering, turkey-gobbler strut."[64]

Conkling's "Stalwarts" and Blaine's "Half-Breeds" long battled for control of the national Republican party. The New Yorker generally stayed behind the scenes, emerging only to fall short with his Presidential bid in 1876. But he retained his arrogance to the end. A tremendous blizzard shut down New York City in March 1888. Conkling haughtily insisted on going about his business, hiking for three hours through the drifts rather than pay the $50 a cabdriver insisted on. He collapsed at the end of what he called "an ugly tramp in the dark." Six weeks later, he died of complications from exposure and exhaustion.

CALVIN COOLIDGE (R 1924)

Coolidge felt he had reached the summit of his career in 1918. After more than a decade of working his way up through the Massachusetts government, he was elected Governor. There was no reason to expect higher honor.

A series of unlikely events propelled Coolidge into the White House within a half-decade. The first was the decision of police officers in Boston to form a union. Their organizers were suspended, so most of the force went on strike. It fell on local officials to handle the crisis, but Coolidge received national acclaim for his declaration, "There is no right to strike against the public safety by anybody, anywhere, any time."[65] Delegates to the 1920 Republican convention remembered those brave words. When party leaders tried to push through their choice of a running mate for Warren Harding, a spontaneous revolt led instead to Coolidge's selection. The seemingly robust Harding died in 1923.

The new President appeared to be a stereotypical native Vermonter. He was conservative, frugal, and a man of few words. He said his first thought on replacing Harding was, "I believe I can swing it." His withdrawal from the 1928 race was accomplished with a one-sentence statement. He left the White House for good in 1929 by saying, "Time to go," and simply walking out the door. Perhaps the most legendary story about Coolidge's taciturnity had him being approached by a woman who said she had made a bet that she could entice him to say more than two words. Coolidge smiled. "You lose," he said.[66]

JAMES COX (D 1920, 1924)

Cox entered journalism as a reporter, was able to buy the Dayton Daily News in 1898, and owned a chain of papers by his death. His reputation as a reform-minded editor grew, providing him a ticket into politics in Ohio. Cox was elected to Congress in 1908, then benefited from Republican dissension in 1912 to become Governor. He went on to be the first Ohio Democrat to serve three terms in that office.

    Cox's progressive record and political success made him a logical Democratic Presidential nominee in 1920, but it was certainly not the party's year. Years later, Cox was introduced at a meeting by a humorist who joked about his landslide loss to Warren Harding. The former Governor replied that considering Harding's record of scandal and incompetence, the joke wasn't on him. It was on the country.

JACOB COXEY (R 1932)

Coxey made his mark in history decades before his Republican protest candidacy against Herbert Hoover in 1932. He remains best known for leading the 1894 march of the unemployed from Ohio to Washington. Only about 500 marchers were in "Coxey's Army" when it reached the Capitol, but Congress was fearful. The chief of the small band was arrested as soon as he tried to speak. Coxey's proposals for soft money and public-works programs to employ the jobless were dismissed with scarcely a hearing.

    A small fortune from his ownership of a sandstone quarry gave Coxey the freedom to promote his ideas. He ran often for public office, beginning as a Populist. His only win came as a Republican, a 1931 election as Mayor of Massillon, Ohio. Coxey enhanced his image as an eccentric during these years by selling something he called, "Cox-E-Lax," on his many speaking tours. But he also showed a certain precision. On May 1, 1944, he returned to Capitol Hill and delivered the speech he had been prevented from giving exactly fifty years earlier.

WILLIAM CRAWFORD (DR 1824)

Crawford was known for his candidness. One of his predecessors as Secretary of the Treasury, Albert Gallatin, described the Georgian as having "united to a powerful mind a most correct judgment and an inflexible integrity -- which last quality, not sufficiently tempered by indulgence and civility, has prevented his acquiring general popularity."[67] Critics also insisted it barred Crawford from the Presidency. They delighted in recounting his 1816 proposal "to incorporate, by humane and benevolent policy, the natives of our forests in the great American family of freemen."[68] He even suggested that whites intermarry with Indians. It was considered a shockingly irresponsible idea.

It was ironic that Crawford's uncharacteristic caution in 1816 also kept him from the White House. Well known as a Senator, Minister to France, Secretary of War, and Secretary of the Treasury, he had developed a strong personal following. He refused pleas that he capitalize by running for President. His narrow loss in the Democratic-Republican caucus led to questions of what might have been. By the time Crawford launched a serious candidacy in 1824, he had been paralyzed by a stroke. Newer, healthier candidates passed him by.

ALBERT CUMMINS (R 1916)

Cummins seemed miscast as a man of the people, but that was his reputation as Iowa's Governor and Senator. It was an image fostered by his role in the five-year legal battle against the barbed-wire monopoly and sustained by his support of progressive legislation. The railroads particularly feared Cummins. They were instrumental in defeating his first two attempts to be elected to the Senate. But Cummins' 1901 race for Governor was successful. He served three terms in that post, then three more in the Senate.

The irony of Cummins' common-man image is that he was a wealthy corporation lawyer. His firm was the largest in Iowa. He belonged to exclusive clubs. Long after the automobile became popular, he was still driven to his office in a luxurious carriage by a liveried coachman. Nor did he have the common touch. Most people found him to be aloof.

Cummins came more into tune with his social position after World War I, growing increasingly conservative. That was enough for the people of Iowa. They voted him out of the Senate in 1926.

CHARLES CURTIS (R 1928)

Curtis was one-eighth Indian, but while a boy, he considered himself fullblooded. He lived for a while with his grandmother on the Kaw Indian reservation. It was a heritage Curtis was always fond of recalling. His 1928 campaign biography was titled, <u>The Life Story of Charles Curtis, Indian, Who Has Risen to High Estate</u>.

But his ancestry did not imbue Curtis with radical beliefs. He served fifteen years in the House of Representatives and twenty-two in the Senate as an Old Guard Republican. One observer joked that the Trinity for Curtis was the protective tariff, the Grand Army of the Republic, and the Republican party. The Kansan couldn't abide insurgents. He once said he respected the Republican dissidents who formed the Progressive party in 1912 because they at least "had the stamina or manliness to get out of the party they chose to fight."[69]

Curtis' skill was as a manipulator. He served as Republican floor leader in the Senate for five years. After the failure of his 1928 Presidential candidacy, he was chosen to be Herbert Hoover's Vice President.

DAVID DAVIS (D-LR none)

Davis was a Maryland native and Yale Law School graduate whose most fateful decision was to move to Illinois. He established a law practice in Bloomington and rose to become the presiding judge of his judicial circuit. Among the lawyers who argued cases before him was one who became a great friend, Abraham Lincoln. It was Davis who headed Lincoln's team at the 1860 Republican convention. The candidate sent a wire, "I authorize no bargains and will be bound by none." Davis rasped, "Lincoln ain't here."[70] He swung the deals that secured the nomination.

Davis was repaid in 1862 when Lincoln appointed him to the Supreme Court. But the Justice insisted he was not as close to the President as most believed. "I know it was the general opinion in Washington that I knew all about Lincoln's thoughts," he said. "But I knew nothing. Lincoln never confided to me anything."[71]

Davis drifted from the Republicans after his friend's assassination. He was a leading contender for the Liberal Republican nomination in 1872, but lost to Horace Greeley. Democrats considered him one of them by 1877, electing him to the Senate. That vote may have cost Samuel Tilden the Presidency, since it removed Davis from the panel being established to award disputed electoral votes from the election of 1876. He was replaced by a Republican.

JOHN DAVIS (D 1920, 1924)

Davis was heralded as the leading lawyer of his age. Supreme Court Justice Oliver Wendell Holmes insisted he had never heard anyone "more elegant, more clear, more concise, or more logical."[72] The West Virginia native also won rave notices for his diplomatic skills as Ambassador to Great Britain. King George V called Davis "the most perfect gentleman" he had ever known.

But what worked before judges and royalty was hardly a success with American voters. Davis' urbanity and reason came across as dullness and lack of commitment. Franklin Roosevelt advised Davis that one of his speeches had been "charming and beautifully expressed," but it needed more fire.

Davis was never as liberal as most Democrats, and he grew more conservative in his later years as a Wall Street lawyer. He helped found the Liberty League, an organization dedicated to the destruction of the New Deal. He usually endorsed Republicans for President after his own candidacy failed in 1924. And reflecting his belief in segregation, he argued unsuccessfully against integrated schools in the landmark case of Brown v. Board of Education. Differences in race and viewpoint could not dull the admiration of the winning lawyer in that case. Thurgood Marshall said of Davis, "He was a great advocate, the greatest."[73]

EUGENE DEBS (SOC 1904, 1908, 1912, 1920)

Debs´ personality was two-faceted. One side was the kindly neighbor who was a respected citizen of Terre Haute, Indiana, and once had been its city clerk. The other was the fiery labor leader who declared, "The issue is socialism versus capitalism. I am for socialism because I am for humanity."[74] Debs maintained both images throughout his life. When he was released from prison after World War I, 25,000 met his train at Terre Haute. Neighbors and Socialists alike were on hand.

Debs was the head of the American Railway Union when he was jailed for his coordination of the 1894 strike against the Pullman Company. Long days in his cell left him little to do but read. He was converted by books making the case for socialism. Debs was instrumental in creating the Socialist party, running five times as its Presidential candidate. His final candidacy was conducted from federal prison, where he had been sent for violating the Espionage Act during the war. "They tell us that we live in a great free republic," he declared in the offending speech. "This is too much, even for a joke."[75] Many non-Socialists doubted there had been any reason to arrest him. President Harding released Debs in 1921 and he returned to his beloved Terre Haute, living out his years as the grand old man of American socialism.

CHAUNCEY DEPEW (R 1888)

Depew was a promising young Republican when he was forced to make a crucial decision in 1866. He had already been promised appointment as the first American Minister to Japan when Cornelius Vanderbilt made a less-than-stunning counteroffer. He would give Depew less money to be the attorney for his railroads. "Railroads are the career for a young man; there is nothing in politics," Vanderbilt blustered. "Don´t be a damned fool."[76] Depew took the advice, beginning a career that would make him head of the New York Central by 1885.

However, politics retained its allure. Depew was often mentioned as a possible Senator or Cabinet officer. He abandoned his 1888 Presidential candidacy because he doubted a railroad man could be elected, but was instrumental in the selection of Benjamin Harrison. He finally became a Senator in 1899.

Depew was a famed storyteller. James Garfield once said that "he might be President if he did not tell funny stories." But those same stories made Depew a favorite at Republican conventions. He was called on to speak as late as 1916. Eight years later, he was back as a delegate at the age of 90.

THOMAS DEWEY (R 1940, 1944, 1948)

Dewey was a young man determined to race his way up the ladder of success. He was the U.S. Attorney for New York City at 31, District Attorney of Manhattan at 35. His successful prosecution of some of the nation's most notorious organized-crime figures earned him the nickname, "Gangbuster." "If you don't think Dewey is Public Hero No. 1," suggested the Philadelphia Inquirer, "listen to the applause he gets everytime he is shown in a newsreel."[77]

A Republican party smarting under quadrennial whippings from Franklin Roosevelt was looking for new heroes. Dewey fit the bill, becoming in 1940 the only District Attorney ever seriously considered for a Presidential nomination. He helped his standing by winning the first of three terms as Governor of New York in 1942. But despite his success at the polls, Dewey was never comfortable with politics. His formal bearing in public led Clare Boothe Luce to say Dewey "looks like the bridegroom on a wedding cake." The Governor seemed unable to change, but understood his image problem. One night after his 1948 loss to Harry Truman, he went outside to pitch pennies with his sons. His wife suggested he might want to stop before any photographers saw him. "Maybe if I had done this during the campaign," he sighed, "I would have won."[78]

JAMES DOOLITTLE (D 1868)

Doolittle was one of the great Senate orators during the Civil War. The Wisconsin Republican was able to fire up crowds with his emotional denunciations of slavery. He proudly wrote his wife that the publisher of Congressional transcripts "says of my voice and pronunciation that it is the finest and clearest he ever heard on the floor of the Senate."[79] Those talents were often used in the defense of Doolittle's friend, Abraham Lincoln. Asked to participate in a public debate over whether Lincoln should be renominated in 1864, he stated his case in two sentences, "I believe in God Almighty! Under Him, I believe in Abraham Lincoln!"[80]

Doolittle maintained his faith in Lincoln's lenient Reconstruction blueprints after the President's assassination. He fell out with the Radicals, voting for the acquittal of Andrew Johnson at his impeachment trial. It was a vote that ended his careers as a Republican and a Senator. "You have turned Traitor to your State and gone over to Johnson and the rebels," wrote one constituent. "Come home and put a ball through your rotten head."[81] Doolittle ran for President and Governor as a Democrat, but never held public office again.

STEPHEN DOUGLAS (D 1852, 1856, 1860)

Douglas compensated for his lack of height with an overdose of self-confidence. He was commonly known as the Little Giant. One of his early friends in Illinois remembered, "It was as natural and spontaneous with him to reason, to argue, to seek to convince, as it is to all men to eat."[82] It was also natural for Douglas to seek public office. By the time he was 30, he had already been a State's Attorney, Illinois Supreme Court Justice, state legislator, Illinois Secretary of State, and Congressman. He entered the Senate at the tender age of 34.

Douglas' elders handed him an innocuous assignment, the chairmanship of the Committee on Territories. No one envisioned the public outcry that would accompany Douglas' bill to allow the settlers in Kansas and Nebraska to decide whether to permit slavery. "I passed the Kansas-Nebraska Act myself," he typically boasted in 1854. "I had the authority and power of a dictator throughout the whole controversy in both houses. The speeches were nothing."[83] Reality set in when Douglas returned home. He remarked that he traveled the whole way by the light of his own burning effigies. This Northern dissatisfaction was coupled by the late 1850s with Southern mistrust of Douglas' refusal to take firm steps to protect slavery. The Little Giant's Presidential hopes were dashed forever. The job passed instead to the man he had defeated in his famous 1858 campaign for reelection to the Senate, Abraham Lincoln.

GEORGE EDMUNDS (R 1880, 1884)

Edmunds was an unusual Senator in the Gilded Age. He was incorruptible. The Vermont Republican was feared by many of his colleagues. He thought nothing of bringing the work of the Senate to a halt while he mercilessly questioned the sponsor of a bill designed to enrich private interests. Harper's Weekly noted approvingly, "There is, in fact, no member of Congress and no conspicuous public man in the country who has been longer or more steadfastly the friend of the reform system than Senator Edmunds."[84] He introduced civil-service legislation as early as 1871.

Edmunds was chairman of the Senate Judiciary Committee for seventeen years. He was so highly regarded as a legal expert that he was once called to testify on a technical matter before a committee of the British House of Lords. Despite the demands of supporters such as Theodore Roosevelt, Edmunds saw little reason to trade this lofty status for the White House. But a friend remembered that the sharp-tongued Senator "beamed all over with satisfaction" when discussing one aspect of the Presidency. Edmunds admitted that despite all his reservations about the job, he wouldn't mind getting his hands on the veto power.

EDWARD EDWARDS (D 1920)

One didn´t win state office in New Jersey in the early 20th Century without the help of political bosses. Woodrow Wilson cut a deal with them, and so did Edwards. The Jersey City banker´s benefactor was the infamous "Boss" Frank Hague. Edwards was elected Governor in 1919 by a margin of 14,500 votes. It was all thanks to Hague, who delivered a margin of 35,000 in his and Edwards´ home county.

Edwards was a bit ahead of the game with his 1920 Presidential candidacy. He advocated repeal of Prohibition, the only major contender to make it an issue. The Volstead Act had just gone into effect early in the year. The nation was certainly not ready to elect someone to dismantle it. Not yet.

DWIGHT EISENHOWER (R 1952, 1956)

A reporter at one of Eisenhower´s Presidential press conferences referred to him as an "old soldier," then hastened to add he meant no disrespect. The man known since his childhood as Ike just laughed, "Make no mistake. I am proud of the title."[85] His thirty-seven years in the Army had brought him worldwide acclaim, not to mention the Presidency.

Eisenhower graduated from West Point in 1915. He became a brigadier general in 1941 after a tour of duty that included a long stretch as an aide to the flamboyant Douglas MacArthur. "I studied dramatics under him for five years in Washington and four years in the Philippines," Ike once joked.[86] He was the easygoing opposite of his former boss, but no less rehearsed. Eisenhower once told George Patton that "a certain sphinx-like quality will do a lot toward enhancing one´s reputation." He played his role well. The New York Times said one of General Eisenhower´s 1942 meetings with reporters was "an excellent demonstration of the art of being jovially outspoken without saying much of anything."[87]

Ike became a worldwide figure that year, taking command of Allied forces in Europe. He held the reins through V-E Day. Both political parties fought to enlist the man who combined a likable grin with the aura of military victory. Eisenhower refused to consider running for President in 1948, but relented four years later. He became the first Republican to serve two full terms in the White House since another revered commander, Ulysses Grant.

JAMES ENGLISH (D 1868)

English was the epitome of the self-made man. Starting as a carpenter´s apprentice, he worked his way to become a designer and contractor. He used his savings to establish a profitable lumber company, then bought a clock company and branched into real estate and banking. He became one of the richest men in Connecticut.

English was also interested in politics. He was a Congressional War Democrat during the Lincoln Administration. That made him a natural candidate for Governor after the war, as Connecticut Democrats scrambled to fight charges of disloyalty. English secured a one-year term in 1867, winning again in 1868 and 1870. He lost a disputed contest in 1871 because of an unfortunately terse telegram. The Governor wired New York's Boss Tweed to send him a Democrat to help in his campaign, "Do not disappoint us. Nothing could be more disastrous."[88] The Republicans obtained a copy and published it with their own lurid interpretations. Voters returned English to private life, where he stayed except for a brief spell as an appointed Senator.

CHARLES FAIRBANKS (R 1908, 1916)

When William McKinley was gunned down by an assassin in 1901, Fairbanks' best chance for the Presidency died with him. The conservative Indiana Senator was one of the President's favorites and was also an influential member of the Republican National Committee. There had even been whispers that McKinley wanted Fairbanks to succeed him in the White House in 1905.

Fairbanks was a leader of the Old Guard. As a lawyer specializing in railroad cases, he eventually became a director or general counsel for many of the nation's leading rail lines. He was worth more than $5 million. The new President, Theodore Roosevelt, needed a bridge to conservatives and the wealthy. He chose Fairbanks in 1904 to perform that duty as his Vice President, but had no intention of advancing his career any further. Asked about Fairbanks as a possible Republican Presidential nominee in 1908, Roosevelt snorted that he was nothing more than "a reactionary machine politician." Out of step with the Progressive era, Fairbanks failed in his two attempts to prove Roosevelt wrong.

JAMES FARLEY (D 1940)

Most contemporaries associated Farley solely with Franklin Roosevelt, figuring him to be nothing more than a worshiper of the President's cult of personality. It was never true. "I was born a Democrat," Farley was fond of saying, "and I expect to die a Democrat."[89] He remembered being an eight-year-old torchbearer in a parade for William Jennings Bryan. The party always came first.

Farley was a county Democratic leader when he met Roosevelt in 1920. FDR elevated him to state party chairman a decade later, but Farley's major task was laying the groundwork for Roosevelt's Presidential campaign. He was rewarded for his success by appointment as Democratic national chairman and Postmaster General. The President's landslide reelection in 1936 was Farley's pinnacle, taken as a sign of his political genius.

Relations with Roosevelt cooled during the late 1930s. Farley objected to plans to purge conservative Democrats from Congress. They were, after all, Democrats. He strenuously protested a third term, launching a weak challenge to his boss. There would be no reconciliation. As a delegate to the 1944 convention that again renominated Roosevelt, Farley voted for Harry Byrd.

STEPHEN FIELD (D 1880)

Field was a prominent man in his time, a Supreme Court Justice for thirty-four years. But he never had a realistic chance of fulfilling his desire to be President. The Democratic party in his home state of California took care of that, opposing him at every turn. "My judicial opinions on subjects of interest in California...have, I am aware, given offense to a large number of people who whould have had me disregard the law, the treaties with China and Mexico, and the Constitution," he conceded.[90] The biggest outpouring of hatred gushed forth in 1879 when Field struck down a San Francisco law requiring all prisoners to be given short haircuts. He charged it was aimed at the Chinese, who took pride in wearing their hair in long queues. White Californians were aghast at Field's defense of a despised minority group. They never forgot it, particularly not when his name was presented to the 1880 Democratic convention.

His Presidential dreams thwarted, Field contented himself with the Court. He became famous for his dissents, some of which led to revisions of constitutional law. The elderly Justice hung on to his seat until 1897, barely able to work at the end. But he reached his goal of surpassing John Marshall's record for the longest term on the nation's highest court.

MILLARD FILLMORE (W 1852, A-W 1856)

Fillmore was an accidental President, but it was no accident that he was unable to win a term in his own right. He doomed his career with a stroke of the pen. The former Congressman and New York Comptroller was determined to save the Union by signing every component of the Compromise of 1850. That included the controversial Fugitive Slave Act. Fillmore confessed signing it would "draw down upon [my] head vials of wrath" from Northerners. He was correct.

His actions in 1850 were typical of Fillmore's lifetime desire for moderation in an age of political excess. He had little use for extremists of any stripe. He blamed abolitionists for costing him the Governor's race in 1844. Slavery seemed to Fillmore to be "an evil, but one with which the national government had nothing to do."[91] As the nominee of the xenophobic American party in 1856, he stressed maintenance of the Union rather than restrictions on immigration. He did best in the South that year. Much of the North would not forgive him for requiring the return of runaway slaves. But Fillmore never doubted he had been correct. He later wrote, "The man who can look upon a crisis without being willing to offer himself upon the altar of his country is not fit for public trust."[92]

CLINTON FISK (PROH 1888)

Fisk was unusual among the generals in the Union Army. He was a teetotaler who demonstrated a strong concern with social issues. President Andrew Johnson knew the perfect position for such a person after Appomattox. He ordered Fisk detailed to the Freedman's Bureau to strive for elusive racial harmony in Kentucky and Tennessee. "Fisk ain't a fool," Johnson said. "He won't hang everybody."[93]

But white Southerners thought Fisk had plenty of foolish ideas. He founded a college for blacks. It is now Fisk University. He also wrote a book for former slaves, Plain Counsels for Freedmen. It advised that "white people have old, strong prejudices." Fisk also sneaked in a temperance lecture, "You will waste your time at drinking saloons, fall into bad company, and, ten chances to one, become a miserable, bloated, wheezing, blear-eyed drunkard."[94]

Fisk was a prosperous banker after his military service, but he retained his social zeal. The rise of the Prohibition party found him a willing convert from the Republicans. His prominence and military record made him a natural standard-bearer for state office in New Jersey and for the Presidency.

JOHN FLOYD (ID 1832)

Floyd underwent a political conversion not unusual in the South of the 1830s. His early career as a state legislator and a Congressman was distinguished by strong nationalist feeling. The Virginian backed the Missouri Compromise, supported increases in the power of the federal government, and advocated western expansion. He introduced a bill to organize Oregon Territory in 1821, twenty-seven years before it actually happened.

A black preacher named Nat Turner triggered a sudden shift in Floyd's thinking. Turner instigated his famous slave rebellion in southeastern Virginia in 1831, killing fifty-seven whites. Floyd was Governor at the time. He had previously expressed sympathy for a gradual end to slavery, but suddenly called for new laws "to preserve in due subordination the slave population of our state." The growth of abolitionist spirit in the North became an irritant to him. Floyd began to see issues solely through a Southern perspective. When his old hero, Andrew Jackson, threatened to use troops against a recalcitrant South Carolina, Floyd wrote, "If he uses force, I will oppose him with a military force. I nor my country will not be enslaved without a struggle."[95] A grateful South Carolina cast its electoral votes for him in 1832, a symbol of defiance to Floyd's once-beloved nationalism.

GERALD FORD (R 1976)

Ford never attained his goal in public life. Soon after entering the House of Representatives in 1949, the former college football star resolved to become Speaker someday. He advanced as far as Minority Leader, the post from which Richard Nixon plucked him in 1973 to be the nation´s first appointed Vice President. Ford moved up to the Presidency upon Nixon´s resignation the following year. "Our long national nightmare is over," he declared in launching America on the road back from Watergate.[96] He was the first President who had not been elected to either of the top two offices.

Ford was a Republican party man first, last, and always. The exception was his first victory, his 1948 unseating of the Republican Congressman in his Michigan district. Senator Arthur Vandenberg gave his tacit support to the overthrow of the isolationist incumbent. After that, Ford showed few renegade impulses. He campaigned tirelessly for fellow Republicans and skewered Democrats. Lyndon Johnson, who Ford accused of "shocking mismanagement" of the Vietnam War, grew weary of it after a while. "There´s nothing wrong with Jerry Ford," he said, "except that he played football too long without a helmet."[97]

HENRY FORD (R 1916)

Contrary to popular belief, Ford did not invent the automobile. The former machine-shop apprentice´s contribution was in bringing the assembly line to its production, making possible what he called "a motorcar for the great multitude," the Model T. The auto was suddenly within the means of the workingman. Ford added to his mass appeal by announcing in 1914 that he would pay some of his workers the astronomical sum of $5 a day. It seemed too good to be true.

Talk began that America needed such a humanitarian as President. Thomas Edison thought it a bad idea. He said, "I would hate to see Henry Ford President because it would spoil a good man."[98] Others thought him anything but a good man, citing his anti-Semitism and strange causes, such as his 1915 Peace Ship that took neutrality advocates to Europe with their vague hope of ending World War I. Ford seemed undisciplined to many. He played hunches in his business and once said, "I don´t like to read books. They muss up my mind."[99]

Ford never announced for President. His only race was a 1918 Senate contest as a Democrat. He barely lost. In his later years, he grew more conservative, becoming locked in a pitched battle with the organized labor he came to hate. He was no longer called a man of the people.

JOSEPH FRANCE (R 1932)

Republican leaders never quite knew what to make of France. The Maryland doctor-turned-Senator seemed to have a need to do the dramatic, even at the expense of political common sense. He went to the Soviet Union in 1921 to visit Bolshevik leaders, the first Senator to do so. Most of his colleagues considered him audacious for dealing with the Communist regime still unrecognized by the American government. It was too soon after the "Red Scare."

France wanted to run for President as early as 1920, but Maryland party leaders refused to support him. He later insisted that if they had pitched in, he, not Warren Harding, would have been the compromise nominee. That memory, coupled with his excessive desire for attention, fueled France's quixotic challenge to Herbert Hoover in 1932. He insisted his was not "a personal candidacy." At the convention, he rushed to withdraw in favor of Calvin Coolidge, but was intercepted at the podium. A reporter described France with "his hair in slight disarray and his arms waving windmill fashion."[100] The police hustled him off the stage and out of Presidential politics.

JOHN FREMONT (R 1856)

Fremont was a romantic figure, the "Pathfinder of the West." His expeditions for the U.S. Topographical Corps in the 1840s brought back valuable geographic and scientific information. His wife helped Fremont write vivid reports that captured the fancy of a country straining west. "The interest of the scene soon dissipated fatigue," he wrote of a Western landscape.[101] Thousands of readers wanted to see it, too.

Fremont's third expedition came on the eve of the Mexican War. He and his men assisted the insurrection of California settlers, the Bear Flag Revolt. Fremont became enmeshed in a jurisdictional dispute between Army and Navy commanders. He was found guilty of mutiny by a court-martial, but President Polk remitted the sentence. The affair surprisingly raised Fremont's public standing. Most people admired his decisiveness, while admitting they wouldn't have known how to traverse the California thicket any better than Fremont had.

Both parties courted the Pathfinder in 1856, but his hostility to slavery drew him to the new Republicans. It was the pinnacle of his career. He served without distinction in the Civil War, flirted with an 1864 challenge to Abraham Lincoln, and suffered business losses in his final years.

JAMES GARFIELD (R 1880)

"The people are responsible for the character of their Congress," Garfield once wrote. "If that body be ignorant, reckless, and corrupt, it is because the people tolerate ignorance, recklessness, and corruption."[102] Garfield certainly was not ignorant, but his critics felt the other two labels were applicable.

The nine-term Congressman from Ohio was accused of involvement in two questionable deals. One involved his being on retainer from a company that was trying to sell paving blocks to the federal government. The more serious was an accusation that Garfield accepted stock in Credit Mobilier, a dummy construction company that bribed several Congressmen. Garfield nervously insisted that he had only received a loan of $329. He later wrote, "Take it all in all, it has been...a most uncomfortable winter."[103] The people in his district nonetheless reelected him.

Garfield`s ability to skirt such dangerous situations was rooted in his amiable nature. He always sought in Congress to find the middle ground, a tendency that some thought would have hounded his Presidency had he not been assassinated. Former President Ulysses Grant certainly thought the record justified that conclusion. He huffed, "Garfield has shown that he is not possessed of the backbone of an angleworm."[104]

JOHN NANCE GARNER (D 1932, 1940)

Garner spent thirty years in the House of Representatives, most of that time looking forward to becoming Speaker. The occupant of that office, Republican Nicholas Longworth, gave Minority Leader Garner a ride home in the Speaker´s car every night. The Democrat usually joked that it would soon be his. On election night, 1930, Garner received a telegram: WHOSE CAR IS IT. He replied: THINK IT MINE WILL BE PLEASURE TO LET YOU RIDE.[105] But Longworth died soon and his successor spent only two years in the driver´s seat.

Garner grudgingly took the Vice Presidency to prevent a Democratic convention deadlock in 1932. His Texas conservatism was sorely out of place in the New Deal. President Franklin Roosevelt began making sarcastic references to Garner and his "antediluvian friends." The Vice President in turn opposed many of Roosevelt´s programs. He appeared in public holding his nose with one hand and turning the other thumbs down on the plan to pack the Supreme Court. The third term was the final blow. Garner challenged Roosevelt, then gladly left the administration. The Vice Presidency, he said, was not worth "a warm barrel of piss."

WALTER GEORGE (D 1928)

George believed above all in two things: the Democratic party and the interests of the white South. The two usually coincided during his thirty-five years in the Senate. "When we fail to stand by President Roosevelt," he lectured a fellow Georgia Democrat early in the New Deal, "we shall be ready to forsake the best of our friends."[106]

The President felt the same way. He watched George and other conservatives later turn against his liberal programs.

He decided to "purge" them from Congress in 1938. Roosevelt announced George´s inclusion on his list at a joint appearance in Georgia. He said the Senator was opposed to the "broad objectives of the party and of the government as they are constituted today." George replied that the President had undertaken a "second march through Georgia."[107] His 1928 conservative Presidential candidacy had flopped and he was becoming accustomed to being on the losing side in the Senate, but George still had the magic in his home state. He was easily reelected.

BARRY GOLDWATER (R 1964)

Goldwater lived up to his 1964 Presidential campaign slogan throughout his Senate career. While most of his colleagues, including many Republicans, accepted the tenets of the New Deal, he offered "a choice, not an echo."

Goldwater`s willingness to buck the crowd was evidenced as early as 1930. His father and uncle were among the founders of the Democratic organization in Arizona, but he registered Republican. Goldwater promised after his election to the Senate in 1952 that he would not be "a me-too Republican." He quickly became a national hero to conservatives with his frank talk. He declared in 1960, "The apostles of the welfare state...[have turned Uncle Sam] into a national wet nurse, dispensing a cockeyed kind of patent medicine labeled `something for nothing,´ passing out the soothing syrup and rattles and pacifiers in return for grateful votes on election day."[108]

Goldwater was treated in his later years as an elder statesman. Even liberals professed to admire his consistent stand for his principles, but they certainly hadn´t felt that way in 1964. "The whole campaign was run on fear of me," the Senator later said of that election. "In fact, if I hadn´t known Goldwater, I´d have voted against the s.o.b. myself."[109]

ARTHUR GORMAN (D 1892)

Gorman received early training for a career that would include twenty-two years in the Senate. As a young page in the House and Senate, he watched the great prewar debates on the Kansas-Nebraska Act and other sectional disputes. He returned as a member in 1881.

Gorman was convervative, but he believed in party loyalty regardless of ideology. He helped run Grover Cleveland´s winning Presidential campaigns in 1884 and 1892, the latter despite having lost to Cleveland at the Democratic convention. But Gorman was disappointed that the President failed to see the need to reward his friends, "He has been so careful of [patronage] that he has scarcely done his party justice."[110] The two finally fell out over tariff revision. Cleveland said those who backed Gorman´s proposals were guilty of "party perfidy and party dishonor." The Maryland Senator replied on the floor that the President was "consumed with vanity and desired to set his judgment above that of his fellows."[111]   Attacking his party's leader was a new step for Gorman, but he didn't make it a practice. Fellow Eastern Democrats deserted the ticket in droves when William Jennings Bryan was nominated in 1896. Gorman swallowed hard and worked for him.

ULYSSES GRANT (R 1864, 1868, 1872, 1880)

Grant was an unlikely hero. A West Point graduate, he never intended to make the army his career. He resigned in 1854, spending the next six years as a farmer, a real-estate agent, and a clerk. He rose from that obscurity in the following decade to command the Union Army and reach the White House.

"I can't spare this man. He fights," Abraham Lincoln said of Grant, whose victories in the western theater were a shining exception to the bleak news in the early months of the Civil War. Grant was given overall command in late 1863. He showed a dogged persistence, wiring Washington in 1864, "I propose to fight it out on this line if it takes all summer."[112] It took longer, but he clinched his place in history at Appomattox.

Grant was no politician. He had only voted once, joking that he supported James Buchanan in 1856 "because I knew Fremont." His lack of political experience hampered his Presidency. "Mistakes have been made, as all can see and I admit," he conceded in his farewell address, "but it seems to me oftener in the selection made of the assistants appointed to aid in carrying out the various duties of administering the Government."[113] His scandal-ridden administrations tarnished his image. The Republican party was able to resist the old hero when he sought a third term in 1880.

GEORGE GRAY (D 1908)

Gray got along well with members of both parties, a little too well for some Democrats. The fourteen-year Senator first came to widespread attention with a fiery speech nominating Thomas Bayard at the 1880 Democratic convention. He thundered, "Who will best lead the Democratic hosts in the impending struggle for the restoration of honest government and the constitutional rights of the states and of their people?"[114] It was the kind of partisan bombast that delegates loved.

But Gray later showed political flexibility. A Republican President, William McKinley, thought him so safely conservative that he appointed Gray to the U.S. Circuit Court of Appeals. Another Republican, Theodore Roosevelt, asked him to mediate the 1902 anthracite coal strike. Gray's success made him a national figure, but many Democrats remembered how his fame had been attained. They preferred a Presidential nominee who believed in fighting the GOP.

HORACE GREELEY (D-LR 1872)

Greeley's sole stint in public office was a three-month appointment to warm a vacant Congressional seat in 1848, but he was one of the most influential men of his era. His New York _Tribune_ was widely read throughout the North. When Greeley advised, "Go West, young man, go West!" thousands did. His editorials were often ahead of their time, opposing capital punishment, terming women's suffrage "a natural right," supporting the creation of labor unions. He also lashed out at slavery. Greeley contended the Supreme Court's Dred Scott decision was "entitled to just so much moral weight as would be the judgment of a majority of those congregated in any Washington barroom."[115]

The power of the printed word was not sufficient. Greeley lusted for public office, often running without success on the state level before his losing 1872 Presidential effort. He conceded he was probably too opinionated to fit in very well as a politician, joking about the enemies he managed to make during his short Congressional stay, "I have divided the House into two parties, one that would like to see me extinguished, and the other is one that couldn't be satisfied without a hand in doing it."[116]

DWIGHT GREEN (R 1948)

Green's biggest victory came long before he won two terms as Governor of Illinois. As an Assistant U.S. Attorney in 1931, he prosecuted Al Capone for income-tax evasion. Green's success put Capone behind bars and himself in the public spotlight. President Herbert Hoover soon rewarded him with appointment as U.S. Attorney for Chicago.

Green later had opportunities to reclaim national glory, but failed to capitalize. Elected Governor in 1940, he gave the welcoming address to the 1944 Republican convention. Delegates dozed through the longest greeting to any convention, thirty-two minutes. His 1948 keynote also failed to arouse any excitement. Green had other worries that year, facing a tough fight for a third term. His loss had more impact on Presidential politics than any speech he ever gave. His replacement as Governor of Illinois was Adlai Stevenson.

WALTER GRESHAM (R 1888)

Gresham was a Republican for most of his life, but he was never very comfortable about his party membership. He also sought office a number of times, but wrote, "There is nothing so unsatisfactory as political life."[117] The Indianan was happiest when he was above the partisan fray during his two tours as a federal judge.

Gresham was elected to the Indiana legislature in 1860 by only 60 votes. It was the only political win of his life; his judgeships and his three Cabinet posts were all appointive. He entered the legislature full of enthusiasm, but soon wrote his wife that most of his colleagues were "perfect asses." Gresham chafed under Republican party discipline, writing by the mid-1870s that the GOP had turned "arrogant, extravagant, and corrupt." He became a bitter enemy of Benjamin Harrison, fighting with him for the hearts of Indiana Republicans. When Harrison beat him for the 1888 Presidential nomination, Gresham was to the point, "I must be frank. I do not like him."[118]

Gresham's judicial decisions were often to the favor of organized labor. The Populists courted him as a possible candidate in 1892, but he endorsed Democrat Grover Cleveland. One relieved Indiana Republican leader said Gresham had "at last torn off the mask and gone into the Democratic party, where he should have been years ago."[119]

JAMES GUTHRIE (D 1860)

Some considered Guthrie to be arrogant and domineering. None could dispute that he was successful in business. The Kentucky lawyer made his fortune by investing in canals and real estate. Guthrie was among the founders of the University of Louisville. He promoted the Louisville and Nashville Railroad, becoming its president by the outbreak of the Civil War. He remained loyal to the Union, using his rail lines to transport men and supplies to the western theater.

Guthrie also made his mark in state politics. He served fourteen years in the Kentucky legislature and headed the 1849 constitutional assembly that repulsed strong efforts to end slavery in that state. His service to the Democratic party and his success in business were recognized by President Franklin Pierce, who named Guthrie his Secretary of the Treasury. The former Secretary tried for the Presidency himself in the volatile year of 1860, but made little headway. Northerners considered him a Southerner. Southern firebrands dismissed him as a Unionist.

JOHN HALE (FS 1852)

Hale faced a moment of truth in 1844. A Democratic Congressman from New Hampshire, he was expected to follow his party's line and support the annexation of Texas. It was something he could not do. Hale took the floor and blasted annexation as a pro-slavery move "eminently calculated to provoke the scorn of earth and the judgment of heaven."[120] He was immediately read out of the Democratic party, but was suddenly a hero to abolitionists and Whigs. They combined to elect him to the Senate.

Hale became known in the Senate as a man with a quick mind and a fine voice. His attacks on slavery were among the first heard in that chamber. But he had a streak of laziness, never compiling a record to match his rhetoric. He was proudest of his two bills that abolished Navy traditions: flogging and the issuance of a grog ration. The Free Soilers nominated him for President in 1852 because of his effectiveness in spreading the anti-slavery message. He became a Republican before the election of 1856.

WINFIELD HANCOCK (D 1868, 1876, 1880)

Hancock neither knew nor cared much about politics, but his Presidential candidacy was perhaps inevitable. The Democratic party was desperately struggling to remove the stain of disloyalty after the Civil War. Hancock, who had valiantly held the line against Pickett's charge at Gettysburg, was one of the few Democratic war heroes.

Hancock was named for another warrior who pursued the Presidency, Winfield Scott. He was strikingly handsome in uniform. Ulysses Grant admiringly said Hancock "presented an appearance that would attract the attention of an army as he passed." He also attracted the enmity of Republicans for his lenient handling of Reconstruction in Louisiana and Texas. They removed him from that post. His wife later complained, "Naturally his ideas of administration would conflict with this arbitrary class, whose harsh measures and extreme views were in perfect sympathy with the radical wing of the party."[121] Ohio Congressman James Garfield unsuccessfully pushed a bill to reduce the number of major generals. It was obviously aimed at Hancock.

The General remained in the army for the rest of his life. His wife recalled that he followed the disputed 1876 election "with intense interest and anxiety." But when he was nominated in 1880, she said he didn't seem interested in the least.

WARREN HARDING (R 1920)

Harding gave fair warning. He wrote a friend before the 1920 election that he was not qualified to be President, "I should really be ashamed to presume myself fitted to reach out for a place of such responsibility."[122] His record bore out that assessment: brief tours in the Ohio legislature and as Lieutenant Governor, less than a full term as a Senator. Harding had never authored any significant legislation. He would have been happy staying in the Senate, "a very pleasant place." His campaign manager, Harry Daugherty, and his wife pushed him higher.

Harding's resonant voice and dignified appearance made him look to be a natural leader. He was gregarious, fitting easily into political circles. His indiscriminate friendships haunted him in the White House. The "Ohio Gang" became infamous as scandal after scandal was revealed following Harding's death, a merciful end to a tortured Presidency. "I don't know what to do or where to turn in this taxation matter," Harding once burst out to an aide. "Somewhere there must be a book that tells all about it, where I could go to straighten it out in my mind. But I don't know where the book is, and maybe I couldn't read it if

I found it!...My God, this is a hell of a place for a man like me to be!"[123]

JUDSON HARMON (D 1912)

Harmon played an important role in the careers of two future Presidents. He served nine years as a local judge in Cincinnati, then recommended William Howard Taft as his replacement in 1887. Later a two-term Governor of Ohio, he defeated Warren Harding in his 1910 reelection. It was commonly assumed to be the end of Harding´s political career.

Harmon served Grover Cleveland as his Attorney General. It was an appropriate match. The Ohioan was always Cleveland´s type of Democrat: willing to undertake a few reforms, but essentially conservative. His administration as Governor was mildly progressive. Harmon signed into law Ohio´s workmen´s compensation act and a public utility commission. His advisers also wanted him to support the initiative and referendum, contending it would increase his national appeal. But Harmon thought the measures dangerous. He deliberately spoke against them at the state´s constitutional convention. The influential William Jennings Bryan cited that speech while blasting him as "a reactionary and the choice of the predatory interests of the country." Harmon´s chances of becoming President in the progressive era were ended.

AVERELL HARRIMAN (D 1952, 1956)

Harriman spent most of his career assisting Democratic Presidents. A millionaire at 17 through inheritance of his father´s financial and railroad interests, he had the freedom to accept a broad range of assignments. His friend Franklin Roosevelt asked him to head the National Recovery Administration. Harriman´s financial and transportation experience then made him the choice to administer Lend-Lease. He established diplomatic contacts in that post that led to his ambassadorships to the Soviet Union and Great Britain. He was Harry Truman´s Secretary of Commerce. John Kennedy, who used Harriman for special missions, said he had held "probably as many important jobs as any American in our history, with the possible exception of John Quincy Adams."[124]

Harriman´s ventures into politics were not nearly as successful. He squeaked through by 11,000 votes in 1954 to become Governor of New York, but was trounced by Nelson Rockefeller four years later. Two Presidential races fell woefully short. Harriman left an outstanding legacy of appointive service, but there was little doubt of his preference for the elective power he so briefly held. Of all the titles he could use in his retirement, he preferred that people call him "Governor."

BENJAMIN HARRISON (R 1888, 1892)

Harrison's accession to the Presidency surprised him as much as anyone. He was a successful Indiana lawyer, but had compiled only a mixed record in politics. Two bids for the governorship failed before he was elected to the Senate in 1880. The Republicans subsequently lost control of the state legislature, guaranteeing his defeat for reelection. Harrison wrote a family friend resignedly, "I was born to be a drudge, I think, and don't look for any rest until the Democrats beat me for the Senate next fall."[125] Three years later, he was living in the White House.

Harrison possessed political attributes, but blunted them with a cold personal style. On the positive side, he was a Civil War general, a powerful speaker, and the grandson of William Henry Harrison. A friend once remarked that if Harrison spoke to a crowd of 10,000, he would make all his friends. But if he were introduced to each afterward, all would be his enemies. Most Republican leaders eventually joined the latter category. One aptly compared the 1892 Harrison bandwagon to an "ice-cart."

WILLIAM HENRY HARRISON (W 1836, 1840)

Benjamin Harrison heard so much about his grandfather during the 1888 campaign that he joked the Harrison family was like a potato plant: the best part was underground. William Henry Harrison was already entrenched in American mythology. His legend dated to his tenure as Territorial Governor of Indiana, when he led an attack on the Indian settlement at Tippecanoe in 1811. Harrison's men won, a cause for rejoicing on the frontier. Overlooked were the facts that the whites sustained heavy losses and the Indians reoccupied the site within a few months. Harrison himself did not grasp the importance of the battle to his career. He misspelled it "Teppecanoe."

"Old Tip" began a slow voyage from the battlefield into obscurity. He served in the War of 1812, spent six undistinguished years in the House and Senate, and descended to the post of clerk of the courts of Hamilton County, Ohio, by 1834. The Whig party, looking for an old hero, nonetheless thought him Presidential material. "If General Harrison is taken up as a candidate," the National Bank's Nicholas Biddle offered in 1835, "it will be on account of the past, not on the future. Let him then rely entirely on the past."[126] It was advice that would elect a President in 1840.

GARY HART (D 1984)

Hart was a Colorado Senator who styled himself a prophet of the Democratic party's future. "The New Deal has run its course," he declared in 1983. "The party is over."[127] His message that a new generation was ready for power was treated as a revelation by the national press in 1984, but Hart had been playing variations on the theme for more than a decade. He managed George McGovern's upstart Presidential campaign in

1972. Two years later, he was elected to the Senate on the slogan, "They had their turn. Now it´s our turn."[128]

Hart´s vision of the future was too cold and cerebral for many old-line Democrats. The head of the AFL-CIO, Lane Kirkland, said he vastly preferred Walter Mondale to be the Democratic nominee in 1984. "He is not some synthetic Masked Marvel or Mystery Man," Kirkland sputtered in a thinly veiled slap at Hart. "He [Mondale] is not made of silicon and micro-chip flakes."[129] But Hart, calling himself an "independent Western Jeffersonian Democrat," insisted his party would eventually be forced to discard the legacy of Franklin Roosevelt and begin anew.

JOHN HARTRANFT (R 1876)

Hartranft was known throughout his career for the use of force. He attained small prominence as a brigadier general during the Civil War, cited for gallantry at Spotsylvania Court House. He based a postwar political career on that military reputation, being elected Governor of Pennsylvania in 1872. Governor Hartranft frequently used the militia to put down strikes and labor disturbances. He later admitted he wasn´t certain he handled those situations correctly.

Hartranft´s 1876 Presidential candidacy was among the most modest on record. The speaker putting his name before the Republican convention conceded the other contenders had "a great intellectual superiority over my candidate." But he insisted Hartranft would make an acceptable President because he knew how to follow advice, was honest, and "the people of Pennsylvania love him."[130]

RUTHERFORD HAYES (R 1876)

Hayes surprised many visitors with his calm demeanor in the winter of 1877. The nation was in an uproar over the disputed election of the previous November. Democrats hinted at renewed civil war if Hayes were declared the winner over Samuel Tilden. But the Ohio Governor quietly bargained to clinch his victory, assembled a Cabinet, and mused over his inaugural address. He had a well-deserved faith in his ability to win close races.

Hayes launched his amazing streak in 1858. The Cincinnati City Council elected him city solicitor by a single vote. After serving as a general in the Civil War and filling two terms in Congress, he was three times elected Governor. Hayes´ combined margin in those statewide races was only 16,000 votes out of more than 1.5 million cast. The three Democrats he edged all ran for President at some point: Allen Thurman, George Pendleton, and William Allen. There was talk that Hayes´ electoral record showed he should do likewise. "Several suggest that if elected Governor now, I will stand well for the Presidency next year," he wrote in his diary in 1875. "How wild! What a queer lot we are becoming!"[131] But the Hayes luck held. He was declared the winner over Tilden by a single electoral vote. Perhaps not tempting fate, the President declined to seek reelection.

WILLIAM RANDOLPH HEARST (D 1904)

Hearst was accustomed to thinking big. He convinced his
father to give him control of the moribund San Francisco
Examiner in 1887. His brand of sensationalism, soon known as
"yellow journalism," produced a sizable profit. Hearst
exported his controversial style to New York City, reviving
the feeble _Journal_. It was the base of the greatest
publishing empire of the age.

Hearst was long fascinated by politics, though he was at
first too shy to get involved overtly. When a bored _Journal_
reporter cabled that nothing was going on in Cuba, Hearst
allegedly wired back, "You furnish the pictures and I´ll
furnish the war!"[132] His papers´ constant agitation probably
hastened the Spanish-American War. He later summoned the
courage to play a direct role, serving two terms in Congress,
losing races for Mayor and Governor of New York, and
scandalizing traditional Democrats by running for President
in 1904.

Hearst´s activities brought him into bitter conflict
with another New York Democrat, Al Smith. The Governor
labeled Hearst´s paper "the Mud-Gutter Gazette" and called
the publisher "a particularly low type of man." But words
were Hearst´s business. He characterized one of Smith´s
attacks as "a vulgar tirade that any resident of Billingsgate
or any occupant of the alcoholic ward in Bellevue could have
written in fifteen minutes in quite the same style, but with
more evidence of education and intelligence."[133] The last
laugh belonged to Smith, who by the 1920s ended Hearst´s
influence in the state party.

THOMAS HENDRICKS (D 1872, 1876, 1880, 1884)

Hendricks was a Democrat through and through, too much for
his own good. The Indianan served in the Senate in the
volatile years from 1863 to 1869. He compiled a record of
opposition to Republican war and Reconstruction policies that
would later haunt him. "The Negro is inferior and no good
would come from his freedom," Hendricks once said.[134] He
opposed emancipation, then voted against black citizenship
and voting rights. He condemned the military draft, tried to
reduce war expenditures, and routinely excoriated military
Reconstruction. Many Democrats later shied from nominating a
man whose candidacy would have played right into Republican
charges of disloyalty.

Hendricks´ ambition was to be Governor of Indiana. He
squeaked through by 1,100 votes on his third try in 1872.
But he was disappointed in the office. "Any man competent to
be a notary public could be Governor of Indiana," he
grumbled.[135] His victory did impress many Democrats, who had
few winners anywhere after the Civil War. It provided
Hendricks a base for repeated tries for the Presidency. He
had to settle for being Grover Cleveland´s first Vice

President, dying nine months after taking office.

DAVID HILL (D 1892)

Hill was not at all like Grover Cleveland, yet he was one of Governor Cleveland´s strongest supporters in the 1884 Presidential race. The reason was simple. Hill was Cleveland´s Lieutenant Governor. If his boss became President, he would be the Governor of New York. The differences between the two became obvious soon after each was promoted. Cleveland disliked heavy use of patronage. Hill campaigned for a term in his own right with the slogan, "I am a Democrat." It became famous as his subtle promise to reward loyal party workers.

The President and the Governor carried out a long feud over control of the state Democratic party. Cleveland succeeded in preventing Hill from being a delegate to the 1888 convention, but he failed to stop the Governor´s elevation to the Senate in 1892. "I have received no favors at his hands," Hill once said in classic understatement. "I have my political grievances."[136] He ran to stop Cleveland´s third Presidential nomination in 1892, but his campaign fell apart at the end. The two men found some common ground in the twilight of their careers, with each condemning the wave of reform that swept from the West. The stolid Cleveland grumbled at William Jennings Bryan´s nomination in 1896, but the ever-witty Hill put it better. "I am a Democrat still," he joked with reporters. "Very still."[137]

HERBERT HOOVER (R 1920, 1928, 1932)

Hoover was a blunt individualist. He rose from orphanhood to become a millionaire businessman and mining engineer. His practical nature was legendary, earning the nickname, "The Great Engineer." His passion for conservative order persisted through the Depression, when he accused those who offered liberal relief bills of "playing politics with human misery."

Hoover ended up in government partly through boredom. Having amassed his fortune, he sought another challenge. He found it in administering European relief efforts during World War I. It was estimated that he eventually arranged to feed more than 10,000,000 people. Hoover became an adviser to President Woodrow Wilson, attending the peace conference. John Maynard Keynes wrote that Hoover was "the only man who emerged from the ordeal of Paris with an enhanced reputation." Everything he touched seemed to be a success. "He is certainly a wonder," Franklin Roosevelt wrote before 1920. "I wish we could make him President. There couldn´t be a better one."[138] His stint as Secretary of Commerce during the 1920s only seemed to confirm that assessment. Business had never enjoyed such a boom.

Hoover was a logical Republican nominee in 1928, but he found campaigning unenjoyable. "I have never liked the clamor of crowds," he recalled. "I intensely dislike superficial social contacts....I was terrorized at the opening of every speech."[139] The nation soon reciprocated the antipathy as the Depression set in. Hoover retreated to the Waldorf-Astoria after his single term, penning books that kept the individualistic faith in an increasingly bureaucratic world.

JOHN HOSPERS (LIB none)

Hospers wanted to dismantle much of the government he was seeking to lead. The California professor and author was the unofficial philosopher of the new Libertarian party. "Individuals often try to use force against others: murderers, rapists, robbers, burglars, and sundry other criminals. So do groups of individuals like the Mafia," he wrote. "But by far the most numerous and most flagrant violations of personal liberty and individual rights are performed by governments."[140] Largely because of that 1971 book, Libertarianism: A Political Philosophy For Tomorrow, Hospers received the party's Presidential nomination the following year.

CHARLES EVANS HUGHES (R 1908, 1916)

Hughes was always driven by his desire for perfection, and sometimes came startlingly close to his ideal. He scored an amazing 99.5 on his bar exam in 1884, then went on to the outstanding legal career everyone expected. His drive for personal efficiency seemingly knew no bounds. Hughes started growing his famous beard in 1890 merely to save the time it took to go to the barbershop every morning. Not everyone enjoyed his intensity. Theodore Roosevelt, himself not an easy man, dismissed Hughes as a "bearded iceberg."

   Hughes' love was the law. It was as the counsel for state legislative investigations into utilities and the life-insurance business that he came to public attention. Roosevelt encouraged him to run for Governor of New York. He won in 1906. But Hughes was happiest on the Supreme Court, where he served seventeen years in two stretches between 1910 and 1941. He resigned his first term to run for President in 1916. His second tenure finally got him to the podium on inauguration day. As Chief Justice, he administered the oath to Franklin Roosevelt three times. After the ceremony in 1941, he showed a sense of humor that few saw, telling the President, "I had an impish desire to break the solemnity of the occasion by remarking, `Franklin, don't you think this is getting to be a trifle monotonous?'"[141]

CORDELL HULL (D 1928)

Hull struggled for decades to increase conservative influence in the Democratic party. It was the irony of his career that he helped set the stage for liberal dominance. The Tennessee Democrat served twenty-two years in the House of Representatives. While there, he also accepted the task of rebuilding his party following its 1920 trouncing. His chairmanship of the Democratic National Committee was hailed for three years, but his handiwork was lost in the debris of the infamous 1924 convention. His conservative Presidential candidacy in 1928 was nothing but a minor irritation to Al Smith.

Hull's great miscalculation came in 1932. Now a Senator, he sought a candidate to repudiate Smith's liberalism and prevent another setback. Hull's choice was Franklin Roosevelt. FDR made him Secretary of State out of gratitude, a post Hull would hold longer than anyone. But he watched with dismay as the liberal New Deal unfolded. The National Recovery Administration, in particular, made him so angry that he wouldn't mention it in public. Roosevelt encouraged Hull to consider a 1940 Presidential candidacy, but then pulled the rug out by running again himself. His disillusioned deputy hung on until 1944, when he resigned because of exhaustion.

HURBERT HUMPHREY (D 1960, 1968, 1972)

Humphrey would always be remembered for the way he closed his announcement of candidacy in 1968. "Here we are," he declared in his typically ebullient manner, "the way politics ought to be in America, the politics of happiness, the politics of purpose, the politics of joy!"[142]   Joy was somehow always missing at the end of Humphrey's Presidential campaigns. He ran out of money in 1960, had a badly divided party in 1968, and was considered damaged goods by 1972. Old supporters urged him forward again in 1976. He later recalled that he contemplated it for a while, then "I thought: `Why do it? I have a good life.'"[143]   He died two years later.

Critics said Humphrey was too talkative and too naive. Democratic liberals thought of him as their spokesman. Arizona Congressman Morris Udall called him "the premier political stump orator of this generation." His apparent innocence masked a burning ambition. In 1948, while still Mayor of Minneapolis, he quite seriously sought Eleanor Roosevelt's advice on whether he should accept the Vice Presidential nomination if offered. The thought apparently never crossed Harry Truman's mind. That year was still important for Humphrey. He was elected to the Senate in 1948, launching a twenty-three year tour, interrupted by four years as Lyndon Johnson's Vice President. Even through stormy years, he remained the self-styled prophet of the "politics of joy."

ROBERT HUNTER (D 1860)

Hunter was always willing to leap to the defense of his native South. The son of a Virginia planter and a disciple of John Calhoun, he never questioned who was correct as sectional hostility became more common. He wrote in 1860, "If there be a remedy for the catastrophe, which now seems so imminent, it rests chiefly with the North to provide it."[144]

A former Speaker of the House, Hunter entered the Senate in 1847, already doubting that the Union could be saved. He attained prominence as a member of the "Southern Triumvirate." Hunter, Jefferson Davis, and Robert Toombs were ever ready to reciprocate any aspersions cast by Northern Senators. Words were useless after Fort Sumter. Hunter willingly advocated secession, wrongly insisting the Union would not resist "unless madness ruled the hour and passion raged where reason ought to govern."[145] He served as Confederate Secretary of State and as a Senator. After the war, he was Virginia´s Treasurer for six years.

ANDREW JACKSON (DR 1824, 1828, D 1832)

Jackson fought politicians, the wealthy, and land barons all his career. Yet he was each of those things. The "hero of the common man" was actually a lawyer who served as a judge and as a member of the House of Representatives and the Senate. He speculated in land, enabling him to live comfortably. His large estate, "The Hermitage," sat on the outskirts of Nashville.

But farmers and laborers remembered Jackson as the "Hero of New Orleans," the man who repulsed the British at the close of the War of 1812. They admired him for his decisiveness, a quality he had in abundance. It was in evidence after a confrontation with South Carolina had been averted during his Presidency. "I thought I would have to hang some of [South Carolina´s leaders]," he wrote, "and I would have done it."[146] Jackson relied on the support of average Americans for his bold moves. He knew it was the source of his political strength. After lawmakers rejected a number of his early appointments, he snapped, "Let Congress go home and the people will teach them the consequence of neglecting my measures and opposing my nominations."[147] Jackson framed issues, such as the recharter of the National Bank, as tests of popular democracy. But he was capable of ignoring democratic principles when necessary, as in forcing the nomination of Martin Van Buren as his replacement. He left office as revered as when he entered. An opponent was probably correct in guessing that if he wanted, Jackson could have been President for life.

HENRY JACKSON (D 1972, 1976)

Jackson was a New Deal liberal who shifted to the right during his forty-two years in Congress: twelve in the House, thirty in the Senate. His opposition to Senator Joseph McCarthy during televised hearings in 1954 drew him the enmity of conservatives. But Jackson drifted increasingly into their camp in the 1960s, as he became one of the last Democratic Senators to back the Vietnam War. Cynics said Jackson´s strong defense posture stemmed from the presence of a large contractor in his state of Washington. He was ridiculed as "the Senator from Boeing." But Republican President Richard Nixon was so impressed that he asked Jackson to be his Secretary of Defense in 1969. The Democrat declined.

Jackson´s two Presidential candidacies were backed by conservative Democrats and those who believed in strong American support for Israel. But his lack of charisma was fatal in the television age. One national magazine insisted Jackson´s speaking style "would put a No-Doz addict to sleep."

JESSE JACKSON (D 1984)

"I was born to lead," Jackson said in a 1975 interview. The Baptist minister spent most of his career in the forefront of the civil rights movement. He came to the attention of Martin Luther King Jr. during the 1965 march on Selma, Alabama. King placed Jackson in charge of Operation Breadbasket, a self-help program run by the Southern Christian Leadership Conference in Chicago. He broke away from the SCLC after King´s assassination, creating PUSH: People United to Save Humanity.

Jackson´s 1984 Presidential candidacy was not welcomed by all of his fellow blacks. "Jesse, first of all, has no experience," said Detroit Mayor Coleman Young. "And he has no platform. And he has no chance. As a politician, he´s out of his league."[148] That last assessment had been true of Jackson´s one previous attempt for elective office. He was thrown off the ballot in the 1971 race for Mayor of Chicago on a technicality. But 1984 was a different story. Jackson´s intensity spread contagiously among minority voters. He spoke with religious fervor, often in rhyme. He implored the young to put "hope in their brains, not dope in their veins." Jackson began the year as an unknown political entity, but ended it as a power in the national Democratic party.

ARTHUR JAMES (R 1940)

James did in Pennsylvania what the Liberty League and conservative Republicans lunged to do in Washington. The corporation lawyer was elected Governor in 1938, an implied repudiation of the state´s Little New Deal, a program on the Roosevelt model. James had declared in his campaign that he intended to "make a bonfire of all the laws passed by the 1937 legislature."[149] He did his best, scaling back state departments, cutting 2,000 jobs, reducing relief appropriations, and watering down the powers of the state labor relations board.

James became a favorite of the corporate world with such tactics, as well as his pledge to "bring business back to Pennsylvania." His Presidential effort was bankrolled by multimillionaire oil man Joseph Pew. After his term as Governor, James quietly went back to his law practice.

THOMAS JEFFERSON (DR 1796, 1800, 1804)

Jefferson was the Renaissance man among the Founding Fathers. James Madison praised him as "a luminary of

Science, as a votary of liberty, as a model of patriotism, and as a benefactor of human kind."[150] The Sage of Monticello had seemingly hundreds of interests outside of government. He was an American pioneer in many sciences, a philosopher, a planter, an architect, and a bibliophile. His personal collection formed the core of the Library of Congress.

His contemporaries sometimes wondered why the shy Jefferson, with his many talents, would adopt the gregarious profession of politics. A poor public speaker, he was at his best with the pen. He had little to say in the Continental Congress, but when it came time to draft the Declaration of Independence, he did most of the work. He went on to serve as Governor of Virginia, Minister to France, and Secretary of State. Despite all of his protests against political parties, he was the spokesman for the new Democratic-Republicans. Many Federalists feared him as an undisciplined radical, but fellow Virginian John Marshall was more charitable. "The democrats are divided into speculative theorists and absolute terrorists," he huffed. "With the latter, I am not disposed to class Mr. Jefferson."[151]

Jefferson was not sorry to leave the White House for his beloved Monticello after two terms. He made no mention of the Presidency when drafting his epitaph, citing instead his writing of the Declaration and the Virginia Statute for Religious Freedom, and his founding of the University of Virginia.

CHARLES JENKINS (D 1872)

Jenkins began to fight when the rest of the South was giving up. The Georgian was a Union Whig during his fifteen years in the state legislature before the Civil War. After losing a race for Governor, he was appointed to the State Supreme Court. He opposed secession, but stayed at his post through Appomattox. The job of picking up the pieces fell to him in 1865, with his election as civilian Governor. "The smoke of a hundred battles does not vanish in a moment," he promised in his inaugural address. "But the atmosphere will clear ere long."[152]

Jenkins soon lost his optimism, falling out with military Reconstruction officials. He tried to press a case against them in the U.S. Supreme Court, but was rebuffed. General George Meade finally had his fill by 1868, removing Jenkins from office. "Had I adequate force, I would resist you to the last extremity!" Jenkins declared.[153] He did what he could, stealing state documents and hiding the state seal, all to the applause of unregenerate Southerners. He didn't give back the seal until the return of civilian rule in 1872.

ANDREW JOHNSON (D 1868)

Johnson compensated for his lack of formal schooling with a powerful speaking style and a firm adherence to his beliefs.

Once a tailor's apprentice, he always spoke for the common man. Comparisons to a fellow Tennessean, Andrew Jackson, were not uncommon. Johnson commanded fierce loyalty from voters the same way Old Hickory had. He served in the House of Representatives and as Governor before his election to the Senate on the eve of the Civil War.

Johnson stunned the nation shortly after South Carolina seceded. "I am unwilling voluntarily to walk out of the Union," he thundered.[154] He was the only Southern Senator to keep his seat, scorned by the others as a traitor. Abraham Lincoln rewarded his loyalty by appointing him Military Governor of Tennessee, then recalling him to be his second Vice President.

Johnson's obstinacy quickly irritated the Radical Republicans. As President he insisted on lenient Reconstruction. Two Congressmen went to the White House to urge him to compromise, but one later remembered, "He received us politely enough, and without mincing any words, he gave us to understand that we were on a fool's errand and that he would not yield."[155] Neither would the Radicals, falling just one vote short in the Senate of convicting Johnson of impeachable offenses. Many of the Tennessean's avowed enemies were still in the Senate when he returned there in 1875, serving five months before his death.

HIRAM JOHNSON (R 1920, 1924)

Johnson advanced in politics by refusing to honor his father. The two were on opposite sides of the key issue in California at the turn of the century. The elder Johnson was a lawyer for the powerful Southern Pacific Railroad. The son was elected Governor on the slogan, "Kick the Southern Pacific out of politics!" The two were estranged ever after.

Johnson brought progressive government to California. He declared he was fighting "against the interests and the system, and for true democracy." Californians were given a direct voice in their government through his sponsorship of the initiative and referendum. Commitment to these reforms exceeded Johnson's loyalty to the Republican party. He ran for Vice President as a Progressive in 1912, shunned the GOP ticket in 1916, and later endorsed Franklin Roosevelt for President.

Johnson was elected to the Senate in 1916, still a leading progressive. But in the 1930s, he veered toward conservatism and isolationism. His already legendary irritability seemed to get worse. "When a man opposes me, I do not become angry at him. On the next issue, he may agree with me," Idaho Senator William Borah once commented. "When a man opposes Johnson, he hates him."[156]

JOHN JOHNSON (D 1908)

Johnson's career as a Democrat was testimony to the power of the press. As a 25-year-old, he became editor and half-owner of the Saint Peter, Minnesota, _Herald_. There were four papers in town. Three were Republican, as was Johnson. The _Herald_ was traditionally Democratic. Since Johnson's main interest was in making a living, he became a Democrat, too. There weren't very many in Minnesota in the late 19th Century.

The young editor's business helped him make contacts all over the state. He was personable and a witty public speaker. The Minnesota Publishers Association made him its president in 1893. Democrats soon convinced him to run for the state legislature and then, in 1904, for Governor. He was elected because of a serious Republican schism, realistically expecting to serve only one term. "I'll be back in two years," he told his colleagues at the _Herald_. "Try to keep the subscribers in line, and don't let the ads get away from you."[157] His vibrant personality captivated Minnesotans. He was twice reelected. Johnson was not well-known when he ran for President in 1908, but he was determined to make a full-scale campaign in 1912. Many thought he had an excellent chance, one taken away by his sudden death in 1909.

LYNDON JOHNSON (D 1956, 1960, 1964, 1968)

Johnson was a Congressional aide when he decided he deserved to be a member of the House himself. He was intoxicated by Washington. "And there was the _smell_ of power," he later recalled. "It's got an odor, you know, power I mean."[158] He was elected to the House in 1937, off on a pursuit of power for the next three decades. He spent eleven years as a Congressman, then was elevated to the Senate in 1948, winning the crucial Democratic primary by only 87 votes. Johnson was henceforth known as "Landslide Lyndon."

The new Texas Senator quickly demonstrated a genius for legislative wheeling and dealing. His Democratic colleagues made him the youngest floor leader in history in 1953. Johnson's word became absolute law in the Senate, even as he often brought the Democrats in line behind Republican President Dwight Eisenhower. He insisted, "I have never agreed with the statement that it is the business of the opposition to oppose."[159] Liberals disagreed, becoming further horrified when Johnson was chosen as John Kennedy's Vice President. They viewed him as a conservative infiltrator on the New Frontier.

Johnson later proved his liberalism with his Great Society, the dying gasp of the New Deal spirit. But the Vietnam War destroyed his administration. Protesters chanted, "Hey, hey, LBJ, how many kids did you kill today?" The President had scored one of the great landslides in history in 1964, but felt national discord sapping his beloved power. He declined to seek another term in 1968, retiring to his ranch.

RICHARD JOHNSON (D 1844)

Johnson's career was sedately respectable on the surface: twenty years in the House and ten in the Senate, capped by a term as Vice President. But his contemporaries considered him one of the true eccentrics of his age.

Johnson's larger-than-life reputation dated from the Battle of the Thames in the War of 1812. The Indian, Tecumseh, fought for the British. It was never determined who killed him, but Johnson quickly claimed the honor. His supporters solidified the legend in later political campaigns, chanting, "Rumpsey, Dumpsey, Rumpsey, Dumpsey, Colonel Johnson killed Tecumseh." The Kentuckian shocked the nation with another campaign technique. He actually went on a national tour in 1843 to drum up support for his Presidential aspirations, the first pre-convention stumping by a contender. One Indiana Democrat wrote that Johnson always desperately needed an audience: "I doubt whether he would be more happy in the full possession of the Executive Chair, than he is in stating his prospects."[160]

Critics considered Johnson's biggest transgression his fathering of two daughters by a mulatto mistress. The United States Telegraph called her "a jet-black, thick-lipped, odoriferous negro wench, by whom he has reared a family of children whom he has endeavored to force upon society as equals."[161] His domestic situation cost him what should have been a natural Southern base of support.

WALTER JONES (ID none)

Jones was proud of his father, a Confederate veteran whom he said carried a flag of truce from Robert E. Lee to Ulysses Grant at Appomattox. His father went on to become Governor of Alabama, but Jones concentrated on a different branch of government. He spent more than four decades as an Alabama Circuit Court Judge.

Jones' decisions upheld the white establishment in his state. He once issued an order banning the NAACP from doing business in Alabama. A Democratic elector recognized his service in 1956 by casting a symbolic vote for Jones. His fellow Alabama electors argued that he was obligated to vote for Adlai Stevenson. "I have fulfilled my obligations to the people of Alabama," the renegade replied. "I'm talking about the white people."[162]

ESTES KEFAUVER (D 1952, 1956)

Kefauver always did things his own way, a trait that gained attention, but also cost him any chance for the Presidency. The Tennessean's bullheadedness first came to national notice in 1948. A nine-year veteran of the House, he ran for the Senate against the handpicked candidate of state Democratic boss Edward Crump. "I may be a pet coon, but I ain't Mr. Crump's pet coon," Kefauver said.[163] A coonskin cap was his symbol as he marched to an upset win.

Kefauver obstinately took liberal stands on civil rights, hurting him badly in his native South. Florida Senator George Smathers once explained his refusal to back Kefauver for President, "The South is always more apt to go for a Northerner who doesn´t know any better than for a Southerner who should know better, but doesn´t."[164]

Democratic leaders also thought Kefauver should have known better than to undertake a nationwide committee probe of organized crime in 1950-51. His panel exposed serious problems in fourteen cities, most of them run by Democratic machines. Many of the hearings were televised, drawing enormous audiences. Con Edison had to add a generator in New York City because of all the TV sets being used. The hearings even won an Emmy, which Kefauver accepted by telephone from New Hampshire, already in his first Presidential campaign. Party bosses and Southerners combined to twice prevent his nomination, despite his strong primary performances.

EDWARD KENNEDY (D 1980)

Kennedy´s future course was set on the night in 1960 that his brother, John, was elected President. Young Edward had campaigned for his brother in the West and had become fond of the region. He later mused that if John had lost, he might have moved beyond the Mississippi. But his brother won and Edward Kennedy was groomed to replace him in the Senate from Massachusetts. "If your name was simply Edward Moore instead of Edward Moore Kennedy, your candidacy would be a joke," shouted his opponent in the 1962 Democratic primary.[165] But Kennedy won, entering the Senate at the youngest permissible age of thirty.

The assassinations of John and Robert Kennedy elevated Edward to the status of champion of those who yearned for a return to the New Frontier. He acknowledged picking up a "fallen standard" and was mentioned for every Democratic nomination from 1968 on. But an infamous accident on Chappaquiddick Island in 1969 cast a permanent shadow on his career. The death of a young woman and Kennedy´s failure to report the fatality for nine hours raised serious questions. The Senator subsequently seemed willing to forgo higher office. "[People] say, `Well, you have to be spending all your time worrying about [being President],´" Kennedy told an interviewer in the 1970s. "I don´t. I enjoy the work that I´m involved in and what I´m doing."[166] Only in 1980 did he seek the nomination his brothers had chased in earlier days.

JOHN KENNEDY (D 1960)

Kennedy was the youngest elected President, bringing such grace to the White House that his idolaters were moved to compare his administration to Camelot. His past did have a storybook quality: heir to a fortune, a war hero, a Congressman at the age of 29, a Senator at 35 after unseating the well-known Henry Cabot Lodge, a contender for Vice President at 39, winner of a Pulitzer Prize. Kennedy enhanced his luster with a sparkling wit. Asked how he attained brief fame in the Navy, he replied, "It was involuntary. They sank my boat."[167] A reporter suggested in 1962 that the business world was winning its war of words with the liberal President, that it had him where it wanted him. Kennedy laughed back, "I can't believe I'm where business, big business, wants me."[168]

But critics wondered if there was anything below the surface. They pointed out that Kennedy's record as a lawmaker was average at best. His refusal to condemn the Red-baiting of Joseph McCarthy rankled many liberals. Eleanor Roosevelt, noting that Kennedy's award-winning book was <u>Profiles In Courage</u>, said the White House should not go to "someone who understands what courage is and admires it, but has not quite the independence to have it."[169] Kennedy, who always called himself "an idealist without illusions," later proved his mettle during the Cuban missile crisis in 1962. Hie assassination a year later spawned an enduring myth.

ROBERT KENNEDY (D 1968)

John Kennedy hoped to mute the cries of outrage he knew would greet the appointment of his brother, Robert, as Attorney General. He joked, "I think I'll open the front door of the Georgetown house some morning about 2 a.m., look up and down the street, and if there's no one there, I'll whisper, `It's Bobby.'"[170] But Robert Kennedy was willing to face the critics. He was already accustomed to controversy, having served as counsel to Senate committees investigating Communism and labor racketeering. He was his brother's closest adviser in the White House.

Robert Kennedy emerged as a political figure after John's assassination. Elected a Senator from New York, he became a leading critic of the Vietnam War. His campaign speeches were more searing and emotional than his brother's. He always ended with a paraphrase of George Bernard Shaw: "Some men see things as they are and say, `Why?' I dream things that never were and say, `Why not?'" Reporters came to depend on that passage in 1968 as their signal to be ready to move to the next stop. Kennedy didn't let them down, once shouting in a sudden rainstorm, "As George Bernard Shaw once said....Run for the buses!"[171]

ROBERT KERR (D 1952)

Kerr was not shy of boasting in his early years that he wanted three things: a family, a million dollars, and to be Governor of Oklahoma. Those dreams seemed only to mock him in the early 1920s. His wife and three children died. His wholesale produce business burned. The young man was wiped out.

Kerr painstakingly rebuilt his life. He remarried. With his brother-in-law, he launched a drilling company. It grew into the mammoth Kerr-McGee Oil Industries. Kerr was now able to make large contributions to the state Democratic party, which in turn nominated him for Governor. He attained the final of his three goals in 1942. He loved to tell constituents, "I´m just like you, only I struck oil."

Kerr moved on to the Senate in 1948. He quickly became a conservative power, repelling liberals with his staunch support of the oil and gas industries. "If Oklahomans didn´t like it," he insisted, "they wouldn´t elect me."[172] His connections had a much different impact on the national level, killing his chances of becoming President. Kerr satisfied himself with his considerable influence, wielded without a formal leadership post. He loved it when a reporter wrote of a bill in 1963, "Mr. Kennedy asked; Mr. Kerr decided."[173]

RUFUS KING (F 1816)

"You never heard such a speaker," Daniel Webster, no slouch himself, once wrote of King. "In strength, and dignity, and fire; in ease, in natural effect, and gesture as well as in matter, he is unequalled."[174] King was widely considered the most eloquent debater at the Constitutional Convention. He was an eager signer of the document it created. It was the start of a career in which he was a spokesman for an ever-decreasing band of Federalists.

King was a member of the first Senate, quickly emerging as a leading defender of Alexander Hamilton´s blueprints for a strong federal government. After seven years as Minister to Great Britain and two unsuccessful runs for Vice President, King returned to the Senate during the War of 1812, a conflict he condemned as "a war of party, and not of the country." Unlike most Federalists, he eventually supported the war effort when it degenerated into a struggle of self-defense. The end of the war saw his party in the throes of a fatal illness, but King agreed to carry its standard in 1816. A New England Federalist, Harrison Gray Otis, wrote him in gratitude a few years later, "Whoever writes your epitaph...may be able to say that you continued many years at your post, the last of the Romans."[175]

FRANK KNOX (R 1936)

Knox was a member of the famed Rough Riders, but he missed his unit´s charge up San Juan Hill. He wrote home that he got separated in the battle, "but I joined a troop of the Tenth Cavalry, colored, and for a time fought with them shoulder to shoulder....I must say that I never saw braver men anywhere."[176] Not to say that Knox thought less of his outfit´s leader, Theodore Roosevelt. He wrote editorials vigorously supporting the new President after returning to his job as an editor in Michigan. Knox rose to be chairman of the state Republican party, but his backing of Roosevelt´s 1912 Progressive party cost him his influence.

Knox followed the itinerant life of a journalist after the collapse of his Michigan empire: papers in New Hampshire and Boston, two years as general manager of the Hearst chain, then his purchase of the Chicago Daily News. He became conservative over the years and turned the Daily News into a leading anti-New Deal organ. Knox dreamed of using his pen as an instrument for the 1936 Republican nomination, but settled for being Alfred Landon´s running mate. Four years later, he was named Secretary of the Navy by the man he once vilified, Franklin Roosevelt.

PHILANDER KNOX (R 1908)

Knox was a shrewd lawyer who was eventually recognized as one of the best in the country. Most of his clients were large corporations, such as the Carnegie Steel Company. He shared the conservative politics of the businessmen he represented, a quality that convinced William McKinley to appoint him Attorney General in 1901.

Knox argued trust-busting suits for Theodore Roosevelt, but he was more comfortable in the relatively sedate administration of William Howard Taft, whom he served as Secretary of State. He also put in two stretches as a Senator from Pennsylvania. His spadework was influential in the successful fight to keep the United States out of the League of Nations.

Conservative Republicans admired Knox for his consistent support of their principles, but members of the progressive wing grew to greatly dislike him. Hiram Johnson sputtered after Roosevelt´s funeral that Knox had "hated Roosevelt as mediocrity and cowardice always hate real ability and fearless courage."[177]

ROBERT LA FOLLETTE (R 1912, 1916, P 1924)

La Follette was the firebrand of the progressive movement, a grim opponent of what he once called a "gang of corporation knaves." His refusal to follow the dictates of political bosses was evident from his very first race. He was elected District Attorney at 25 against the wishes of the Republican machine in Madison, Wisconsin. Then came three terms in Congress, followed by two failures to buck the GOP establishment to be elected Governor.

La Follette finally triumphed on his third try in 1900. As Governor, he quickly attained national prominence for his "Wisconsin Idea," the forerunner of progressivism. He won legislative approval of primary elections, regulatory commissions, and tax reform. The man known as "Fighting Bob" moved to the Senate in 1906, where he was a thorn in the side of the conservative Republican leadership for a generation. "The supreme issue," he declared, "is the encroachment of the powerful few upon the rights of the many."[178] It was an unusual stand for a member of what was considered the nation´s business party. He received additional heat for his vote against American entrance in World War I. One colleague declared on the floor that La Follette belonged either in Germany or in jail. After the war, despairing of ever turning the GOP in a more liberal direction, La Follette sought the Presidency on the ticket of the Progressive party.

ALFRED LANDON (R 1936)

Landon's brief fling with fame came for the classic reason: he was in the right place at the right time. Kansas was the most solidly Republican state on the plains during the Depression. Landon's election as its Governor would normally have caused nary a stir across the country. But in 1932, he was the only Republican Governor elected west of the Mississippi. He received a small boost shortly before the crucial primary that year from the publicity given the birth of his daughter, Nancy. Two years later, without such assistance, he was nationally known, the only Republican Governor reelected anywhere.

Landon was an unassuming man, a self-made millionaire in the oil business. He had a monotonous speaking delivery and admitted he was taken aback by his sudden elevation to the 1936 Republican nomination. He said he felt "like the country boy going to take a job in Toronto for the first time."[179] On election night, having proven that his magic in Kansas didn't carry nationally, Landon beckoned his wife to join him in front of a photographer. "Come on, Mother, and get your picture took," he said. "It will be the last chance."[180] But Landon lived for many more pictures. He saw his daughter twice elected to the Senate.

JOSEPH LANE (D 1852)

Lane seemed out of place in the West as the Civil War neared. The Senator from Oregon was one of the most vociferous defenders of Southern rights. His feelings could be partly explained by the fact that he was raised in North Carolina and Kentucky. He went West only after serving as a Senator from Indiana and a general in the Mexican War. President James Polk named him Territorial Governor of Oregon in 1848. That latter experience only strengthened Lane's belief that Congress had no right to decide the fate of slavery in the territories. "Slavery is a thing that will regulate itself," he said. "Climate, soil, products, commerce, business, profit on investments: these are the things that must settle the question of slavery or no slavery."[181]

Lane entered the Senate when Oregon became a state. Southerners considered him such a strong ally that he was nominated for Vice President on the Southern Democratic ticket in 1860. "If we will not deal fairly by our Southern friends," he said that year in the Senate, "for God's sake, let them, if they must go, depart in peace."[182] Lane soon retired to Oregon, but one of his sons kept the faith. He resigned from West Point to enlist in the Confederate Army.

FRANK LAUSCHE (D 1956)

Lausche always ran as a Democrat, but leaders of his own party often tried as hard as the Republicans to defeat him. The five-term Governor and two-term Senator from Ohio cared nothing about party labels. He irritated Democratic officials with his conservatism and apostasy. Lausche gave tacit support to the 1950 reelection campaign of Republican Senator Robert Taft, then said a few years later that he had "a certain affinity" for President Dwight Eisenhower. "My strength has been that no one has been able to dictate to me," Lausche said in brushing off criticism from fellow Democrats. "Bankers on down to labor leaders, strip miners, truckers, the utilities, and the whole rest of them: I can tell them all to go to hell except the people whom I´ve tried to represent."[183]

Lausche remained popular with those common people, in no small part due to his speaking ability. One national magazine called him "a great orator, a spellbinder of the William Jennings Bryan tradition." But the dogged Democratic party leadership caught up to him. It recommended his defeat in the 1968 Senatorial primary and finally succeeded in sending Lausche to retirement.

WILLIAM LEMKE (U 1936)

Lemke labeled himself a progressive in the mold of Robert La Follette, but his critics considered him a dangerous radical. He appeared harmless, with an artificial eye, a face pockmarked from smallpox, and a monotonous speaking style. But the things he said bothered conservatives and businessmen. "Because he was unorganized, the farmer has been made the financial shock absorber," Lemke once said. "He fed the nation and he lost his home."[184] The North Dakotan aimed to harness the political power of agrarian discontent. He was one of the leaders of his state´s Nonpartisan League, which rose to power during World War I. It passed a legislative program that many felt verged on socialism.

The NPL faded, but Lemke revived his career in 1932, being elected to Congress as a Republican. He hailed Franklin Roosevelt´s inaugural address as "the greatest speech ever made by a President." But it soon became evident the New Deal didn´t want his advice. Lemke complained, "These New York professors do not understand the agricultural problem of the nation."[185] He was further alienated when Roosevelt called Lemke´s bill to allow refinancing of farm mortgages "wild legislation." The Congressman´s opposition as the Union party´s nominee resulted, but he also retained his seat in the House as a Republican until his death.

ABRAHAM LINCOLN (R 1860, 1864)

Legend portrays Lincoln as a diamond in the rough, a man who lived in obscurity until his unexpected elevation to the Presidency. Nothing is further from the truth. He was a lawyer with a statewide reputation, a man who rose to be minority leader of the Whigs in the Illinois legislature, a one-term Congressman, and an orator who was in demand as far away as New York by 1860. Lincoln's law partner remembered him as a calculating politician. "His ambition was a little engine that knew no rest," wrote William Herndon.[186] The campaign of 1860 provided ample proof. Far from his supposedly aloof nature, Lincoln actively sought the Presidency. He admitted well before the Republican con-vention, "The taste is in my mouth a little."[187] It was a major understatement.

Lincoln owed much of his later success to Stephen Douglas. It was his opposition to Douglas' Kansas-Nebraska Act that inspired Lincoln to end his self-imposed political retirement. And it was the classic Lincoln-Douglas debates in the 1858 Senate campaign that made the Republican a national figure. Douglas won the election, but he conceded that his opponent was "the best stump speaker, with his droll ways and dry jokes, in the West."[188]

Lincoln was an unpopular President for much of his tenure. The Civil War went badly. Democrats called him a dictator for his strong exercise of wartime powers. But a string of Union victories in late 1864 turned things around. Lincoln's assassination in 1865 ensured martyrdom. Secretary of War Edwin Stanton intoned, "Now he belongs to the ages."

HENRY CABOT LODGE (R 1964)

Lodge began in the footsteps of his namesake, his famous grandfather who masterminded the destruction of Woodrow Wilson's plans for the League of Nations. The younger Massachusetts Republican was first elected in 1936 to the Senate, where he generally toed the expected isolationist line. But service in World War II changed Lodge. He returned with an outlook that would have horrified his grandfather. Now an internationalist, he called the fledgling United Nations "our best hope." Lodge became Dwight Eisenhower's UN Ambassador after losing his Senate reelection bid to John Kennedy in 1952.

Lodge was not forgotten as he held diplomatic posts in New York and South Vietnam. Many felt his moderate views and political experience were exactly what the Republicans needed in a Presidential candidate. Eisenhower said of Lodge, "He talks more common sense than anyone."[189] But two factors worked against any candidacy. One was Lodge's candor. He shocked Republicans in 1960 when, as the party's Vice Presidential nominee, he pledged that a black would be named to Richard Nixon's Cabinet. The other consideration was more important. Lodge never showed any real interest in the White House.

JOHN LOGAN (R 1884)

The Civil War transformed Logan from an obscure Democratic Congressman to a Republican war hero. The Illinois native had served two terms in the House when he joined the Union Army as a colonel. He proved to be one of the best volunteer soldiers the North had. William Tecumseh Sherman praised Logan as "perfect in combat." Rising to become a major-general, he briefly commanded the Army of the Tennessee. But politics was always on his mind, a trait that annoyed some of his fellow officers. There were even rumors that Logan convinced artists to give him prominent display in the enormous cyclorama later painted of the Battle of Atlanta. He thought the sight of him galloping forward, waving his black felt hat, might win votes.

Logan switched to the GOP after the war, serving as a Congressman, Senator, and the 1884 Vice Presidential nominee. He never failed to emphasize his war record, while showing a continuing interest in veterans´ affairs. Logan was among the founders of the Grand Army of the Republic. He served three times as its president.

FRANK LOWDEN (R 1920, 1928)

Lowden seemed to be different men in his two tries for the Presidency. The Illinois Republican built up to his 1920 candidacy by amassing solidly conservative credentials. Marrying George Pullman´s daughter, he became the manager of several of the sleeping-car czar´s enterprises. Lowden served two terms in the House of Representatives, then was elected Governor in 1916. He earned national praise for abolishing or consolidating 125 state boards and commissions. He left a $15,000,000 surplus after a single term.

Lowden drifted from the Republican mainstream after 1920. He astounded party leaders by rejecting a series of job offers: Secretary of the Navy, Ambassador to Great Britain, the 1924 Vice Presidential nomination. Turning attention instead to his farms in seven states, Lowden became alarmed by the agricultural depression of the mid-1920s. He was an outspoken supporter of the defeated McNary-Haugen bill, a forerunner of later New Deal measures. Lowden by 1928 was considered an agrarian radical, as he again sought the Republican nomination. He refused to support Herbert Hoover in the fall, predicting a depression would hit during his administration.

DOUGLAS MacARTHUR (R 1944)

MacArthur always seemed larger than life. His troops remembered his daring tactics and distinctive style of dress as a colonel in World War I. The nation watched as he rolled tanks through downtown Washington in 1932 to disperse the Bonus Army, a ragtag collection of ex-servicemen and their families. The Allies thrilled to his declaration, "I shall return," on his departure from the Philippines in 1942, a promise made good two-and-a-half years later.

MacArthur held almost every top military position: superintendent of West Point, Army Chief of Staff, commander of U.S. forces in the Far East, commander again in Korea. But he coveted the White House, actively encouraging his conservative supporters back home. MacArthur naturally assumed others had motivations similar to his. When Dwight Eisenhower honestly told him after World War II that he had no interest in the Presidency, MacArthur just nodded. "That's the way to play it, Ike," he agreed.[190]

MacArthur's flamboyance and egotism were his undoing. Harry Truman got an early taste after replacing Franklin Roosevelt. He encouraged the General to return home to be honored for his war performance, but MacArthur refused. "If I returned for only a few weeks," he explained to a subordinate, "word would spread through the Pacific that the United States is abandoning the Orient."[191] Even many Republicans doubted an ego that large would fit in the Oval Office. Truman, after enduring six years of such insolence, recalled MacArthur from Korea in 1951.

JAMES MADISON (DR 1808, 1812)

Madison did as much as anyone to create the Democratic-Republican party, but his commitment to the cause was never pure enough for many of its followers. They remembered his early leanings toward Federalism, particularly evident in his defense of strong government at the 1787 Constitutional Convention. Some called Madison "the father of the Constitution," but he insisted it had been a group effort. "You give me a credit to which I have no claim...," he wrote one idolater. "This was not like the fabled goddess of wisdom the offspring of a single brain. It ought to be regarded as the work of many heads and many hands."[192]

Madison eventually rebelled against Alexander Hamilton's financial program, becoming the focus of the coalescing opposition in Congress. Thomas Jefferson was among those who expected Madison to be the first Democratic-Republican Presidential candidate. He wrote his friend in 1794, "There I should rejoice to see you; I hope I may say, I shall rejoice to see you."[193] But Jefferson was the first. Madison was his Secretary of State, then his successor in the White House. Not all Democratic-Republicans were pleased with his policies, particularly his support for protective tariffs and the new Second Bank of the United States. John Randolph groused that things hadn't changed. Madison, he complained, still "out-Hamiltons Alexander Hamilton."

WILLIE PERSON MANGUM (IW 1836)

Mangum believed so strongly in Andrew Jackson that he cast an electoral vote for Old Hickory in 1828. Two years later, he was elected to the Senate from North Carolina, pledging to give solid support to the President's policies. It was a promise Mangum did not keep. He became a leading critic of Jackson within four years.

The nullification crisis in South Carolina triggered the split. Mangum disagreed with state officials who contended they could ignore offensive federal laws, but he also accused the President of overreacting by preparing for military action. Calling Jackson's plan "violent and dangerous in its principles," Mangum wrote he "would sooner resign than sanction the mad project of the administration."[194]   He switched to the Whigs in 1834, serving in the Senate until 1853 with one hiatus. Although a strong orator, he rarely spoke from the floor. Mangum rose to be President pro tem of the Senate before leaving office.

WILLIAM MARCY (D 1852)

Marcy served in high office for more than two decades, but he is perhaps best remembered for adding "spoils system" to the American political lexicon. The New Yorker was a founding member of his state's famed Democratic machine, the Albany Regency, headed by Martin Van Buren. Marcy was a Senator in 1832 when Van Buren came under attack for his distribution of patronage in New York. Critics said his activities were unbecoming to a man nominated to be Minister to Great Britain. "It may be, sir, that the politicians of the United States are not so fastidious as some gentlemen are, as to disclosing the principles on which they act," Marcy thundered. "They see nothing wrong in the rule that to the victor belong the spoils of the enemy!"[195]   Van Buren lost the subsequent vote, but a saying was born.

Besides his service in the Senate, Marcy was also Governor of New York, Secretary of War, and Secretary of State. The Presidency escaped him, as it did another leading contemporary. A friend wrote Marcy that he saw a parallel, "You labour under one of Mr. Webster's difficulties, that you are almost universally conceded to be the ablest man among the candidates."[196]

JOSEPH MARTIN (R 1940)

Martin emerged as a powerful Republican while his party was suffering from a fissure between moderates and conservatives. But the Massachusetts Congressman avoided taking sides in the dispute. An amiable man, he thought personality was more important than ideology. "If the voters meet you, and like you," he once advised, "they don't worry too much about the issues."[197] It was a philosophy that helped him bridge the intraparty gap. Martin served as House Minority Leader, then Speaker for four years. He chaired every Republican convention from 1940 to 1956.

Martin's talents seemed best suited for political management on the national scale. Besides his forty-two years in Congress, he headed the Republican National Committee from 1940 to 1942 and was high in party councils for decades. But Martin's bland rhetoric, so suited for handling the gavel or swinging the backroom deal, smothered his Presidential dreams. Republican delegates waged ideological war when choosing a nominee in those years. They had little interest in selecting a noncombatant.

WILLIAM GIBBS McADOO (D 1920, 1924)

Transportation systems were three times influential in McAdoo's rise from being a Tennessee speculator to being a Presidential prospect. The first instance was a Chattanooga streetcar venture that went bankrupt, dragging him to the same status. Needing a large amount of money to pay his debts, McAdoo headed for the big city, New York. He often crossed the Hudson River for his law practice, growing increasingly irritated by the costly, twenty-minute ferry trips. McAdoo organized a company that completed the first Holland Tunnel in 1904, cutting twelve minutes off the passage and making him rich and famous. His third transit-related episode occurred on a train platform five years later. McAdoo met a fellow ticketholder, Woodrow Wilson.

McAdoo's career was testimony to his statement, "I like movement and change...to reshape old forces and worn-out ideals into new and dynamic forms."[198] He was a forceful Secretary of the Treasury, one of Wilson's key advisers. He was also the President's son-in-law after 1914. McAdoo's energy made him an attractive candidate to succeed his wife's father. He moved to California in 1922 to increase his appeal to Southern and Western Democrats. But he failed to make headway in the turbulent politics of the 1920s. McAdoo's only political success came in 1932, when he was elected to his single term in the Senate.

EUGENE McCARTHY (D 1968)

McCarthy was a proven votegetter in his native Minnesota, but swam a bit outside of the national political mainstream. He was studious, a former economics professor who was interested in poetry. Democratic leaders often had difficulty in getting along with or even understanding him. Lyndon Johnson gave long thought to making McCarthy his running mate in 1964, but rejected the idea. "There's something sort of stuck up about Gene," he was quoted as saying. "You get the impression that he's got a special pipeline to God and that they talk only Latin to each other."[199]

McCarthy entered politics as part of the brigade of fresh faces led by Hubert Humphrey that revitalized Minnesota's Democratic-Farmer-Labor party. He served ten years in the House and twelve in the Senate. McCarthy was pegged by Washington insiders as a bright newcomer. He warned against political cynicism in a 1954 article, saying "it...eats away the will to attack difficult political problems."[200] But critics later charged that he ignored his own advice. A sharp edge crept into McCarthy's rhetoric in the 1960s, prominently in his 1968 Democratic antiwar crusade. It was even more evident in his independent Presidential candidacy eight years later.

GEORGE McCLELLAN (D 1864)

McClellan's rise to national prominence was truly meteoric. He was the president of the Ohio and Mississippi Railroad in

1860, convinced that his military career was forever behind him. A year later, he was General-in-Chief of the Union Army. He wrote his wife that people were already speaking of him as Presidential material. "By some strange operation of magic, I seem to have become the power of the land," he told her.[201]

McClellan entered the war in charge of the Ohio Volunteers. He scored early victories in western Virginia that were not particularly impressive, but were stunning when compared to the embarrassing rout at Bull Run. His startling promotion to overall command quickly followed, but Abraham Lincoln came to consider McClellan overcautious. The General was also unsympathetic to Republican war aims, warning Lincoln against "radical views" on slavery. The President twice removed him from his post.

McClellan dropped from sight almost as quickly as he rose. After his 1864 Presidential defeat, he settled down to engineering projects and a stint as Governor of New Jersey. He conceded he might have been better off if his fame had not come so quickly, writing, "It probably would have been better for me personally had my promotion been delayed a year or more."[202]

JOSEPH McDONALD (D 1884)

McDonald never truly emerged from national obscurity during his political career. He served as Indiana´s Attorney General, a Congressman, and a one-term Senator. A likable man, he was nicknamed "Old Saddle Bags" because of his early days as a saddler´s apprentice. Even though he was unseated from the Senate by Benjamin Harrison in 1880, and despite his lack of identity, McDonald ran for President as Indiana´s Democratic favorite son in 1884. It soon became obvious his candidacy was merely a front for former Governor Thomas Hendricks, who gave McDonald´s nominating speech at the convention, seizing the chance to speak directly to the delegates. Indiana led the hasty switches to Hendricks on the second ballot, but it wasn´t enough to stop Grover Cleveland. McDonald was, as usual, forgotten in the shuffle.

GEORGE McGOVERN (D 1968, 1972)

McGovern was a political moralist in a volatile period. Although a recipient of the Distinguished Flying Cross as a World War II bomber pilot, he was a caustic opponent of the Vietnam War. "Every Senator in this chamber is partly responsible for the sending of 50,000 young Americans to an early grave," he preached in a 1970 address. "Every Senator here is partly responsible for that human wreckage at Walter Reed and Bethesda Naval Hospitals and all across the land."[203] His passion motivated an army of youthful supporters in the 1972 Presidential campaign.

McGovern´s rhetoric diverted many from recognizing his political sagacity. He drove the back roads of South Dakota in the 1950s to revive its Democratic party. He went on to win three Senate elections in that predominantly Republican state. When the national Democratic party needed an experienced politician to revise its nominating process after the disastrous 1968 Chicago convention, it turned to McGovern. He wrote the new rules, then used them to seize the nomination in 1972. The landslide general-election defeat that followed was an exception to his record of political success. McGovern explained to the 1973 Gridiron Club dinner that since he was a boy, he had wanted to run for President in the worst possible way. Now, he joked, he had.

WILLIAM McKINLEY (R 1892, 1896, 1900)

McKinley was a Republican preacher in the late 19th Century, and the protective tariff was his gospel. He became a favorite of businessmen by repeatedly declaring, "The protective system meets our wants, our conditions, promotes the national design, and will work out our destiny better than any other." He wedded his panacea to his party, instructing crowds, "Vote the Republican ticket. Stand by the protective policy."204   To him, they were one and the same. His faith didn't waver even after a harsh tariff he devised cost Republicans control of Congress in 1890 and McKinley the seat he had held for twelve years.

Critics considered McKinley's tariff policy to be proof he was under the control of industrialists, particularly the shrewd Mark Hanna. But he demonstrated a native cunning as he launched his comeback in 1891 by being elected Governor of Ohio. McKinley had supported silver legislation in Congress, but adroitly shifted to the gold standard in 1896, sensing the public mood. Illinois Congressman Joseph Cannon, himself a smooth legislative operator, thought the Ohioan too willing to do anything to gain the voters' support. He grumbled that McKinley had his ear so close to the ground it was full of grasshoppers.

McKinley's Presidential administrations went strictly by the orthodox Republican book. He was assassinated in 1901, to be succeeded by a man of considerably more vigor, Theodore Roosevelt.

JOHN McLEAN (R 1856)

McLean spent most of his career on the Supreme Court, thirty-two years from 1829 until his death. He rejected arguments that his position placed him above politics. His healthy appetite for the Presidency led him to seek nominations from the Anti-Masonic, Whig, and Republican parties while on the bench, always falling short. Critics insisted his record as a judge was pedestrian, hardly an indication he could handle the White House. A New York Tribune reporter at the 1856 Republican gathering called McLean "the candidate for the slow and hunkerish part of the convention."

McLean spent four years in Congress and six as

Postmaster General before his elevation to the Supreme Court. His best-remembered decision was a dissent in the Dred Scott case in 1857. The Court ruled that Congress had no power to prohibit slavery in the territories, but McLean disagreed. He called slaveholding a wrong that existed only through force. His dissent, widely quoted by abolitionists, asserted that the government could take steps to halt the further spread of slavery.

JOHN McLEAN (D 1896)

His daughter-in-law once wrote that McLean "loved power and nothing was too much trouble when he saw a chance to extend his reach and his control of other men."[205] The tools he used to fulfill his needs were money and newspapers, both of which he inherited from his father. McLean became a major financial supporter of Democratic candidates in Ohio. A grateful party awarded him a seat on the Democratic National Committee. He took control of his family's Cincinnati Enquirer in 1880, continuing its strong support of the Democrats.

Cincinnati was not large enough for McLean. He moved to Washington in 1884. The new address didn't stop him from absentee campaigns for the Senate and Governor of Ohio. He lost both races. His journalistic fortunes also slumped in the mid-1890s. McLean bought the New York Journal, but lost so much money he had to unload it to a young publisher from San Francisco. William Randolph Hearst had greater success. So did McLean with his next acquisition, the Washington Post.

WALTER MONDALE (D 1984)

Mondale's career was characterized by caution. "He was not a contentious flame thrower," Missouri's Thomas Eagleton remembered of Mondale's years in the Senate.[206] The Minnesota Democrat got along well with his conservative colleagues even though he routinely supported liberal legislation. His voting record mirrored that of his mentor, Hubert Humphrey. "They were tweedle-dum and tweedle-dee," said one Minnesota Congressman. "It would have taken major surgery to separate the two."[207] But while Humphrey was ebullient, Mondale was reticent. He admitted this trait hurt him in his losing 1984 campaign. "Modern politics today requires a mastery of television," Mondale told reporters. "I've never really warmed up to television and, in fairness to television, it's never warmed up to me."[208]

Mondale had plenty of help on his way up the political ladder. He was appointed to fill vacancies as Minnesota Attorney General and Senator before having to run in elections for those offices. Jimmy Carter then designated him for Vice President in 1976. Running on his own for the top spot did not hold heavy appeal. Mondale ended an exploratory candidacy in 1974, saying, "I don't think anyone should be President who is not willing to go through fire."[209] He had greater enthusiasm a decade later, but was unable to transfer it to the electorate.

JAMES MONROE (DR 1816, 1820)

Monroe was strangely cast as President during the "Era of Good Feelings." Much more partisan than his four predecessors, he ruled over a period that lacked party competition. The Virginian had been an early outspoken foe of Federalism, even condemning the Constitution for its centralization of power. He wrote a fellow Democratic-Republican, Thomas Jefferson, in the early 1790s, "To be passive in a controversy of this kind, unless the person had been bred a priest in the principles of the Romish church, is a satisfactory proof he is on the wrong side."[210]

Monroe was neither a fiery speaker nor a deep political thinker, but he filled a series of important posts: Governor of Virginia, Senator, Minister to France, Secretary of War, and Secretary of State. He remained headstrong, ignoring State Department instructions on his French mission, later annoying Jefferson and James Madison by negotiating what they considered an inadequate treaty with Britain. His injured vanity in the latter case led him to challenge Madison's Presidential candidacy in 1808. His old friend did not quickly forgive, but finally named Monroe Secretary of State in 1811, putting him on the track to the White House.

WILLIAM MORRISON (D 1880)

Morrison had an adventurous life before entering Congress. He fought in the Mexican War, prospected for gold in California, then returned to the battlefield in the Civil War. His daring spirit was also evident during his sixteen years representing Illinois in the House. Morrison led the fight against the popular protective tariff, which he called "spoilation, because it takes the earnings of the labor of one person or class of persons and gives these earnings to other persons."[211] He became known as "Horizontal Bill" because of his advocacy of a uniform, horizontal reduction in tariff rates.

Morrison met little success in his crusade. "The Morrison bill is like Bill Morrison, a very much overrated affair," a Saint Louis newspaper once remarked. "It also resembles the Morrison [Presidential] boom and Yankee beans in being composed chiefly of wind."[212] Defeated for reelection to Congress in 1886, he was appointed the following year to the new Interstate Commerce Commission.

LEVI MORTON (R 1896)

Morton was one of the richest bankers in the country, but he never forgot the decision that prevented him from being even more powerful. James Garfield was looking to conciliate New York Republicans after winning the party's Presidential nomination in 1880. His agents asked Morton, then a Congressman, to be his running mate. The boss of the Stalwart faction, Roscoe Conkling, demanded that Morton say "no." He did. Garfield then approached Chester Arthur, who defied Conkling. Morton became Minister to France, knowing full well that a demonstration of backbone would have placed him in the White House instead of Arthur after Garfield's assassination.

A second chance came in 1888. Morton accepted the Vice Presidential nomination under Benjamin Harrison with alacrity. His term in the office was undistinguished and he was denied renomination. He later served a stint as Governor of New York, but irritated the bosses with his refusal to accept their dictates. As far as Morton was concerned, he had listened to them too much already.

OLIVER MORTON (R 1876)

The hardest thing to believe about Morton's career was that he was once a Democrat. His violent opposition to the Kansas-Nebraska Act ended that affiliation. Morton became perhaps the most vituperative Republican orator of his age. He blasted the Democratic party as "a common sewer and loathsome receptacle." He pioneered in tarring the opposition as the party of disloyalty. "Every unregenerate rebel...every deserter, every sneak who ran away from the draft calls himself a Democrat," he shouted in his powerful voice. "Every man who labored for the rebellion in the field, who murdered Union prisoners by cruelty and starvation...calls himself a Democrat."[213]

Morton's hatred for Democrats first showed itself during the Civil War. As Governor of Indiana, he quarreled constantly with the Democratic-controlled legislature, finally bypassing it to maintain his state's financial contribution to the war effort. The opposition bitterly assailed him as a dictator. After the war, Morton was repelled by Andrew Johnson's lenient Reconstruction policies. He became a leading Radical in the Senate. But two strokes slowed Morton's rise. He was unable to walk or stand without two canes after 1865. Many Republicans felt that regardless of his powerful rhetoric, Morton could no longer be considered a realistic Presidential contender.

WILLIAM MURRAY (D 1932)

Murray came of political age in a wild time, the Populist era, in a wild place, Indian Territory, soon to be Oklahoma. His eccentric independence stemmed from those roots, as did his enduring love of rural life. Murray was widely known as "Alfalfa Bill" for his unceasing efforts to prod Oklahoma farmers to plant that crop. Discouraged about the future of agrarian interests after World War I, he moved his family to Bolivia for five years.

Murray served four years in the House before his departure. He returned in the Depression, being elected Governor in 1930. His efforts to aid starving farmers brought national attention, but enemies found his measures bordering on the dictatorial. An Oklahoma City newspaper fought back with a series of articles on Murray´s personal habits, even declaring that his underwear showed below his trouser cuffs. Murray laughed of the reporter, "I want to assure you that I do not know as much about her underwear, and if I did, I would be too much a gentleman to tell it."[214]

After the failure of his 1932 Presidential candidacy, Murray drifted toward conservatism. He capped his conversion by appearing before the 1948 convention of the States´ Rights Democratic party. He told cheering delegates America´s greatness was due to "Christian principles and the white man´s brains."

EDMUND MUSKIE (D 1972)

Muskie was a Democratic trailblazer, but he did most of his early work without national acclaim. The son of a Polish immigrant, he rose to become Governor of Maine in 1954, the first Democrat elected to the post in two decades. Muskie became his state´s first popularly elected Democratic Senator four years later. He was a quiet man in the Senate, but gained the respect of his colleagues. Lyndon Johnson, who knew more than a few things about handling legislation, called Muskie "a real powerhouse...one of the few liberals who´s a match for the Southern legislative craftsmen."[215]

It wasn´t until 1968 that the nation became aware of the man from Maine. His cool performance as Hubert Humphrey´s running mate was exceptional in that volatile year. One columnist called Muskie "the most refreshing figure in the American campaign." But as reporters became more familiar with Muskie, they noted his fierce and unpredictable temper. "I´ve always found it useful to be thought of as an intimidating sort of fellow," he once confessed. "Someone once said that I would intimidate Mount Rushmore."[216] Americans weren´t sure that was the kind of man they wanted in the White House in 1972, so Muskie was forced to stay in the quiet confines of the Senate, later serving briefly as Secretary of State.

RICHARD NIXON (R 1960, 1968, 1972)

There was nothing in Nixon´s introduction to politics that suggested he would be capable of a stunning climb to national prominence. Republicans in his California district were searching for a Congressional candidate in 1946, but without luck. The president of Whittier College mentioned Nixon, a former student-body president who was then in the Navy. An emissary called to ask, "Are you a Republican?" Nixon thought it over. "I guess so," he replied. "I voted for Dewey last time."[217] That was good enough.

Nixon spent just four years in the House, winning acclaim for his dogged investigation into Alger Hiss´ Communist connections. Two years in the Senate were concluded by his selection as Dwight Eisenhower´s running mate in 1952. Nixon would be on the national Republican ticket in every election but one through 1972.

Democrats detested the young Californian, believing him too quick to blame the Communists for every problem. Adlai Stevenson warned in 1956 that if Eisenhower were reelected, Nixon would probably become President. Harry Truman called him one of the two men he hated in politics. "He not only doesn´t give a damn about the people," the former President insisted, "he doesn´t know how to tell the truth."[218]

All that seemed irrelevant after Nixon´s political comeback failed miserably in 1962. Two years after an unsuccessful Presidential effort, he lost the race for Governor of California by 300,000 votes. He bitterly told reporters, "You won´t have Nixon to kick around anymore because, gentlemen, this is my last press conference."[219] There were actually hundreds in his future. A second comeback brought two Presidential victories. It also brought the Watergate scandal that gave the Democrats the satisfaction of seeing their old nemesis resign in disgrace.

GEORGE NORRIS (R 1928)

Norris´ name was listed on the ballot in the Republican column for most of his career, but he insisted that didn´t mean very much. The Nebraskan lashed out at "this wicked, nonsensical, illogical, and I think I can say unpatriotic, spirit of party."[220] During his ten years in the House and thirty in the Senate, he held true only to progressivism.

Norris came to national attention in a natural role, that of insurgent. He introduced the resolution in 1910 that stripped Speaker Joseph Cannon of his power over the House Rules Committee. Its passage broke the iron grip of "Cannonism." Norris moved to the Senate two years later, drifting ever further from Republican orthodoxy. He supported much of Woodrow Wilson´s legislative program, then later endorsed the Democratic Presidential candidacies of Al Smith and Franklin Roosevelt, the latter all four times.

Norris withstood repeated Republican attempts to dump him from the Senate, but finally conceded to logic in 1936. He was elected to his fifth term as an independent. He had no more fervent supporter than the President. Franklin Roosevelt once called Norris "the very perfect, gentle knight of American progressive ideals."[221]

ASA PACKER (D 1868)

Packer was a living definition of the self-made man. He had little luck as a farmer in his native Connecticut, so he hiked to Pennsylvania, where he hired out as a carpenter´s apprentice. The young man lived for a decade in a cabin he built himself, saving enough money to buy a canal boat. He shipped coal in the boat, the start of a fortune that would make him the richest man in Pennsylvania. The Lehigh Valley Railroad was the cornerstone of his empire.

Packer was also interested in politics, but didn't fare nearly as well as he did in business. He served a stretch in the state legislature and four years in the House. But higher office escaped him. His last try came in 1869, when he was nominated for Governor by the Democrats, but lost.

MITCHELL PALMER (D 1920)

Palmer was one of Woodrow Wilson's earliest supporters in the 1912 campaign. The President-elect sought to reward the Pennsylvania Congressman by naming him Secretary of War. But Palmer, citing religious reasons, declined. That didn't mean he shied from a battle, as demonstrated by his nickname of "The Fighting Quaker." He was Wilson's most controversial subordinate during the President's second term.

Palmer was appointed Alien Property Custodian in 1917, charged with selling the American possessions of enemy aliens. It was a task that attracted considerable attention and criticism, a good warmup for his next assignment, Attorney General. Palmer was perhaps the earliest Red-baiter, charging that the Bolshevik revolution had been managed by "a small clique of outcasts from the East Side of New York."[222] He aimed to eliminate American Communism, directing mass arrests and deportations of radicals. Palmer dismissed critics of his tactics as "pale-pink parlor Bolsheviks." His house was bombed in 1919, and the Attorney General said more Communist-inspired violence was coming. But when May Day, 1920, was quiet, Palmer's warnings were dismissed by many as those of an alarmist. His Presidential hopes dribbled away with his credibility.

ALTON PARKER (D 1904)

Parker's image during his 1904 Presidential campaign was that of a nonpolitical, conservative stuffed shirt. It was not true. Parker was actually an experienced politician. He was once chairman of the New York Democratic party and had been elected Chief Justice of the state Court of Appeals by a then-startling margin of 60,000 votes. It was his view of judicial ethics that prevented him from campaigning for the Democratic Presidential nomination while still on the bench. "You may be right in thinking that an expression of my views is necessary to secure the nomination," he wrote a friend. "If so, let the nomination go."[223]

Parker's judicial record actually had its liberal aspects, but he downplayed them in 1904. His aim was to appeal to the party's right wing. Conservatives also found Parker's sedate lifestyle comforting, but they were unaware of his idiosyncrasies. Prominent in that category was his faith in the intelligence of pigs. The supposedly austere jurist loved to train them to play games and to answer to their names.

JOEL PARKER (D 1868)

Parker was one of the few Democrats who heaped severe criticism on the Lincoln Administration, yet managed to maintain political careers after Appomattox. The New Jersey Governor had two saving graces. He was always popular in his state, and there was no doubting his desire to maintain the Union.

Parker disagreed with Lincoln on the methods used to defeat the South. He insisted the Emancipation Proclamation would only encourage the rebels to fight harder. Slavery was not an issue with Parker. "The Union should be the sole condition of peace," he asserted, "and that must be adhered to with unswerving fidelity." The Governor charged that "the fatal policy of those in power" was an obstacle to Union every bit as formidable as the rebel armies.[224]

Parker´s term expired in 1866. He returned to his law practice, but was inaugurated as Governor again in 1872. He was appointed to the state Supreme Court in 1880, serving until his death.

ROBERT PATTISON (D 1896)

Pattison was a boy-wonder City Controller who helped rescue Philadelphia from bankruptcy before he was 30. His resulting reputation for honesty and tough administration won him election as Governor of Pennsylvania in 1882 at age 32. He cut the state´s debt and instituted tougher controls on railroads. Pattison was not legally allowed to succeed himself in 1886, but returned as Governor in 1890 for another four years.

Pattison´s Presidential hopes were dashed by the fight over bimetallism. He was a gold Democrat in a party infested by the silver bug. The Governor was also hurt by charges that he was insensitive to labor. He had steadfastly refused to get involved when violence broke out in the famous strike against the Carnegie Steel Company in Homestead, Pennsylvania, in 1892. The sheriff wired for help when a gunfight began. Pattison cooly replied, "Local authorities must exhaust every means at their command for the preservation of peace."[225] He reluctantly sent the militia five days later, allowing strikebreakers to enter the plant to resume production.

HENRY PAYNE (D 1880)

Payne was at the fringes of Democratic party power for nearly four decades, but he had little luck breaking into the top ranks. Success in business and the law gave Payne the money and time to enter politics. He formally placed James Buchanan´s name before the 1856 convention. Four years later, he reported out the platform plank on slavery that triggered the Southern walkout.

Payne was not comparably successful in drawing attention

when it came to advancing his own fortunes. He managed a single term in the Ohio legislature and another in the House, but lost an 1857 race for Governor. When Payne finally hit the big time, winning a Senate seat in 1885, his victory came under circumstances he would just as soon have forgotten. The Senate investigated charges that Payne´s son, the treasurer of the Standard Oil Company, spent $100,000 to convince state legislators to elect his father. The probe never turned up sufficient proof, but the stain of the accusations remained with Payne for the rest of his life.

GEORGE PENDLETON (D 1868)

Pendleton often advanced ideas his critics found outrageous, but he had such a courteous and dignified manner that he made few enemies. He was commonly known as "Gentleman George." His tact was essential as he orchestrated Congressional criticism of the Lincoln Administration during the Civil War and emerged as the chief postwar proponent of soft money.

Pendleton spent eight years in the House, including most of the war years. He was a leader of the Democratic peace wing and a friend of the famous Copperhead, Clement Vallandigham, the mere mention of whose name caused Republican hackles to rise. Pendleton never apologized for the peace views that won him his party´s 1864 Vice Presidential nomination. He said optimistically at Vallandigham´s funeral in 1871, "I thank God he has lived long enough to see...that many who had maligned him most were beginning to see their error and to do him justice."[226]

Pendleton´s faith in greenbacks, a concept known as the "Ohio Idea," cost him Eastern support for his 1868 Presidential campaign. He continued his decline the following year, losing the race for Governor of Ohio to Rutherford Hayes. But he rebounded to sponsor his lasting achievement during his only term in the Senate. The Pendleton Act created the Civil Service Commission in 1883.

FRANKLIN PIERCE (D 1852, 1856)

Pierce thought he was bidding farewell to his political career when he resigned from the Senate in 1842. His wife wanted nothing more to do with Washington after her husband´s four years in the House and five in the Senate. She feared that Pierce, in his biographer´s words, "was too easily a prey to the jovial and reckless life of the politicians."[227] Some used plainer speech. The Whigs would later call Pierce "a hero of many a well-fought bottle."

The next decade was largely passed in quiet New Hampshire. Pierce refused Democratic offers to return to the Senate. His stint as a brigadier general in the Mexican War was generally uneventful. But his interest in politics remained. Pierce, a lifelong Northerner who always had an unusually strong Southern inclination, publicly blasted abolitionists as "reckless fanatics." He drew Southern praise for his support of the Fugitive Slave Act. This appeal in regions other than his own was a secret to Pierce's dark-horse Presidential victory in 1852.

The President was a convivial man, but had difficulty making decisions. That deficiency proved dangerous in the wake of the 1854 passage of the Kansas-Nebraska Act. Pierce was helpless to restrain the mushrooming menace of sectional hatred. The Democratic party felt it necessary to look elsewhere for its nominee in 1856.

CHARLES COTESWORTH PINCKNEY (F 1804, 1808)

Pinckney served with distinction in the Revolutionary War and was later given peacetime command of all troops south of Maryland. But a single utterance did more than all of his battlefield exploits to advance his political career. Pinckney was dispatched with two other commissioners to negotiate an agreement that would prevent a war with France in 1797. The French ruling body, the Directory, demanded a $250,000 bribe as one of its conditions. Pinckney cried, "No, no, not a sixpence!"[228] Publication of the correspondence dealing with what became known as the XYZ Affair made Pinckney a national hero.

Up to this point, the South Carolinian had avoided government service. George Washington, whom Pinckney had served as an aide during the Revolution, offered three Cabinet posts, a Supreme Court seat, or command of the Army. Pinckney declined all. But after the episode in France, the Federalist party insisted. Pinckney was its Vice Presidential nominee in 1800, then ran for President the next two times. All three campaigns ended in defeat.

JAMES POLK (D 1844)

Polk had many character traits that normally spell doom for a politician. He was introverted, invariably somber, and lacking in personal magnetism. He compensated by developing an amazing memory. Polk once said, "I don't think I was ever introduced to a man and talked with him ten minutes, that I ever afterwards forgot him."[229] He also worked diligently to improve his stump speaking.

Another key to Polk's rise was his lasting friendship with a fellow Tennessean, Andrew Jackson. He became a leader of administration forces during his fourteen years in the House, including a stint as Speaker. Democrats called him home in 1839 to become Governor. Polk served one uneventful term, then lost two tries for reelection. The Nashville Banner crowed, "HENCEFORTH HIS CAREER WILL BE DOWNWARDS."[230]

Polk hoped to turn his fortunes around with a Vice Presidential nomination in 1844. It was Jackson who suggested he aim higher. A Democratic convention deadlock provided the opportunity to do so, and sent him on to the White House.

MATTHEW QUAY (R 1896)

Quay held public office for much of his adult life, but he made his mark in political backrooms. He was elected to a number of positions in his native Pennsylvania, including Secretary of the Commonwealth and State Treasurer. Quay capped his career with service in the Senate from 1887 to 1904, with one hiatus. But his real power was derived from his talent for organization. He served as chairman of both the Pennsylvania and national Republican parties.

Quay considered patronage the fuel that powered political machines. He disliked those who disagreed. "Arthur has a great many apples in his basket," he once grumbled of the President who was trying to prove his commitment to civil service. "If he is not careful, some of them will rot on his hands."[231] Quay avoided similar indecision. He kept copious card files, known as "Quay's Coffins." They contained records of all favors granted and any indiscretions committed by those seeking his help. "This man runs the Republican party," the New York Globe wailed of his power in 1890. "He is now running it in Congress, as he has hitherto run it in the greatest Republican state of the Union. He has organized the House in the interest of trusts and the tariff monopolies."[232]

SAMUEL RANDALL (D 1884)

Randall served twenty-seven years as a Congressman. "The devil can't beat me in my own district," he liked to boast.[233] But there was a price. The Republican-controlled Pennsylvania legislature would almost certainly have gerrymandered him out of his comfortable position if he hadn't been a staunch supporter of the protective tariff. As it was, he was the only Democrat representing Philadelphia in the House.

Randall was once a Whig and retained many of that party's conservative principles. "If there be one evil greater than another today in this country," he said, "it is that we have too much legislation."[234] He put a stopper on many bills during his stint as Speaker from 1876 to 1881. That term was the peak of Randall's influence. Fellow Democrats angered by his stand on the tariff prevented his reelection as Speaker. Southern and Western foes of protection then blocked his two tries for the White House. President Grover Cleveland, who declared tariff reduction his main issue, delivered the final blow. He stripped Randall of all control of Pennsylvania patronage in 1887.

RONALD REAGAN (R 1968, 1976, 1980, 1984)

Reagan spent nearly three decades as a movie actor before entering politics. The skills he acquired in his first career helped greatly in his second. His ease on television earned Reagan the nickname, "The Great Communicator." Critics noted he often made remarks or cited statistics that were incorrect, but there was no mistaking his popularity with the electorate.

Reagan, later the nemesis of organized labor and liberals, was once in each of their camps. He headed the Screen Actors Guild for six years. He recalled he was then "a near-hopeless hemophiliac liberal. I bled for `causes.´"[235] A conversion to conservatism was capped by his 1964 nationally televised endorsement of Barry Goldwater. Impressed Republicans urged him to run for Governor of California two years later. Reagan campaigned as a "citizen politician," a tag that infuriated Governor Pat Brown. "This is your citizen pilot," Brown mocked him. "I´ve never flown a plane before, but don´t worry. I´ve always had a deep interest in aviation."[236] Reagan won by nearly a million votes.

The Californian did not always follow through on his promises in his state´s highest office. He raised taxes and boosted university funding after an original cut. But he emerged as the leading national spokesman for conservative Republicans. Reagan´s first two Presidential efforts fell short, but the nation was shifting to the right. The political climate was congenial by the 1980s, allowing him to score two landslide victories.

JAMES REED (D 1928)

One journalist described Reed as the "roughest and hardest hitter" in the Senate during his eighteen years there. Few disagreed. The acid-tongued Missouri Democrat, once the reform Mayor of Kansas City, didn´t care who he battled. Reed backed Woodrow Wilson´s early programs, but broke with the President over his handling of World War I and his later insistence on American participation in the League of Nations. Reed declared anyone who blindly followed "the dictation of some other man is too contemptible to send to Congress." Wilson retorted that Reed was "a discredit to the party to which he pretends to belong."[237] He lent his support to the 1922 "Rid Us of Reed" movement organized by mainstream Democrats. The Senator was nonetheless reelected.

Reed was no kinder to the Republican administrations of the 1920s. He blasted Attorney General Harry Daugherty for his role in the scandals of the Harding years. Daugherty, Reed said, was the "vilest insect that ever crawled across the page of time." A reporter asked the Senator if he was worried that he would be remembered for nothing more than such criticism of others and their legislation. "I have done a lot of that, thank God!" he replied. "My only regret is that I was not given the power to do more of it."[238]

THOMAS REED (R 1896)

Henry Cabot Lodge once called Reed "the finest, most effective debater that I have ever seen or heard." There was no doubting the Maine Congressman´s ability to use wit and sarcasm. His six-foot-three, nearly 300-pound bulk made him appear to be even more imposing. Many of his colleagues took great pains to avoid tangling with him on the House floor. One who took the chance compounded his error by protesting that he would rather be right than be President. "The gentleman need not be disturbed," Reed coolly replied. "He will never be either."[239]

Reed spent twenty-three years in the House, rising to the position of Speaker. He masterminded rules changes that consolidated his power, saying they were necessary to break "the tyranny of the minority." Democrats bitterly called him "Czar" Reed. The Speaker paid little attention. He likewise dismissed the abilities of his rivals for the Republican Presidential nomination. Asked if his party might choose him in 1892, he said, "They might do worse and I think they will."[240] Reed was never fond of William McKinley and opposed his annexation of Puerto Rico and the Philippines. He resigned from Congress in protest.

JAMES RHODES (R 1968)

Rhodes was in many ways a forerunner of the Republican budget-cutters of the 1980s. The onetime "boy Mayor" of Columbus, Ohio, was elected Governor in 1962 on his second try. His slogan was "Jobs and Progress" and he quickly made it clear he intended to reach those goals by shrinking the role of the state government. "It´s not what we need," Rhodes insisted, "it´s what we can afford to spend that counts."[241] He laid off state workers and cut taxes. Other states sent representatives to study this unusual program in the years of the Great Society. Critics complained that the poor were suffering under Rhodes. "Listening to this administration is like holding an audience with the Wizard of Oz," said a Cleveland mental-health official.[242]

Rhodes won four terms as Governor, but his penchant for wheeling and dealing hurt his image on the national level. Even leading Republicans dismissed him as a clubhouse politician. They never gave serious consideration to nominating him for higher office.

NELSON ROCKEFELLER (R 1964, 1968)

Rockefeller spent more than a decade in appointive posts before deciding elective politics was where the action was. The New York multimillionaire made the switch in a big way, ousting Governor Averell Harriman in 1958 by a margin of almost 600,000 votes. He was instantly discussed as a Presidential possibility.

Scant days after that first election, Barry Goldwater warned that Rockefeller would become a national force in the Republican party only "if he doesn´t introduce a lot of radical ideas." Conservatives came to feel he badly flunked the test. They watched with horror as Rockefeller initiated expensive programs during his fourteen years as Governor, such as a $2 billion renovation of the State Capitol grounds.

Rockefeller´s Presidential hopes always were halted by

unexpected obstacles. He was blocked in 1960 by Richard Nixon's excellent advance work, stymied in 1964 by negative public reaction to his divorce and remarriage, and crippled in 1968 by his own indecision. Rockefeller had a simpler explanation. He blamed conservative Republicans. "I think if I'd been nominated, I would have been elected," he mused.[243] He had to settle for being appointed Vice President by Gerald Ford.

FRANKLIN ROOSEVELT (D 1932, 1936, 1940, 1944)

Clare Boothe Luce once insisted it was simple to identify prominent leaders: they had easily recognized gestures. She cited Winston Churchill's V-for-victory and Adolf Hitler's stiffly extended arm. What, someone asked, about Roosevelt? Luce just wet her index finger and held it to the wind.

There was no doubt Roosevelt was a master at reading and shaping public opinion. His election in 1932 after two terms as Governor of New York fired the optimism of a country deep in the Depression. The President was determined to give the appearance of action. "Above all, try something," he implored subordinates. The result was the massive growth of the federal government under the New Deal. Critics lamented the "alphabet soup" of new agencies. Herbert Hoover moaned that his successor had no fixed principles, changing like "a chameleon on plaid."[244] Others used stronger language.

Roosevelt's easy manner, his undistinguished career before becoming Governor, and his confinement to a wheelchair by polio led observers to underestimate him. Walter Lippmann dismissed him in 1932 as "a pleasant man who, without any important qualifications for the office, would very much like to be President."[245] Roosevelt confounded the experts by winning an unprecedented four terms, leading the country through the Depression and World War II. Most Americans came to think of him simply as <u>the</u> President and found it impossible to imagine anyone filling his role after his death in 1945. "He was just like a daddy always," sobbed one Congressman on that final day. "He was the one person I ever knew, anywhere, who was never afraid. God, God -- how he could take it for us all!"[246] The young lawmaker temporarily despairing of the future was Lyndon Johnson of Texas.

THEODORE ROOSEVELT (R 1904, 1912, P 1912, R 1916)

Roosevelt guaranteed future political success when he and his Rough Riders made their highly publicized dash up Cuba's San Juan Hill during the brief Spanish-American War. America warmed to the vigorous New Yorker who combined a gift for self-promotion with his advocacy of "the strenuous life." Roosevelt had served on the Civil Service Commission and as Assistant Secretary of the Navy before the war. Now a hero, he was quickly drafted for bigger things. He was elected Governor of New York in 1898, then chosen to be Vice President just two years later. New York's Republican bosses eased his elevation. They wanted the reform-minded Governor out of their way.

Roosevelt pledged to "continue, absolutely unbroken, the policy of President McKinley" after the 1901 assassination.[227] But it was against his nature. Finding the Presidency "a bully pulpit," Roosevelt pushed a mildly progressive program. He also demonstrated a characteristic impatience. When negotiations with Colombia over land rights for construction of the Panama Canal bogged down, he helped create a revolution. "I took the Canal Zone and let Congress debate," he later boasted. "While the debate goes on, the canal does also."[248] Such an action-oriented person could hardly be satisfied with retirement. Roosevelt left the White House in 1909, but he schemed for the rest of his life to return.

ELIHU ROOT (R 1916)

Root called himself "a lawyer first and all the time." He became known as one of the country´s finest, but his preoccupation with his profession may have cost him the Presidency.

William McKinley turned to Root in 1899 to be his Secretary of War. He wanted a lawyer who could answer the tricky legal questions resulting from America´s new role as the possessor of colonies. Theodore Roosevelt elevated Root to Secretary of State in 1905. Other Cabinet members were impressed with his performance. "He is certainly one of the strongest men intellectually whom I ever met," marveled Secretary of War William Howard Taft. "He has a judicial cast of mind and power of analysis that are much like Lincoln´s."[249] But Root´s ambition was certainly not similar to Lincoln´s. Roosevelt suggested grooming the Secretary of State to succeed him, but Root was barely interested. The President turned to Taft.

Root later served a term in the Senate, but otherwise devoted himself to the law. He insisted he had no desire for further government service, just asking for "enough incidental intellectual occupation...to ward off softening of the brain."[250]

RICHARD RUSSELL (D 1948, 1952)

Russell was a true power of the Senate in the mid-20th Century. He served thirty-eight years in that body, eighteen as chairman of the Armed Services Committee. The Georgian entered in 1933 as a confirmed New Dealer, but rebelled at what he considered Franklin Roosevelt´s excesses. He gradually became the leader of the bloc of conservative Southern Democrats.

Russell´s conception of regional interests doomed his Presidential hopes. He introduced a bill in 1948 to permit draftees to request that they be assigned to units only of their own race. He proposed a year later that the federal government spend $4.5 billion for the voluntary relocation of Southern blacks to the North. Harry Truman considered Russell a victim of his upbringing. He wrote, "I believe that if Russell had been from Indiana or Missouri or Kentucky, he may very well have been the President of the United States."[251]   But he was from Georgia, limiting his base of substantial support to the white South.

WINFIELD SCOTT (W 1840, 1848, 1852)

Scott was often likened to Andrew Jackson. It was true that each ran for President after capturing the public's fancy in the War of 1812. But it was otherwise a poor comparison. Jackson was a professional politician who had already served in the House and Senate before his stirring victory as a volunteer general at New Orleans. Scott was the reverse: a professional soldier, but an amateur politician. The difference showed at the ballot box.

Scott won acclaim for putting up a spirited fight against the British at Lundy's Lane in 1814. He then settled into the routine of the peacetime Army, rising to become General-in-Chief in 1841. Scott had by that time been infected by the Presidential bug, but was deemed to have little hope of a Whig nomination. The Mexican War saved him. His capture of Vera Cruz and Mexico City renewed his hero status. "His campaign was unsurpassed in military annals," gushed the Duke of Wellington. "He is the greatest living soldier."[252] He may also have been the vainest, as evidenced by his nickname, "Old Fuss and Feathers." Scott's failure to take the White House always hurt him, sometimes prompting him to mutter about the ingratitude of republics.

WILLIAM SCRANTON (R 1964)

Scranton was a reluctant participant in politics. An heir to a fortune made in iron and coal, he devoted himself after World War II to the family businesses. He was also a leader in efforts to attract new industry to the city that bore the family name: Scranton, Pennsylvania.

Scranton took leave in 1959 to serve on the staff of the Secretary of State. His mother heard rumors that he would run for Congress the following year, but he assured her they were groundless. Republican leaders forced him into it. Two years later, Dwight Eisenhower was among those pressuring the Congressman into a candidacy for Governor. Scranton finally consented and won. It was a familiar story by 1964. Moderate Republicans, dismayed by the collapse of Nelson Rockefeller's Presidential campaign, looked for a new champion to stop Barry Goldwater. Scranton waffled for so long that reporters dubbed him "the Hamlet of Harrisburg." After his defeat at the convention, he completed his term as Governor, never to run for elective office again.

WILLIAM SEWARD (R 1860)

It was rarely difficult to know where Seward stood. The New Yorker was convivial, but he also had a stubborn streak of independence. He distrusted slaveholders throughout his career, which he began as an Anti-Mason, later to be a Whig and a Republican.

Seward's severest pronouncements came during his twelve years in the Senate. He blasted the Compromise of 1850, assailing all legislative bargains as "radically wrong and essentially vicious." The South never forgot his ominous declaration during that famous debate, "But there is a higher law than the Constitution...."[253] One Southern newspaper labeled him "a wretch whom it would be a degradation to name." The editorial abuse continued through the decade, as Seward warned of an "irrepressible conflict" between North and South.

It was ironic that the same remarks also made many Republicans skittish. They preferred a candidate of less extreme rhetoric. "I am half a mind to go back [home]," Seward wrote, "where it seems they don't think it an objection to a man that he is identified with their own party."[254] But he stayed on to serve as Secretary of State under Abraham Lincoln and Andrew Johnson.

HORATIO SEYMOUR (D 1864, 1868)

Seymour's love of private life was so intense that he refused one Democratic designation for Governor of New York and tried vigorously to dodge the party's 1868 Presidential nomination. He sighed that his acceptance of the latter honor was the greatest mistake of his life. Seymour's critics enjoyed the spectacle of a politician trying to avoid public office. They nicknamed him "The Great Decliner."

Seymour got his fill of campaigning in five other races for Governor. He won two. He was an occupant of the state's highest office in 1863 when the key event of his career took place. Seymour opposed the institution of a military draft, but he hustled to New York City to quell a riot against conscription. He went to City Hall to speak to an orderly crowd; the riot was elsewhere. Horace Greeley reported the next morning that Seymour began, "My friends...." The implication that he addressed the mob in such a fashion was never dispelled. Seymour, although protesting that he didn't see a single rioter that day, was dogged by accusations of disloyalty for the rest of his career.

THOMAS SEYMOUR (D 1864)

Seymour was cited for bravery in the Mexican War. Two years after its conclusion, he was elected Governor of Connecticut by a coalition that included the antislavery Free Soil party. These would seem to be the roots of a conservative Republican. But Seymour became a prominent Peace Democrat during the Civil War. He denied that he had an emotional attachment to the Confederacy, but based his politics on economics. Seymour insisted an immediate armistice was needed because Connecticut, especially the New Haven carriage industry, did a large amount of business with the South. He also warned that conquering the rebel states would prove to be impossible.

Seymour´s controversial stands ended his hopes for political success. He ran for Governor again in 1860 and 1863, but lost both times. The Connecticut State Senate was so disgusted by his position on the war that it voted to remove his portrait from its chamber, saying the honor should be reserved only for former Governors who knew the meaning of loyalty.

JOHN SHERMAN (R 1880, 1888)

Sherman represented Ohio, but his true home was Washington, D.C. He spent forty-three years of continuous service in the capital. He entered the House in 1855, toiling six years there. That stint was followed by sixteen years in the Senate, four as Secretary of the Treasury, another sixteen in the Senate, and a final year as Secretary of State.

Sherman compiled his impressive record despite the largest handicap a politician could suffer, a colorless personality. He overcame it with a native shrewdness and the power of his national identity as the apostle of the gold standard. "There must be a day of reckoning," he warned soft-money advocates after the Civil War. "Order must be wrought out of a chaotic currency."[255] He turned out to be the man who did it. Sherman was Secretary of the Treasury in 1879 when the government officially backed paper money with gold. He declared, "There is but one par, and that par is gold."[256] But soft-money Republicans disagreed. They joined forces with those who considered Sherman a tired face, shooting down his Presidential candidacies.

LAWRENCE SHERMAN (R 1916)

Sherman was one of Woodrow Wilson´s harshest critics. The Illinois Republican entered the Senate after a 1913 special election, serving until the day Wilson left the White House eight years later. He castigated the President prior to World War I for what Sherman believed was a lack of military preparedness. The pendulum swung in the other direction after American troops landed in France. Sherman charged that Wilson was creating a "Presidential dictatorship" of a socialistic nature under "executive whip and spur."

Sherman returned to Illinois after his voluntary retirement from the Senate. But in 1924, he joined that decade´s rush to Florida, establishing himself as a lawyer and an investor.

ALFRED SMITH (D 1920, 1924, 1928, 1932)

"I don´t know those people out there," an exasperated Smith admitted privately during his 1928 campaign. "I don´t speak their language."[257] The man raised on Manhattan´s Lower East Side never established a rapport with middle Americans beyond the Hudson. They found his accent unusual and his urban background offensive. Many were repelled by his Catholicism.

Another strike against Smith was his close affiliation
with Tammany Hall. He began as an errand runner for the
Democratic machine, rising to become its chief in the New
York legislature. He won the first of four terms as Governor
in 1918. Smith's record was a strange mixture of progressive
legislation and Tammany patronage. Southerners and
Westerners were particularly offended by his willingness to
assist New York's bosses, but Smith refused to change. He
also refused to apologize for his roots. During a state
legislative session in 1911, one member proudly announced
that his college had just won an intercollegiate boat race.
Smith took the floor, "Mr. Chairman, if my old alma mater had
been represented in the race, we would have won....We were,
and I say it without boasting, strong on the water."
Colleagues asked his school. "I'm an old FFM man," Smith
replied, "the Fulton Fish Market."[258]

Smith watched jealously as his successor as Governor
leapfrogged past him to the Presidency. He emerged as a
leading conservative critic of Franklin Roosevelt. "All the
things we have done in the federal government are like the
things Al Smith did as Governor," a perplexed Roosevelt
said. "What in the world is the matter?"[259]

WILLIAM SPROUL (R 1920)

Sproul inherited two things that greatly shaped his
career: his family's money and its devotion to the Republican
party. The money came from an ironworks, augmented by his
wife's own wealth. Her father owned a large shipbuilding
firm. Sproul branched from this base into publishing,
railroads, manufacturing, real estate, and banking. His
solid Republican roots were best demonstrated by his middle
name, Cameron, in honor of Simon Cameron.

Sproul was interested in politics from his college days,
when he was Mitchell Palmer's roommate at Swarthmore. His
large bank account allowed him the freedom to occasionally
defy Pennsylvania's powerful Republican machine during his
twenty-two years in the state legislature, such as when he
voted against Matthew Quay's reelection to the Senate. But
Sproul hewed increasingly through the years to the party
line. He was elected to his sole term as Governor in 1918.
Republican bosses meeting in the infamous "smoke-filled room"
gave thought to Sproul as a possible compromise Presidential
nominee in 1920. They informally agreed to give him a whirl,
but only after trying Warren Harding.

HAROLD STASSEN (R 1948, 1952)

Few politicians emerged from World War II with brighter
futures than Stassen. Only 38 years old, he had already
served three terms as Governor of Minnesota, followed by Navy
duty on the staff of the famous Admiral William Halsey.
Stassen's organizational ability was conceded by his rivals.
They remembered how he shrewdly assembled a coalition of

young Republicans to seize control of the state party when he was only 31.

Stassen's first Presidential campaign was respectable, but fell short in 1948. He became president of the University of Pennsylvania, biding his time before running again in 1952. His loss that year seemed to end his political hopes, but Stassen denied it. "When God ends my life, that's when my career will end," he once said.[260] He proceeded to prove his persistence, losing races for Governor of Pennsylvania, Mayor of Philadelphia, and Senator from Minnesota. He returned to the Presidential wars in 1964, prompting Philadelphia magazine to give him its facetious Norman Thomas Candidate of the Year Award. It wrote, "The unquenchable Republican also wins a palm-leaf cluster for holding press conferences in hotel lobbies where the potted palms outnumbered the reporters."[261] The indefatigable Stassen nonetheless kept to his self-appointed task, running three more times for President. His name, once synonymous with youthful success, had been reduced to a punch line in jokes about political failure.

ADLAI STEVENSON (D 1952, 1956, 1960)

Stevenson was a hero to a generation of liberal Democrats, but he attained that status largely by chance. The grandson of Grover Cleveland's second Vice President, Stevenson held a number of appointive posts in the Roosevelt Administration, concluding as a member of the American delegation to the first meeting of the United Nations. Foreign affairs intrigued him more than domestic policy. He hoped in 1948 to pursue that interest by running for the Senate, but Illinois Democratic leaders forced him to settle for Governor. Stevenson's resounding win, coupled with the progressive administration that followed, made him a national figure.

Stevenson planned to run for reelection in 1952, but reluctantly accepted the Presidential nomination. "Let's talk sense to the American people," he declared, launching a campaign that received high marks for its intellectual content. The candidate's bald pate gave rise to a new word, "egghead." He was noted for a spontaneous wit, but the Chicago Tribune grumbled that he should leave the comedy to professionals. It compared "Adlai, the side-splitter," unfavorably to Abraham Lincoln, the rail-splitter.[262]

Stevenson's way with words never translated into national victory. He passed the Democratic torch to John Kennedy in 1960. "Do you remember that in classical times when Cicero had finished speaking, the people said, `How well he spoke,'" Stevenson noted in a speech that year. "But when Demosthenes had finished speaking, the people said, `Let us march.'"[263] With that, the modern-day Cicero yielded to a more vigorous type of liberalism, on the march toward the New Frontier.

STUART SYMINGTON (D 1960)

Symington was given an early look at the wild side of politics. As an eleven-year-old in Baltimore, he landed a job as a peanut and popcorn vendor at the chaotic 1912 Democratic convention. The young boy obviously was not intrigued. Symington avoided politics, growing up to be an executive with steel and radio businesses, landing at the Emerson Electric Manufacturing Company in Saint Louis during World War II. It was there that he came to the attention of Missouri Senator Harry Truman. President Truman later appointed Symington to a series of federal posts, capped by his nomination to be Secretary of the Air Force.

Symington entered politics in 1952, winning a Senate seat. The Missouri Democrat kept it for twenty-four years. He was noted for his insistence that the Soviets had opened a "missile gap" with the United States, a gap that was later disproved. He authored few pieces of legislation. One national magazine called him "a man with a grey flannel mind." But Symington remained proud of the business background that others attacked. He maintained it was the best training for a potential President.

ROBERT TAFT (R 1940, 1948, 1952)

Taft was an inflexible man in a profession that thrives on compromise. Conservatives admired what they saw as his steadfast commitment to principle. Herbert Hoover called the Ohio Republican "more nearly the irreplaceable man in American life than we have seen in three generations."[264] Liberals scoffed at such praise. They considered Taft to be pigheadedly clinging to antiquated theories. Organized labor never forgave him for the Taft-Hartley Act, which outlawed the closed shop.

Taft was the son of William Howard Taft. He did not share his father's preference for the judicial life, instead capping his career with fourteen years in the Senate. The younger Taft was an uninspiring, colorless speaker. Many found him unnecessarily frank. A Wisconsin politician once thanked him for sending a congratulatory telegram. "Oh, that," Taft coldly replied. "Never saw that wire myself, you know. [My staff] sends those things out by the dozen."[265] It was not unusual for him to interrupt a fellow Republican Senator in caucus by exclaiming, "Why, that's nonsense!" Some of his colleagues feared him.

Taft's power was derived from his consistency and personal strength. His tightly reasoned defense of conservative ideals in a liberal era earned him the nickname, "Mr. Republican." But it could not win him a Presidential nomination. Those were reserved for more congenial, less rigid candidates.

WILLIAM HOWARD TAFT (R 1908, 1912)

Taft was a large, good-natured man, well suited for the relatively placid life of a judge. That was the focus of much of his early career: three years on the local bench in Cincinnati, eight on the federal circuit court. But appointment as Territorial Governor of the Philippines ended the reverie. Taft was drawn closer to the partisan world. He didn´t like it. "Politics, when I am in it, makes me sick," he once said.266

Taft was recalled after four years in the Far East. Theodore Roosevelt named him Secretary of War, soon deciding to groom Taft to be his successor. The President one night pretended to fall into a trance in front of Taft and his wife, saying of the Cabinet officer, "There is something hanging over his head. I cannot make out what it is....At one time, it looks like the Presidency; then again, it looks like the Chief Justiceship." Taft´s wife immediately pleaded for the former; Taft whispered his hopes for the latter.267 He ended up with both. His one term as President was unhappy, marked by the celebrated split with Roosevelt. But Taft was overjoyed when Warren Harding placed him in charge of the Supreme Court in 1921. It was a dream come true.

ZACHARY TAYLOR (W 1848)

Taylor was one of the unlikeliest Presidential nominees ever. A career Army officer, he served thirty-eight years before the Mexican War elevated him to sudden glory. "Old Rough and Ready" scored two quick victories over the Mexicans in 1846. A grateful Congress authorized a medal for Taylor, but no one knew what he looked like. An artist had to be sent to his camp in Mexico to sketch a portrait. The inevitable talk began of running the faceless General for President in 1848. Taylor laughed that no sane person would envision him as a politician. He had never even voted in a Presidential election.

The Whigs persisted in running Taylor, but found him an eccentric candidate. He refused the letter notifying him of his nomination because there was postage due. The party had to send a second one. Even with his Whig endorsement, Taylor told anyone who listened that he would be a President "independent of party domination." It was expected that as a slaveholder, he would be incapable of escaping the influence of Southern Whigs. He surprised all by siding with the Northern branch of the party on the question of slavery in the territories. He might well have vetoed the Compromise of 1850, but died before it reached his desk.

NORMAN THOMAS (SOC 1932)

Thomas was introduced to capitalism while still a schoolboy. He earned spending money by delivering his hometown newspaper, the Marion, Ohio, Star. Its young publisher was Warren Harding. From that truly middle American background, Thomas went to Princeton, where one of his professors was Woodrow Wilson. He followed college with ordination as a Presbyterian minister in 1911, assigned to New York City.

World War I intruded on Thomas´ orderly progression. His opposition to the war led him to join the Socialist party in 1918. He decried the "grotesque inequalities, conspicuous waste, gross exploitation, and unnecessary poverty all about me."[268] He resigned his ministry, devoting his life to spreading the gospel of socialism.

Thomas willingly ran for almost any office as a Socialist: alderman, Mayor of New York City, state legislator, Governor of New York, and six times for President. He never won, but called his losses meaningless. "I suppose it is an achievement to live to my age and feel that one has kept the faith, or tried to," he said in 1961. "That´s the kind of achievement that I have to my credit. As the world counts achievement, I have not got much."[269]

ALLEN THURMAN (D 1880, 1884)

Thurman moved from his native Virginia at the age of six, but he never lost his devotion to the political principles rooted in the soil of the Old Dominion. The Ohio Democrat served two years in the House before the Civil War and twelve in the postwar Senate. He spoke for the doctrine of states´ rights, with one exception. He was against secession. Thurman belonged to Ohio´s influential corps of Peace Democrats during the war. He vehemently opposed black suffrage, promising in his unsuccessful 1867 campaign for Governor to free Ohio "from the thraldom of niggerism."

Thurman was among the most popular Democrats in the country after the war. He was known as "The Old Roman" and, because of his habit of theatrically mopping his brow, "The Knight of the Red Bandana." His last campaign came eight years after he lost his bid for reelection to the Senate. While hundreds of delegates waved red bandanas, the 1888 Democratic convention nominated Thurman for Vice President. The ticket lost in November.

STROM THURMOND (SRD 1948)

Thurmond´s career was a barometer of political changes in the South following World War II. The former lieutenant colonel was elected Governor of South Carolina in 1946 as a rabid white supremacist. He carried those views nationally two years later as the nominee of the States´ Rights Democratic party. Thurmond demonstrated a talent for invective. He charged that "the parlor pinks and subversives" were behind Harry Truman´s civil-rights program. A proposed federal law against lynching was dismissed because it "would provide the opening wedge for federal control of our police powers."[270]

Thurmond returned to the Democratic party, but never really felt at home after 1948. He and his running mate, Fielding Wright of Mississippi, were conspicuously absent from a luncheon of Democratic governors hosted by Truman in 1950. Asked if they had refused to come, Truman snapped, "They were not invited. I only invited Democrats."[271] Thurmond, who entered the Senate in 1955, presaged the

South's shift to the Republican party by switching his affiliation in 1964. He became a regional senior statesman by the 1980s, but was still obliged to keep up with the times. His later Senate campaigns featured appeals for the support of black voters, unthinkable in the past but a necessity in the new South.

SAMUEL TILDEN (D 1876, 1880)

Tilden grew up in a household steeped in Democratic party mythology. His father was connected with New York's Democratic organization, the Albany Regency. Tilden, while still young, therefore met kingpins such as Martin Van Buren. He worked for the party all his life, including eight years as state Democratic chairman. His own political ambitions were unfulfilled. Tilden served one term in the state legislature, but lost a race for New York Attorney General. He concentrated on his career as a railroad lawyer, becoming wealthy in the process.

The boss of Tammany Hall, William Tweed, provided the opportunity for Tilden's quick rise from obscurity. The infamous Tweed Ring was plundering New York City's treasury. Tilden lent his legal talents to the investigation that ended in Tweed's jailing in 1872. The resulting publicity catapulted Tilden to Governor in 1874. "I do not care a snap of my fingers for the Presidency," he insisted of the likely next step in his career.[272] His exposure of additional political corruption, in the form of the Canal Ring, virtually forced his nomination. Tilden always believed the 1876 election was stolen from him, joking that he had the best of both worlds: the honor of being elected President without the cares of office.

HARRY TRUMAN (D 1948)

Truman was the personification of the American dream, a hardworking man from a small town who was rewarded with unimagined success. He became noted for a fierce, independent spirit. All of this shocked those who followed Truman's early struggles, when two descriptions routinely applied by critics were "failure" and "subservient."

Truman farmed for twelve years as an adult. After serving in World War I, he opened a haberdashery. It folded, leaving him $35,000 in the red. It took fifteen years to pay off the debts. Truman was rescued by Kansas City's Democratic boss, Tom Pendergast, who decided to run him for Jackson County Court Judge. Truman held the administrative post for ten years, eight as Presiding Judge. He moved up to the Senate in 1934, but found Washington unimpressed. Colleagues laughingly referred to him as "the Gentleman from Pendergast." One of his opponents in the 1934 campaign predicted Truman would get "calluses on his ears listening on the long-distance telephone to his boss." Franklin Roosevelt tried to stop Truman from running for reelection in 1940 by offering him another job. The Senator barked at an emissary, "Tell them to go to hell!"[273] He won a second term.

The wartime panel known as the Truman Committee rehabilitated the Senator´s image. He was suddenly seen as a feisty watchdog over defense contractors. Roosevelt now considered him an asset, choosing the man from Missouri as his last Vice President. After only eighty-three days in that post, Truman received his final promotion, struggling to emerge from Roosevelt´s enormous shadow. It was a job not completed until his storybook triumph over Thomas Dewey in 1948.

MORRIS UDALL (D 1976)

Udall replaced his brother in Congress. Stewart Udall was chosen by John Kennedy to be his Secretary of the Interior. Morris launched a House career that would run more than twenty years, eventually establishing him as an expert on conservation. Democratic leaders in the 1960s could not foresee his accomplishments. They considered Udall to be a troublemaker. He blasted Lyndon Johnson´s Vietnam policy in 1967 as "a mistaken and dangerous road." He constantly criticized the House´s seniority system, sacrosanct to the leadership. The Arizonan committed the ultimate heresy in 1969, challenging the reelection of Speaker John McCormack. He lost.

Udall eventually rose to Congressional power the old-fashioned way, by accumulating seniority. But he never ditched the sense of humor that had bothered his elders. After losing his 1970 race for House Majority Leader, he turned his "MO" button upside down. It read "OW." Losing was also the rule in his 1976 Presidential campaign. The networks projected a breakthrough in the Wisconsin primary. "It looks like we are winners tonight," Udall shouted to supporters. "How good it is!" The next morning´s final returns showed Jimmy Carter the hairbreadth victor. "You may amend my statement of last night," Udall told reporters. "Insert the word `losers´ where I had `winners.´"[274]

OSCAR UNDERWOOD (D 1912, 1924)

Underwood was born in Kentucky and spent his adult life in Alabama, but he was never a typical Southern politician. Critics blamed his apostasy on the fact that he spent much of his childhood in Minnesota and later briefly returned to that state as a lawyer. No matter how conservative his voting record, he still seemed to have a touch of the Northerner in him. William Jennings Byran once marveled, "He is a New York candidate living in the South."[275]

Underwood served nineteen years in the House and twelve in the Senate. He rose to be Democratic floor leader in each chamber. But his lack of orthodoxy prevented any promotion to the White House. Underwood called for the repeal of Prohibition and excoriated the Ku Klux Klan, at the peak of its power in 1924. "It is either the Klan or the United States," he declared.[276] The South abandoned him, with the exception of Alabama, which led every roll call at the marathon convention by supporting its native son. A weary nation listening by radio grew to know the voice of Governor William Brandon, shouting, "Alabama casts twenty-four votes for Oscar W. Underwood!" Will Rogers joked that Brandon's litany became better known than the Lord's Prayer.

MARTIN VAN BUREN (D 1836, 1840, 1844, FS 1848)

Van Buren may have been the master political tactician of his age. Known as the "Little Magician," the charming New Yorker was an expert at manipulating people. He assembled his state's formidable Albany Regency, then formed an ironclad alliance with Andrew Jackson. Congressman Edward Everett was convinced that Jackson's 1828 victory was accomplished "directly under the wand of the great magician." Horace Greeley, trying to discover Van Buren's secret, found that the politician lacked personal magnetism and was neither a great orator nor administrator. "I believe his strength lay in his suavity," Greeley concluded. "He was the reconciler of the estranged, the harmonizer of those who were at feud, among his fellow partisans. An adroit and subtle, rather than a great man."[277]

Van Buren served eight years in the Senate, then rode Jackson's coattails to become Secretary of State, Vice President, and President. His downfall resulted from two explosive issues that not even his great political sagacity could defuse. An economic depression convinced voters to depose the President in 1840. His comeback in 1844 was wrecked by the furor over the proposed annexation of Texas. Van Buren opposed it, but a majority of Democrats was on the other side. It was rare proof that even magicians could make political mistakes.

ARTHUR VANDENBERG (R 1940, 1948)

Vandenberg ran twice for President, presenting himself on two substantially different platforms. His 1940 campaign carried the standard of isolationism. Eight years later, the Michigan Senator was a proponent of internationalism. Neither effort caught the fancy of Republican delegates.

Vandenberg was a newspaper editor for twenty-two years before being appointed to the Senate in 1928. He advanced to Minority Leader by the mid-1930s, never missing a chance to advocate neutrality legislation. He asserted in 1939, "We all have our sympathies and our natural emotion in behalf of the victims of national or international outrage all around the globe. But we are not, we cannot be, the world's protector or the world's policeman."[278]

Conversion came suddenly with the bombing of Pearl Harbor. "That day ended isolation for any realist," Vandenberg conceded.[279] He switched completely, becoming a leading advocate of the United Nations and the Marshall Plan. Democratic Presidents counted on him to lead the bipartisan battle against the small band of enduring isolationists, a group he once led, but now scorned.

GEORGE WALLACE (D 1964, AI 1968, D 1972, 1976)

Wallace came to national prominence in 1963. He literally stood in the schoolhouse door to prevent the admission of blacks to the University of Alabama. President John Kennedy federalized the National Guard, forcing Wallace to back down. But the Governor was a hero across the South. He had demonstrated his commitment to the pledge he made in his inaugural address, "I say segregation now, segregation tomorrow, segregation forever!"[280]

Wallace was, above all else, a shrewd politician. He first ran for Governor as a racial moderate in 1958 and lost. Telling friends he had been "outniggered," he vowed not to let it happen again. His 1962 victory as a white supremacist was the first of four times he was chosen to be Governor. Wallace's wife was once elected when he was constitutionally barred from running again.

Wallace was out of place in the liberal national Democratic party. He toyed with becoming a Republican in 1964, then formed the American Independent party four years later. His Presidential campaigns were marked by populist rhetoric. "There is nothing wrong with America," he would shout, "but there is something wrong with leadership that refuses to listen to average citizens."[281] Observers who dismissed Wallace as an aberration were astounded at his broad appeal outside the South. Paralyzed after a 1972 assassination attempt, Wallace never regained the vigor that marked his early efforts. The rise of fellow Southerner Jimmy Carter ended his final try for the Democratic nomination.

HENRY WALLACE (P 1948)

Franklin Roosevelt often called Wallace "the philosopher of the New Deal." Even the Iowan's critics conceded his penchant for abstract thought, sometimes bordering on mysticism. Professional politicians were uncomfortable with what they considered his peculiar blend of naivete and outspokenness. While others portrayed World War II as a deadly struggle with Germany and Japan, Wallace said, "The object of this war is to make sure everybody in the world has the privilege of drinking a quart of milk a day."[282] Cynics just shook their heads.

Wallace's training was in agriculture. He conducted experiments and wrote for his family's farm journal. His father had been Warren Harding's Secretary of Agriculture and the son filled the same position for Roosevelt in 1933. The President surprised nearly everyone by tapping Wallace to be his running mate in 1940. "He's a philosopher, he's got ideas, [and] he'll help the people think," Roosevelt assured James Farley.[283] Opponents' thoughts turned sour after Wallace called them "American fascists." They helped unseat him in 1944. Wallace thereafter drifted away from the Democratic party, accusing it of abandoning Roosevelt's principles.

THOMAS WALSH (D 1924, 1928)

Walsh was a prototype for Sam Ervin. Each labored long in the Senate without public acclaim, then vaulted to prominence by investigating a political scandal. Walsh headed the probe into the Harding Administration's Teapot Dome, while Ervin conducted the inquiry into the Nixon Administration's Watergate. Both became popular heroes for a time, even though critics ridiculed them as muckrakers. "Of course I am," Walsh replied to the charges. "I have been wallowing in the muck in which the late [Interior] Secretary [Albert] Fall and his associates sought to hide themselves."[284]

Walsh left a prosperous Montana law practice to serve the last twenty years of his life in the Senate. His record was progressive, including early support for women's suffrage and the League of Nations. Franklin Roosevelt named Walsh his Attorney General, but the Montanan died on a Washington-bound train two days before the inaugural. The Saint Louis Post-Dispatch mourned his passing by comparing him to a famous Italian social reformer. "As Florence had its Savonarola," it editorialized, "so Washington had its Walsh."[285]

EARL WARREN (R 1948, 1952)

Warren was a Republican in name only. He used the party label to win fourteen years as a local prosecutor, four as California Attorney General, and ten as Governor. His commitment went little further. Warren refused to campaign for other Republicans or even share stages with them. He went so far as to secure the nomination of both major parties when running for reelection as Governor in 1946. He scorned the Republican tag, preferring the seemingly contradictory label of "progressive conservative." Harry Truman laughed that Warren was really a Democrat. He just didn't know it.

Warren's liberal credentials became glaringly apparent during his sixteen-year stint as Chief Justice. Dwight Eisenhower praised his "middle-of-the-road philosophy" when announcing the appointment. Ike then watched helplessly as the Warren Court ordered school desegregation, outlawed school prayer, and broadened defendants' rights. Republicans were livid. Thomas Dewey, who chose Warren as his running mate in 1948, began calling him "that big dumb Swede." Eisenhower just grumbled that naming Warren Chief Justice was "the biggest damnfool mistake I ever made."[286]

GEORGE WASHINGTON (F 1789, 1792)

Life for Washington was an almost constant struggle between his wishes to be a gentleman farmer in Virginia and the demands of others that he provide public service. His experience in the French and Indian War and the Continental Congress' desire to give the South a stake in the Revolutionary War led Congress to place him in command of the Continental Army. Washington left Mount Vernon on what proved to be an eight-year odyssey to freedom. He called himself a "wearied traveler" when peace finally returned in 1783, insisting he had no "wish beyond that of living and dying an honest man on my own farm."[287]

Washington´s dreams were dashed by the failure of the Articles of Confederation. He reluctantly emerged from semi-retirement to preside over the Constitutional Convention. Some thought he needed the challenge. James Madison wrote privately that "a mind like his, capable of grand views, and which has long been occupied with them, cannot bear a vacancy."[288]   The call soon sounded again, with Washington´s election as the first President. His contemporaries first feared he would refuse the honor, then worried he would resign in mid-term. The man known as "the Father of His Country" surprised almost everyone by serving two full terms before heading home for the last time.

JAMES WATSON (R 1928)

Watson was an unbending member of the Republican Old Guard. He represented Indiana in the House for twelve years and the Senate for sixteen. His record was consistently conservative, isolationist, and pro-business. Watson´s 1928 Presidential candidacy was fueled by these principles, but was also motivated by his dislike of Herbert Hoover. Their relationship was further strained in 1929, when Hoover moved into the White House and Watson was elevated to Senate Majority Leader. The President tried to oust his nemesis, but failed.

Watson was always on the lookout for impurity in the Republican party. He opposed the Presidential nomination of a fellow Indiana native, Wendell Willkie, in 1940 because the candidate had once been a Democrat. Willkie jokingly asked Watson if he believed in conversion. "Yes, Wendell, if the town whore truly repented and wanted to join my church, I´d welcome her," came the reply. "I would greet her personally and lead her up the aisle to the front pew. But I´d be damned if I´d ask her to lead the choir the first night."[289] Willkie just grinned at Watson and shook his head.

JAMES WEAVER (GR 1880, POP 1892)

Weaver came full circle in his political career, beginning and ending as a Democrat, but traveling through three other parties on the way. His strong antislavery views triggered his first switch. He joined the Republican party before the Civil War, in which he rose to be a major-general. The GOP turned sour on soft money after the war, causing Weaver to write the party´s candidate for Governor of Iowa in 1877, "Differing, as I do, so widely with the Republican party upon questions of finance, I find it impossible for me to go before the people and advocate a continuance of that policy."[290] He joined the new Greenback party, being elected to the first of his three terms in the House the following year.

Weaver´s dynamic, almost evangelical speaking style made

him a logical Presidential nominee for the Greenbackers in 1880 and for the Populist party in 1892. He was instrumental in leading the latter to fusion with the Democrats in 1896 behind the candidacy of William Jennings Bryan. A grateful Bryan called him "a man who was in advance of most of the people of his time in regard to the things that stood in the way of the people's good."[291] His political odyssey completed, Weaver remained with the Democrats from that point on.

DANIEL WEBSTER (W 1836, 1848, 1852)

Webster was a legend in his own time, one of the greatest orators in American history. His booming voice and theatrical presence commanded large audiences in Congressional galleries or on the stump. John Quincy Adams, who disliked the man, still found his speeches "brilliant." A Harvard student who was spellbound by a Webster oration later wrote, "I was never so excited by public speaking before in my life. Three or four times I thought my temple would burst with the rush of blood."[292] His 1830 speech against the concept of secession was a classic. It ended with the immortal line, "Liberty and Union, now and forever, one and inseparable!"[293]

Webster served eight years in the House, nineteen in the Senate, and four as Secretary of State. First as a Federalist, then a Whig, he defended the commercial interests of New England. He believed in the protective tariff and vigorously supported the Second Bank of the United States. Grateful businessmen often supplemented Webster's income or helped rescue him from the debts that always threatened. He saw nothing wrong with such arrangements.

Webster dreamed of the Presidency for decades, but never got close to the White House. "How will this look in history?" he cried of what he considered the ultimate injustice.[294] But he had failed to create a political base to right the perceived wrong. The Northern masses disliked his affiliation with the commercial classes. Southerners never forgot his contempt for secession and slavery.

JOHN WEEKS (R 1916)

Weeks established himself with a banking and brokerage firm in Boston, acquiring both a fortune and conservative Republican principles. He entered local politics in Newton, Massachusetts, at the turn of the 20th Century. He later served eight years in the House and six in the Senate.

Weeks always sided with the Old Guard. In the debate over the strict, some said dictatorial, rule of Speaker Joseph Cannon, he defended Cannon as "the best-fitted man in the House to occupy that place." The reform element nonetheless triumphed. Weeks fought another losing battle in the Senate against expanding the electorate. "I cannot see anything but harm coming from woman suffrage," he wrote in 1917. "What we want is a more intelligent suffrage rather than a less intelligent one."[295]   The times were obviously passing him by, proved by his defeat for reelection in 1918. Weeks returned to Washington in an appointive post, Secretary of War, in 1921. He filled the position for four years.

HUGH WHITE (W 1836)

White and Andrew Jackson were great friends during the early years of Tennessee. When White ran for a state judgeship in 1801, Jackson declared, "To have this done [White elected], is my greatest wish."[296]   Likewise, when Old Hickory sought the Presidency, his friend was among his most ardent supporters. Jackson left the Senate in 1825, the year after his first national campaign. He was replaced by White, who promised to follow his predecessor's voting record. The only real difference between the two seemed to be in personality. Jackson was fiery, but White had little imagination. He was a colorless man in a colorful age.

White eventually drifted from President Jackson. The Senator charged that "the foolish advice of small men" was causing his friend to take unintelligent stands. He was especially upset by the rising star of Martin Van Buren. Jackson warned White that he would ruin the Senator if he joined the evolving Whig opposition. White did anyway. He and Jackson were thereafter enemies. The feud was so strong it outlived them. The Tennessee legislature discussed placing a statue of White in its new state capitol in 1858. The debate was so heated that a fist fight broke out in a corridor between supporters of the two men, both long dead.

WENDELL WILLKIE (R 1940)

Willkie was a lawyer for Firestone Tire and Rubber after World War I, but resolved to go into private practice. "Young man, I like you," Harvey Firestone said on his departure, "but I don't think you will ever amount to a great deal." Willkie asked why not. "Because I understand you're a Democrat," Firestone replied.[297]   It was certainly true. Willkie turned his graduation speech from Indiana University in 1916 into a defense of Woodrow Wilson. He was a delegate to the chaotic 1924 Democratic convention. He remained a registered Democrat until 1938.

Willkie's political metamorphosis was triggered by a career change. He became president of a large utility, Commonwealth and Southern Corporation, in 1933. For six years, he struggled against the Roosevelt Administration's plans to add C&S property to the Tennessee Valley Authority. Willkie lost the battle, only after being recognized as an outspoken and articulate critic of the New Deal. He joked that he was just "the best gadget salesman in the country," but the Republicans thought he was the fresh face they needed in 1940. His increasingly virulent attacks against big businessmen, such as calling them "economic Tories," destroyed any hopes for a second nomination in 1944. Willkie died of a heart attack before the end of the year.

WOODROW WILSON (D 1912, 1916)

Wilson´s switch from the academic life to politics had the appearance of an impulsive move, but it was actually the culmination of a lifelong dream. While still a student, he fantasized by making business cards that read, "Thomas Woodrow Wilson, Senator from Virginia." He later went to law school, but not to become a lawyer. "The profession I chose was politics, the profession I entered was the law," Wilson wrote. "I entered the one because I thought it would lead to the other."298 It didn´t. Bored with the law, Wilson became a professor. He was chosen president of Princeton in 1902, reconciled to the death of his political ambitions.

Wilson was determined to deemphasize athletics and social clubs at Princeton. He was only partly successful, but attracted public attention as a crusader. His warning that colleges were in danger because they served "the classes, [not] the masses," added to his reputation. New Jersey Democrats wanted such a popular figure to be their candidate for Governor in 1910. Wilson won, then pushed a highly publicized progressive package through the state legislature. He attained the Presidency two years later.

Washington expected the man from quiet campuses to be overwhelmed by the hectic atmosphere of the White House. But Wilson employed a strong will and a more than normal-sized ego in battles over his progressive bills and the League of Nations. The President maintained he was well prepared. "Compared with the college politician," he wrote, "the real article seems like an amateur."299

WILLIAM WIRT (AM 1832)

Wirt was a talented lawyer, but was never fond of hard work. Legend has it that his fiancee´s father disapproved of their proposed marriage and went to confront Wirt one morning. He was dismayed to find his future son-in-law playing Falstaff after a night of revelry, using a tin basin for a helmet and a poker for a sword. Wirt´s tendency to be a showman extended to the courtroom. He wrote a colleague about one of his cases, "Come down and hear it....It will be a combat worth witnessing."300

Wirt´s natural skills nonetheless propelled him upward. He was one of the best-known lawyers in Virginia after his role in the unsuccessful prosecution of Aaron Burr for treason in 1807. Following a stint as a U.S. Attorney, Wirt was named Attorney General by President James Monroe. He served for twelve years.

Wirt was a Baltimore lawyer when he was nominated for President by the Anti-Masonic party. He was chosen mainly because of his availability and his dislike for Andrew Jackson. It was ironic that Wirt had once been a Mason himself and never saw any evil in Freemasonry. He returned to private practice after his defeat.

LEONARD WOOD (R 1920)

Wood put in years of routine service in the Army Medical Corps before a fateful meeting in 1897. He made the acquaintance of someone remarkably similar to himself, Theodore Roosevelt. Both men were ambitious, energetic, and strong nationalists. Together, they formed the Rough Riders when the Spanish-American War broke out. Roosevelt charged up San Juan Hill to the White House. Wood was eventually named Military Governor of Cuba. He grew to be such a popular figure on the island that when he died in 1927, Cuba voted his widow a pension before Congress did.

Wood's Cuban service launched him to the highest ranks of the Army. He became Chief of Staff in 1910. After the outbreak of World War I, Wood was a leading agitator for preparedness. He often cited Henry Lee's words, "A government is the murderer of its people which sends them to the field uninformed and untaught."[301] Woodrow Wilson disliked the implication. He made certain that Wood did not receive an overseas command when America entered the war.

Roosevelt suggested Wood as his political heir for 1920. The General exasperated his advisers by campaigning for President in uniform and raising the volatile issue of Communism. Republican bosses looked for someone safer and more prone to take direction. They found Warren Harding.

LEVI WOODBURY (D 1848)

Woodbury was his region's Democratic leader in the party's early years. The New Hampshire resident was nicknamed, "The Rock of New England Democracy." Hannibal Hamlin, later to be Vice President as a Republican, backed Woodbury for President in 1848, calling him "a wheelhorse of the Democracy." Everyone agreed Woodbury's long friendship with Andrew Jackson was one of the sources of his power. His conservative beliefs gave him broad appeal, particularly in the South.

Woodbury was elected Governor at age 34. He later served eleven years in the Senate, and occupied the Cabinet posts of Secretary of the Navy and Secretary of the Treasury. In the latter office, he was the point man for Jackson's continuing battle against the Second Bank of the United States. Woodbury was appointed in 1846 to the Supreme Court, where he served the rest of his life. His decisions upheld the rights of slaveholders, labeling slavery "a political question, settled by each state for itself."[302] He continued to be admired in the South, but saw his Northern popularity dwindle as the nation edged closer to the Civil War.

Charts for Chapter 7

John Adams (1735-1826)

General	PV	%	EV	%	personal
1796*F (Q)	----	----	71	51.4	Mass. 61
1800 F (Q)	----	----	65	47.1	Mass. 65
Career	----	----	136	49.3	

John Quincy Adams (1767-1848)

General	PV	%	EV	%	personal
1820 IDR	----	----	1	0.4	Mass. 53
1824*DR (Q)	113,122	30.9	84	32.2	Mass. 57
1828 NR (Q)	500,897	43.6	83	31.8	Mass. 61
Career	614,019	40.6	168	32.0	

Russell Alger (1836-1907)

Convention	FB	%	LB	%	personal
1888 R (Q)	84	10.1	100	12.0	Mich. 52

William Allen (1803-1879)

Convention	FB	%	LB	%	personal
1876 D (Q)	54	7.3	54	7.3	Ohio 73

William Boyd Allison (1829-1908)

Convention	FB	%	LB	%	personal
1888 R (Q)	72	8.7	0	0.0	Iowa 59
1896 R	35½	3.8	----	----	Iowa 67
Career	107½	8.7	0	0.0	

John Anderson (1922-   )

Primaries	W	%	PV	%	personal
1980 R (Q)	0	0.0	1,572,174	12.2	Ill. 58

Convention	FB	%	LB	%	personal
1980 R	37	1.9	----	----	

General	PV	%	EV	%	personal
1980 NU (Q)	5,720,060	6.6	0	0.0	
1984 NU	1,479	0.0	0	0.0	Ill. 62
Career	5,721,539	6.6	0	0.0	

Chester Arthur (1830-1886)

Convention	FB	%	LB	%	personal
1884 R (Q)	278	33.9	207	25.2	N.Y. 54

John Ashbrook (1928-1982)

Primaries	W	%	PV	%	personal
1972 R (Q)	0	0.0	311,543	5.0	Ohio 44

Alben Barkley (1877-1956)

Convention	FB	%	LB	%	personal
1948 D	1	0.1	----	----	Ky. 71
1952 D (Q)	48½	3.9	67½	5.5	Ky. 75
Career	49½	3.9	67½	5.5	

Edward Bates (1793-1869)

Convention	FB	%	LB	%	personal
1860 R (Q)	48	10.3	0	0.0	Mo. 67

Thomas Bayard (1828-1898)

Convention	FB	%	LB	%	personal
1872 D	15	2.0	----	----	Del. 44
1876 D (Q)	33	4.5	4	0.5	Del. 48
1880 D (Q)	153½	20.8	2	0.3	Del. 52
1884 D (Q)	170	20.7	81½	9.9	Del. 56
Career	371½	15.5	87½	3.8	

John Bell (1797-1869)

General	PV	%	EV	%	personal
1860 CU (Q)	590,901	12.6	39	12.9	Tenn. 63

Allan Benson (1871-1940)

General	PV	%	EV	%	personal
1916 SOC (Q)	589,924	3.2	0	0.0	N.Y. 45

John Bidwell (1819-1900)

General	PV	%	EV	%	personal
1892 PROH (Q)	270,770	2.2	0	0.0	Cal. 73

James Birney (1792-1857)

General	PV	%	EV	%	personal
1840 LTY	6,797	0.3	0	0.0	N.Y. 48
1844 LTY (Q)	62,103	2.3	0	0.0	Mich. 52
Career	68,900	2.3	0	0.0	

Joseph Blackburn (1838-1918)

Convention	FB	%	LB	%	personal
1896 D (Q)	82	8.8	0	0.0	Ky. 58

James Blaine (1830-1893)

Convention	FB	%	LB	%	personal
1876 R (Q)	285	37.7	351	46.4	Me. 46
1880 R (Q)	284	37.6	42	5.6	Me. 50
1884*R (Q)	334½	40.8	541	66.0	Me. 54
1888 R (Q)	35	4.2	5	0.6	Me. 58
1892 R (Q)	$182\frac{1}{6}$	20.1	----	----	Me. 62
Career	$1,120\frac{2}{3}$	27.5	939	29.7	

General	PV	%	EV	%	personal
1884 R (Q)	4,848,936	48.2	182	45.4	

Richard Bland (1835-1899)

Convention	FB	%	LB	%	personal
1896 D (Q)	235	25.3	11	1.2	Mo. 61

Horace Boies (1827-1923)

Convention	FB	%	LB	%	personal
1892 D (Q)	103	11.3	----	----	Iowa 65
1896 D (Q)	67	7.2	0	0.0	Iowa 69
Career	170	9.2	0	0.0	

William Borah (1865-1940)

Primaries	W	%	PV	%	personal
1936*R (Q)	5	41.7	1,474,152	44.4	Ida. 71

Convention	FB	%	LB	%	personal
1916 R	2	0.2	0	0.0	Ida. 51
1920 R	2	0.2	0	0.0	Ida. 55
1936 R	19	1.9	----	----	
Career	23	----	0	----	

John Breckinridge (1821-1875)

Convention	FB	%	LB	%	personal
1860 D	0	0.0	7½	2.5	Ky. 39

General	PV	%	EV	%	personal
1860 SD (Q)	848,019	18.1	72	23.8	

Benjamin Bristow (1832-1896)

Convention	FB	%	LB	%	personal
1876 R (Q)	113	14.9	21	2.8	Ky. 44

Gratz Brown (1826-1885)

General	PV	%	EV	%	personal
1872 D-LR (Q)	----	----	18	5.2	Mo. 46

Jerry Brown (1938-   )

Primaries	W	%	PV	%	personal
1976 D (Q)	3	11.1	2,449,374	15.3	Cal. 38
1980 D	0	0.0	575,296	2.9	Cal. 42
Career	3	11.1	3,024,670	15.3	

Convention	FB	%	LB	%	personal
1976 D (Q)	300½	10.0	----	----	
1980 D	1	0.0	----	----	
Career	301½	10.0	----	----	

William Jennings Bryan (1860-1925)

Convention	FB	%	LB	%	personal
1896*D (Q)	137	14.7	652	70.1	Neb. 36
1900*D (Q)	936	100.0	----	----	Neb. 40
1908*D (Q)	888½	88.7	----	----	Neb. 48
1912 D	1	0.1	0	0.0	Neb. 52
1920 D	1	0.1	0	0.0	Neb. 60
Career	1,963½	68.4	652	70.1	

General	PV	%	EV	%	personal
1896 D-POP (Q)	6,511,495	46.7	176	39.4	
1900 D (Q)	6,358,345	45.5	155	34.7	
1908 D (Q)	6,406,801	43.0	162	33.5	
Career	19,276,641	45.1	493	35.8	

James Buchanan (1791-1868)

Convention	FB	%	LB	%	personal
1844 D	4	1.5	0	0.0	Pa. 53
1848 D (Q)	55	19.0	33	11.4	Pa. 57
1852 D (Q)	93	32.3	0	0.0	Pa. 61
1856*D (Q)	135½	45.8	296	100.0	Pa. 65
Career	287½	32.4	329	37.6	

General	PV	%	EV	%	personal
1856*D (Q)	1,836,072	45.3	174	58.8	

Theodore Burton (1851-1929)

Primaries	W	%	PV	%	personal
1916 R (Q)	2	10.0	122,165	6.4	Ohio 65

Convention	FB	%	LB	%	personal
1916 R (Q)	77½	7.9	0	0.0	

George Bush (1924-   )

Primaries	W	%	PV	%	personal
1980 R (Q)	6	17.1	3,075,449	23.9	Tex. 56

Convention	FB	%	LB	%	personal
1980 R	13	0.7	----	----	

Nicholas Murray Butler (1862-1947)

Convention	FB	%	LB	%	personal
1920 R (Q)	69½	7.1	2	0.2	N.Y. 58

Harry Byrd (1887-1966)

Convention	FB	%	LB	%	personal
1932 D	25	2.2	0	0.0	Va. 45
1944 D (Q)	89	7.6	----	----	Va. 57
Career	114	7.6	0	----	

General	PV	%	EV	%	personal
1956 SR	2,657	0.0	0	0.0	Va. 69
1960 ID (Q)	116,248	0.2	15	2.8	Va. 73
Career	118,905	0.2	15	2.8	

Simon Cameron (1799-1889)

Convention	FB	%	LB	%	personal
1860 R (Q)	50½	10.8	0	0.0	Pa. 61

Joseph Cannon (1836-1926)

Convention	FB	%	LB	%	personal
1908 R (Q)	58	5.9	----	----	Ill. 72

Jimmy Carter (1924-   )

Primaries	W	%	PV	%	personal
1976*D (Q)	17	63.0	6,235,609	38.8	Ga. 52
1980*D (Q)	24	68.6	10,043,016	51.2	Ga. 56
Career	41	66.1	16,278,625	45.6	

Convention	FB	%	LB	%	personal
1976*D (Q)	2,238½	74.4	----	----	
1980*D (Q)	2,123	63.7	----	----	
Career	4,361½	68.8	----	----	

General	PV	%	EV	%	personal
1976*D (Q)	40,830,763	50.1	297	55.2	
1980 D (Q)	35,483,883	41.0	49	9.1	
Career	76,314,646	45.4	346	32.2	

Lewis Cass (1782-1866)

Convention	FB	%	LB	%	personal
1844 D (Q)	83	31.2	29	10.9	Mich. 62
1848*D (Q)	125	43.1	179	61.7	Mich. 66
1852 D (Q)	116	40.3	2	0.7	Mich. 70
1856 D	5	1.7	0	0.0	Mich. 74
Career	329	38.4	210	24.9	

General	PV	%	EV	%	personal
1848 D (Q)	1,223,460	42.5	127	43.8	

Salmon Chase (1808-1873)

Convention	FB	%	LB	%	personal
1860 R (Q)	49	10.5	2	0.4	Ohio 52

Shirley Chisholm (1924-   )

Primaries	W	%	PV	%	personal
1972 D	1	4.8	430,703	2.7	N.Y. 48

Convention	FB	%	LB	%	personal
1972 D (Q)	$151\frac{95}{100}$	5.0	----	----	

Frank Church (1924-1984)

Primaries	W	%	PV	%	personal
1976 D (Q)	4	14.8	830,818	5.2	Ida. 52

Convention	FB	%	LB	%	personal
1976 D	19	0.6	----	----	

Sanford Church (1815-1880)

Convention	FB	%	LB	%	personal
1868 D (Q)	34	10.7	0	0.0	N.Y. 53

Champ Clark (1850-1921)

Primaries	W	%	PV	%	personal
1912 D (Q)	5	41.7	405,537	41.6	Mo. 62

Convention	FB	%	LB	%	personal
1912 D (Q)	440½	40.3	84	7.7	
1920 D	9	0.8	0	0.0	Mo. 70
Career	449½	40.3	84	7.7	

Henry Clay (1777-1852)

Convention	FB	%	LB	%	personal
1832*NR (Q)	167	99.4	----	----	Ky. 55
1840 W (Q)	103	40.6	90	35.4	Ky. 63
1844*W (Q)	275	100.0	----	----	Ky. 67
1848 W (Q)	97	34.6	32	11.4	Ky. 71
Career	642	65.7	122	22.8	

General	PV	%	EV	%	personal
1824 DR (Q)	47,531	13.0	37	14.2	Ky. 47
1832 NR (Q)	484,205	37.4	49	17.1	
1844 W (Q)	1,300,004	48.1	105	38.2	
1848 IW	89	0.0	0	0.0	
Career	1,831,829	42.0	191	23.2	

Grover Cleveland (1837-1908)

Convention	FB	%	LB	%	personal
1884*D (Q)	392	47.8	683	83.3	N.Y. 47
1888*D (Q)	822	100.0	----	----	N.Y. 51
1892*D (Q)	$617\frac{1}{3}$	67.8	----	----	N.Y. 55
Career	$1,831\frac{1}{3}$	71.8	683	83.3	

General	PV	%	EV	%	personal
1884*D (Q)	4,874,621	48.5	219	54.6	
1888 D (Q)	5,534,488	48.6	168	41.9	
1892*D (Q)	5,551,883	46.1	277	62.4	
Career	15,960,992	47.7	664	53.3	

DeWitt Clinton (1769-1828)

General	PV	%	EV	%	personal
1812 F-IDR (Q)	----	----	89	41.0	N.Y. 43

George Clinton (1739-1812)

General	PV	%	EV	%	personal
1808 IDR (Q)	----	----	6	3.4	N.Y. 69

Francis Cockrell (1834-1915)

Convention	FB	%	LB	%	personal
1904 D (Q)	42	4.2	----	----	Mo. 70

Roscoe Conkling (1829-1888)

Convention	FB	%	LB	%	personal
1876 R (Q)	99	13.1	0	0.0	N.Y. 47

Calvin Coolidge (1872-1933)

Primaries	W	%	PV	%	personal
1924*R (Q)	15	88.2	2,410,363	68.4	Mass. 52
1928 R	0	0.0	12,985	0.3	Mass. 56
Career	15	88.2	2,423,348	68.4	

Convention	FB	%	LB	%	personal
1920 R	34	3.5	5	0.5	Mass. 48
1924*R (Q)	1,065	96.0	----	----	
1928 R	17	1.6	----	----	
1932 R	4½	0.4	----	----	Mass. 60
Career	1,120½	96.0	5	----	

General	PV	%	EV	%	personal
1924*R (Q)	15,717,553	54.1	382	71.9	

James Cox (1870-1957)

Primaries	W	%	PV	%	personal
1920 D (Q)	1	6.3	86,194	15.1	Ohio 50
1924 D	1	7.1	74,183	9.7	Ohio 54
Career	2	6.3	160,377	15.1	

James Cox (continued)

Convention	FB	%	LB	%	personal
1920✻D (Q)	134	12.2	699½	63.9	
1924 D (Q)	59	5.4	0	0.0	
1932 D	0	0.0	1	0.1	Ohio 62
Career	193	8.8	700½	31.9	

General	PV	%	EV	%	personal
1920 D (Q)	9,140,884	34.2	127	23.9	

Jacob Coxey (1854-1951)

Primaries	W	%	PV	%	personal
1932 R (Q)	1	7.1	100,844	4.3	Ohio 78

General	PV	%	EV	%	personal
1932 F-L	7,431	0.0	0	0.0	

William Crawford (1772-1834)

General	PV	%	EV	%	personal
1824 DR (Q)	40,856	11.2	41	15.7	Ga. 52

Albert Cummins (1850-1926)

Primaries	W	%	PV	%	personal
1916 R (Q)	5	25.0	191,950	10.0	Iowa 66

Convention	FB	%	LB	%	personal
1912 R	17	1.6	----	----	Iowa 62
1916 R (Q)	85	8.6	0	0.0	
Career	102	8.6	0	0.0	

Charles Curtis (1860-1936)

Convention	FB	%	LB	%	personal
1928 R (Q)	64	5.9	----	----	Kan. 68

David Davis (1815-1886)

General	PV	%	EV	%	personal
1872 D-LR	----	----	1	0.3	Ill. 57

John Davis (1873-1955)

Convention	FB	%	LB	%	personal
1920 D (Q)	32	2.9	52	4.8	W.Va. 47
1924*D (Q)	31	2.8	844	76.9	W.Va. 51
Career	63	2.9	896	40.9	

General	PV	%	EV	%	personal
1924 D (Q)	8,386,169	28.8	136	25.6	

Eugene Debs (1855-1926)

General	PV	%	EV	%	personal
1900 SOC	86,935	0.6	0	0.0	Ind. 45
1904 SOC (Q)	402,489	3.0	0	0.0	Ind. 49
1908 SOC (Q)	420,380	2.8	0	0.0	Ind. 53
1912 SOC (Q)	900,369	6.0	0	0.0	Ind. 57
1920 SOC (Q)	913,664	3.4	0	0.0	Ind. 65
Career	2,723,837	3.8	0	0.0	

Chauncey Depew (1834-1928)

Convention	FB	%	LB	%	personal
1888 R (Q)	99	11.9	0	0.0	N.Y. 54

Thomas Dewey (1902-1971)

Primaries	W	%	PV	%	personal
1940*R (Q)	6	46.2	1,605,754	49.7	N.Y. 38
1944 R (Q)	3	23.1	262,746	11.6	N.Y. 42
1948 R (Q)	2	16.7	304,394	11.5	N.Y. 46
Career	11	28.9	2,172,894	26.7	

Convention	FB	%	LB	%	personal
1940 R (Q)	360	36.0	11	1.1	
1944*R (Q)	1,056	99.7	----	----	
1948*R (Q)	434	39.7	1,094	100.0	
Career	1,850	58.7	1,105	52.8	

General	PV	%	EV	%	personal
1944 R (Q)	22,013,372	45.9	99	18.6	
1948 R (Q)	21,970,017	45.1	189	35.6	
Career	43,983,389	45.5	288	27.1	

James Doolittle (1815-1897)

Convention	FB	%	LB	%	personal
1868 D (Q)	13	4.1	0	0.0	Wis. 53

Stephen Douglas (1813-1861)

Convention	FB	%	LB	%	personal
1852 D (Q)	20	6.9	2	0.7	Ill. 39
1856 D (Q)	33	11.1	0	0.0	Ill. 43
1860*D (Q)	145½	48.0	190½	62.9	Ill. 47
Career	198½	22.4	192½	21.7	

General	PV	%	EV	%	personal
1860 D (Q)	1,380,202	29.5	12	4.0	

George Edmunds (1828-1919)

Convention	FB	%	LB	%	personal
1880 R (Q)	34	4.5	0	0.0	Vt. 52
1884 R (Q)	93	11.3	41	5.0	Vt. 56
Career	127	8.1	41	2.6	

Edward Edwards (1863-1931)

Primaries	W	%	PV	%	personal
1920 D (Q)	2	12.5	28,470	5.0	N.J. 57

Convention	FB	%	LB	%	personal
1920 D	42	3.8	0	0.0	

Dwight Eisenhower (1890-1969)

Primaries	W	%	PV	%	personal
1948 R	0	0.0	5,014	0.2	N.Y. 58
1952 R (Q)	5	38.5	2,114,588	27.1	N.Y. 62
1956*R (Q)	15	78.9	5,007,970	85.9	Pa. 66
1960 R	0	0.0	172	0.0	Pa. 70
Career	20	62.5	7,127,744	52.3	

Convention	FB	%	LB	%	personal
1952*R (Q)	845	70.1	----	----	
1956*R (Q)	1,323	100.0	----	----	
Career	2,168	85.7	----	----	

General	PV	%	EV	%	personal
1948 I	1	0.0	0	0.0	
1952*R (Q)	33,936,137	55.1	442	83.2	
1956*R (Q)	35,585,245	57.4	457	86.1	
Career	69,521,383	56.3	899	84.7	

James English (1812-1890)

Convention	FB	%	LB	%	personal
1868 D (Q)	16	5.0	0	0.0	Conn. 56
1880 D	1	0.1	0	0.0	Conn. 68
Career	17	5.0	0	0.0	

Charles Fairbanks (1852-1918)

Primaries	W	%	PV	%	personal
1916 R	1	5.0	176,078	9.2	Ind. 64

Convention	FB	%	LB	%	personal
1908 R (Q)	40	4.1	----	----	Ind. 56
1916 R (Q)	74½	7.5	0	0.0	
Career	114½	5.8	0	0.0	

James Farley (1888-1976)

Primaries	W	%	PV	%	personal
1952 D	0	0.0	77	0.0	N.Y. 64

Convention	FB	%	LB	%	personal
1940 D (Q)	$72\frac{9}{10}$	6.6	----	----	N.Y. 52
1944 D	1	0.1	----	----	N.Y. 56
Career	$73\frac{9}{10}$	6.6	----	----	

Stephen Field (1816-1899)

Convention	FB	%	LB	%	personal
1880 D (Q)	65	8.8	0	0.0	Cal. 64

Millard Fillmore (1800-1874)

Convention	FB	%	LB	%	personal
1852 W (Q)	133	44.9	112	37.8	N.Y. 52

General	PV	%	EV	%	personal
1856 A-W (Q)	873,053	21.5	8	2.7	N.Y. 56

Clinton Fisk (1828-1890)

General	PV	%	EV	%	personal
1888 PROH (Q)	249,819	2.2	0	0.0	N.J. 60

John Floyd (1783-1837)

General	PV	%	EV	%	personal
1832 ID (Q)	----	----	11	3.8	Va. 49

Gerald Ford (1913-   )

Primaries	W	%	PV	%	personal
1976*R (Q)	16	61.5	5,529,899	53.3	Mich. 63

Convention	FB	%	LB	%	personal
1976*R (Q)	1,187	52.5	----	----	

General	PV	%	EV	%	personal
1976 R (Q)	39,147,793	48.0	240	44.6	

Henry Ford (1863-1947)

Primaries	W	%	PV	%	personal
1916 R (Q)	1	5.0	131,889	6.9	Mich. 53
1924 D	1	7.1	48,567	6.4	Mich. 61
Career	2	5.0	180,456	6.9	

Convention	FB	%	LB	%	personal
1916 R	32	3.2	0	0.0	

Joseph France (1873-1939)

Primaries	W	%	PV	%	personal
1932*R (Q)	7	50.0	1,137,948	48.5	Md. 59

Convention	FB	%	LB	%	personal
1932 R	4	0.3	----	----	

John Fremont (1813-1890)

Convention	FB	%	LB	%	personal
1856*R (Q)	520	91.7	----	----	Cal. 43
1860 R	1	0.2	0	0.0	Cal. 47
Career	521	91.7	0	----	

General	PV	%	EV	%	personal
1856 R (Q)	1,342,345	33.1	114	38.5	

James Garfield (1831-1881)

Convention	FB	%	LB	%	personal
1880✶R (Q)	0	0.0	399	52.8	Ohio 49

General	PV	%	EV	%	personal
1880✶R (Q)	4,446,158	48.3	214	58.0	

John Nance Garner (1868-1967)

Primaries	W	%	PV	%	personal
1932 D (Q)	1	6.3	249,816	8.5	Tex. 64
1936 D	0	0.0	108	0.0	Tex. 68
1940 D (Q)	0	0.0	426,641	9.5	Tex. 72
Career	1	3.4	676,565	9.1	

Convention	FB	%	LB	%	personal
1932 D (Q)	90¼	7.8	0	0.0	
1940 D (Q)	61	5.5	----	----	
Career	151¼	6.7	0	0.0	

Walter George (1878-1957)

Convention	FB	%	LB	%	personal
1928 D (Q)	52½	4.8	----	----	Ga. 50

Barry Goldwater (1909-   )

Primaries	W	%	PV	%	personal
1960 R	0	0.0	3,146	0.1	Ariz. 51
1964*R (Q)	5	31.3	2,267,079	38.2	Ariz. 55
Career	5	31.3	2,270,225	38.2	

Convention	FB	%	LB	%	personal
1960 R	10	0.8	----	----	
1964*R (Q)	883	67.5	----	----	
Career	893	67.5	----	----	

General	PV	%	EV	%	personal
1960 IR	1	0.0	0	0.0	
1964 R (Q)	27,177,838	38.5	52	9.7	
Career	27,177,839	38.5	52	9.7	

Arthur Gorman (1839-1906)

Convention	FB	%	LB	%	personal
1892 D (Q)	36½	4.0	----	----	Md. 53

Ulysses Grant (1822-1885)

Convention	FB	%	LB	%	personal
1864 R (Q)	22	4.2	----	----	Ill. 42
1868*R (Q)	650	100.0	----	----	Ill. 46
1872*R (Q)	752	100.0	----	----	Ill. 50
1880 R (Q)	304	40.2	306	40.5	Ill. 58
Career	1,728	64.5	306	40.5	

Ulysses Grant (continued)

General	PV	%	EV	%	personal
1868*R (Q)	3,013,650	52.7	214	72.8	
1872*R (Q)	3,598,235	55.6	286	81.9	
Career	6,611,885	54.2	500	77.8	

George Gray (1840-1925)

Convention	FB	%	LB	%	personal
1904 D	12	1.2	----	----	Del. 64
1908 D (Q)	59½	5.9	----	----	Del. 68
Career	71½	5.9	----	----	

Horace Greeley (1811-1872)

Convention	FB	%	LB	%	personal
1872*D (Q)	686	93.7	----	----	N.Y. 61

General	PV	%	EV	%	personal
1872 D-LR (Q)	2,834,761	43.8	----	----	

Dwight Green (1897-1958)

Convention	FB	%	LB	%	personal
1948 R (Q)	56	5.1	0	0.0	Ill. 51

Walter Gresham (1832-1895)

Convention	FB	%	LB	%	personal
1888 R (Q)	107	12.9	59	7.1	Ind. 56

James Guthrie (1792-1869)

Convention	FB	%	LB	%	personal
1860 D (Q)	35½	11.7	5½	1.8	Ky. 68

John Hale (1806-1873)

General	PV	%	EV	%	personal
1852 FS (Q)	155,210	4.9	0	0.0	N.H. 46

Winfield Hancock (1824-1886)

Convention	FB	%	LB	%	personal
1868 D (Q)	33½	10.6	0	0.0	Pa. 44
1876 D (Q)	75	10.2	58	7.9	Pa. 52
1880*D (Q)	171	23.2	705	95.5	Pa. 56
Career	279½	15.6	763	42.6	

General	PV	%	EV	%	personal
1880 D (Q)	4,444,260	48.3	155	42.0	

Warren Harding (1865-1923)

Primaries	W	%	PV	%	personal
1920 R (Q)	1	5.0	144,762	4.5	Ohio 55

Convention	FB	%	LB	%	personal
1920*R (Q)	65½	6.7	$644\frac{7}{10}$	65.5	

General	PV	%	EV	%	personal
1920*R (Q)	16,133,314	60.3	404	76.1	

Judson Harmon (1846-1927)

Primaries	W	%	PV	%	personal
1912 D (Q)	1	8.3	116,294	11.9	Ohio 66

Convention	FB	%	LB	%	personal
1912 D (Q)	148	13.5	12	1.1	

Averell Harriman (1891-1986)

Primaries	W	%	PV	%	personal
1952 D	1	6.3	17,820	0.4	N.Y. 61
1956 D	0	0.0	2,281	0.0	N.Y. 65
Career	1	----	20,101	----	

Convention	FB	%	LB	%	personal
1952 D (Q)	123½	10.0	0	0.0	
1956 D (Q)	210	15.3	----	----	
Career	333½	12.8	0	0.0	

Benjamin Harrison (1833-1901)

Convention	FB	%	LB	%	personal
1888*R (Q)	85	10.2	544	65.4	Ind. 55
1892*R (Q)	$535\frac{1}{6}$	59.1	----	----	Ind. 59
Career	$620\frac{1}{6}$	35.7	544	65.4	

General	PV	%	EV	%	personal
1888*R (Q)	5,443,892	47.8	233	58.1	
1892 R (Q)	5,179,244	43.0	145	32.7	
Career	10,623,136	45.3	378	44.7	

William Henry Harrison (1773-1841)

Convention	FB	%	LB	%	personal
1840*W (Q)	91	35.8	148	58.3	Ohio 67

General	PV	%	EV	%	personal
1836 W (Q)	550,816	36.6	73	24.8	Ohio 63
1840*W (Q)	1,275,390	52.9	234	79.6	
Career	1,826,206	46.6	307	52.2	

Gary Hart (1937-   )

Primaries	W	%	PV	%	personal
1984 D (Q)	16	53.3	6,501,612	35.8	Colo. 47

Convention	FB	%	LB	%	personal
1984 D (Q)	1,200½	30.5	----	----	

John Hartranft (1830-1889)

Convention	FB	%	LB	%	personal
1876 R (Q)	58	7.7	0	0.0	Pa. 46

Rutherford Hayes (1822-1893)

Convention	FB	%	LB	%	personal
1876*R (Q)	61	8.1	384	50.8	Ohio 54

General	PV	%	EV	%	personal
1876*R (Q)	4,034,311	48.0	185	50.1	

William Randolph Hearst (1863-1951)

Convention	FB	%	LB	%	personal
1904 D (Q)	181	18.1	----	----	N.Y. 41
1920 D	1	0.1	0	0.0	N.Y. 57
Career	182	18.1	0	----	

Thomas Hendricks (1819-1885)

Convention	FB	%	LB	%	personal
1868 D	2½	0.8	0	0.0	Ind. 49
1876 D (Q)	140½	19.0	85	11.5	Ind. 57
1880 D (Q)	49½	6.7	30	4.1	Ind. 61
1884 D (Q)	1	0.1	45½	5.5	Ind. 65
Career	193½	8.3	160½	7.0	

General	PV	%	EV	%	personal
1872 D (Q)	----	----	42	12.0	Ind. 53

David Hill (1843-1910)

Convention	FB	%	LB	%	personal
1892 D (Q)	114	12.5	----	----	N.Y. 49
1896 D	1	0.1	1	0.1	N.Y. 53
Career	115	12.5	1	----	

Herbert Hoover (1874-1964)

Primaries	W	%	PV	%	personal
1920 R (Q)	0	0.0	303,212	9.5	Cal. 46
1928*R (Q)	7	46.7	2,020,325	49.2	Cal. 54
1932 R (Q)	2	14.3	781,165	33.3	Cal. 58
1936 R	0	0.0	7,276	0.2	Cal. 62
1940 R	0	0.0	1,082	0.0	Cal. 66
Career	9	18.4	3,113,060	32.2	

Convention	FB	%	LB	%	personal
1920 R	5½	0.6	10½	1.1	
1928*R (Q)	837	76.9	----	----	
1932*R (Q)	1,126½	97.6	----	----	
1940 R	17	1.7	10	1.0	
Career	1,986	87.5	20½	----	

General	PV	%	EV	%	personal
1928*R (Q)	21,411,991	58.2	444	83.6	
1932 R (Q)	15,758,397	39.6	59	11.1	
Career	37,170,388	48.6	503	47.4	

John Hospers (1918-   )

General	PV	%	EV	%	personal
1972 LIB	3,671	0.0	1	0.2	Cal. 54

Charles Evans Hughes (1862-1948)

Primaries	W	%	PV	%	personal
1916 R (Q)	2	10.0	80,737	4.2	N.Y. 54

Convention	FB	%	LB	%	personal
1908 R (Q)	67	6.8	----	----	N.Y. 46
1912 R	2	0.2	----	----	N.Y. 50
1916*R (Q)	253½	25.7	949½	96.2	
1928 R	1	0.1	----	----	N.Y. 66
Career	323½	16.3	949½	96.2	

General	PV	%	EV	%	personal
1916 R (Q)	8,546,789	46.1	254	47.8	

Cordell Hull (1871-1955)

Convention	FB	%	LB	%	personal
1924 D	0	0.0	1	0.1	Tenn. 53
1928 D (Q)	$50\frac{5}{6}$	4.6	----	----	Tenn. 57
1940 D	$5\frac{2}{3}$	0.5	----	----	Tenn. 69
Career	56½	4.6	1	----	

Hubert Humphrey (1911-1978)

Primaries	W	%	PV	%	personal
1952 D	1	6.3	102,527	2.1	Minn. 41
1960 D (Q)	2	12.5	590,410	10.4	Minn. 49
1964 D	0	0.0	323	0.0	Minn. 53
1968 D	0	0.0	166,463	2.2	Minn. 57
1972*D (Q)	4	19.0	4,121,372	25.8	Minn. 61
1976 D	0	0.0	61,992	0.4	Minn. 65
Career	7	16.2	5,043,087	21.7	

Convention	FB	%	LB	%	personal
1952 D	26	2.1	0	0.0	
1960 D	41½	2.7	----	----	
1968*D (Q)	1,759¼	67.1	----	----	
1972 D	$66\frac{7}{10}$	2.2	----	----	
1976 D	10	0.3	----	----	
Career	$1,903\frac{45}{100}$	67.1	0	----	

General	PV	%	EV	%	personal
1968 D (Q)	31,274,503	42.7	191	35.5	

Robert Hunter (1809-1887)

Convention	FB	%	LB	%	personal
1860 D (Q)	42	13.9	0	0.0	Va. 51

Andrew Jackson (1767-1845)

Convention	FB	%	LB	%	personal
1832*D (Q)	283	100.0	----	----	Tenn. 65

General	PV	%	EV	%	personal
1824 DR (Q)	151,271	41.3	99	37.9	Tenn. 57
1828*DR (Q)	642,553	56.0	178	68.2	Tenn. 61
1832*D (Q)	701,780	54.2	219	76.6	
Career	1,495,604	53.3	496	61.4	

Henry Jackson (1912-1983)

Primaries	W	%	PV	%	personal
1972 D	0	0.0	505,198	3.2	Wash. 60
1976 D (Q)	1	3.7	1,134,375	7.1	Wash. 64
Career	1	3.7	1,639,573	7.1	

Convention	FB	%	LB	%	personal
1972 D (Q)	525	17.4	----	----	
1976 D	10	0.3	----	----	
Career	535	17.4	----	----	

Jesse Jackson (1941-   )

Primaries	W	%	PV	%	personal
1984 D (Q)	2	6.7	3,281,992	18.1	Ill. 43

Convention	FB	%	LB	%	personal
1984 D (Q)	465½	11.8	----	----	

Arthur James (1883-1973)

Primaries	W	%	PV	%	personal
1940 R	0	0.0	8,172	0.3	Pa. 57

Convention	FB	%	LB	%	personal
1940 R (Q)	74	7.4	0	0.0	

Thomas Jefferson (1743-1826)

General	PV	%	EV	%	personal
1796 DR (Q)	----	----	68	49.3	Va. 53
1800*DR (Q)	----	----	73	52.9	Va. 57
1804*DR (Q)	----	----	162	92.0	Va. 61
Career	----	----	303	67.0	

Charles Jenkins (1805-1883)

General	PV	%	EV	%	personal
1872 D (Q)	----	----	2	0.6	Ga. 67

Andrew Johnson (1808-1875)

Convention	FB	%	LB	%	personal
1860 D	12	4.0	0	0.0	Tenn. 52
1868 D (Q)	65	20.5	0	0.0	Tenn. 60
Career	77	20.5	0	0.0	

Hiram Johnson (1866-1945)

Primaries	W	%	PV	%	personal
1920*R (Q)	7	35.0	965,651	30.3	Cal. 54
1924 R (Q)	1	5.9	1,007,833	28.6	Cal. 58
Career	8	21.6	1,973,484	29.4	

Convention	FB	%	LB	%	personal
1920 R (Q)	133½	13.6	$80\frac{4}{5}$	8.2	
1924 R	10	0.9	----	----	
Career	143½	13.6	$80\frac{4}{5}$	8.2	

John Johnson (1861-1909)

Convention	FB	%	LB	%	personal
1908 D (Q)	46	4.6	----	----	Minn. 47

Lyndon Johnson (1908-1973)

Primaries	W	%	PV	%	personal
1960 D	0	0.0	15,691	0.3	Tex. 52
1964 D (Q)	8	50.0	1,106,999	17.7	Tex. 56
1968 D (Q)	1	6.7	383,048	5.1	Tex. 60
Career	9	29.0	1,505,738	10.8	

Convention	FB	%	LB	%	personal
1956 D (Q)	80	5.8	----	----	Tex. 48
1960 D (Q)	409	26.9	----	----	
1964*D (Q)	2,318	100.0	----	----	
Career	2,807	53.9	----	----	

Lyndon Johnson (continued)

General	PV	%	EV	%	personal
1964*D (Q)	43,126,584	61.1	486	90.3	

Richard Johnson (1780-1850)

Convention	FB	%	LB	%	personal
1844 D (Q)	24	9.0	0	0.0	Ky. 64

Walter Jones (1888-1963)

General	PV	%	EV	%	personal
1956 ID	----	----	1	0.2	Ala. 68

Estes Kefauver (1903-1963)

Primaries	W	%	PV	%	personal
1952*D (Q)	12	75.0	3,169,448	64.3	Tenn. 49
1956 D (Q)	9	47.4	2,283,172	39.1	Tenn. 53
Career	21	60.0	5,452,620	50.6	

Convention	FB	%	LB	%	personal
1952 D (Q)	340	27.6	275½	22.4	

Edward Kennedy (1932-   )

Primaries	W	%	PV	%	personal
1964 D	0	0.0	1,259	0.0	Mass. 32
1968 D	0	0.0	4,052	0.1	Mass. 36
1972 D	0	0.0	16,693	0.1	Mass. 40
1976 D	0	0.0	19,805	0.1	Mass. 44
1980 D (Q)	10	28.6	7,381,693	37.6	Mass. 48
Career	10	28.6	7,423,502	37.6	

Convention	FB	%	LB	%	personal
1968 D	$12\frac{3}{4}$	0.5	----	----	
1972 D	$12\frac{7}{10}$	0.4	----	----	
1976 D	1	0.0	----	----	
1980 D (Q)	1,150½	34.5	----	----	
Career	$1,176\frac{95}{100}$	34.5	----	----	

John Kennedy (1917-1963)

Primaries	W	%	PV	%	personal
1956 D	0	0.0	949	0.0	Mass. 39
1960✻D (Q)	10	62.5	1,847,259	32.5	Mass. 43
Career	10	62.5	1,848,208	32.5	

Convention	FB	%	LB	%	personal
1960✻D (Q)	806	53.0	----	----	

General	PV	%	EV	%	personal
1960✻D (Q)	34,221,344	49.7	303	56.4	

Robert Kennedy (1925-1968)

Primaries	W	%	PV	%	personal
1964 D	0	0.0	33,810	0.5	Mass. 39
1968 D (Q)	5	33.3	2,304,542	30.6	N.Y. 43
Career	5	33.3	2,338,352	30.6	

Robert Kerr (1896-1963)

Primaries	W	%	PV	%	personal
1952 D	0	0.0	42,467	0.9	Okla. 56

Convention	FB	%	LB	%	personal
1952 D (Q)	65	5.3	0	0.0	

Rufus King (1755-1827)

General	PV	%	EV	%	personal
1816 F (Q)	----	----	34	15.7	N.Y. 61

Frank Knox (1874-1944)

Primaries	W	%	PV	%	personal
1936 R (Q)	1	8.3	493,562	14.9	Ill. 62

Philander Knox (1853-1921)

Convention	FB	%	LB	%	personal
1908 R (Q)	68	6.9	----	----	Pa. 55
1916 R	36	3.6	0	0.0	Pa. 63
1920 R	0	0.0	1	0.1	Pa. 67
Career	104	6.9	1	----	

Robert La Follette (1855-1925)

Primaries	W	%	PV	%	personal
1912 R (Q)	2	16.7	327,357	14.5	Wis. 57
1916 R (Q)	2	10.0	133,426	6.9	Wis. 61
1924 R	1	5.9	82,492	2.3	Wis. 69
Career	5	12.5	543,275	11.0	

Convention	FB	%	LB	%	personal
1908 R	25	2.6	----	----	Wis. 53
1912 R	41	3.8	----	----	
1916 R	25	2.5	3	0.3	
1920 R	24	2.4	24	2.4	Wis. 65
1924 R	34	3.1	----	----	
Career	149	----	27	----	

General	PV	%	EV	%	personal
1924 P (Q)	4,814,050	16.6	13	2.4	

Alfred Landon (1887-   )

Primaries	W	%	PV	%	personal
1936 R (Q)	2	16.7	729,908	22.0	Kan. 49

Convention	FB	%	LB	%	personal
1936*R (Q)	984	98.1	----	----	

General	PV	%	EV	%	personal
1936 R (Q)	16,679,543	36.5	8	1.5	

Joseph Lane (1801-1881)

Convention	FB	%	LB	%	personal
1852 D (Q)	13	4.5	0	0.0	Ore. 51
1860 D	6	2.0	0	0.0	Ore. 59
Career	19	4.5	0	0.0	

Frank Lausche (1895-   )

Primaries	W	%	PV	%	personal
1956 D (Q)	1	5.3	276,923	4.7	Ohio 61

Convention	FB	%	LB	%	personal
1956 D	5½	0.4	----	----	

William Lemke (1878-1950)

General	PV	%	EV	%	personal
1936 U (Q)	892,492	2.0	0	0.0	N.D. 58

Abraham Lincoln (1809-1865)

Convention	FB	%	LB	%	personal
1860*R (Q)	102	21.9	350	75.1	Ill. 51
1864*R (Q)	494	95.2	----	----	Ill. 55
Career	596	60.5	350	75.1	

General	PV	%	EV	%	personal
1860*R (Q)	1,865,908	39.8	180	59.4	
1864*R (Q)	2,218,388	55.0	212	91.0	
Career	4,084,296	46.9	392	73.1	

Henry Cabot Lodge (1902-1985)

Primaries	W	%	PV	%	personal
1960 R	0	0.0	373	0.0	Mass. 58
1964 R (Q)	3	18.8	386,661	6.5	Mass. 62
Career	3	18.8	387,034	6.5	

Convention	FB	%	LB	%	personal
1964 R	2	0.2	----	----	

John Logan (1826-1886)

Convention	FB	%	LB	%	personal
1884 R (Q)	63½	7.7	7	0.9	Ill. 58

Frank Lowden (1861-1943)

Primaries	W	%	PV	%	personal
1920 R (Q)	1	5.0	389,127	12.2	Ill. 59
1928 R (Q)	2	13.3	1,283,535	31.2	Ill. 67
Career	3	8.6	1,672,662	22.9	

Convention	FB	%	LB	%	personal
1920 R (Q)	211½	21.5	28	2.8	
1928 R (Q)	74	6.8	----	----	
Career	285½	13.8	28	2.8	

Douglas MacArthur (1880-1964)

Primaries	W	%	PV	%	personal
1944*R (Q)	2	15.4	662,127	29.1	Wis. 64
1948 R	0	0.0	87,839	3.3	Wis. 68
1952 R	0	0.0	44,209	0.6	Wis. 72
Career	2	15.4	794,175	29.1	

Convention	FB	%	LB	%	personal
1944 R	1	0.1	----	----	
1948 R	11	1.0	0	0.0	
1952 R	4	0.3	----	----	
Career	16	----	0	----	

General	PV	%	EV	%	personal
1952 CONST	17,200	0.0	0	0.0	

James Madison (1751-1836)

General	PV	%	EV	%	personal
1808*DR (Q)	----	----	122	69.7	Va. 57
1812*DR (Q)	----	----	128	59.0	Va. 61
Career	----	----	250	63.8	

Willie Person Mangum (1792-1861)

General	PV	%	EV	%	personal
1836 IW (Q)	----	----	11	3.7	N.C. 44

William Marcy (1786-1857)

Convention	FB	%	LB	%	personal
1852 D (Q)	27	9.4	0	0.0	N.Y. 66

Joseph Martin (1884-1968)

Primaries	W	%	PV	%	personal
1948 R	0	0.0	974	0.0	Mass. 64

Convention	FB	%	LB	%	personal
1940 R (Q)	44	4.4	0	0.0	Mass. 56
1948 R	18	1.6	0	0.0	
Career	62	4.4	0	0.0	

William Gibbs McAdoo (1863-1941)

Primaries	W	%	PV	%	personal
1920 D (Q)	2	12.5	74,987	13.1	N.Y. 57
1924*D (Q)	9	64.3	456,733	59.8	Cal. 61
1928 D	0	0.0	213	0.0	Cal. 65
Career	11	36.7	531,933	39.8	

Convention	FB	%	LB	%	personal
1920 D (Q)	266	24.3	270	24.7	
1924 D (Q)	431½	39.3	11½	1.0	
Career	697½	31.8	281½	12.8	

Eugene McCarthy (1916-   )

Primaries	W	%	PV	%	personal
1968*D (Q)	6	40.0	2,914,933	38.7	Minn. 52
1972 D	0	0.0	553,955	3.5	Minn. 56
Career	6	40.0	3,468,888	38.7	

Convention	FB	%	LB	%	personal
1968 D (Q)	601	22.9	----	----	
1972 D	2	0.1	----	----	
Career	603	22.9	----	----	

General	PV	%	EV	%	personal
1968 ID	25,552	0.0	0	0.0	
1976 I	756,691	0.9	0	0.0	Minn. 60
Career	782,243	----	0	----	

George McClellan (1826-1885)

Convention	FB	%	LB	%	personal
1864*D (Q)	174	77.0	----	----	N.Y. 38
1880 D	2	0.3	0	0.0	N.J. 54
Career	176	77.0	0	----	

General	PV	%	EV	%	personal
1864 D (Q)	1,812,807	45.0	21	9.0	

Joseph McDonald (1819-1891)

Convention	FB	%	LB	%	personal
1880 D	3	0.4	0	0.0	Ind. 61
1884 D (Q)	56	6.8	2	0.2	Ind. 65
Career	59	6.8	2	0.2	

George McGovern (1922-   )

Primaries	W	%	PV	%	personal
1972 D (Q)	8	38.1	4,053,451	25.3	S.D. 50
1984 D	0	0.0	335,372	1.8	S.D. 62
Career	8	38.1	4,388,823	25.3	

Convention	FB	%	LB	%	personal
1968 D (Q)	146½	5.6	----	----	S.D. 46
1972*D (Q)	$1,728\frac{35}{100}$	57.3	----	----	
1984 D	4	0.1	----	----	
Career	$1,878\frac{85}{100}$	33.3	----	----	

General	PV	%	EV	%	personal
1972 D (Q)	29,171,791	37.5	17	3.2	

William McKinley (1843-1901)

Convention	FB	%	LB	%	personal
1888 R	2	0.2	4	0.5	Ohio 45
1892 R (Q)	182	20.1	----	----	Ohio 49
1896*R (Q)	661½	71.6	----	----	Ohio 53
1900*R (Q)	926	100.0	----	----	Ohio 57
Career	1,771½	64.2	4	----	

General	PV	%	EV	%	personal
1896*R (Q)	7,108,480	51.0	271	60.6	
1900*R (Q)	7,218,039	51.7	292	65.3	
Career	14,326,519	51.3	563	63.0	

John McLean (1785-1861)

Convention	FB	%	LB	%	personal
1848 W	2	0.7	0	0.0	Ohio 63
1856 R (Q)	37	6.5	----	----	Ohio 71
1860 R	12	2.6	½	0.1	Ohio 75
Career	51	6.5	½	----	

John McLean (1848-1916)

Convention	FB	%	LB	%	personal
1896 D (Q)	54	5.8	0	0.0	Ohio 48

Walter Mondale (1928-   )

Primaries	W	%	PV	%	personal
1984*D (Q)	11	36.7	6,943,429	38.3	Minn. 56

Convention	FB	%	LB	%	personal
1972 D	1	0.0	----	----	Minn. 44
1980 D	1	0.0	----	----	Minn. 52
1984*D (Q)	2,191	55.7	----	----	
Career	2,193	55.7	----	----	

General	PV	%	EV	%	personal
1984 D (Q)	37,565,334	40.5	13	2.4	

James Monroe (1758-1831)

General	PV	%	EV	%	personal
1816*DR (Q)	----	----	183	84.3	Va. 58
1820*DR (Q)	----	----	231	99.6	Va. 62
Career	----	----	414	92.2	

William Morrison (1824-1909)

Convention	FB	%	LB	%	personal
1880 D (Q)	62	8.4	0	0.0	Ill. 56
1892 D	3	0.3	----	----	Ill. 68
Career	65	8.4	0	0.0	

Levi Morton (1824-1920)

Convention	FB	%	LB	%	personal
1896 R (Q)	58	6.3	----	----	N.Y. 72

Oliver Morton (1823-1877)

Convention	FB	%	LB	%	personal
1876 R (Q)	124	16.4	0	0.0	Ind. 53

William Murray (1869-1956)

Primaries	W	%	PV	%	personal
1932 D (Q)	1	6.3	226,392	7.7	Okla. 63

Convention	FB	%	LB	%	personal
1932 D	23	2.0	0	0.0	

Edmund Muskie (1914-   )

Primaries	W	%	PV	%	personal
1972 D (Q)	2	9.5	1,840,217	11.5	Me. 58

Convention	FB	%	LB	%	personal
1972 D	$24\frac{3}{10}$	0.8	----	----	
1980 D	1	0.0	----	----	Me. 66
Career	$25\frac{3}{10}$	----	----	----	

Richard Nixon (1913-   )

Primaries	W	%	PV	%	personal
1956 R	0	0.0	316	0.0	Cal. 43
1960*R (Q)	11	73.3	4,975,938	89.9	Cal. 47
1964 R	0	0.0	197,212	3.3	N.Y. 51
1968 R (Q)	9	60.0	1,679,443	37.5	N.Y. 55
1972*R (Q)	18	90.0	5,378,704	86.9	Cal. 59
Career	38	76.0	12,231,613	74.3	

Convention	FB	%	LB	%	personal
1960*R (Q)	1,321	99.2	----	----	
1968*R (Q)	692	51.9	----	----	
1972*R (Q)	1,347	99.9	----	----	
Career	3,360	83.7	----	----	

General	PV	%	EV	%	personal
1960 R (Q)	34,106,671	49.6	219	40.8	
1968*R (Q)	31,785,148	43.4	301	55.9	
1972*R (Q)	47,170,179	60.7	520	96.7	
Career	113,061,998	51.4	1,040	64.5	

George Norris (1861-1944)

Primaries	W	%	PV	%	personal
1928 R (Q)	2	13.3	259,548	6.3	Neb. 67
1932 R	1	7.1	139,514	5.9	Neb. 71
Career	3	13.3	399,062	6.3	

Convention	FB	%	LB	%	personal
1928 R	24	2.2	----	----	

Asa Packer (1805-1879)

Convention	FB	%	LB	%	personal
1868 D (Q)	26	8.2	0	0.0	Pa. 63

Mitchell Palmer (1872-1936)

Primaries	W	%	PV	%	personal
1920 D (Q)	1	6.3	91,543	16.0	Pa. 48

Convention	FB	%	LB	%	personal
1920 D (Q)	254	23.2	1	0.1	

Alton Parker (1852-1926)

Convention	FB	%	LB	%	personal
1904*D (Q)	679	67.9	----	----	N.Y. 52

General	PV	%	EV	%	personal
1904 D (Q)	5,082,898	37.6	140	29.4	

Joel Parker (1816-1888)

Convention	FB	%	LB	%	personal
1868 D (Q)	13	4.1	0	0.0	N.J. 52
1876 D	18	2.4	0	0.0	N.J. 60
1880 D	1	0.1	0	0.0	N.J. 64
Career	32	4.1	0	0.0	

Robert Pattison (1850-1904)

Convention	FB	%	LB	%	personal
1892 D	1	0.1	----	----	Pa. 42
1896 D (Q)	97	10.4	95	10.2	Pa. 46
1904 D	4	0.4	----	----	Pa. 54
Career	102	10.4	95	10.2	

Henry Payne (1810-1896)

Convention	FB	%	LB	%	personal
1880 D (Q)	81	11.0	0	0.0	Ohio 70

George Pendleton (1825-1889)

Convention	FB	%	LB	%	personal
1868 D (Q)	105	33.1	0	0.0	Ohio 43

Franklin Pierce (1804-1869)

Convention	FB	%	LB	%	personal
1852*D (Q)	0	0.0	279	96.9	N.H. 48
1856 D (Q)	122½	41.4	0	0.0	N.H. 52
Career	122½	21.0	279	47.8	

General	PV	%	EV	%	personal
1852*D (Q)	1,607,510	50.8	254	85.8	

Charles Cotesworth Pinckney (1746-1825)

General	PV	%	EV	%	personal
1804 F (Q)	----	----	14	8.0	S.C. 58
1808 F (Q)	----	----	47	26.9	S.C. 62
Career	----	----	61	17.4	

James Polk (1795-1849)

Convention	FB	%	LB	%	personal
1844*D (Q)	0	0.0	231	86.8	Tenn. 49

General	PV	%	EV	%	personal
1844*D (Q)	1,339,494	49.5	170	61.8	

Matthew Quay (1833-1904)

Convention	FB	%	LB	%	personal
1896 R (Q)	61½	6.7	----	----	Pa. 63

Samuel Randall (1828-1890)

Convention	FB	%	LB	%	personal
1880 D	6	0.8	0	0.0	Pa. 52
1884 D (Q)	78	9.5	4	0.5	Pa. 56
Career	84	9.5	4	0.5	

Ronald Reagan (1911-   )

Primaries	W	%	PV	%	personal
1968*R (Q)	1	6.7	1,696,270	37.9	Cal. 57
1976 R (Q)	10	38.5	4,758,325	45.9	Cal. 65
1980*R (Q)	29	82.9	7,709,793	59.9	Cal. 69
1984*R (Q)	24	100.0	6,176,274	98.8	Cal. 73
Career	64	64.0	20,340,662	59.9	

Convention	FB	%	LB	%	personal
1968 R (Q)	182	13.7	----	----	
1976 R (Q)	1,070	47.4	----	----	
1980*R (Q)	1,939	97.2	----	----	
1984*R (Q)	2,233	99.9	----	----	
Career	5,424	69.4	----	----	

General	PV	%	EV	%	personal
1976 IR	----	----	1	0.2	
1980*R (Q)	43,904,153	50.7	489	90.9	
1984*R (Q)	54,451,521	58.8	525	97.6	
Career	98,355,674	54.9	1,015	94.2	

James Reed (1861-1944)

Primaries	W	%	PV	%	personal
1928 D (Q)	1	6.3	207,367	16.4	Mo. 67

Convention	FB	%	LB	%	personal
1928 D (Q)	52	4.7	----	----	
1932 D	24	2.1	0	0.0	Mo. 71
Career	76	4.7	0	----	

Thomas Reed (1839-1902)

Convention	FB	%	LB	%	personal
1892 R	4	0.4	----	----	Me. 53
1896 R (Q)	84½	9.1	----	----	Me. 57
Career	88½	9.1	----	----	

James Rhodes (1909-   )

Primaries	W	%	PV	%	personal
1964 R	1	6.3	615,754	10.4	Ohio 55
1968 R	1	6.7	614,492	13.7	Ohio 59
Career	2	----	1,230,246	----	

Convention	FB	%	LB	%	personal
1968 R (Q)	55	4.1	----	----	

Nelson Rockefeller (1908-1979)

Primaries	W	%	PV	%	personal
1960 R	0	0.0	30,639	0.6	N.Y. 52
1964 R (Q)	2	12.5	1,304,204	22.0	N.Y. 56
1968 R	1	6.7	164,340	3.7	N.Y. 60
Career	3	12.5	1,499,183	22.0	

Convention	FB	%	LB	%	personal
1964 R (Q)	114	8.7	----	----	
1968 R (Q)	277	20.8	----	----	
Career	391	14.8	----	----	

General	PV	%	EV	%	personal
1968 IR	69	0.0	0	0.0	

Franklin Roosevelt (1882-1945)

Primaries	W	%	PV	%	personal
1932*D (Q)	9	56.3	1,314,366	44.5	N.Y. 50
1936*D (Q)	12	85.7	4,814,978	92.9	N.Y. 54
1940*D (Q)	7	53.8	3,204,054	71.7	N.Y. 58
1944*D (Q)	7	50.0	1,324,006	70.9	N.Y. 62
Career	35	61.4	10,657,404	73.6	

Convention	FB	%	LB	%	personal
1932*D (Q)	666¼	57.7	945	81.9	
1936*D (Q)	1,100	100.0	----	----	
1940*D (Q)	$946\frac{13}{30}$	86.0	----	----	
1944*D (Q)	1,086	92.3	----	----	
Career	$3,798\frac{41}{60}$	83.9	945	81.9	

General	PV	%	EV	%	personal
1932*D (Q)	22,825,016	57.4	472	88.9	
1936*D (Q)	27,747,636	60.8	523	98.5	
1940*D (Q)	27,263,448	54.7	449	84.6	
1944*D (Q)	25,611,936	53.4	432	81.4	
Career	103,448,036	56.5	1,876	88.3	

Theodore Roosevelt (1858-1919)

Primaries	W	%	PV	%	personal
1912*R (Q)	9	75.0	1,164,765	51.5	N.Y. 54
1916 R (Q)	1	5.0	80,019	4.2	N.Y. 58
Career	10	31.3	1,244,784	29.7	

Theodore Roosevelt (continued)

Convention	FB	%	LB	%	personal
1904*R (Q)	994	100.0	----	----	N.Y. 46
1908 R	3	0.3	----	----	N.Y. 50
1912 R (Q)	107	9.9	----	----	
1916 R (Q)	65	6.6	18½	1.9	
Career	1,169	38.1	18½	1.9	

General	PV	%	EV	%	personal
1904*R (Q)	7,626,593	56.4	336	70.6	
1912 P (Q)	4,119,207	27.4	88	16.6	
Career	11,745,800	41.1	424	42.1	

Elihu Root (1845-1937)

Convention	FB	%	LB	%	personal
1916 R (Q)	103	10.4	0	0.0	N.Y. 71

Richard Russell (1897-1971)

Primaries	W	%	PV	%	personal
1952 D (Q)	1	6.3	369,671	7.5	Ga. 55

Convention	FB	%	LB	%	personal
1948 D (Q)	266	21.6	----	----	Ga. 51
1952 D (Q)	268	21.8	261	21.2	
Career	534	21.7	261	21.2	

General	PV	%	EV	%	personal
1964 ID	50	0.0	0	0.0	Ga. 67

Winfield Scott (1786-1866)

Convention	FB	%	LB	%	personal
1840 W (Q)	57	22.4	16	6.3	N.J. 54
1848 W (Q)	43	15.4	63	22.5	N.J. 62
1852*W (Q)	131	44.3	159	53.7	N.J. 66
Career	231	27.8	238	28.7	

General	PV	%	EV	%	personal
1852 W (Q)	1,386,942	43.9	42	14.2	

William Scranton (1917-   )

Primaries	W	%	PV	%	personal
1964 R (Q)	1	6.3	245,401	4.1	Pa. 47

Convention	FB	%	LB	%	personal
1964 R (Q)	214	16.4	----	----	

William Seward (1801-1872)

Convention	FB	%	LB	%	personal
1856 R	1	0.2	----	----	N.Y. 55
1860 R (Q)	173½	37.2	111½	23.9	N.Y. 59
Career	174½	37.2	111½	23.9	

Horatio Seymour (1810-1886)

Convention	FB	%	LB	%	personal
1864 D (Q)	12	5.3	----	----	N.Y. 54
1868*D (Q)	0	0.0	317	100.0	N.Y. 58
1880 D	8	1.1	0	0.0	N.Y. 70
Career	20	2.2	317	100.0	

General	PV	%	EV	%	personal
1868 D (Q)	2,708,744	47.3	80	27.2	

Thomas Seymour (1807-1868)

Convention	FB	%	LB	%	personal
1864 D (Q)	38	16.8	----	----	Conn. 57

John Sherman (1823-1900)

Convention	FB	%	LB	%	personal
1880 R (Q)	93	12.3	3	0.4	Ohio 57
1884 R	30	3.7	0	0.0	Ohio 61
1888 R (Q)	229	27.5	118	14.2	Ohio 65
Career	352	20.3	121	7.6	

Lawrence Sherman (1858-1939)

Primaries	W	%	PV	%	personal
1916 R	1	5.0	155,945	8.1	Ill. 58

Convention	FB	%	LB	%	personal
1916 R (Q)	66	6.7	0	0.0	

Alfred Smith (1873-1944)

Primaries	W	%	PV	%	personal
1924 D	0	0.0	16,459	2.2	N.Y. 51
1928＊D (Q)	9	56.3	499,452	39.5	N.Y. 55
1932 D (Q)	2	12.5	406,162	13.8	N.Y. 59
1936 D	0	0.0	2,974	0.1	N.Y. 63
Career	11	34.4	925,047	21.5	

Convention	FB	%	LB	%	personal
1920 D (Q)	109	10.0	0	0.0	N.Y. 47
1924 D (Q)	241	21.9	7½	0.7	
1928＊D (Q)	849$\frac{2}{3}$	77.2	----	----	
1932 D (Q)	201$\frac{3}{4}$	17.5	190½	16.5	
Career	1,401$\frac{5}{12}$	31.5	198	5.9	

General	PV	%	EV	%	personal
1928 D (Q)	15,000,185	40.8	87	16.4	

William Sproul (1870-1928)

Convention	FB	%	LB	%	personal
1920 R (Q)	84	8.5	0	0.0	Pa. 50

Harold Stassen (1907-   )

Primaries	W	%	PV	%	personal
1944 R	1	7.7	67,508	3.0	Minn. 37
1948 R (Q)	4	33.3	449,713	16.9	Minn. 41
1952 R (Q)	1	7.7	881,702	11.3	Minn. 45
1964 R	0	0.0	113,803	1.9	Pa. 57
1968 R	0	0.0	31,598	0.7	Pa. 61
1980 R	0	0.0	24,753	0.2	N.Y. 73
1984 R	0	0.0	12,755	0.2	Minn. 77
Career	6	20.0	1,581,832	12.7	

Convention	FB	%	LB	%	personal
1948 R (Q)	157	14.4	0	0.0	
1968 R	2	0.2	----	----	
Career	159	14.4	0	0.0	

Adlai Stevenson (1900-1965)

Primaries	W	%	PV	%	personal
1952 D	0	0.0	78,583	1.6	Ill. 52
1956*D (Q)	7	36.8	3,058,470	52.3	Ill. 56
1960 D	0	0.0	51,665	0.9	Ill. 60
1964 D	0	0.0	452	0.0	Ill. 64
Career	7	36.8	3,189,170	52.3	

Convention	FB	%	LB	%	personal
1952*D (Q)	273	22.2	617½	50.2	
1956*D (Q)	905½	66.0	----	----	
1960 D (Q)	79½	5.2	----	----	
Career	1,258	30.5	617½	50.2	

Adlai Stevenson (continued)

General	PV	%	EV	%	personal
1952 D (Q)	27,314,649	44.4	89	16.8	
1956 D (Q)	26,030,172	42.0	73	13.7	
Career	53,344,821	43.2	162	15.3	

Stuart Symington (1901-   )

Primaries	W	%	PV	%	personal
1960 D	0	0.0	29,557	0.5	Mo. 59

Convention	FB	%	LB	%	personal
1956 D	45½	3.3	----	----	Mo. 55
1960 D (Q)	86	5.7	----	----	
Career	131½	5.7	----	----	

Robert Taft (1889-1953)

Primaries	W	%	PV	%	personal
1940 R (Q)	1	7.7	516,428	16.0	Ohio 51
1948 R	0	0.0	37,974	1.4	Ohio 59
1952*R (Q)	6	46.2	2,794,736	35.8	Ohio 63
Career	7	26.9	3,349,138	30.0	

Convention	FB	%	LB	%	personal
1940 R (Q)	189	18.9	318	31.8	
1948 R (Q)	224	20.5	0	0.0	
1952 R (Q)	280	23.2	----	----	
Career	693	21.0	318	15.2	

William Howard Taft (1857-1930)

Primaries	W	%	PV	%	personal
1912 R (Q)	1	8.3	766,326	33.9	Ohio 55

Convention	FB	%	LB	%	personal
1908*R (Q)	702	71.6	----	----	Ohio 51
1912*R (Q)	556	51.6	----	----	
1916 R	14	1.4	0	0.0	Ohio 59
Career	1,272	61.1	0	----	

General	PV	%	EV	%	personal
1908*R (Q)	7,676,258	51.6	321	66.5	
1912 R (Q)	3,486,333	23.2	8	1.5	
Career	11,162,591	37.3	329	32.4	

Zachary Taylor (1784-1850)

Convention	FB	%	LB	%	personal
1848*W (Q)	111	39.6	171	61.1	La. 64

General	PV	%	EV	%	personal
1848*W (Q)	1,361,393	47.3	163	56.2	

Norman Thomas (1884-1968)

General	PV	%	EV	%	personal
1928 SOC	266,453	0.7	0	0.0	N.Y. 44
1932 SOC (Q)	883,990	2.2	0	0.0	N.Y. 48
1936 SOC	187,785	0.4	0	0.0	N.Y. 52
1940 SOC	116,827	0.2	0	0.0	N.Y. 56
1944 SOC	79,000	0.2	0	0.0	N.Y. 60
1948 SOC	138,973	0.3	0	0.0	N.Y. 64
Career	1,673,028	2.2	0	0.0	

Allen Thurman (1813-1895)

Convention	FB	%	LB	%	personal
1876 D	3	0.4	2	0.3	Ohio 63
1880 D (Q)	68½	9.3	0	0.0	Ohio 67
1884 D (Q)	88	10.7	4	0.5	Ohio 71
Career	159½	10.0	6	0.3	

Strom Thurmond (1902-   )

General	PV	%	EV	%	personal
1948 SRD (Q)	1,169,134	2.4	39	7.3	S.C. 46

Samuel Tilden (1814-1886)

Convention	FB	%	LB	%	personal
1876*D (Q)	401½	54.4	535	72.5	N.Y. 62
1880 D (Q)	38	5.1	1	0.1	N.Y. 66
1884 D	1	0.1	0	0.0	N.Y. 70
Career	440½	29.8	536	36.3	

General	PV	%	EV	%	personal
1876 D (Q)	4,288,546	51.0	184	49.9	

Harry Truman (1884-1972)

Primaries	W	%	PV	%	personal
1948*D (Q)	8	57.1	1,375,452	63.9	Mo. 64
1952 D	0	0.0	62,345	1.3	Mo. 68
Career	8	57.1	1,437,797	63.9	

Convention	FB	%	LB	%	personal
1948*D (Q)	926	75.0	----	----	
1952 D	6	0.5	0	0.0	
Career	932	75.0	0	----	

General	PV	%	EV	%	personal
1948*D (Q)	24,105,587	49.5	303	57.1	

Morris Udall (1922-   )

Primaries	W	%	PV	%	personal
1976 D (Q)	0	0.0	1,611,754	10.0	Ariz. 54

Convention	FB	%	LB	%	personal
1976 D (Q)	329½	11.0	----	----	

Oscar Underwood (1862-1929)

Convention	FB	%	LB	%	personal
1912 D (Q)	117½	10.7	0	0.0	Ala. 50
1920 D	½	0.0	0	0.0	Ala. 58
1924 D (Q)	42½	3.9	102½	9.3	Ala. 62
Career	160½	7.3	102½	4.7	

Martin Van Buren (1782-1862)

Convention	FB	%	LB	%	personal
1836*D (Q)	265	100.0	----	----	N.Y. 54
1840*D (Q)	244	100.0	----	----	N.Y. 58
1844 D (Q)	146	54.9	0	0.0	N.Y. 62
Career	655	84.5	0	0.0	

General	PV	%	EV	%	personal
1836*D (Q)	764,176	50.8	170	57.8	
1840 D (Q)	1,128,854	46.8	60	20.4	
1848 FS (Q)	291,501	10.1	0	0.0	N.Y. 66
Career	2,184,531	32.2	230	26.2	

Arthur Vandenberg (1884-1951)

Primaries	W	%	PV	%	personal
1940 R	0	0.0	100,651	3.1	Mich. 56
1948 R	0	0.0	18,924	0.7	Mich. 64
Career	0	----	119,575	----	

Convention	FB	%	LB	%	personal
1940 R (Q)	76	7.6	0	0.0	
1948 R (Q)	62	5.7	0	0.0	
Career	138	6.6	0	0.0	

George Wallace (1919-   )

Primaries	W	%	PV	%	personal
1964 D (Q)	0	0.0	672,984	10.8	Ala. 45
1968 D	0	0.0	33,520	0.4	Ala. 49
1972 D (Q)	5	23.8	3,755,424	23.5	Ala. 53
1976 D (Q)	0	0.0	1,995,388	12.4	Ala. 57
Career	5	7.8	6,457,316	16.8	

Convention	FB	%	LB	%	personal
1968 D	$\frac{1}{2}$	0.0	----	----	
1972 D (Q)	$381\frac{7}{10}$	12.7	----	----	
1976 D	57	1.9	----	----	
Career	$439\frac{1}{5}$	12.7	----	----	

General	PV	%	EV	%	personal
1964 ID	60	0.0	0	0.0	
1968 AI (Q)	9,901,151	13.5	46	8.6	
Career	9,901,211	13.5	46	8.6	

Henry Wallace (1888-1965)

Primaries	W	%	PV	%	personal
1948 D	0	0.0	4,416	0.2	Iowa 60

General	PV	%	EV	%	personal
1948 P (Q)	1,157,057	2.4	0	0.0	

Thomas Walsh (1859-1933)

Primaries	W	%	PV	%	personal
1928 D (Q)	0	0.0	59,871	4.7	Mont. 69

Convention	FB	%	LB	%	personal
1924 D (Q)	0	0.0	58	5.3	Mont. 65

Earl Warren (1891-1974)

Primaries	W	%	PV	%	personal
1936 R	1	8.3	350,917	10.6	Cal. 45
1944 R	1	7.7	594,439	26.2	Cal. 53
1948*R (Q)	1	8.3	771,295	29.1	Cal. 57
1952 R (Q)	1	7.7	1,349,036	17.3	Cal. 61
Career	4	8.0	3,065,687	20.3	

Convention	FB	%	LB	%	personal
1948 R (Q)	59	5.4	0	0.0	
1952 R (Q)	77	6.4	----	----	
Career	136	5.9	0	0.0	

George Washington (1732-1799)

General	PV	%	EV	%	personal
1789*F (Q)	----	----	69	100.0	Va. 57
1792*F (Q)	----	----	132	100.0	Va. 60
Career	----	----	201	100.0	

James Watson (1864-1948)

Primaries	W	%	PV	%	personal
1928 R	1	6.7	228,795	5.6	Ind. 64

Convention	FB	%	LB	%	personal
1928 R (Q)	45	4.1	----	----	

James Weaver (1833-1912)

General	PV	%	EV	%	personal
1872 I	309	0.0	0	0.0	Iowa 39
1880 GR (Q)	305,997	3.3	0	0.0	Iowa 47
1892 POP (Q)	1,024,280	8.5	22	5.0	Iowa 59
Career	1,330,586	6.3	22	2.7	

Daniel Webster (1782-1852)

Convention	FB	%	LB	%	personal
1848 W (Q)	22	7.9	14	5.0	Mass. 66
1852 W (Q)	29	9.8	21	7.1	Mass. 70
Career	51	8.9	35	6.1	

General	PV	%	EV	%	personal
1836 W (Q)	41,201	2.7	14	4.8	Mass. 54
1852 IW	6,994	0.2	0	0.0	
Career	48,195	2.7	14	4.8	

John Weeks (1860-1926)

Convention	FB	%	LB	%	personal
1916 R (Q)	105	10.6	3	0.3	Mass. 56

Hugh White (1773-1840)

General	PV	%	EV	%	personal
1836 W (Q)	146,107	9.7	26	8.8	Tenn. 63

Wendell Willkie (1892-1944)

Primaries	W	%	PV	%	personal
1940 R	0	0.0	21,140	0.7	N.Y. 48
1944 R	0	0.0	27,097	1.2	N.Y. 52
Career	0	----	48,237	----	

Convention	FB	%	LB	%	personal
1940*R (Q)	105	10.5	655	65.5	

General	PV	%	EV	%	personal
1940 R (Q)	22,336,260	44.8	82	15.4	

Woodrow Wilson (1856-1924)

Primaries	W	%	PV	%	personal
1912*D (Q)	5	41.7	435,169	44.6	N.J. 56
1916*D (Q)	20	100.0	1,173,220	98.8	N.J. 60
Career	25	78.1	1,608,389	74.4	

Convention	FB	%	LB	%	personal
1912*D (Q)	324	29.6	990	90.5	
1916*D (Q)	1,092	100.0	----	----	
Career	1,416	64.8	990	90.5	

General	PV	%	EV	%	personal
1912*D (Q)	6,293,152	41.8	435	81.9	
1916*D (Q)	9,126,300	49.2	277	52.2	
Career	15,419,452	45.9	712	67.0	

William Wirt (1772-1834)

General	PV	%	EV	%	personal
1832 AM (Q)	100,715	7.8	7	2.4	Md. 60

Leonard Wood (1860-1927)

Primaries	W	%	PV	%	personal
1920 R (Q)	8	40.0	710,863	22.3	N.H. 60

Convention	FB	%	LB	%	personal
1920 R (Q)	287½	29.2	181½	18.4	

Levi Woodbury (1789-1851)

Convention	FB	%	LB	%	personal
1844 D	2	0.8	0	0.0	N.H. 55
1848 D (Q)	53	18.3	38	13.1	N.H. 59
Career	55	18.3	38	13.1	

8.
The Parties

AMERICAN INDEPENDENT (1968)

The American Independent party stemmed from events on the campus of the University of Alabama in September 1963, five years before it ran a candidate. Governor George Wallace failed to prevent the integration of the university and resolved to challenge the Northern Democrats who had ordered it. He fared surprisingly well in three Democratic primaries the following year. It was too late to mount an independent candidacy that fall, but he began planning for 1968.

Wallace's strategy was predicated on the then-minority belief that racial tension was not confined to the South. "When they start catching this mess up North and everywhere else," he predicted, "then you're going to see this whole country Southernized, from Boston to Los Angeles."[1] Journalists began noting signs of a white backlash to the civil-rights movement. Wallace planned to capitalize on it.

The American Independents were listed on all fifty state ballots in 1968. Wallace's coalition of right-wingers and Southerners brought him the highest popular vote ever for a third-party candidate. But the Alabaman had scant interest in the painstaking task of developing local party organizations. He returned to the Democratic fold in 1970. The 1972 American Independent nominee, California Congressman John Schmitz, polled only 1.4 percent of the vote, slightly better than one-tenth of what Wallace had received. The party was split soon thereafter by internal conflicts, yielding separate American and American Independent parties. Neither passed the one-percent mark in subsequent elections.

AMERICAN-WHIG (1856)

The American party was formed because of fear. The Protestant poor and lower-middle classes watched with dismay as millions of immigrants, a large proportion of them Catholic, poured into the United States. The rush began in 1845, bringing nearly 3,000,000 newcomers in the following decade. A nativist society, the Order of United Americans, rose in response to this perceived threat. Its members were bound to secrecy. Asked if they belonged, they were to reply, "I know nothing."

The private order went public in 1855, forming the American party. Its motto was straightforward: "Americans must rule America." It proposed a twenty-one-year waiting period before immigrants could become citizens. The Catholic Church was condemned as "essentially a foreign power...fed and strengthened as it is from alien sources."[2] The new party quickly became popular in the South and New England. Its members were often called Know-Nothings.

The American party's momentum was broken by the slavery dispute. The party's refusal to condemn involuntary servitude triggered heavy Northern defections to the Republicans. Former Whigs under Millard Fillmore, not really interested in the immigration controversy, captured the remaining organization for their own uses. The weak remnants of the Whig party quickly endorsed Fillmore. His coalition ticket carried only one state in 1856. The young party survived in some areas until 1859, but never ran a national candidate again.

ANTI-MASONIC (1832)

The Anti-Masonic party had an unlikely genesis. It was created in reaction to the disappearance in 1826 of William Morgan, an Upstate New Yorker who was planning to make public the secret rituals of Freemasonry. There were whispers he had been kidnaped and drowned by Masons. The New York legislature refused to investigate. Local probes turned up nothing. Aware that many government figures belonged to the secret order, critics charged conspiracy. They formed a new political organization to fight back.

The Anti-Masonic party began in New York, but spread by 1830 to much of the North. Party literature blasted Masonry as "an organized kingdom within the limits of the Republic." All forms of privilege and elitism were attacked, but the focus never varied. "The offences of Freemasonry upon our individual and national rights, if they had been committed by a foreign nation would, by the law of nations, have justified a public war to avenge them," declared an 1831 party resolution.[3]

The Anti-Masons were perhaps too effective in their propagandizing. The hated secret order lost its attractiveness to the upper class. The number of Masonic lodges in New York dropped 90 percent from 1826 to 1832. Such a precipitous decline destroyed the party's reason for being. Most of its members left to join the Whigs after the 1832 campaign. But the Anti-Masons had one enduring legacy: Their 1831 national convention was the first ever held, establishing the nominating mechanism to be used by all subsequent parties.

CONSTITUTIONAL UNION (1860)

The Constitutional Union party was based on the premise that some things are better left unsaid. It was created in 1859 by survivors of the American and Whig parties who despaired of ever resuscitating those lifeless forms. The organizers hoped to keep their new party healthy by avoiding the controversy that had been fatal to its predecessors. It was a forlorn wish in the volatile year of 1860.

Constitutional Unionists scorned platforms, contending they would only widen the nation's regional fissures. The party satisfied itself with pledging loyalty to "the Constitution of the Country, the Union of the States, and the Enforcement of the Laws."[4] Former Tennessee Senator John Bell, the Constitutional Union nominee, refused to commit himself further.

The new party's straddle had no appeal to extremists, either North or South. It did best in the border states, where secession fever was still of a mild strain. Bell's ticket carried Kentucky, Tennessee, and Virginia. But after Fort Sumter, compromise was an empty hope. The Constitutional Union party died with the coming of the conflict it had hoped to smother with a cloud of vague phrases.

DEMOCRATIC (1832, 1984)

The Democratic party has survived longer than any other in the United States. The organization stakes a fuzzy claim to direct descent from Thomas Jefferson's Democratic-Republicans. It actually was born after the Jeffersonian coalition splintered in the 1824 election. Supporters of Andrew Jackson called themselves Democratic-Republicans in 1828, but recognizing the new character of their party, began using the Democratic label in the early 1830s.

Jackson's party was dominant in the years before the Civil War. It had strong appeal in rural areas, particularly in the South. The Democratic philosophy was conservative, opposing federal interference with slavery. The party embraced the doctrine of states' rights. "The Federal Government is one of limited power, derived solely from the Constitution," asserted the 1856 party platform. "The grants of power made therein ought to be strictly construed by all the departments and agents of the government."[5] Democrats steadfastly opposed the use of federal money for public-works projects.

The party's majority vanished with the Civil War. Republican orators delighted in reminding Northern audiences that many prominent Democrats had favored peaceful secession and later had harassed Abraham Lincoln's prosecution of the war. Only a grateful South stuck with the party. The Democrats lost fourteen of the eighteen elections between

1860 and 1928. Their only victories resulted from Republican schisms in 1884 and 1912, and the candidacies of a former Democratic President in 1892 and an incumbent in 1916.

A self-confident New York politician came to the rescue in 1932, the centennial of the Democrats´ first national victory. Franklin Roosevelt remade the party in his image. The Jacksonian emphasis on states´ rights and opposition to public works were dropped. Rural areas and the South saw their intraparty power wash away. Dominance passed to urban politicians and their constituencies, among them organized labor, ethnic groups, and blacks. Conservative Virginia Senator Carter Glass surveyed the wreckage. "The New Deal is not only a mistake," he complained, "it is a disgrace to the nation."[6]   It was also a political success. The Democrats won seven of the nine elections from 1932 to 1964. Roosevelt attributed those victories to the party´s new liberalism. "We ought to have two real parties: one liberal and the other conservative," he remarked. "As it is now, each party is split by dissenters."[7]

Those dissenters began to move away in the 1960s. The white South, livid at Democratic civil-rights programs, defected to the Republicans in national contests. A country tired of foreign wars and high government spending drifted to the right. The Democrats were quadrennially buried in landslides, with the exception being 1976, an election in the wake of the Republican Watergate scandal. "The New Deal has run its course," asserted Colorado Senator Gary Hart in 1984. "The party is over."[8]   Others agreed after the Democrats sustained yet another shocking defeat that fall.

DEMOCRATIC-REPUBLICAN (1796, 1828)

Tensions within George Washington´s original Cabinet set in motion the forces that created the Democratic-Republican party. Secretary of the Treasury Alexander Hamilton and Secretary of State Thomas Jefferson disagreed vehemently on the course of the new nation. Hamilton favored a strong federal government. He accused his rival of wishing "to narrow the federal authority." Jefferson retorted that Hamilton had "the purpose of subverting step by step the principles of the Constitution, which he has so often declared to be a thing of nothing which must be changed."[9] Hamilton´s backers became known as Federalists. Jefferson´s were Democratic-Republicans, often informally called Republicans.

The anti-Hamilton faction was an unofficial coalition at first. It developed throughout the 1790s. Jefferson was the first Democratic-Republican candidate for President, losing in 1796. He had often ridiculed the idea of party, but now confessed that when "the principle of difference is as substantial and as strongly pronounced as between the Republicans and the Monocrats of our country, I hold it...honorable to take a firm and decided part."[10]   His victory in 1800 was the first of eight straight for the new party.

The Democratic-Republicans glorified the agrarian life. They also defended the concept of states´ rights. These two stands made the party especially popular in the South and on the trans-Appalachian frontier. The Federalists, slowly retreating to their New England stronghold, watched gloomily as Jefferson arranged the Louisiana Purchase. The vast territory appeared certain to be someday carved into a number of safely Democratic-Republican states. It was a foreshadowing of Federalist doom. The Republicans sealed it by ending the War of 1812 with battlefield victories that obscured two years of failure, then co-opting Federalist causes such as the Second Bank of the United States. Jefferson´s coalition was the only remaining party after 1816.

Optimistic Democratic-Republicans settled in for a long political summer. President James Monroe said hopefully, "Surely our government may go on and prosper without the existence of parties."[11] But others knew politics abhors a vacuum. Jefferson had written as early as 1807, "I had always expected that when the Republicans should have put all things under their feet, they would schismatize among themselves."[12] It eventually came to pass, as four candidates presented themselves in 1824. Backers of the victorious John Quincy Adams and Henry Clay combined to form the National Republican party after the election. Supporters of Andrew Jackson and William Crawford kept the Democratic-Republican label for their new coalition. But after Jackson´s win in 1828, his organization changed its name to the simpler Democratic party.

FEDERALIST (1789, 1816)

The Federalist party got a sizable jump on its competition. It had the advantage of association with the immortal George Washington. It also was blessed with the support of the nation´s powerful commercial interests. These factors seemed the formula for a long reign, but the Federalists dissipated it after just three elections. The party then retired very slowly from the national stage.

The Federalist movement was launched in 1787 to convince state legislatures to ratify the Constitution. The name was passed to that faction in the new government that believed in strong federal authority. Many politicians belonged to both groups. Some, such as James Madison, were in the first, but objected to the economic blueprints of Secretary of the Treasury Alexander Hamilton. They helped form the Democratic-Republican party.

Hamilton was the founder of the Federalist party. Washington was elected with Federalist support in 1789 and 1792, but denied formal involvement with the organization. He nonetheless was labeled a Federalist because of the obvious favor he accorded Hamiltonian programs. Washington´s successor, John Adams, likewise kept his distance from party machinations. The Federalists suffered from this inattention. Their political network was soon dwarfed by that of the Democratic-Republicans.

The Federalist party never returned to power after Adams´ loss in 1800. Its image as the tool of aristocrats hurt badly. So did the growing talk of secession by some New England Federalists, culminating in the 1815 Hartford Convention. Critics labeled it a gathering of traitors, a false charge that was nonetheless effective. Adams noted that his party, once known for its nationalism, had evolved into little more than a New England organization. "Our two great parties have crossed over the valley and taken possession of each other´s mountain," he marveled.[13] It was true that in the wake of the War of 1812, the newly nationalistic Democratic-Republicans had broad support. The Federalists mounted one final ineffectual challenge in 1816, then faded into the history books.

FREE SOIL (1848, 1852)

The Free Soil party advertised itself as a party of principle, but it was formed largely out of political expedience. The Democratic party in New York was torn into two factions in 1848. The Hunkers endorsed the policies of President James Polk. The Barnburners lined up behind former President Martin Van Buren and against the extension of slavery into newly acquired Mexican territory. The spurned Barnburners bolted the Democratic national convention to form the Free Soil party. Most members of the Liberty party and a few Northern Whigs joined as well.

The new party took a strong stand on its key issue. Its 1848 platform condemned slavery in the territories, "Congress has no more power to make a SLAVE than to make a KING; no more power to institute or establish SLAVERY, than to institute or establish a MONARCHY."[14] The party´s other aim was to punish the Polk wing of the Democratic party, which it did. Defections to the Free Soilers clinched the defeat of Lewis Cass by throwing New York´s crucial electoral votes to the Whigs. Their point made, Van Buren and his Barnburners returned to the Democratic fold in 1849.

A vastly different group of Free Soilers made a second try in 1852. The party now consisted largely of disaffected Whigs. It was crippled by the exit of the Van Burenites and by the temporary political calm resulting from the Compromise of 1850. Most Free Soilers abandoned the organization after its poor 1852 showing. They soon joined the new Republican party.

GREENBACK (1880)

The Greenback party was in its key respects a prototype for the better-known Populist party. Greenbackers and Populists both outspokenly supported soft money. Both advanced packages of reform legislation that were ridiculed at the time, but later were enacted. And both dreamed of assembling a powerful coalition of farmers and labor, a task that proved impossible.

The Greenback party was formed in 1875. The nation was

then deep in an economic depression. Congress chose that moment to decide to put the nation back on the gold standard by 1879. Critics warned that the money supply would dry up, further harming those who were already suffering. They wanted the nation to continue to use unsecured greenbacks, the paper money pressed into service during the Civil War.

The hastily organized Greenbackers polled less than one percent of the vote in 1876, but aimed for success in 1880, when they would have time to prepare. The party's platform boldly accused the Republicans of running government "of the bondholder, by the bondholder, and for the bondholder."[15] It pledged support for shorter workdays and women's suffrage, as well as its revered greenbacks. But two factors hurt the party badly in 1880. Its labor and farmer elements were constantly feuding. Worse, good times returned, decreasing public interest in soft money. The party made one last try in 1884, then faded away. Most of its leading figures, including 1880 nominee James Weaver, soon were reincarnated as Populists.

LIBERAL REPUBLICAN (none)

The Liberal Republican party was never destined to be long-lived. Its founders were motivated largely by a specific short-term problem, corruption in the Grant Administration. They then arranged a coalition with the Democrats that submerged the Liberal Republican identity. The party did not survive the year of its birth, 1872.

The new national organization modeled itself on the successful Liberal movement in Missouri, which had elected Gratz Brown as Governor in 1870. Liberals wanted to put the Civil War behind them, striving for reconciliation in their divided state. The Liberal Republicans felt the same way, demanding an end to military Reconstruction. They also wanted civil-service reform. "Federal office-holders have...usurped the organization of the Republican party," cried the editor of Harper's Weekly, George William Curtis. "They have banded themselves into an odious and intolerable oligarchy which menaces the very system of our government."[16]

Coalition with the Democrats was the key to the Liberal win in Missouri, so the Liberal Republicans followed the pattern. But the unexpected triumph of Horace Greeley at the new party's convention destroyed any hope of unseating Ulysses Grant. Democrats showed little enthusiasm for the publisher who had spent so much of his career skewering them. Greeley's resulting landslide defeat killed the movement. Most Liberal Republicans returned to the major parties in 1876, supporting Republican Benjamin Bristow or Democrat Samuel Tilden.

LIBERTARIAN (none)

Most political parties are primarily motivated by the desire for patronage. The Libertarian party takes the opposite tack, aiming to eliminate thousands of government jobs.

Formed in 1971, it preaches the gospel of free enterprise more energetically than any party in American history. Libertarian platforms have promised to dismantle such agencies as the Federal Trade Commission and the Federal Bureau of Investigation. The party wants to greatly reduce America´s international commitments. The Pentagon would be subjected to a massive budget cut under a Libertarian administration. Social programs would also get the ax. The 1984 Presidential nominee, David Bergland, said simply, "The government should not be in the charity business."[17]

The Libertarian party has attracted both former conservatives and ex-members of radical leftist organizations. It received national attention in 1972 when a Republican elector bolted Richard Nixon to vote for the Libertarian ticket. But acceptance of the party has been minimal. It has never attracted more than 1.1 percent of the popular vote.

LIBERTY (1844)

The abolitionist movement was torn by a great dispute in the late 1830s. One faction of the American Anti-Slavery Society, headed by founder William Lloyd Garrison, wanted nothing to do with politics. Garrison didn´t even vote because he felt doing so would admit the legitimacy of a government that allowed slaveholding. The other group, led by James Birney, insisted abolition could only be achieved with political muscle. It formed the Liberty party in 1839, the first anti-slavery party in America.

Subsequent national debate would center on the extension of slavery in the territories, but the Liberty party denied that was the true issue. Its 1844 platform demanded "the absolute and unqualified divorce of the General Government from Slavery." The same document condemned slaveholding, whether in territories or states, as "the grossest form and most revolting manifestation of Despotism."[18]

Birney did poorly in 1840, receiving fewer than 7,000 votes. But the climate for the Liberty party was much improved in 1844, as the nation heatedly debated the proposed annexation of Texas as a slave state. Birney polled 2.3 percent of the vote. He had hopes of doing better in 1848, but his thunder was stolen by the emergence of the less militant Free Soil party. No one in the Liberty party could match the high public profile of Free Soil nominee Martin Van Buren, so the older organization melded with the new. A few hardcore Liberty partisans ran their own 1848 campaign before folding their tent for good.

NATIONAL REPUBLICAN (1828, 1832)

The National Republican party was the ideological heir to Federalism. It advocated strong federal authority, protection for the nation´s commercial interests, and federal spending for public-works projects such as canals and roads. "The spirit of improvement is abroad upon the earth and the

United States must take the lead in furthering it," declared President John Quincy Adams in 1825.[19] His party also rode to the defense of the Second Bank of the United States, calling it "this great and beneficial institution."

The National Republican party was a by-product of the 1824 election that pitted four Democratic-Republicans against one another. Two, Adams and Henry Clay, formed the new party the following year. Their opponents retained the Democratic-Republican label through 1828, then shortened it to Democratic.

The National Republicans suffered as the Federalists had with the tag of "elitists." The two also had in common an electoral weakness everywhere except New England. And both suffered from poor party organization. But the National Republicans carried an important additional burden. Their opponent in the 1828 and 1832 elections was a national hero, Andrew Jackson. Critics vilified him as a dictator, but his popularity was unrivaled. Both campaigns against him ended in landslide defeats. After Henry Clay´s loss in 1832, National Republicans joined Anti-Masons and disaffected Democrats under a new banner, that of the Whig party.

NATIONAL UNITY (1980)

The National Unity party was a patchwork affair, really not a party at all. It was hastily formed by Illinois Congressman John Anderson in April 1980 after it became obvious he had no hope of winning the Republican Presidential nomination. Anderson´s liberal stands on social issues were out of tune with a party that was soon to nominate Ronald Reagan. He promised a middle-of-the-road alternative to Reagan and Jimmy Carter, denying he was a spoiler. "What´s to spoil?" he asked about his two opponents.

The National Unity party surprised observers by qualifying for ballot status in all fifty states. But Anderson´s standing in the public-opinion polls dwindled through the fall. He ended with only 6.6 percent in November. "This campaign must not, shall not, and will not end for me!" he shouted to supporters on election night. "That [losing] was a decision deferred."[20]

The brave talk vanished by 1984. Anderson refused to run again, even though he was now eligible for $6 million in federal campaign funding. The National Unity party appeared on the ballot only in Kentucky. Its leader endorsed Democrat Walter Mondale. Anderson said he hoped his organization would regain its national status in 1988 by running a candidate again, but added he would not be the man.

POPULIST (1892)

Hard times on the plains spawned the Populist party in 1891. Farmers were becoming desperate as their financial losses mounted. Thousands lost their property in foreclosure sales. Economic theorists said low commodity prices were a result of overproduction and strong world competition. Farmers saw two different villains. They accused railroads of charging excessively high rates and Eastern financiers of restricting the money supply.

The Populists intended to tap this agrarian discontent. One party speaker, Mary Elizabeth Lease, exhorted farmers "to raise less corn and more hell."[21] Feelings against the moneyed East were strong. The East reciprocated. The New York _Tribune_ said the Populists were "engineered and directed by the most notorious political hacks and chronic office-seekers."[22] Most leaders actually came from farmers' associations or the late Greenback party.

The Populist party won 22 electoral votes in 1892. It was the first third-party to break into the Electoral College since the Civil War. But two decisions in 1896 halted the strong Populist momentum. The party abandoned its package of reforms to concentrate on advocacy of free coinage of silver. It then endorsed the silver Democratic ticket headed by William Jennings Bryan. The return of prosperity by 1900 killed silver as an issue, and the Populists never regained their identity after fusion with the Democrats. The party ran candidates through 1908, but they received no more than a handful of votes.

PROGRESSIVE (LA FOLLETTE) (1924)

The Progressive party of Robert La Follette was ahead of its time. Its reform program presaged much of the New Deal. La Follette's difficulty was in trying to sell his message in the midst of prosperity. Franklin Roosevelt was much more successful with a similar program after the crash on Wall Street.

The Progressive coalition was formed of four elements in 1922: organized labor, farmers' associations, the Socialist party, and members of Theodore Roosevelt's late Progressive party. La Follette rallied them with blistering attacks on corporate monopolies. "They would like to see the farmer happy and the city man with loose change in his pocket," La Follette thundered, "provided, and here is the point, provided it can be done without reducing the swollen profits of these interests."[23] The financial world looked with horror on a platform that called for strong trust-busting, a lower tariff, and government takeover of the railroads.

The Progressive party did its best in the 1924 election in a belt stretching from the Great Lakes to the Pacific Coast. Overall, it received nearly 17 percent of the popular vote. La Follette dreamed of supplanting the Democrats as the nation's second party, but he died in 1925. Labor union members lined the tracks as a train carried his body from Washington to his native Wisconsin. They were paying last respects not only to their champion, but also to a Progressive party that perished with its leader.

PROGRESSIVE (ROOSEVELT) (1912)

This Progressive party was the sole property of Theodore Roosevelt. His anger fueled its creation in 1912. His annoyance dictated its death in 1916. The party served the former President primarily as a tool of retribution, but also advanced a reform platform that included some truly radical ideas.

Roosevelt consented to a third-party race in 1912 after losing the Republican nomination to William Howard Taft. He called GOP leaders "pocket-picking, porch-climbing bandits" for ruling against his credentials challenges at the convention. His supporters marched to a second hall, where Roosevelt vowed to fight back. "We stand at Armageddon and we battle for the Lord!" he shouted.[24]

Roosevelt's popularity carried the Progressives to a higher vote total than the Republicans achieved in the fall. He insisted he would continue to battle for such innovative concepts as social insurance and popular ratification of judicial decisions. But without patronage or entrenched local organizations, the former President found it difficult to keep his coalition together. He had condemned the major parties in 1912 as "husks, with no real soul within either," but he secretly plotted to return to the Republican side in 1916.[25] Roosevelt hoped for fusion that would result in his nomination. The Republicans spoiled his plan by insisting on Charles Evans Hughes. An irritated Roosevelt then spurned the Progressive nomination. The young party received scattered votes without a candidate in November before vanishing.

PROGRESSIVE (WALLACE) (1948)

"We have assembled a Gideon's Army, small in number, powerful in conviction, ready for action!"[26] So declared former Vice President Henry Wallace in 1947, as he announced the creation of the nation's third Progressive party. Wallace's infantry consisted largely of former New Dealers who feared Harry Truman had abandoned the sacred tenets of Franklin Roosevelt. But it also included the Communist party, whose endorsement Wallace refused to repudiate.

Wallace began his trek toward a third-party candidacy in 1946. Truman dismissed him as Secretary of Commerce after he publicly questioned the President's strict stance against the Soviets. "The tougher we get with Russia," Wallace insisted, "the tougher they will get with us."[27] He wanted a return to Roosevelt's wartime policy of coexistence. Public-opinion polls showed millions agreeing with him. The new Progressives expected to receive more than 10 percent of the vote in 1948.

The issue of Communism deflated those hopes. Asked why his platform was much like that of the Communists, Wallace joked, "I'd say they have a good platform." He later said, "The Communists are the closest things to the early Christian martyrs."[28] Wallace's insistence that he was a capitalist could not stem massive defections from the Progressive banner. He ended with only 2.4 percent of the vote.

The new party was never well organized. It split in 1950 when the United States entered the Korean War. Wallace was among the Progressives who resigned their memberships after the party decided to oppose the war effort. It disappeared following a poor showing in 1952.

PROHIBITION (1888, 1892)

The Prohibition party has been around since 1869, but it has little to show for its longevity. The nation's oldest third-party has never won an electoral vote. It also had no real claim to the big victory of the temperance movement, passage of the 18th Amendment in 1919. That success was largely the result of lobbying by the Women's Christian Temperance Union and the Anti-Saloon League. Those organizations were better suited to gain the cooperation of lawmakers because they didn't run candidates against them.

The Prohibition party contended that many of society's problems resulted directly from alcohol. Its 1880 platform said those who drank were "necessarily tending to form intemperate habits, increasing greatly the number, severity, and fatal termination of diseases, weakening and deranging the intellect, polluting the affections, hardening the heart and corrupting the morals, depriving many of reason and more of its healthful exercise, and annually bringing down large numbers to untimely graves."[29] The party sometimes backed reform proposals, as shown by its early support of women's suffrage, but temperance was always foremost.

The Prohibition party reached its peak in 1888 and 1892, crossing the two-percent mark. But the passage of the Volstead Act reduced it to insignificance. Americans saw no need for a Prohibition party while the country was dry. They wanted nothing to do with it after repeal. The party's nominees have not surpassed 0.2 percent of the popular vote since 1924.

REPUBLICAN (1856, 1984)

The Republican party has been the most successful of all. It has won more national elections and drawn more popular and electoral votes than any of its competitors. With the exception of the period of 1932-1956, it has dominated Presidential politics.

There was little in the Republican party's origins to suggest its eventual success. Its formation was convulsive. Congress' passage of the Kansas-Nebraska Act in 1854 ignited a political firestorm. The Whig party perished in the flames of renewed sectional conflict. The prospect of slavery in the new territories infuriated abolitionists and worried laborers who dreaded competition from unpaid workers. These Free Soilers, Northern Whigs, and anti-Nebraska Democrats held organizational meetings in 1854. The Northern wing of the American party soon joined. The result was a sectional party with no support in the South.

The 1860 Democratic split provided the Republicans the chance to win the White House despite their inadequate political base. Abraham Lincoln drew only 39.8 percent of the vote in his first victory. He then struggled for four years to hold the fractious elements of his party together, but clinched Republican dominance with victory in the Civil War, followed by his assassination. Party orators reminded Northern audiences for decades of the martyrdom of Lincoln. They "waved the bloody shirt" at Democrats who had criticized the war effort. Indiana Governor Oliver Morton was a master of the art. He blasted the Democratic party as "a common sewer and loathsome receptacle, into which is emptied every element of treason North and South."[30] Such rhetoric kept the nationalist, pro-business Republicans in power. They won fourteen of the eighteen elections between 1860 and 1928.

Voters quickly dropped the Republican habit in the Depression. Herbert Hoover insisted on upholding his party's conservative views in the midst of crisis. He condemned calls for massive government-sponsored relief efforts. "Prosperity cannot be restored by raids on the public treasury," he declared.[31] The Democrats took over in 1932, winning seven of the next nine elections. Hoover furnished the Democratic version of the "bloody shirt," his name invoked in every campaign as evidence of Republican insensitivity.

The party spent these bleak years fighting among itself. Conservatives led by Robert Taft battled Eastern moderates marshaled by Thomas Dewey. The Easterners pushed through the nomination of Dwight Eisenhower, who scored the party's first wins after Hoover. But the conservatives retaliated in 1964 with Barry Goldwater, who spoke of luring the "forgotten American" to the Republicans. Goldwater was trounced that fall, but his philosophy slowly gained favor in a nation sick of the Vietnam War and urban riots. Richard Nixon's victory in 1968 launched a Republican streak of four wins in five contests, marred only in 1976 because of the Watergate scandal. Goldwater's "forgotten American" had turned Republican, particularly in the South. The party that began with a woefully small base in the 1850s boasted of broad appeal 130 years later.

SOCIALIST (1904, 1932)

The Socialist party had reason to believe that it was taking hold in capitalist America during the first two decades of the 20th Century. The informal coalition that backed Eugene Debs for President in 1900 formed the party in 1901. It began with about 10,000 members. Debs polled three percent of the vote in the next election.

Optimism was rampant by 1912. The Socialist party said it had 118,000 members. Debs had doubled his share of the popular vote to six percent. Better yet, 1,200 Socialist candidates were elected to office on the state and local levels, 79 as mayors. "The class of privilege and pelf has had the world by its throat and the working class beneath its iron-shod hoofs long enough," Debs crowed. "The magic word of freedom is ringing through the nation and the spirit of intelligent revolt is finding expression in every land beneath the sun."[32]

The Socialists proposed collective ownership of all large American industries. Their promise of social upheaval appealed to workers and intellectuals alike, but it became much less popular with the advent of World War I. The party's anti-war harangues were considered by many to be treasonous. Debs was thrown in prison after delivering one such vitriolic address. Socialists added to their problems with intraparty squabbles. Norman Thomas led a brief revival in 1932, but then watched as much of his platform was co-opted by the New Deal. The Socialist party never again played a significant role in a national election.

SOUTHERN DEMOCRATIC (1860)

The Democratic party mirrored the nation in the late 1850s. Each was torn by the dispute over slavery in the territories. Each was in danger of being permanently split. The principals in the Democratic argument were President James Buchanan and Illinois Senator Stephen Douglas. Buchanan wanted to admit Kansas as a slave state. Douglas, once a Southern favorite for his advocacy of popular sovereignty, was opposed.

Southerners decided to settle the question at the 1860 Democratic convention. They insisted on a platform plank guaranteeing federal protection for slavery in all territories. When Douglas' forces defeated the proposal, delegates from eight Southern states walked out. They later held a rump convention that nominated Vice President John Breckinridge.

This Southern Democratic party actually drew some Northern and Western support. Buchanan, former President Franklin Pierce, and former Democratic nominee Lewis Cass all backed Breckinridge. They thought he had a better chance of victory than did the regular Democratic nominee, the outspoken Douglas. But the fact remained that the party's base was in slave states. "Breckinridge may not be for disunion," sniffed Douglas, "but all the disunionists are for Breckinridge."[33] The Vice President indeed spoke for Union in 1860, but changed his mind after he was defeated, joining the Confederate Army as a general. The Southern Democratic party he had briefly headed disappeared with the outbreak of the Civil War.

STATES´ RIGHTS DEMOCRATIC (1948)

The States´ Rights Democratic party bore a startling resemblance to the Southern Democratic party that had existed eighty-eight years earlier. Each was created following the walkout of Southern delegates from a Democratic convention after a dispute over racial issues. The 1948 party was a protest against a strong civil-rights plank successfully promoted by Northern liberals. Dissidents held a rump convention that nominated South Carolina Governor Strom Thurmond for President.

Followers of the new party were commonly known as Dixiecrats. But they insisted they had done nothing disloyal. "This is not a bolt. This is not a fourth party," maintained Mississippi Governor Fielding Wright. "I say to you that we are the true Democrats of the Southland and the United States."[34] Most Southern Democratic leaders, fearing reprisals from Harry Truman, refused to endorse the Thurmond ticket. The South Carolinian carried only the four states where the Dixiecrats had arranged to be listed simply as Democrats.

The States´ Rights Democratic party hoped to deprive the real Democrats of the electoral votes they took for granted, showing them how important the South was. "If the South should vote for Truman this year," Thurmond said, "we might just as well petition the government to give us colonial status."[35] Truman won, anyway. Most Dixiecrats returned to the Democratic party after the election, but they weren´t made to feel welcome. Thurmond finally became a Republican in 1964, continuing his search for a party congenial to white Southerners.

UNION (1936)

The first talk about the Union party sent shivers up the spine of James Farley. The chairman of the Democratic National Committee commissioned a poll that showed a leftist challenge could draw 4,000,000 votes from Franklin Roosevelt in 1936. The candidate of this new party was almost certain to be the charismatic Senator from Louisiana, Huey Long. Long had formed the Share Our Wealth Society in 1934 to spread his populist message. He estimated he had 7.5 million members.

Long´s assassination in September 1935 removed the Union party as a legitimate threat. Noted radio priest Charles Coughlin nonetheless went ahead with the plan. "My friend, there is a way out, a way to freedom!" he told his listeners. "There is an escape from the dole standard of Roosevelt."[36] Coughlin was joined by a well-known advocate of old-age pensions, Francis Townsend, and a former Long aide, Gerald L.K. Smith, in spreading the Union gospel. Coughlin and Smith became increasingly vituperative in the fall, drawing attention away from their nominee, William Lemke. Many Americans were repelled by the spokesmen´s attacks on Jews and Roosevelt. The President meanwhile deftly shifted his policies to the left, preempting Union positions. The new party polled less than 900,000 votes in what proved to be its only national campaign.

WHIG (1836, 1852)

It was obvious from its beginning in 1834 that the Whig party was an uneasy coalition. One Democratic newspaper gleefully labeled it an incongruous mix of "Federalists, nullifiers, and Bank men." There was truth in the joke. Federalists who had joined the National Republican party were indeed now Whigs. Southern believers in nullification were led into the party by South Carolina´s John Calhoun. And defenders of the Second Bank of the United States, such as Henry Clay, also called it home. Most members of the late Anti-Masonic party added their support for good measure.

These disparate elements originally were held together by their hatred of President Andrew Jackson. They scorned him as "King Andrew I" for his "monarchical" use of the veto and the spoils system. The party´s name was borrowed from Britain´s Whigs, who had sworn to oppose tyranny.

Most American Whigs were conservative nationalists. More important were their differences. The party was considered an improvement over the National Republican party it supplanted because it had broader geographical appeal. But the result was widespread internal disagreement over such crucial issues as states´ rights and slavery. When John Tyler assumed the Presidency in 1841, Northern Whigs were horrified to learn of the Virginian´s strong aversion to federal control. They eventually read him out of the party. Henry Clay was nominated to succeed Tyler in 1844. He spent an uncomfortable year tailoring his stand on Texas annexation to appeal to both abolitionist Whigs and slaveholding Whigs. It was a thankless task that left him a laughingstock.

Whig leaders tried to keep their party together by avoiding controversy at all costs. They didn´t even hold a convention in 1836, fearful the young coalition would rupture. Their only two victories came behind military heroes whose views were virtually unknown. Neither had much sense of identification with the Whig party. William Henry Harrison asked in 1840, the year he was elected, "Can anything be more ruinous in its tendency to our institutions than this high party spirit, which looks to the shadow, and not to the substance of things? Nothing, nothing."[37] Zachary Taylor insisted eight years later, "If elected, I would not be the President of a party."[38] The Whigs elected both, particularly Harrison, with campaigns long on hoopla and short on issues.

The Whig shell game could not last forever. It was ended by Congress´ passage of the Kansas-Nebraska Act in 1854. Renewed sectional passions drew most Northern Whigs to the fledgling Republican party. Southern Whigs chose to defend slavery by joining the American or Democratic parties. A few diehards insisted on holding a Whig convention in 1856 to endorse the American ticket headed by Millard Fillmore. They then looked for new parties of their own.

Charts for Chapter 8

American Independent

Elections	5	PV	11,384,192
Qualified	1	PV % (Q)	13.5
W	0	EV	46
		EV % (Q)	8.6

	PV	PV % (Q)	EV	EV % (Q)
1960-1984	11,384,192	13.5	46	8.6

Top PV, one year	George Wallace (1968), 9,901,151
Top PV %, one year	George Wallace (1968), 13.5
Top EV, one year	George Wallace (1968), 46
Top EV %, one year	George Wallace (1968), 8.6

Note: The American Independent party split into two
factions for the 1976 election and those that followed.
Votes for both (the American party and the American
Independent party) are included in the figures above.

American-Whig

Elections	1		PV	873,053
Qualified	1		PV % (Q)	21.5
W	0		EV	8
			EV % (Q)	2.7

	PV	PV % (Q)	EV	EV % (Q)
1856-1900	873,053	21.5	8	2.7

Top PV, one year	Millard Fillmore (1856), 873,053
Top PV %, one year	Millard Fillmore (1856), 21.5
Top EV, one year	Millard Fillmore (1856), 8
Top EV %, one year	Millard Fillmore (1856), 2.7

Anti-Masonic

Elections	1		PV	100,715
Qualified	1		PV % (Q)	7.8
W	0		EV	7
			EV % (Q)	2.4

	PV	PV % (Q)	EV	EV % (Q)
1820-1852	100,715	7.8	7	2.4

Top PV, one year	William Wirt (1832), 100,715
Top PV %, one year	William Wirt (1832), 7.8
Top EV, one year	William Wirt (1832), 7
Top EV %, one year	William Wirt (1832), 2.4

Constitutional Union

Elections	1	PV	590,901
Qualified	1	PV % (Q)	12.6
W	0	EV	39
		EV % (Q)	12.9

	PV	PV % (Q)	EV	EV % (Q)
1856-1900	590,901	12.6	39	12.9

Top PV, one year	John Bell (1860), 590,901
Top PV %, one year	John Bell (1860), 12.6
Top EV, one year	John Bell (1860), 39
Top EV %, one year	John Bell (1860), 12.9

Democratic

Elections	39	PV	546,910,533
Qualified	39	PV % (Q)	46.4
W	17	EV	7,745
		EV % (Q)	45.1

	PV	PV % (Q)	EV	EV % (Q)
1820-1852	6,765,274	48.5	1,000	57.6
1856-1900	48,136,224	46.3	1,684	38.7
1904-1928	59,436,389	38.4	1,364	37.7
1932-1956	180,898,444	50.9	2,341	63.0
1960-1984	251,674,202	45.7	1,356	36.0

Top PV, one year	Lyndon Johnson (1964), 43,126,584
Top PV %, one year	Lyndon Johnson (1964), 61.1
Top EV, one year	Franklin Roosevelt (1936), 523
Top EV %, one year	Franklin Roosevelt (1936), 98.5

Democratic-Republican

Elections	9		PV	995,333
Qualified	9		PV % (Q)	65.7
W	8		EV	1,406
			EV % (Q)	77.5

	PV	PV % (Q)	EV	EV % (Q)
1789-1816	----	----	736	69.3
1820-1852	995,333	65.7	670	88.9

Top PV, one year	Andrew Jackson (1828), 642,553
Top PV %, one year	Andrew Jackson (1828), 56.0
Top EV, one year	James Monroe (1820), 231
Top EV %, one year	James Monroe (1820), 99.6

Federalist

Elections	8		PV	----
Qualified	8		PV % (Q)	----
W	3		EV	521
			EV % (Q)	41.3

	PV	PV % (Q)	EV	EV % (Q)
1789-1816	----	----	521	41.3

Top PV, one year	none
Top PV %, one year	none
Top EV, one year	George Washington (1792), 132
Top EV %, one year	George Washington (1789), 100.0
	George Washington (1792), 100.0

Free Soil

Elections	2	PV	446,711
Qualified	2	PV % (Q)	7.4
W	0	EV	0
		EV % (Q)	0.0

	PV	PV % (Q)	EV	EV % (Q)
1820-1852	446,711	7.4	0	0.0

Top PV, one year	Martin Van Buren (1848), 291,501
Top PV %, one year	Martin Van Buren (1848), 10.1
Top EV, one year	none
Top EV %, one year	none

Greenback

Elections	3	PV	557,066
Qualified	1	PV % (Q)	3.3
W	0	EV	0
		EV % (Q)	0.0

	PV	PV % (Q)	EV	EV % (Q)
1856-1900	557,066	3.3	0	0.0

Top PV, one year	James Weaver (1880), 305,997
Top PV %, one year	James Weaver (1880), 3.3
Top EV, one year	none
Top EV %, one year	none

Liberal Republican

Elections	1	PV	----
Qualified	----	PV % (Q)	----
W	0	EV	----
		EV % (Q)	----

	PV	PV % (Q)	EV	EV % (Q)
1856-1900	----	----	----	----

Top PV, one year	none
Top PV %, one year	none
Top EV, one year	none
Top EV %, one year	none

Note: The Liberal Republican party put forward the ticket that was later endorsed by the Democrats in 1872. The Democratic party is classified as the lead party in the resulting coalition. The votes are included in its listing.

Libertarian

Elections	4	PV	1,325,149
Qualified	0	PV % (Q)	----
W	0	EV	1
		EV % (Q)	----

	PV	PV % (Q)	EV	EV % (Q)
1960-1984	1,325,149	----	1	----

Top PV, one year	Edward Clark (1980), 921,299
Top PV %, one year	Edward Clark (1980), 1.1
Top EV, one year	John Hospers (1972), 1
Top EV %, one year	John Hospers (1972), 0.2

Liberty

Elections	3	PV	71,445
Qualified	1	PV % (Q)	2.3
W	0	EV	0
		EV % (Q)	0.0

	PV	PV % (Q)	EV	EV % (Q)
1820-1852	71,445	2.3	0	0.0

Top PV, one year	James Birney (1844), 62,103
Top PV %, one year	James Birney (1844), 2.3
Top EV, one year	none
Top EV %, one year	none

National Republican

Elections	2	PV	985,102
Qualified	2	PV % (Q)	40.3
W	0	EV	132
		EV % (Q)	24.1

	PV	PV % (Q)	EV	EV % (Q)
1820-1852	985,102	40.3	132	24.1

Top PV, one year	John Quincy Adams (1828), 500,897
Top PV %, one year	John Quincy Adams (1828), 43.6
Top EV, one year	John Quincy Adams (1828), 83
Top EV %, one year	John Quincy Adams (1828), 31.8

National Unity

Elections	2		PV	5,721,539
Qualified	1		PV % (Q)	6.6
W	0		EV	0
			EV % (Q)	0.0

	PV	PV % (Q)	EV	EV % (Q)
1960-1984	5,721,539	6.6	0	0.0

Top PV, one year	John Anderson (1980), 5,720,060
Top PV %, one year	John Anderson (1980), 6.6
Top EV, one year	none
Top EV %, one year	none

Populist

Elections	5		PV	1,217,047
Qualified	1		PV % (Q)	8.5
W	0		EV	22
			EV % (Q)	5.0

	PV	PV % (Q)	EV	EV % (Q)
1856-1900	1,074,620	8.5	22	5.0
1904-1928	142,427	----	0	----

Top PV, one year	James Weaver (1892), 1,024,280
Top PV %, one year	James Weaver (1892), 8.5
Top EV, one year	James Weaver (1892), 22
Top EV %, one year	James Weaver (1892), 5.0

Note: The Populist party endorsed the 1896 nomination of the Democrats. The Democratic party is classified as the lead party in that coalition. The votes are included in its listing.

Progressive (La Follette)

Elections	1	PV	4,814,050
Qualified	1	PV % (Q)	16.6
W	0	EV	13
		EV % (Q)	2.4

	PV	PV % (Q)	EV	EV % (Q)
1904-1928	4,814,050	16.6	13	2.4

Top PV, one year	Robert La Follette (1924), 4,814,050
Top PV %, one year	Robert La Follette (1924), 16.6
Top EV, one year	Robert La Follette (1924), 13
Top EV %, one year	Robert La Follette (1924), 2.4

Progressive (Roosevelt)

Elections	2	PV	4,154,441
Qualified	1	PV % (Q)	27.4
W	0	EV	88
		EV % (Q)	16.6

	PV	PV % (Q)	EV	EV % (Q)
1904-1928	4,154,441	27.4	88	16.6

Top PV, one year	Theodore Roosevelt (1912), 4,119,207
Top PV %, one year	Theodore Roosevelt (1912), 27.4
Top EV, one year	Theodore Roosevelt (1912), 88
Top EV %, one year	Theodore Roosevelt (1912), 16.6

Progressive (Wallace)

Elections	2		PV	1,297,473
Qualified	1		PV % (Q)	2.4
W	0		EV	0
			EV % (Q)	0.0

	PV	PV % (Q)	EV	EV % (Q)
1932-1956	1,297,473	2.4	0	0.0

Top PV, one year	Henry Wallace (1948), 1,157,057
Top PV %, one year	Henry Wallace (1948), 2.4
Top EV, one year	none
Top EV %, one year	none

Prohibition

Elections	29		PV	2,834,375
Qualified	2		PV % (Q)	2.2
W	0		EV	0
			EV % (Q)	0.0

	PV	PV % (Q)	EV	EV % (Q)
1856-1900	1,021,935	2.2	0	0.0
1904-1928	1,218,132	----	0	----
1932-1956	471,841	----	0	----
1960-1984	122,467	----	0	----

Top PV, one year	John Bidwell (1892), 270,770
Top PV %, one year	John Bidwell (1892), 2.25
Top EV, one year	none
Top EV %, one year	none

Note: The Prohibition party was known as the Statesman party in 1980. It returned to the Prohibition label in 1984. Statesman party totals are included in this listing.

Republican

Elections	33		PV	576,938,691
Qualified	33		PV % (Q)	49.5
W	20		EV	8,359
			EV % (Q)	54.1

	PV	PV % (Q)	EV	EV % (Q)
1856-1900	50,317,586	48.4	2,528	58.1
1904-1928	80,598,831	52.1	2,149	59.5
1932-1956	168,278,971	47.3	1,336	35.9
1960-1984	277,743,303	50.4	2,346	62.3

Top PV, one year	Ronald Reagan (1984), 54,451,521
Top PV %, one year	Richard Nixon (1972), 60.7
Top EV, one year	Ronald Reagan (1984), 525
Top EV %, one year	Ronald Reagan (1984), 97.6

Socialist

Elections	16		PV	5,021,834
Qualified	6		PV % (Q)	3.2
W	0		EV	0
			EV % (Q)	0.0

	PV	PV % (Q)	EV	EV % (Q)
1856-1900	86,935	----	0	----
1904-1928	3,493,279	3.6	0	0.0
1932-1956	1,428,684	2.2	0	0.0
1960-1984	12,936	----	0	----

Top PV, one year	Eugene Debs (1920), 913,664
Top PV %, one year	Eugene Debs (1912), 6.0
Top EV, one year	none
Top EV %, one year	none

Southern Democratic

Elections	1		PV	848,019
Qualified	1		PV % (Q)	18.1
W	0		EV	72
			EV % (Q)	23.8

	PV	PV % (Q)	EV	EV % (Q)
1856-1900	848,019	18.1	72	23.8

Top PV, one year	John Breckinridge (1860), 848,019
Top PV %, one year	John Breckinridge (1860), 18.1
Top EV, one year	John Breckinridge (1860), 72
Top EV %, one year	John Breckinridge (1860), 23.8

States' Rights Democratic

Elections	1		PV	1,169,134
Qualified	1		PV % (Q)	2.4
W	0		EV	39
			EV % (Q)	7.3

	PV	PV % (Q)	EV	EV % (Q)
1932-1956	1,169,134	2.4	39	7.3

Top PV, one year	Strom Thurmond (1948), 1,169,134
Top PV %, one year	Strom Thurmond (1948), 2.4
Top EV, one year	Strom Thurmond (1948), 39
Top EV %, one year	Strom Thurmond (1948), 7.3

Union

Elections	1		PV	892,492
Qualified	1		PV % (Q)	2.0
W	0		EV	0
			EV % (Q)	0.0

	PV	PV % (Q)	EV	EV % (Q)
1932-1956	892,492	2.0	0	0.0

Top PV, one year	William Lemke (1936), 892,492
Top PV %, one year	William Lemke (1936), 2.0
Top EV, one year	none
Top EV %, one year	none

Whig

Elections	6		PV	6,061,853
Qualified	5		PV % (Q)	47.9
W	2		EV	657
			EV % (Q)	45.3

	PV	PV % (Q)	EV	EV % (Q)
1820-1852	6,061,853	47.9	657	45.3

Top PV, one year	Winfield Scott (1852), 1,386,942
Top PV %, one year	William Henry Harrison (1840), 52.9
Top EV, one year	William Henry Harrison (1840), 234
Top EV %, one year	William Henry Harrison (1840), 79.6

Note: The remnants of the Whig party endorsed the 1856
ticket of the American party. The American party is
classified as the lead party in that coalition, and the
votes are included in the American-Whig listing.

9.
The States

ALABAMA (SOUTH, 1820)

Alabama has always had a soft spot for politicians who put up a good fight. It was a frontier state at the dawn of Jacksonian Democracy. The bellicose populism of Andrew Jackson was wildly popular in a society that, unlike many other Southern states, did not yet have a dominant planter class. The Democratic party entrenched itself for more than a century.

Racial fear was the force that kept Alabamans in line behind the Democrats. The state party constantly raised the specter of black Republican rule. It eventually masterminded the disenfranchisement of most blacks in 1901. One black editor wrote, "It is goodbye with poor white folks and niggers now, for the train of disenfranchisement is on the rail and will come thundering upon us like an avalanche."[1] The Alabama Democratic party boldly printed its slogan on the ballot well into the 1960s: "White Supremacy -- For The Right." These twin traditions of populism and racism produced Presidential candidate George Wallace, first known for his fierce effort to keep the state university lily white.

Alabama´s commitment to the national Democratic party began to flag in 1948, when half of its delegation stalked out of the party´s convention to protest a strong civil-rights platform plank. The state supported the States´ Rights Democratic ticket that fall. It has been carried by the Democrats only three times in the nine subsequent elections.

ALASKA (WEST, 1960)

Alaska trumpets itself as America´s "last frontier." Its residents hold with religious fervor to frontier ideals, individualism foremost among them. The Republican party naturally has the upper hand in such a political climate. The GOP has carried the state all but once since its admission to the Union.

The irony is that Alaska sought statehood because of its desire for a greater slice of the federal government's largesse. Ernest Gruening, later to be a Senator, stressed in 1946 that Alaska would never get its share until it was allowed to deal in the currency all mainland politicians understood: votes. He blasted "this [territorial] government by remote control, this government by distant absentees, this government by a changing personnel in Congress."[2]

Many Alaskans have more recently had similarly unkind words about Washington, particularly because of a 1980 bill that declared millions of acres off-limits to development. His support of the legislation only worsened Democrat Jimmy Carter's already dismal prospects of carrying the state that year. Alaska has been more comfortable with pro-development Republicans, such as pipeline supporter Gerald Ford and fellow Westerner Ronald Reagan.

ARIZONA (WEST, 1912)

There was considerable sentiment in Congress early in the 20th Century to admit Arizona and New Mexico to the Union under one government. Former President Theodore Roosevelt was among those who thought it senseless to create two sparsely populated states. Outraged citizens of Phoenix immediately demanded the renaming of their city's Roosevelt Street. They had no desire to be joined with New Mexicans, whom they considered much too conservative.

Times have changed. Arizona is now one of the most solidly conservative Republican states in the country, certainly much more so than New Mexico. Its early support of Woodrow Wilson, Franklin Roosevelt, and Harry Truman has been long forgotten. Water projects and air conditioning made possible a large influx of new Arizonans, beginning in the 1950s. These immigrants have been mainly Midwestern Republicans and Southern conservatives. They have remade the face of Arizona politics.

Barry Goldwater's ascension to the Senate in 1952 signaled his state's rightward change of heart. Arizona also voted for Dwight Eisenhower that year, its first electoral votes for a Republican Presidential candidate in twenty-four years. It has not been carried by any other party since.

ARKANSAS (SOUTH, 1836)

Arkansas has always had a split personality. It is a Southern state. But like Oklahoma and Texas, it also has characteristics of the West. This divided Arkansas sat on the sidelines as fiercely Southern states left the Union in 1861. It seceded almost a month after the firing on Fort Sumter, slower than all but two states of the Confederacy. Thousands of Arkansans found even that decision hasty. They volunteered to fight for the North.

Reconstruction forced a hesitant Arkansas deep into the Southern fold. Occupation by Northern troops had the same effect as it did elsewhere, engendering a white conservative opposition that retained power by playing racial politics. Senator J. William Fulbright, famed for his liberal opposition to the Vietnam War, knew better than to buck the tide even a century after the Civil War. "I did not vote for civil-rights legislation prior to the late 1960s for two very simple reasons," the Arkansas Democrat said. "First, I doubted its efficacy. Second, my constituents would not have tolerated it."[3]

Arkansas was a Democratic state from its inception, largely because of that party's agrarian orientation prior to the Civil War. Memories of Reconstruction maintained the Democrats' dominance. No other party carried Arkansas in a Presidential election from 1876 through 1964. The state has since reconsidered that devotion, following the Southern trend to the Republicans in recent years.

CALIFORNIA (WEST, 1852)

California has replaced New York as the most cherished prize in Presidential elections. Its allocation of 47 electoral votes following the 1980 census ties the record for the most ever held by one state. Projections indicate the figure could grow to an unprecedented 54 by the election of 2004.

Parties fighting to control this key state face a difficult task. California has long had laws that severely constrain traditional politics. Most were the work of Hiram Johnson's Progressive movement in the early 20th Century. Party organizations are deliberately kept weak, and voters have become accustomed to circumventing the legislature through referendums. Theodore Roosevelt called the Johnson program "the greatest advance ever made by any state for the betterment of its people."[4] But an angry San Francisco Chronicle dissented by headlining a contemporary editorial, "A Legislature of Progressive Cranks: It is Likely to Do Infinitely More Mischief Than a Legislature of Rascals Would Ever Attempt."[5]

Professional politicians agree with the latter assessment. Ticket-splitting is the rule in California's liberated environment. Candidates' personal campaigns are usually more important than anything their parties do. Californians accustomed to these conditions are becoming increasingly popular Presidential candidates as party structures erode countrywide. State residents have won three of the four national elections since 1972. All ran as Republicans, the party that has usually held the upper hand in California, particularly since the state began shifting to the right in the mid-1960s.

COLORADO (WEST, 1876)

Colorado's wild Populist past does not seem to square with its complacent Republicanism for most of the 20th Century, but there is a common thread. Self-interest motivated both attachments. Populism, which stirred emotions elsewhere with its calls for agrarian reform, was beloved in Colorado for its monetary policy. A state dependent on mining lusted for the free coinage of silver. William Jennings Bryan received almost 85 percent of its popular votes in 1896. Four years later, when free coinage was generally considered a dead issue, the Denver Rocky Mountain News still editorially declared, "The future of silver depends on the vote of this year."[6] Bryan carried Colorado in all three of his losing races.

The decline of the mining industry ended Colorado's fling with the political fringe. The state settled in with the repository of individualism, the Republican party, which was also more interested than the Democrats in the development of the West. Colorado voted twice for Franklin Roosevelt, but turned against him in 1940 and 1944. Democratic nominees have carried the state in only two of the ten subsequent elections. The party has done better in races for state and local office, thanks to a recent influx of liberal and moderate immigrants. But their impact has yet to be felt in Presidential contests.

CONNECTICUT (EAST, 1789)

Party labels changed, but Connecticut remained a bastion of conservatism for almost a century and a half. It voted for the Federalist ticket in all eight of that party's campaigns, then switched in turn to the National Republicans, the Whigs, and the Republicans. The attachment to the GOP became so strong that Connecticut was one of only six states to stand by Herbert Hoover in the Depression election of 1932.

Protestant Anglo-Saxons dominated the state's politics over this lengthy period. These Yankees insisted on property requirements for voting eligibility long after most other states abandoned similar laws as undemocratic. Their powerful Republican machine routinely outgunned the poorly organized Democrats. But the numbers caught up to the Yankee Republicans in the 1930s. Immigrants, largely Catholic, were streaming into Connecticut's cities. They tripped the balance to the Democrats by 1936. Franklin Roosevelt scored an easy victory.

Tight two-party competition has been the rule ever since. Republicans have won seven elections dating from 1936, the Democrats six. Republican survival is the result of the party's willingness to adapt. The Hartford Courant demanded "new blood and a new outlook" for the state Republican leadership after the 1936 debacle.[7] It got it. Moderate GOP nominees such as Dwight Eisenhower have consequently fared better than the once popular conservatives in the new Connecticut.

DELAWARE (EAST, 1789)

Delaware has had three distinct phases in its political history. The first state to ratify the Constitution, it was strongly conservative during the nation's early decades. The Federalists, National Republicans, and Whigs were favored. But Delaware was also a slave state. It switched its loyalty to the Southern-oriented Democratic party in phase two, beginning in 1852. The Republicans carried Delaware only once in the next forty years. Memories of the Civil War dimmed by 1892, when the state entered its third phase, that of mirroring the nation's Presidential vote. Delaware has been carried by the same party that won the White House in twenty-one of the twenty-four most-recent elections.

One of the reasons for the state's tight partisan balance is its largest employer, the du Pont Company. It's estimated that more than 400 du Pont heirs live in Delaware, but they are not of a single mind. "Du Pont has people on both sides of the fence; often they are diametrically opposed," one family member told a Ralph Nader research group in the 1970s.[8] Money and influence therefore flow to both parties. Delaware's blend of urban North and rural South helps further to maintain the balance, making the nation's second-smallest state in area one of the best predictors of its Presidential choices.

DISTRICT OF COLUMBIA (EAST, 1964)

Few things may be certain in politics, but the District of Columbia's support for Democratic Presidential candidates comes awfully close. The District has voted Democratic in all six elections since being granted national voting privileges in 1961. It was the only "state" to support both George McGovern and Walter Mondale in their landslide defeats. Mondale surpassed 85 percent of the District's popular vote while being buried almost everywhere else in 1984 by Ronald Reagan.

The District of Columbia was created by the Constitution, which provided for a "District (not exceeding ten Miles square)" to serve as the seat of government. Its residents were placed under federal control, even denied local elections between 1874 and 1974. Southerners who controlled the Senate and House District committees, repelled by its large black population, kept the reins tight on the District. Mississippi Senator Theodore Bilbo was among those chairmen. He contended he would rather see civilization "blotted out with the atomic bomb than to see it slowly but surely destroyed in the maelstrom of miscegenation, interbreeding, intermarriage, and mongrelization." Bilbo had no intention of letting District residents vote for President, coyly explaining his opposition by predicting "the alleys would outvote the avenues."[9] It wasn't until the 23rd Amendment in 1961 that the District of Columbia finally was allowed to help determine who would live in its most distinguished residence.

FLORIDA (SOUTH, 1848)

Florida was a standard-issue Southern state before 1950. It had voted for Democratic Presidential nominees in seventeen of the previous eighteen elections. Stereotypical conservative courthouse politicians held the reins of power. Blacks were seen on the streets, but were rarely heard through the ballot box. Change of almost any kind was discouraged.

A virtually unprecedented immigration killed the old Florida. The state's population grew by an amazing 251 percent between 1950 and 1980. Millions of Northerners accustomed to voting Republican brought their party south with them. Conservative natives, alarmed at the increasingly liberal civil-rights stands of the national Democratic party, joined the vivified GOP. Republican nominees carried Florida in seven of the nine elections from 1952. The state Democratic party changed drastically in character, picking up blacks and Caribbean refugees as new constituencies.

Florida grew by 1980 to be the seventh most populous state, making it the largest to have never produced a full-scale Presidential candidate. Then-Senator Claude Pepper ran briefly in 1948. He was called "Red Pepper" by Southerners who thought him too liberal. Ex-Governor Reubin Askew tried for the Democratic nomination in 1984. Neither came close to statistical qualification levels.

GEORGIA (SOUTH, 1789)

No state has voted Democratic more often in national elections than Georgia, but it's unlikely to be in that party's column much in the future. Georgia has given its electoral votes to thirty Democratic nominees, a record grounded in the distant past. The only Democrat to carry the state since 1964 was native son Jimmy Carter, twice. Republicans won three elections, George Wallace's American Independent party took the other.

Georgia's perpetual bond to the Democrats was sliced by the sharp edge of the national party's liberal civil-rights policy. Virulent racism was long the hallmark of the state Democratic organization. Its champions included Governor Eugene Talmadge, Senator Richard Russell, and Governor Lester Maddox. "[Once blacks] are secure in their right to vote in [the Democratic] primary," Talmadge warned in 1946, "Negro candidates for public office will be as thick as flies around a jug of molasses."[10] Russell wanted the federal government to pay in the 1950s to relocate blacks in the North. Maddox's chief claim to fame was his use of an ax handle to keep blacks out of his Atlanta restaurant a decade later.

Conservative Democrats switched wholesale to the Republicans in 1964 when the latter nominated Barry Goldwater, an opponent of the 1964 Civil Rights Act. Newly enfranchised blacks have helped revitalize the Democratic base in the past two decades. But white Georgia voters, once automatically Democrats, are building a new tradition. Most now pull the Republican lever in Presidential elections.

HAWAII (WEST, 1960)

Hawaii has surprised some politicians by proving not to be a breeding ground for revolution. The only state where Caucasians are in a distinct minority, its admission to the Union was tied up for years by Southern Democrats who dreaded the thought of nonwhites in Congress. Mississippi Senator James Eastland warned during the 1959 debate, "Many good patriotic people support Hawaii's admission. But there are those who do have a selfish interest -- including the Communist world conspiracy -- and it is the selfish interests alone which will be served by a grant of statehood."[11] Fourteen of the fifteen Senators who on the final roll call opposed making Hawaii a state were from the South.

There was resentment in Hawaii against the Democrats for allowing such opposition, but the anger quickly dissipated. The Democratic party has carried the state in five of seven Presidential elections. It's a switch from territorial days, when the Republicans controlled Hawaii's legislature for fifty-one consecutive years. The Caucasian business community dominated the islands through the GOP in that period. The Democrats only gained power when they reached out to Asian voters. The national Democratic party's liberal stands on civil rights and social issues, politically harmful in so many places, have merely strengthened its now-healthy standing in Hawaii.

IDAHO (WEST, 1892)

Two Idaho Senators have run for President: Republican William Borah in 1936, Democrat Frank Church in 1976. The two men may have belonged to different parties, but they were otherwise remarkably alike. Each ignored the textbook advice for Senate longevity while representing a rural state. Borah and Church seemed less interested in state matters than foreign affairs, and each took liberal stands destined to be unpopular back home. Borah called for American recognition of the Soviet Union in the 1920s. Church was one of the first critics of the Vietnam War. Each Senator was nonetheless often reelected. Borah once easily defeated an opponent who employed the provocative slogan, "From Idaho, For Idaho, Not Russia." It was oddly ineffective.

Idaho voters showed a similarly open mind in Presidential elections. From 1896 until 1972, they went Democratic ten times and Republican ten times. The New Deal was particularly popular, with Franklin Roosevelt carrying Idaho in all four of his races. But John Kennedy's New Frontier and Lyndon Johnson's Great Society were different. Both seemed to many Idahoans to go beyond economic recovery, to trigger social upheaval. One-quarter of the state's residents are Mormons, many of whom came to blame the Democrats for society's growing permissiveness. Idaho has reacted by turning sharply conservative. No Democrat has carried the state since 1964. In fact, none has come close.

ILLINOIS (MIDWEST, 1820)

Illinois triggers two contradictory memories of Presidential campaigns. The first is the extraordinary eloquence of some of the candidates it has produced. Stephen Douglas and Abraham Lincoln displayed their awesome forensic skills in their immortal debates on the prairie during the 1858 Senate campaign. They met again for the Presidency two years later. Adlai Stevenson inspired a generation of liberals in 1952 with his promise to "talk sense to the American people." Jesse Jackson, the first black man to be taken seriously as a Presidential candidate, brought religious intensity to the 1984 campaign.

But Illinois is also well-known for its grimy political machines. Chicago Democrats and downstate Republicans have often been accused of flagrant vote stealing. Republicans screamed that John Kennedy was elected President in 1960 by the votes from Democratic graveyards in Chicago.

The state's voting record in Presidential elections is as split as its image. Illinois was solidly Democratic before the Civil War, enthralled by the frontier image of the party of Andrew Jackson. It was just as completely in the Republican camp from 1860 through 1928, wedded to the party of Lincoln. The two sides have evenly split the fourteen elections since then. But the Republicans are showing signs of renewed dominance, having won every contest since 1968. The famed Chicago machine is no longer able to deliver Illinois to the Democrats as it once could.

INDIANA (MIDWEST, 1816)

Indiana residents have not had much success in the Presidential sweepstakes. Eight Hoosiers have run for the office a total of sixteen times, but Benjamin Harrison's 1888 effort was the only one to succeed. Historian William Wilson has suggested, "With baseball offering a better metaphor than the state pasttime of basketball, it must be admitted that Indiana politics has been largely a sandlot game and those few players reaching the big leagues have enjoyed no more than a moderate success."[12] Hopefuls from Indiana were often shunted to the second spot. Only New York has produced more Vice Presidents than Indiana's four.

Both state political parties have long been regarded as among the strongest and best organized in the country. The Democratic machine was known as the "Tammany of the Middle West" in the early 20th Century. It was a poor allusion, since the Democrats never achieved anything in Indiana that rivaled their ironclad control of New York City. Their best performances were way back during the state's frontier period before the Civil War. But since 1860, Indiana has generally supported Republican Presidential candidates. It has voted for twenty-five GOP nominees in that period, only seven Democrats.

IOWA (MIDWEST, 1848)

One observer of Iowa after the Civil War said the state was characterized by "corn, cattle, and contentment." He should have added Republicanism. The state was carried by the first fourteen nominees of the new party. It has cast its electoral votes for the GOP in twenty-eight of the thirty-three elections since the party´s founding. Senator Jonathan Dolliver remarked early in the 20th Century that he saw no end to Republican dominance. "When Iowa goes Democratic," he said, "hell will go Methodist."[13]

The roots of Iowa´s Republican strength can be found in the state´s topsoil, among the best in the country. Conservative Northern immigrants established prosperous farms in the 1800s. Although Populist party nominee James Weaver was from Iowa, few of the state´s farmers ever joined that agrarian movement. Most avoided the agricultural depression and happily voted the safe Republican ticket. The same was true in 1984, when three-quarters of the state´s jobs were still related in some way to agriculture.

Democratic Presidential candidates have only carried Iowa twice since 1940. Harry Truman´s surprising win in 1948 resulted from one of his party´s rare efforts to woo the farm vote. "This Republican Congress has already stuck a pitchfork in the farmer´s back," he shouted in a speech at Dexter, Iowa. "They have already done their best to keep the price supports from working!"[14] It was effective rhetoric, but unusual. Iowa switched back to its Republican ways four years after playing a key role in the Truman upset.

KANSAS (MIDWEST, 1864)

Kansas had its most significant impact on American politics before becoming a state. Senator Stephen Douglas´ famous Kansas-Nebraska Act created Kansas Territory in 1854, but more importantly, it revived the national debate over the extension of slavery to the territories. Abolitionists and slaveholders rushed into "Bleeding Kansas" to defend their beliefs. Guerrilla warfare raged across the territory. A national political realignment was among the by-products, marked by the birth of the Republican party.

Presidents Franklin Pierce and James Buchanan favored the admission of Kansas as a slave state, but it didn´t enter the Union until the start of the Civil War removed any question. Republicans were thoroughly in control, and have been virtually ever since, winning twenty-four of thirty-one elections. The only serious deviation came in the 1890s, when destitute farmers briefly placed faith in the Populist party. Prosperity returned in the next decade and Populism hastily vanished.

Safe-and-sane Republicanism has been the rule in Kansas through the 20th Century. It was embodied in Governor Alfred Landon, who said in his 1933 inaugural address, "The pathway from the swamp of despair must be built with planks of economy devoted to the principle that we must not spend that which we do not have."[15]   As Landon paused, the auditorium lights flickered off. Everyone laughed at the coincidence, which had a certain appeal to the fiscal conservatives in the audience. Landon finished his speech in the dark.

KENTUCKY (SOUTH, 1792)

Kentucky was the only Southern state that did not secede during the Civil War, but it sustained damage every bit as serious as that which hit the Confederacy. Families were ripped apart. It was not uncommon for Kentucky brothers to enlist in opposing armies. The state´s political establishment also was sundered. Benjamin Bristow, later to run for President as a Republican, defied his wife´s family to fight for the Union. John Breckinridge, the 1860 nominee of the Southern Democrats, escaped to the South and entered battle as a Confederate General. The Presidents of the two countries, Abraham Lincoln and Jefferson Davis, were both Kentucky natives.

Kentucky entered the Union as a Democratic-Republican stronghold, then became a leading Whig state under the tutelage of Henry Clay. The Civil War destroyed existing political patterns. Some counties are still solidly Democratic or Republican, based on their feelings about secession more than a century ago. The result has been an unusually competitive two-party system in Kentucky since 1872. It was the only Southern state to support Republicans William McKinley in 1896 or Calvin Coolidge in 1924. Democrats still hold a sizable edge in the number of elections won. Kentucky, after all, has Southern heritage. But Republicans established a base in the state earlier than anywhere else in the South. They have built upon it to carry Kentucky in six of the eight most-recent Presidential elections.

LOUISIANA (SOUTH, 1812)

It has been more than a half-century since Huey Long´s assassination, but he remains the dominant figure in Louisiana history, a symbol of the state´s flamboyant, often corrupt politics. Long built the state´s road system, Louisiana State University, and the skyscraper capitol in which he was killed. He also ruled the state with an iron fist that led critics to accuse him of fascism. One reporter asked him if he was like Hitler. "Don´t liken me to that son-of-a-bitch," he barked, then insisted Louisiana was still a democracy. "A perfect democracy can come close to looking like a dictatorship, a democracy in which the people are so satisfied they have no complaint."[16]   Long dreamed of spreading his control over the entire country, but he was shot just months before he was expected to announce his 1936 Presidential candidacy. The enigmatic Zachary Taylor remains the only President from the state.

Louisiana favored the Democratic-Republican party in its early years, then made the easy transition to the Democrats of Andrew Jackson. Republican Reconstruction was long and tumultuous. Union troops weren´t pulled out until 1877. Louisianans registered their discontent by voting Democratic in the next seventeen Presidential elections. The growing liberalism of national Democrats on civil rights broke that streak in 1948. Louisiana has only sided with its traditional party three times in the ten most-recent elections.

MAINE (EAST, 1820)

Politics, like other endeavors, has its inaccurate folk wisdom. One long-time rule-of-thumb was, "As Maine goes, so goes the nation." Maine once held its state elections in September. Politicians earnestly believed the party carrying America´s easternmost state would triumphantly seize the White House two months later. The myth was exploded in 1936. Republicans swept in September, but Alfred Landon was buried in November. Maine was one of only two states to back the Republican national ticket. Democratic leader James Farley joked that a modification was needed. "As Maine goes," he laughed, "so goes Vermont."[17]

Maine is actually one of the worst predictors in the country. It has voted the same way as the nation only two times of every three. That ties it for thirty-sixth place among the states. It was solidly Republican for a century, only voting Democratic once between 1856 and 1960. Maine was much like the rural South, provincially clinging to the politics of its forefathers. Banks, railroads, and lumber interests provided the money to keep the state Republican machine humming.

Democrats, who had strong appeal to Maine voters before the Civil War, have mounted a small comeback since the 1950s. Edmund Muskie directed the party´s resurgence, but there is no doubt who still commands the loyalty of Maine voters. Republicans have carried the state in the four most-recent elections. And in every case, Vermont followed.

MARYLAND (EAST, 1789)

Spiro Agnew came closer to the truth than he knew when he resigned as Governor of Maryland to become Vice President in 1969. "I was a controversial Governor. I have been a controversial candidate for Vice President," he told reporters. "There is no reason to believe that I will be any less controversial as Vice President."[18] Agnew became the point man for the Nixon Administration´s war against liberals, whom he called "radiclibs." But his most con-troversial act was his resignation in October 1973 after pleading no contest to a charge of income-tax evasion. His record reinforced the popular perception that politics in Maryland was among the most corrupt in the country.

Agnew was actually unusual in one sense: a Republican from an historically Democratic state. Maryland allowed slaveholding before the Civil War. Its eventual adherence to the Union was bitterly opposed by a sizable portion of the population. Democrats capitalized on lingering resentment after the war by stressing opposition to Congressional Radicals and their harsh Reconstruction plans. This formed a base that allowed Democrats to carry the state in eleven of thirteen Presidential contests between 1868 and 1916.

Competition has been closer in the ensuing years, as Maryland slowly lost its Southern ties and developed into an urban Eastern state. Democrats have won nine elections since 1920, Republicans eight. But unlike most states, Maryland still seems to give Democrats the benefit of the doubt in close races. It was one of just seven states to stick with Jimmy Carter in 1980. It even rejected the Republicans in 1968, despite the presence of its controversial favorite son, Agnew, on the ticket.

MASSACHUSETTS (EAST, 1789)

Massachusetts has recently gained an image as one of the most liberal states in the Union. Its history belies the current perception. Massachusetts was long a conservative hotbed, all the way back to its passionate affair with Federalism. "Between uncontrolled democracy and uncontrolled despotism in any other shape, there is but a very narrow dividing line," wrote one state Federalist.[19] Massachusetts´ Yankee elite worried constantly about that line. It supported any party that promised to defend wealthy business interests. Massachusetts backed the Federalists in seven of their eight elections, the Whigs in all five of theirs, and the Republicans in seventeen of their first eighteen.

Pitted against the conservative Yankees was the state´s burgeoning immigrant population. The potato famine of the 1840s impelled hundreds of thousands of Irish to move to Boston. Six of every ten city residents were foreign-born at the outbreak of the Civil War. The newcomers were overwhelmingly Democratic. Political tension between the Yankees and the Irish was understandably high.

Al Smith´s 1928 candidacy triggered the breakthrough for Massachusetts Democrats. The chance to support a fellow urban Catholic inspired record numbers of ethnic voters to come to the polls, many for the first time. Smith carried the state. Democrats have won ten of the subsequent fourteen elections. But despite this reversal, Massachusetts still retains traces of its earlier economic conservatism. The state gave its electoral votes to Ronald Reagan in both 1980 and 1984.

MICHIGAN (MIDWEST, 1836)

Henry Ford was a man of firmly held prejudices. He had little use for cities and suburbs. He said he was "born on a farm and have always believed that the real future of America is in the land."[20] Ford also intensely disliked labor unions. And despite a brief fling with the Democratic party, he settled in as a conservative Republican. He enthusiastically endorsed Calvin Coolidge, the man who once said,

"The chief business of the American people is business."

The irony of Ford's life is that he was heavily responsible for destroying the Michigan of his youth. The state was settled by New Englanders, who made it a Republican stronghold. The Democrats did not carry the state between 1856 and 1928. But Ford's innovative assembly-line production of automobiles lured Southerners and foreigners to Michigan for jobs. They settled in cities, joined unions, and voted the Democratic ticket. Nearly 61 percent of the state's residents in 1900 lived in rural areas. The figure dropped to 31.8 percent in just three decades.

Ford was distressed by the forces he had unleashed. He was particularly heartbroken by the emergence of the United Auto Workers union, soon one of the political powers of the new Michigan. The UAW aligned with the Democratic party, making it suddenly competitive. Republicans retain a base in rural areas and the suburbs. They have carried Michigan in eight of the past fourteen elections, the Democrats six.

MINNESOTA (MIDWEST, 1860)

Minnesota was once one of the staunchest Republican states. It is now among the most congenial to the Democrats. The transition, as in so many other states, was the result of the Depression. Minnesota Democrats were unusual in that they harnessed the economic discontent of the 1930s for their long-term benefit. A group of post-World War II idealists built a party organization that remained strong in the 1980s.

Minnesota was settled by New Englanders, Germans, and Scandinavians. The Yankees transported their faith in Republicanism. The foreigners tempered it with a belief in progressive government. Democrats, with their conservative states' rights philosophy, found the political climate uncongenial in the 1800s. "Our people move into a region and make the state," boasted Republican Congressman Ignatius Donnelly in 1864. "We need erect no bulwark of state sovereignty behind which to shelter ourselves."[21] Republicans carried seventeen of Minnesota's first eighteen Presidential elections.

Donnelly eventually became a fiery Populist orator, just one sign of the liberalism always present in Minnesota politics. Another came from Governor Floyd Olson, whose Farmer-Labor party took control in the 1930s. "You bet I'm radical," he told a reporter. "You might say I'm radical as hell."[22] The invigorated national Democratic party was suddenly in tune with this spirit. Hubert Humphrey masterminded a merger of the Democrats and Farmer-Laborites, consolidating his party's new majority status. Republicans have consequently carried Minnesota in only three national elections since 1932.

MISSISSIPPI (SOUTH, 1820)

Mississippi has always been a place of political extremes. The state with the highest percentage of black citizens, it was accordingly the home of the most virulent white-supremacy movement. "The choice is between victory and defeat," Senator James Eastland declared when the Supreme Court ordered school desegregation. "Defeat means death, the death of Southern culture and our aspirations as an Anglo-Saxon people."[23] The Democratic party was the vehicle of defense chosen by whites who were fed a steady diet of horror stories about Republican Reconstruction. Democratic candidates carried the state in eighteen straight Presidential elections between 1876 and 1944.

Voter turnout was deliberately kept extremely low by a requirement that those who wanted to register had to interpret a section of the state constitution. Senator Theodore Bilbo laughed that the document was so convoluted that "damn few white men and no niggers at all can explain [it]."[24] The small group of voters agreed that race was the only real issue. Candidates blessed by the white establishment usually came close to unanimous victories. Mississippi holds the national records for the highest popular-vote percentages given Democratic, Republican, and third-party candidates in one state in single elections.

Democratic support for civil-rights legislation since 1948 killed the national party in Mississippi. Only three Democrats have carried the state in the past ten elections. Whites now generally vote Republican, while the growing black electorate has become important for Democratic hopes.

MISSOURI (MIDWEST, 1820)

The New York _Times_ discovered Missouri's record in 1948. "Missouri might well be the bellwether state for determining Presidential sentiment," wrote reporter William Blair. "It could well supplant Maine, which no longer accurately forecasts the nation's choice."[25] Maine, of course, had never been a good predictor, but Blair was right about Missouri. It had last differed from the national electoral vote in 1900. The _Times_ was certain the streak would continue that fall: "And it appears that Missouri will be Republican in this year's Presidential election." State voters knew better than did the reporters. Missouri stuck with favorite son Harry Truman as he scored a stunning victory.

No state has more closely mirrored the nation's political mood in the 20th Century. Missouri misstepped in 1956, narrowly landing in Adlai Stevenson's column. It has given its electoral votes to the national winners in the other twenty elections from 1904 through 1984. It's a drastic change from the 19th Century. Missouri was then almost automatically Democratic because of its frontier status and slave-state tradition.

Memories of the Civil War faded by the turn of the

century. The growth of Saint Louis and Kansas City provided
an urban balance to the Southern sympathies of rural
Missouri. The state's support of Theodore Roosevelt in 1904
marked its first backing of a Republican in thirty-six
years. It also started the accuracy streak that continues
today.

MONTANA (WEST, 1892)

Democrats have done better in Montana than they had any
reason to expect. They have carried the state in ten of its
twenty-four Presidential elections despite powerful
opposition and a rural electorate that seems tailor-made for
the Republicans. The GOP has been able to capitalize
consistently on these natural advantages only since the
1950s.

    Democrats were active in Montana's territorial days.
One Republican wrote unhappily during the Civil War that he
lived "in a Territory more disloyal as a whole than Tennessee
or Kentucky ever were. Four-fifths of our citizens were
openly declared secessionists."[26] It was an exaggeration,
but also a good indication of Democratic vigor. Miners and
small farmers were particularly attracted to the party when
it entered a coalition with the Populists in the 1890s.

    Mine owners, cattlemen, and power companies threw their
money and influence behind the Republican organization. They
proved no match for the personal appeal of Franklin Roosevelt
during the Depression. Montana Sioux named FDR "Fearless
Blue Eagle" during his visit to the state. The name came
from the symbol for the National Recovery Administration.
Such New Deal measures were so popular that the Democrats
carried Montana in all five elections from 1932 through 1948.

    The Republicans have mounted an impressive comeback
since those days. They have won eight of the nine most-
recent Presidential elections in Montana. The state that was
for so many campaigns a welcome surprise for the Democrats is
now following the West's trend to the right.

NEBRASKA (MIDWEST, 1868)

Nebraska has displayed an electoral consistency that is
gratifying to the Republican party. The plains state was
settled by conservative farmers from the East and Midwest.
The philosophy they planted in the soil of the 1870s and
1880s remains dominant. Republican Presidential candidates
have carried the state twenty-three out of thirty times.
Only one Democrat has received Nebraska's electoral votes
since 1940.

    The irony is that this conservative state's two homespun
Presidential candidates were considered radicals by their
contemporaries. Democrat William Jennings Bryan and
Republican George Norris delighted in attacking the
establishment. Bryan won acclaim for his dramatic 1896
speech for free silver, "You shall not crucify mankind upon a

cross of gold!"[27]   Norris was noted for leading the successful revolt in 1910 against the powerful Speaker of the House,
Joseph Cannon.

A conservative anti-Bryan faction grew in the national
Democratic party.   It also gained popularity in Nebraska,
seizing control in 1912.   Bryan eventually moved to Florida.
Norris stayed home, but the state Republican organization did
its best to end his career.   It even ran a man with the same
name against him in the 1930 primary.   The challenger was
thrown off the ballot on a technicality.   Norris nonetheless
took the hint.   He successfully ran for reelection in 1936 as
an independent.

NEVADA (WEST, 1864)

Nevada fulfilled its mission early in its history.
Republicans were nervous in 1864.   They feared a close
election.   No effort was spared to line up electoral votes
for Abraham Lincoln.   Additional supporters were also needed
in the Senate to guarantee passage of the 13th Amendment to
outlaw slavery.   Republican strategists hit on the idea of
creating a state in the area east of California where the
rich Comstock Lode had recently been discovered.   Nevada was
hastily admitted to the Union, even though almost all of it
was unpopulated desert.   Lincoln signed the statehood papers
just eight days before his reelection.   No one was surprised
when he received Nevada´s wholehearted support in that
contest.

The new state was solidly in the Republican camp in its
early years.   But Populism took Nevada by storm, particularly
with the promise of increased mining that would accompany the
free coinage of silver.   The Republicans, thoroughly locked
to the gold standard, saw their base slip to the Populists
and later the Democrats.   The GOP only carried Nevada four
times in the fifteen elections from 1892 through 1948.

Nevada came close to bankruptcy early in the century,
but the legalization of gambling in 1931 turned its economy
around.   The return of prosperity fostered a conservative
movement.   The state rejoined the Republicans in 1952, voting
for the party´s nominees in seven of the nine elections from
that year on.

NEW HAMPSHIRE (EAST, 1789)

New Hampshire´s quadrennial moment of glory comes at the
start of each Presidential campaign.   "If you want to see the
beginning of it," journalist Charles McDowell once wrote,
"you have to go where the snow is deep and the people are few
and only a fool or a politician would expect to see the
beginning of anything important."[28]   Even though Iowa´s
caucuses now precede it, the New Hampshire primary remains an
important early event on the political calendar.   The
national press descends on this small state for the first
election of an almost endless stream to follow.

The journalistic overkill is a bit difficult to figure. The New Hampshire primary has a particularly poor record of foreshadowing Presidential nominations. Among its ballyhooed winners have been Democrats Estes Kefauver in 1952, Lyndon Johnson in 1968, Edmund Muskie in 1972, and Gary Hart in 1984, and Republican Henry Cabot Lodge in 1964. None came close to nomination. The results in the primary are skewed by New Hampshire's atypical demographics. Almost half of its residents live in rural areas; the national average is about a quarter. Less than one percent of the state's population is black or Hispanic.

New Hampshire's role in the fall is usually to deliver its electoral votes to the Republicans. A strong Democratic state before the Civil War, it has voted with the Republicans in twenty-seven of the thirty-three elections since that party was created. Only one Democrat has carried the state since 1948.

NEW JERSEY (EAST, 1789)

New Jersey has always been a state in search of an identity. One writer complained back in 1834, "The state has been...a hive of nations, constantly sending out swarms, whose labors have contributed largely to build up the two greatest marts of the Union [New York City and Philadelphia]."[29] New Jersey still lived in the shadows of its two large neighbors a century-and-a-half later. Only eight states had larger allocations of electoral votes after the 1980 census, but New Jersey often seemed forgotten as a prize in national elections.

Commercial interests held sway in the state's early years. Its voters usually gave majorities to the Federalist or Whig tickets. The Democrats, harmed in so many states by their opposition to the Civil War, actually increased their power in the latter half of the 19th Century, thanks to a corps of New Jerseyites who retained faith in the doctrine of states' rights. Democrats carried the state seven times in the eight elections between 1864 and 1892.

Republicans rebounded in 1896 and have generally retained the upper hand ever since. GOP nominees have carried New Jersey in sixteen of the most-recent twenty-three elections. The only substantial deviation came under the influence of Franklin Roosevelt, who won the state four times. A recurrence of such Democratic strength becomes increasingly unlikely as the New York and Philadelphia suburbs stretch their tentacles ever farther toward New Jersey's center, carrying Republican voting patterns with them.

NEW MEXICO (WEST, 1912)

New Mexico is unrepresentative of the United States as a whole. The most obvious divergence is in the ethnic composition of their populations. Nearly 37 percent of the state's residents in 1980 were of Spanish origin. The

national figure was only slightly more than six percent. The
distinct character of New Mexico almost kept it out of the
Union. "It comprises the tag end of all that is
objectionable in an imperfect civilization," the Milwaukee
Sentinel protested in 1876. "The scum and dregs of the
American, Spanish, Mexican, and Indian people are there
concentrated."[30] It took the submission of almost fifty
statehood bills before Congress finally passed one.

The surprise about New Mexico has been its uncanny
record of mirroring the results of national elections. Only
once have the state and country differed: in 1976, when New
Mexico supported Gerald Ford, the nation Jimmy Carter. No
other state has a higher percentage of matching Presidential
election outcomes.

The Hispanic community gave substantial support to the
Republicans in New Mexico's early years. The Depression
triggered a switch to the Democrats that has proved to be
permanent. Whites lean toward the Republicans. Growing
white immigration threatens to end the state's two-party
balance in Presidential politics. New Mexico has not gone
Democratic since supporting Lyndon Johnson in 1964.

NEW YORK (EAST, 1792)

John Adams once called New York politics "the devil's own
incomprehensibles."[31] Things only became more complex as the
state grew to be the nation's most powerful, encompassing
diverse ethnic and religious groups. Navigating past the
tricky shoals of a New York campaign was excellent
preparation for a national election. Both major parties came
to depend on the state as a source of talent. Eighteen of
their forty-four nominations between 1864 and 1948 went to
New Yorkers. All but one of the state's Governors from 1923
to 1973 were serious contenders for the Presidency.

New York had the largest allocation of electoral votes
from 1812 through 1968, peaking at 47. Only seven Presidents
have been elected without carrying the state. New York is
also a power in party conventions, generally advocating
policies to the left of both the Democratic and Republican
mainstreams. When conservative Robert Taft lost the 1952 GOP
nomination, he ascribed it to "New York financial interests"
and businessmen "subject to New York influence."[32]

That influence has slipped in recent decades, symbolized
by New York City's fiscal crisis in the mid-1970s. No native
New Yorker has been elected President since Franklin
Roosevelt. The state with the largest package of electoral
votes is now California. This decline in power has been
accompanied by a moderation of New York's liberal politics,
as its largest city shrinks and the suburbs grow. Republican
candidates have carried the state in three of the past four
elections. The GOP has also taken an overall lead in what
was once a Democratic stronghold. Republican nominees have
won New York twenty times, Democrats seventeen.

NORTH CAROLINA (SOUTH, 1792)

North Carolina entered the exalted ranks of the nation´s ten most-populous states after the 1980 census. It was a status that none would have dared to predict in the 19th Century, when North Carolina was sometimes called "the Rip Van Winkle state." A legislative committee reported in 1830 that the state had no major crops, no substantial industries, and no ports from which to ship the few products it had: "in short, without any object to which native industry and active enterprise could be directed."[33] The result was a massive emigration that included two future Presidents, James Polk and Andrew Johnson. This exodus of political talent partly explains why no North Carolina resident has ever received a major-party nomination for President.

North Carolina was never particularly enthusiastic about the Civil War. Having fewer slaves than any seceding state but Tennessee, it was the last to join the Confederacy. Reconstruction had the usual effect, strengthening voters´ already solid ties to the Democratic party. Only one Republican carried the state between 1876 and 1964. Heavy immigration of Northern Republicans and the alienation of natives from the national Democratic party have since switched the balance to the GOP. Jimmy Carter´s 1976 victory was the only instance in the past five elections when the Republican nominee failed to carry North Carolina.

NORTH DAKOTA (MIDWEST, 1892)

There has always been a hint of radicalism behind North Dakota´s staid facade. Populism secured a foothold among the state´s financially distressed farmers. The same constituency embraced the Nonpartisan League a generation later. The NPL advanced a socialist program in the years around World War I. A former Chief Justice of the North Dakota Supreme Court, Andrew Bruce, was no fan of the group. But he wrote that he understood why it came to be: "North Dakota, in fact, always has been, and perhaps always will be in some particulars a province of Saint Paul and of Minneapolis, rather than an economically and politically independent state."[34] The NPL briefly took control of most state offices. It exploited resentment of Minnesota banks and millers with the slogan, "North Dakota for North Dakotans."

Agriculture is almost always the key issue in North Dakota campaigns. Hard times on the farm rouse the state´s latent radical impulses, hence the attraction of Populism, the NPL, and the New Deal. Franklin Roosevelt won the state in both 1932 and 1936. North Dakotans return to their conservative roots in times of prosperity. The Republicans have therefore been dominant, carrying the state in eighteen of its twenty-four Presidential elections. The Democrats have only broken through once in the twelve contests dating from 1940.

OHIO (MIDWEST, 1804)

"Out of the lair of the wolf came the founders of old Rome, and out of the Ohio forest came rulers for young America."[35] Those were the words in 1899 of the Atlantic Monthly, convinced that Ohio truly merited the nickname, "Cradle of the Presidency." Of the twenty-one elections from 1840 through 1920, seven were won by Ohio residents. No other state could boast more than four winners. And over the nation's first two centuries, more Presidential candidates were born in Ohio than in any other state.

Ohio's dominance ended abruptly in the years after World War I. "The Republicans nominated Senator Warren G. Harding of Ohio," Will Rogers joked about the 1920 convention. "Ohio claims they are due a President, as they haven't had one since Taft. Look at the United States, they haven't had one since Lincoln."[36] It was a pleasantry appreciated by a country accustomed to nominees from Ohio. But for whatever reason, there has not been one since. The Presidential cradle has been barren for more than six decades.

Ohio voters strongly supported the Democratic-Republicans and the Democrats in their state's early years, largely because of those parties' frontier influence. The Republicans quickly caught on in 1856, carrying Ohio in their first fourteen tries. Democrats managed to restore competitive balance with the New Deal, holding Republican nominees to eight wins in the most-recent fourteen elections. Democrats have carried the other six. The GOP generally retains the edge in close contests, because of its strength in rural areas and some cities, such as Columbus and Cincinnati.

OKLAHOMA (SOUTH, 1908)

The typical Southern conservatism of modern Oklahoma masks an atypical past. A fiery populist spirit once burned on this edge of the plains, yielding outspoken leaders such as Democrat "Alfalfa Bill" Murray. Socialism also took root. Organizer Oscar Ameringer doubted his party could flourish in what he mistakenly expected to be a prosperous region. He discovered on arriving in rural Oklahoma "an indescribable aggregation of moisture, steam, dirt, rags, unshaven men, slatternly women, and fretting children."[37] Eugene Debs received 16.4 percent of the state's votes in 1912, his second-best performance in any state. Allan Benson took 15.4 percent four years later, the best Socialist record anywhere.

World War I and the "Red Scare" deflated the Socialist boom in Oklahoma. The discovery of oil propped up the state's poor economy, paving the way for conservative Democrats to dominate. Democratic nominees carried Oklahoma in nine of its first eleven elections. But the Democrats' national shift to the left triggered defections on the state level. "Every time they have an earthquake or a hippie rebellion in California," one resident told Time in 1970, "another handful of Okies comes back home."[38] Those descendants of Depression emigrants returned to a more prosperous, more urban state. Those factors have also made Oklahoma more Republican. The GOP has only lost the state once since 1952.

OREGON (WEST, 1860)

No primary election has more consistently foreshadowed Democratic and Republican Presidential nominations than Oregon´s. Thirteen times in each party since 1912, the victor in the state election went on to triumph at the convention. Two factors have contributed to this record of accuracy. Oregon was the first to pass a law requiring all legitimate Presidential contenders to be placed on its ballot; it avoided the succession of favorite sons that rendered other states´ contests meaningless for decades. The Oregon primary also traditionally comes late in the political season, narrowing the field to those popular enough to have already survived a long campaign.

Oregon was settled largely by Midwesterners in the mid-19th Century. It naturally reflected their Republican origins, supporting the GOP nominee in sixteen of the eighteen elections from 1860 through 1928. Oregon switched to Franklin Roosevelt for all four of his victories. An influx of young immigrants from the East was an important factor in loosening the bonds of Oregon´s conservative Republican past. But the state´s current reputation for liberalism is overblown. "This state is like one giant suburb," an exasperated Robert Kennedy grumbled in 1968 after sizing up Oregon´s essentially homogeneous population.[39] These white, middle-class residents support progressive legislation on the state level and admire political independence. But they also reject what they see as the liberal extremes of the Democratic party. Republican nominees have carried Oregon in nine of the past ten Presidential elections.

PENNSYLVANIA (EAST, 1789)

Pennsylvania, the birthplace of the Declaration of Independence and the Constitution, was once so essential to the Union that it was known as the Keystone State. It became nearly as important to the Republican party, which quadrennially anticipated its large package of electoral votes. Americans turned their backs on the despised Herbert Hoover in the grim Depression election of 1932. Pennsylvanians loyally stuck with him. It was the eighteenth time in the nineteen elections since 1860 that they voted for the GOP.

Republican dominance was difficult to foresee prior to the Civil War. Pennsylvania generally supported nominees of the Democratic-Republican and Democratic parties. James Buchanan was typical of the moderate, states´ rights Democrats who held power in the antebellum period. Robert E. Lee ended their influence when he led his Confederate forces into the state in 1863. Pennsylvanians grateful for the Union victory at Gettysburg that repulsed the invaders rallied behind the Republicans. Simon Cameron and Matthew Quay cemented their party´s newfound popularity by assembling one of the most enduring political machines in American history. The situation remained so bleak for the Democrats as late as 1930 that the party´s nominee for Governor withdrew from the race. He said he wanted to concentrate on his effort to be elected Grand Exalted Ruler of the Elks.

The growing popularity of the New Deal and the increasing power of organized labor finally freed the Democrats from their decades in Pennsylvania´s political wilderness. They are now competitive, having carried the state in seven of the thirteen most-recent contests. The Republicans can blindly count on Pennsylvania´s votes no longer.

RHODE ISLAND (EAST, 1792)

The smallest state in area, Rhode Island has always had to cope with its relative insignificance. It was the last of the original thirteen states to ratify the Constitution. No one waited. George Washington was already into his second year as President when Rhode Island finally acknowledged the federal government. The state was allocated a paltry four electoral votes for its first election in 1792, insufficient to warrant the concerns of national candidates. The figure has not varied, with the exception of a brief elevation to five electors from 1912 through 1928. Rhode Island has also proved to be a poor training ground. It is the only one of the original states to have failed to produce a Presidential candidate.

The political transformation of Rhode Island was typical of lower New England. The upper-class Yankees dominated for almost a century-and-a-half. Their allegiance belonged, in turn, to the Federalists, National Republicans, Whigs, and Republicans. GOP Presidential nominees carried the state in seventeen of the eighteen elections from 1856 through 1924. The heavily Catholic working class was politically ineffective until inspired by the 1928 Democratic nomination of Al Smith. The New Deal later encouraged the development of organized labor, which quickly became a power in this heavily industrialized state. Democratic nominees have flourished in the new environment, carrying Rhode Island in eleven of the fifteen most-recent elections. Only the District of Columbia gave a higher percentage of its popular vote to the Democrats from 1960 to 1984.

SOUTH CAROLINA (SOUTH, 1789)

The most important political statistic in South Carolina was racial. Blacks outnumbered whites throughout the 19th Century. The white elite living in the coastal Lowcountry consequently became the most spirited defenders of slavery in the South. Their philosopher was John Calhoun. Slavery, he asserted in the Senate in 1837, "is, instead of an evil, a good -- a positive good."[40] It was predictable that South Carolina would be the first to leave the Union when its beloved institution was threatened in 1860.

Antebellum South Carolina leaned heavily to the Democratic-Republican and Democratic parties. Republican-imposed Reconstruction brought a state legislature controlled by blacks. The Fairfield Herald bemoaned "the hell-born policy which has trampled the fairest and noblest States of our great sisterhood beneath the unholy hoofs of African savages and shoulder-strapped brigands."[41]   The elite clung to the lily-white Democrats after regaining control in 1877. No other party carried the state in a Presidential race until 1948.

That was the year the national Democrats committed themselves to a liberal civil-rights policy. South Carolina's Strom Thurmond ran for President on the rump Dixiecrat ticket, symbol of his region's violent displeasure. Sixteen years later, he astounded the nation with a televised announcement. "The Democratic party has abandoned the people," the Senator said. "It is leading the evolution of our nation to a socialistic dictatorship."[42] Thurmond became a Republican in 1964, viewing the party as the best hope for the conservative white South. South Carolina voted for the GOP that election, and in four of the five that followed.

SOUTH DAKOTA (MIDWEST, 1892)

The uninitiated eye notes little difference between North and South Dakota. They appear to be identical slices of the American plains. Democrats certainly felt that way in the late 19th Century. They pushed for the admission of Dakota Territory as one state. Republicans successfully held out for two. Cynics said the GOP was motivated by the simple desire to have four new Senators, rather than two. Those expectations have generally been fulfilled. Both Dakotas have been strongly Republican in national politics.

But there is a difference. South Dakota has a more conservative history than its northern neighbor. The Nonpartisan League's social program never caught hold in South Dakota. The state Republican party defused the reform spirit by embracing some of the progressivism of Theodore Roosevelt, once a rancher in the other Dakota. Conservatism was entrenched by the 1920s. It has remained the dominant philosophy in this agricultural state.

The Republican party has carried South Dakota in nineteen of its twenty-four elections. Roosevelt's Progressive party won another. The only Democratic successes have come in William Jennings Bryan's first battle, Franklin Roosevelt's first two elections, and Lyndon Johnson's 1964 landslide. Bryan and Roosevelt profited from severe agricultural depressions, Johnson from the reaction against Barry Goldwater's right-wing image. But South Dakota has otherwise been staunchly Republican, even rejecting the 1972 Presidential candidacy of its own Senator, Democrat George McGovern.

TENNESSEE (SOUTH, 1796)

The map shows Tennessee to be a single entity, but even official literature refers to the "Three Great States of Tennessee." East, Middle, and West Tennessee are not only geographically different, but also have dissimilar political histories. The East has long been a Republican stronghold. Residents of that mountainous region were so violently opposed to secession that the Confederate Governor placed them under martial law at the outbreak of the Civil War. The Middle, the home of Andrew Jackson, has traditionally been Democratic. Likewise the West, once home of the great planters. Racial issues have been more important in this river region than the other areas. West Tennessee whites have led the defection to the Republican party as national Democrats veered to the left.

Tennessee was once the American frontier. Jackson, the first President from west of the Appalachians, epitomized its rough spirit. Old Hickory's personal magnetism was instrumental in establishing the early dominance of the Democratic-Republican and Democratic parties in Tennessee. But upon his retirement to the Hermitage, the Whigs took control with their superior organization. The typical Southern reaction to Reconstruction restored the Democrats to power, but Republicans remained active in East Tennessee. "Tennessee ought to be Republican," a Knoxville editor argued in 1900. "There are one hundred thousand white men in the state of Tennessee who would rejoice to have the Republican party triumphant."[43] If so, they had a long wait. The GOP finally gained the upper hand in 1952. It has carried the state in seven of the nine Presidential elections since.

TEXAS (SOUTH, 1848)

The very name of Texas has always conjured up distinct images. Believers in manifest destiny in the 19th Century heralded it as a territorial Golconda. The oil boom of the 20th Century caused millions to envision Texas as a land of great riches. And throughout it all has stood the stereotype of the Texan: haughty, outspoken, larger than life.

The state's voting pattern conformed to the Southern mold for a century. Texas was strongly Democratic from the beginning, for two reasons: admission of the state was most fervently advanced in Congress by Democrats, and a majority of the early settlers were Southerners. Texas followed the Southern pattern: secession, Reconstruction, the strong Democratic backlash upon the restoration of white elite control. No Republican nominee carried the state until Herbert Hoover in 1928, a repudiation of Democrat Al Smith's Catholicism.

Defections from the traditional party began in earnest after World War II. Governor Allan Shivers, a Democrat, did the unthinkable in 1952, endorsing Republican Dwight Eisenhower. "A change must occur in the national trend...," he announced. "I want to help fight that battle from Texas ramparts."[44] Texans were angered by the Democrats'

increasing liberalism on civil rights, but they also had
economic motivations for switching. The oil boom had created
a new affluent class more at home with Republican ideals.
Lyndon Johnson managed to hold his state in the Democratic
column in the 1960s, but his demise foreshadowed his
party's. Republican nominees have carried Texas in three of
the past four national elections.

UTAH (WEST, 1896)

"This is the place!" Those were the famous words uttered by
Brigham Young when he and his band of Mormon followers
reached the Valley of the Great Salt Lake. Democrats felt
the same way. They were certain that Utah would be in their
column permanently. Mormons in the late 19th Century
bitterly remembered the Republican-led war against their
church's practice of polygamy. More than 1,300 polygamists
were sent to prison before the church renounced multiple
marriages. Only then did the Republican-controlled Congress
consent to Utah's admission as a state.

Democrat William Jennings Bryan was wildly triumphant in
Utah's first Presidential election, polling more than 82
percent of its popular vote in 1896. But Republicans soon
pulled to parity, with the influential assistance of Joseph
Smith, nephew and namesake of the founder of the Mormon
church. "Our lot is cast in the world," he wrote, "and we
must...unite on a proper division in the politics of the
day."[45]   That meant not antagonizing the Republicans, then
the national majority party. Democrats and Republicans each
won seven of the state's first fourteen elections.

Utah has veered sharply to the right since World War
II. Nearly three-quarters of its residents are Mormons. The
church takes a strongly conservative line, often advising its
members on political issues. As national Democrats became
increasingly identified with social liberalism, Utah landed
solidly in the Republican camp. GOP nominees have carried it
in eight of the nine most-recent elections.

VERMONT (EAST, 1792)

Many crops would not grow in the hilly, rocky soil of
Vermont, but the Republican party sank its roots deep. The
GOP's conservative philosophy was perfectly in tune with that
of the state's rural, Protestant populace. Vermont remained
the nation's most rural state into the 1980s, with only
one-third of its residents living in cities. Liberal
Democratic nominees had difficulty finding favor with such an
electorate.

Vermont was a disputed territory during the
Revolutionary War, claimed by both New Hampshire and New
York. Unable to join the Union, it declared itself a
republic. The new nation's constitution was unique for that
era because of its clause prohibiting slavery. The state of
Vermont later became known for its zealous support of
abolition. An exasperated Georgia state legislature passed a

resolution suggesting that Irish laborers be hired to dig along Vermont´s borders and float "the thing" out to sea.

After an early flirtation with the Democratic-Republican party, Vermont settled into its conservative pattern. It was carried by Whig nominees in all five of that party´s elections. Then came twenty-seven straight Republican victories, from 1856 through 1960. Vermont proved its colors by sticking with Republican nominees in 1912 and 1936, when the party only carried two states each time. A recent influx of younger, more liberal newcomers to Vermont has cut the GOP´s margins, but the party still carried the state in the five most-recent contests.

VIRGINIA (SOUTH, 1789)

Virginia was the chief fount of leadership for a young America. Eight of the first nine Presidential terms were served by Virginians. Northerners grumped about a dynasty. John Adams groaned that his son, John Quincy, would never be President "till all Virginians shall be extinct."[46]

The dynasty collapsed without warning. No Virginian since James Monroe in 1820 has received a major-party nomination. The state turned inward, consumed by the growing flames of sectional discord. Its politicians became leading proponents of slavery. After the Civil War, much of which was fought on Virginia soil, the state followed the typical Southern pattern. The white elite regained control, embraced the Democratic party, and disenfranchised most blacks. British historian Arnold Toynbee wrote in the 1940s, "Virginia makes the painful impression of a country living under a spell, in which time has stood still."[47]

Virginia was long under the Democratic spell, only breaking from the party´s ranks once between 1876 and 1948. But the new liberal Democratic civil-rights policy angered traditionalists led by Senator Harry Byrd. He refused to endorse Adlai Stevenson in 1952, maintaining what he called a "golden silence." Byrd´s conservative constituents got the message. The state voted Republican that fall, and has done so in seven of the eight elections that followed.

WASHINGTON (WEST, 1892)

Washington is similar in appearance to neighboring Oregon, but different in history. Oregon´s past was placid, with both political parties staying essentially conservative until recent years. Washington was long politically turbulent. The Populist and Socialist parties received strong support in their heydays. The 1912 Progressive ticket carried the state. The 1924 party of the same name garnered more than a third of Washington´s popular vote. Organized labor, which was a potent force in all of these campaigns, conducted a 1919 general strike in Seattle that was viewed by some as a foreshadowing of revolution. James Farley had all this in mind when he said in the 1930s, "There are forty-seven American states -- and the Soviet of Washington."[48]

A manufacturing boom in the 1940s helped calm the waters of Washington politics. The Democratic and Republican parties had split the fourteen Presidential elections between the state´s admission to the Union and 1948. But growing prosperity tilted the balance to the conservatives, even though labor continued to exert considerable influence. Republican nominees have won Washington in seven of the nine elections dating from 1952. Latent Democratic potential was demonstrated by Hubert Humphrey´s surprise victory in 1968, his only triumph in a continental Western state. But Washington has been in the Republican column ever since.

WEST VIRGINIA (EAST, 1864)

Republicans created West Virginia, but it didn´t provide the long-term political support they hoped for. Originally part of Virginia, the region constantly complained about lack of representation in Richmond. Its residents had little in common with the elite slaveholders who ruled Virginia as their collective fiefdom. The Civil War provided a chance to remedy these long-standing grievances. The western counties seceded from the Confederacy, petitioning to be admitted as the state of Kanawha. Many doubted the legality of such a move. But Abraham Lincoln signed the statehood bill. "We can scarcely dispense with the aid of West Virginia in this struggle," he said, using the state´s new name. "Much less can we afford to have her against us, in Congress and in the field."[49]

West Virginia was with Lincoln´s Republicans in the beginning. But the sense of gratitude vanished in the 1870s, a reaction against efforts to disenfranchise former Southern sympathizers, of whom there were many. Even marginal Republicans considered such exclusion unnecessary and heavy-handed. Democrats carried every Presidential election from 1876 through 1892.

Political control has since been cyclical. Republicans were ascendant in 1896, beneficiaries of West Virginia´s industrialization. They won eight of the next nine contests. But the Depression hit harder in coal country than almost anywhere else. Franklin Roosevelt carried the state in 1932. His New Deal then paved the way for organized labor to become the major force in West Virginia that it remains. Democratic Presidential nominees have won the state in eleven of the fourteen most-recent elections.

WISCONSIN (MIDWEST, 1848)

Wisconsin defies political categories. It was the home of Robert La Follette, the dynamic champion of progressivism. It was also the state that produced Joseph McCarthy, the reviled leader of the anti-Communist backlash of the 1950s. Wisconsin today retains the image of being a hotbed of Midwestern liberalism. Its record contradicts, showing a leaning to the Republican party.

La Follette told his campaign managers, "Appeal to the

citizenship of the state to save Wisconsin´s good name from
this gang of corporation knaves."[50]   His election as Governor
in 1900 heralded an unprecedented wave of reform that drew
national attention.   La Follette carried his hard-headed
independence to the Senate, earning Woodrow Wilson´s lasting
enmity for opposing American entry to World War I.   National
observers questioned how a state that revered such a man
could later send McCarthy to Washington.   They underestimated
its German and Scandinavian voters´ love of outspokenness, no
matter the philosophy.   Long after McCarthy was discredited,
the Milwaukee _Sentinel_ would eulogize him as "valiant" and a
"saber-slashing warrior."

    The Republican party naturally won favor in such an
environment during the volatile 1850s.   Wisconsin was
enthusiastically pro-Union and anti-slavery.   The GOP carried
the state in sixteen of its first twenty-one Presidential
contests.   But Franklin Roosevelt tore Wisconsinites from
their Republican roots.   Much of his New Deal was La
Follette´s Wisconsin Idea on a national scale.   The state
Democratic party, long dormant, reorganized after World War
II.   Republicans retain the upper hand, but Presidential
elections are closer.   The GOP has a narrow edge in the past
fourteen contests, eight-to-six.

WYOMING (WEST, 1892)

In Wyoming, the individual is preeminent.   The state´s
residents consider their home the real West, a place of wide
open spaces.   It is the least densely populated continental
state.   The 1980 census reported an average of only 5.3
persons inhabiting each square mile.   Many were descendants
of early settlers who pioneered in ranching or built the
transcontinental railroad across unforgiving terrain.

    Wyoming politics has always mirrored the individualism
of the state´s citizens.   Historian Taft Larson wrote that
Wyoming Democrats have historically found fault with the
federal government, "while Republican politicians often
talked as if they thought the United States were a hostile
foreign power."[51]   Senator Joseph O´Mahoney, though a
Democrat, shared that Republican view while serving during
Franklin Roosevelt´s Administration.   O´Mahoney said during
World War II that "the greatest evil of our time is
centralization of power."[52]   His audience wasn´t sure if he
meant Hitler or Roosevelt, or most likely both.

    The Republican party has been dominant in Wyoming since
the state´s admission to the Union.   The party´s conservative
rhetoric naturally has strong appeal.   Democrats William
Jennings Bryan, Woodrow Wilson, Roosevelt, and Harry Truman
scored isolated Democratic breakthroughs in earlier years,
but only Lyndon Johnson has managed one since 1952.
Republicans have carried Wyoming in eight of the past nine
elections.

Charts for Chapter 9

Alabama

Winners	D 28, R 6, DR 3, SRD 1, AI 1, SD 1, ID 1
General Match	21-20 51.2
Convention Match	D 21-16 56.8 R 23-7 76.7
Primary Match	D 2-5 28.6 R 1-0 100.0
County Sweeps	1 (D 1)

	PV %	EV
1820-1852	DR/D 61.7, NR/W 37.6, other 0.7	D 48, DR 13
1856-1900	D 57.0, R 30.7, other 12.3	D 82, R 18, oth 9
1904-1928	D 66.2, R 29.1, other 4.7	D 82
1932-1956	D 66.0, R 24.7, other 9.3	D 65, other 12
1960-1984	R 49.8, D 36.0, other 14.1	R 37, oth 16, D 14

Top PV %, one year	Andrew Jackson (D-1832), 99.9
Top PV %, Democrat	Andrew Jackson (1832), 99.9
Top PV %, Republican	Richard Nixon (1972), 72.4
Top PV %, third party	Strom Thurmond (SRD-1948), 79.7
Home-State Candidates	2 individuals, 6 qualified
Results	0 nominees, 0 winners, 47 EV

Alaska

Winners	R 6, D 1	
General Match	5-2 71.4	
Convention Match	D 19-6 76.0	R 21-3 87.5
Primary Match	D 1-0 100.0	R 1-0 100.0
District Sweeps	2 (D 1, R 1)	

	PV %	EV
1960-1984	R 55.7, D 36.5, other 7.8	R 18, D 3

Top PV %, one year	Ronald Reagan (R-1984), 66.9
Top PV %, Democrat	Lyndon Johnson (1964), 65.9
Top PV %, Republican	Ronald Reagan (1984), 66.9
Top PV %, third party	George Wallace (AI-1968), 12.1
Home-State Candidates	0
Results	0 nominees, 0 winners, 0 EV

Arizona

Winners	R 12, D 7	
General Match	16-3 84.2	
Convention Match	D 18-8 69.2	R 22-7 75.9
Primary Match	never had primaries	
County Sweeps	6 (D 6)	

	PV %	EV
1904-1928	R 45.8, D 44.0, other 10.2	R 9, D 6
1932-1956	D 52.4, R 46.6, other 1.0	D 17, R 8
1960-1984	R 59.3, D 35.6, other 5.1	R 39

Arizona (continued)

Top PV %, one year	Franklin Roosevelt (D-1936), 69.9
Top PV %, Democrat	Franklin Roosevelt (1936), 69.9
Top PV %, Republican	Ronald Reagan (1984), 66.4
Top PV %, third party	Theodore Roosevelt (P-1912), 29.3
Home-State Candidates	2 individuals, 2 qualified
Results	1 nominee, 0 winners, 52 EV

Arkansas

Winners	D 30, R 4, SD 1, AI 1		
General Match	20-16 55.6		
Convention Match	D 23-13 63.9	R 22-9 71.0	
Primary Match	D 2-0 100.0	R 0-1 0.0	
County Sweeps	3 (D 2, R 1)		

	PV %	EV
1820-1852	DR/D 59.7, NR/W 40.3	D 16
1856-1900	D 57.2, R 34.3, other 8.5	D 54, R 5, oth 4
1904-1928	D 59.4, R 33.9, other 6.6	D 63
1932-1956	D 66.0, R 31.1, other 2.9	D 61
1960-1984	R 47.9, D 45.3, other 6.8	D 20, R 18, oth 6

Top PV %, one year	Franklin Roosevelt (D-1932), 86.3
Top PV %, Democrat	Franklin Roosevelt (1932), 86.3
Top PV %, Republican	Richard Nixon (1972), 68.9
Top PV %, third party	John Breckinridge (SD-1860), 53.1
Home-State Candidates	0
Results	0 nominees, 0 winners, 0 EV

California

Winners	R 22, D 11, P 1	
General Match	29-5 85.3	
Convention Match	D 17-17 50.0	R 23-10 69.7
Primary Match	D 8-11 42.1	R 9-10 47.4
County Sweeps	2 (D 1, R 1)	

	PV %	EV
1820-1852	DR/D 53.0, NR/W 46.8, other 0.2	D 4
1856-1900	R 48.0, D 45.1, other 6.9	R 61, D 18
1904-1928	R 52.9, D 29.8, other 17.3	R 59, D 15, oth 11
1932-1956	D 51.2, R 47.0, other 1.8	D 116, R 64
1960-1984	R 50.9, D 45.1, other 4.0	R 254, D 40

Top PV %, one year	Franklin Roosevelt (D-1936), 67.0
Top PV %, Democrat	Franklin Roosevelt (1936), 67.0
Top PV %, Republican	Warren Harding (1920), 66.2
Top PV %, third party	Theodore Roosevelt (P-1912), 41.8
Home-State Candidates	10 individuals, 18 qualified
Results	7 nominees, 4 winners, 2,372 EV

Colorado

Winners	R 18, D 9, POP 1	
General Match	19-9 67.9	
Convention Match	D 17-11 60.7	R 21-10 67.7
Primary Match	never had primaries	
County Sweeps	1 (R 1)	

Colorado (continued)

	PV %	EV
1856-1900	D 52.2, R 38.0, other 9.9	R 12, D 8, oth 4
1904-1928	R 50.1, D 40.1, other 9.9	R 23, D 17
1932-1956	R 50.7, D 47.9, other 1.4	R 24, D 18
1960-1984	R 55.0, D 40.3, other 4.7	R 41, D 6

Top PV %, one year

William Jennings Bryan (D-POP-1896), 84.9

Top PV %, Democrat	William Jennings Bryan (1896), 84.9
Top PV %, Republican	Herbert Hoover (1928), 64.8
Top PV %, third party	James Weaver (POP-1892), 57.1
Home-State Candidates	1 individual, 1 qualified
Results	0 nominees, 0 winners, 0 EV

Connecticut

Winners	R 22, D 13, F 8, W 3, DR 2, NR 2	
General Match	34-16 68.0	
Convention Match	D 26-12 68.4	R 23-10 69.7
Primary Match	D 0-2 0.0	R 0-1 0.0
County Sweeps	14 (R 11, D 2, W 1)	

	PV %	EV
1789-1816	----	F 70
1820-1852	NR/W 50.0, DR/D 45.5, other 4.5	W 20, DR 17, NR 16, D 14
1856-1900	R 52.5, D 44.5, other 3.0	R 48, D 24
1904-1928	R 55.6, D 37.9, other 6.4	R 42, D 7
1932-1956	R 51.4, D 47.1, other 1.5	R 32, D 24
1960-1984	R 49.4, D 47.3, other 3.3	R 32, D 24

Connecticut (continued)

Top PV %, one year	John Quincy Adams (NR-1828), 71.4
Top PV %, Democrat	Lyndon Johnson (1964), 67.8
Top PV %, Republican	Dwight Eisenhower (1956), 63.7
Top PV %, third party	John Breckinridge (SD-1860), 19.2
Home-State Candidates	2 individuals, 2 qualified
Results	0 nominees, 0 winners, 0 EV

Delaware

Winners	R 17, D 16, F 8, W 4, DR 2, NR 2, SD 1
General Match	31-19 62.0
Convention Match	D 22-16 57.9 R 28-5 84.8
Primary Match	never had primaries
County Sweeps	23 (R 11, D 10, W 1, SD 1)

	PV %	EV
1789-1816	----	F 25
1820-1852	NR/W 51.9, DR/D 47.8, other 0.3	W 12, DR 7, NR 6, D 3
1856-1900	D 48.6, R 44.8, other 6.6	D 24, R 9, oth 3
1904-1928	R 54.9, D 40.9, other 4.2	R 18, D 3
1932-1956	D 50.1, R 49.0, other 0.9	R 12, D 9
1960-1984	R 49.9, D 46.6, other 3.5	R 12, D 9

Top PV %, one year	Herbert Hoover (R-1928), 65.8
Top PV %, Democrat	Lyndon Johnson (1964), 61.0
Top PV %, Republican	Herbert Hoover (1928), 65.8
Top PV %, third party	John Breckinridge (SD-1860), 45.5
Home-State Candidates	2 individuals, 4 qualified
Results	0 nominees, 0 winners, 0 EV

District of Columbia

Winners	D 6		
General Match	2-4 33.3		
Convention Match	D 19-7 73.1	R 21-10 67.7	
Primary Match	D 2-7 22.2	R 2-3 40.0	
County Sweeps	has no counties		

	PV %	EV
1960-1984	D 81.5, R 16.1, other 2.3	D 18

Top PV %, one year	Walter Mondale (D-1984), 85.7
Top PV %, Democrat	Walter Mondale (1984), 85.7
Top PV %, Republican	Richard Nixon (1972), 21.6
Top PV %, third party	John Anderson (NU-1980), 9.3
Home-State Candidates	0
Results	0 nominees, 0 winners, 0 EV

Florida

Winners	D 21, R 11, W 1, SD 1	
General Match	24-10 70.6	
Convention Match	D 19-15 55.9	R 24-6 80.0
Primary Match	D 6-8 42.9	R 6-2 75.0
County Sweeps	11 (D 10, R 1)	

	PV %	EV
1820-1852	DR/D 51.4, NR/W 48.6	D 3, W 3
1856-1900	D 58.2, R 34.3, other 7.5	D 27, R 11, oth 3
1904-1928	D 55.3, R 35.4, other 9.3	D 34, R 6
1932-1956	D 55.4, R 42.2, other 2.4	D 37, R 20
1960-1984	R 55.7, D 39.6, other 4.7	R 79, D 31

Florida (continued)

Top PV %, one year	Grover Cleveland (D-1892), 85.0
Top PV %, Democrat	Grover Cleveland (1892), 85.0
Top PV %, Republican	Richard Nixon (1972), 71.9
Top PV %, third party	John Breckinridge (SD-1860), 62.2
Home-State Candidates	0
Results	0 nominees, 0 winners, 0 EV

Georgia

Winners	D 30, DR 9, W 3, R 3, F 2, SD 1, AI 1		
General Match	28-21 57.1		
Convention Match	D 21-17 55.3	R 22-8 73.3	
Primary Match	D 4-0 100.0	R 2-1 66.7	
County Sweeps	2 (D 1, R 1)		

	PV %	EV
1789-1816	----	DR 36, F 9
1820-1852	DR/D 55.9, NR/W 42.8, other 1.4	W 32, D 31, DR 26
1856-1900	D 59.9, R 27.9, other 12.2	D 112, other 10
1904-1928	D 67.4, R 23.3, other 9.2	D 96
1932-1956	D 74.3, R 22.4, other 3.3	D 84
1960-1984	R 47.7, D 45.8, other 6.5	D 36, R 36, oth 12

Top PV %, one year	Andrew Jackson (D-1832), 100.0
Top PV %, Democrat	Andrew Jackson (1832), 100.0
Top PV %, Republican	Richard Nixon (1972), 75.3
Top PV %, third party	John Breckinridge (SD-1860), 48.9
Home-State Candidates	5 individuals, 7 qualified
Results	3 nominees, 1 winner, 389 EV

Hawaii

Winners	D 5, R 2
General Match	5-2 71.4
Convention Match	D 17-5 77.3 R 18-4 81.8
Primary Match	never had primaries
County Sweeps	5 (D 3, R 2)

	PV %	EV
1960-1984	D 50.8, R 46.6, other 2.6	D 19, R 8

Top PV %, one year	Lyndon Johnson (D-1964), 78.8
Top PV %, Democrat	Lyndon Johnson (1964), 78.8
Top PV %, Republican	Richard Nixon (1972), 62.5
Top PV %, third party	John Anderson (NU-1980), 10.6
Home-State Candidates	0
Results	0 nominees, 0 winners, 0 EV

Idaho

Winners	R 13, D 10, POP 1
General Match	19-5 79.2
Convention Match	D 19-7 73.1 R 20-10 66.7
Primary Match	D 1-2 33.3 R 2-1 66.7
County Sweeps	6 (R 5, D 1)

	PV %	EV
1856-1900	D 49.2, R 39.4, other 11.5	D 6, other 3
1904-1928	R 52.7, D 33.3, other 13.9	R 18, D 8
1932-1956	R 49.8, D 48.9, other 1.3	D 20, R 8
1960-1984	R 61.3, D 33.6, other 5.1	R 24, D 4

Idaho (continued)

Top PV %, one year	William Jennings Bryan (D-POP-1896), 78.1
Top PV %, Democrat	William Jennings Bryan (1896), 78.1
Top PV %, Republican	Ronald Reagan (1984), 72.4
Top PV %, third party	James Weaver (POP-1892), 54.2
Home-State Candidates	2 individuals, 2 qualified
Results	0 nominees, 0 winners, 0 EV

Illinois

Winners	R 23, D 16, DR 3			
General Match	36-6 85.7			
Convention Match	D 25-12 67.6		R 22-11 66.7	
Primary Match	D 12-7 63.2		R 9-10 47.4	
County Sweeps	0			

	PV %	EV
1820-1852	DR/D 52.1, NR/W 42.4, other 5.5	D 44, DR 9
1856-1900	R 51.5, D 45.3, other 3.2	R 198, D 35
1904-1928	R 55.2, D 34.4, other 10.4	R 170, D 29
1932-1956	D 49.8, R 49.3, other 1.0	D 143, R 54
1960-1984	R 50.4, D 46.7, other 2.9	R 128, D 53

Top PV %, one year	Andrew Jackson (D-1832), 68.0
Top PV %, Democrat	Andrew Jackson (1832), 68.0
Top PV %, Republican	Warren Harding (1920), 67.8
Top PV %, third party	Theodore Roosevelt (P-1912), 33.7
Home-State Candidates	13 individuals, 22 qualified
Results	7 nominees, 4 winners, 1,067 EV

Indiana

Winners	R 25, D 12, DR 4, W 2		
General Match	33-10 76.7		
Convention Match	D 29-10 74.4	R 25-8 75.8	
Primary Match	D 4-6 40.0	R 8-4 66.7	
County Sweeps	1 (R 1)		

	PV %	EV
1789-1816	----	DR 3
1820-1852	DR/D 50.6, NR/W 47.1, other 2.3	D 46, W 18, DR 13
1856-1900	R 49.4, D 47.8, other 2.8	R 114, D 58
1904-1928	R 51.3, D 41.5, other 7.1	R 90, D 15
1932-1956	R 51.2, D 47.6, other 1.1	R 66, D 28
1960-1984	R 55.2, D 41.8, other 3.0	R 77, D 13

Top PV %, one year	Richard Nixon (R-1972), 66.1
Top PV %, Democrat	Franklin Roosevelt (1936), 56.6
Top PV %, Republican	Richard Nixon (1972), 66.1
Top PV %, third party	Theodore Roosevelt (P-1912), 24.8
Home-State Candidates	8 individuals, 16 qualified
Results	2 nominees, 1 winner, 420 EV

Iowa

Winners	R 28, D 7		
General Match	26-9 74.3		
Convention Match	D 23-12 65.7	R 24-9 72.7	
Primary Match	D 1-0 100.0	R 0-1 0.0	
County Sweeps	2 (R 2)		

Iowa (continued)

	PV %	EV
1820-1852	DR/D 50.3, NR/W 44.7, other 4.9	D 8
1856-1900	R 55.5, D 40.8, other 3.7	R 122
1904-1928	R 57.0, D 31.3, other 11.7	R 78, D 13
1932-1956	R 51.5, D 47.2, other 1.3	R 41, D 32
1960-1984	R 51.4, D 45.5, other 3.1	R 51, D 9

Top PV %, one year	Warren Harding (R-1920), 70.9
Top PV %, Democrat	Lyndon Johnson (1964), 61.9
Top PV %, Republican	Warren Harding (1920), 70.9
Top PV %, third party	Theodore Roosevelt (P-1912), 32.9
Home-State Candidates	5 individuals, 7 qualified
Results	0 nominees, 0 winners, 22 EV

Kansas

Winners	R 24, D 6, POP 1	
General Match	23-8 74.2	
Convention Match	D 23-8 74.2	R 25-8 75.8
Primary Match	D 1-0 100.0	R 1-0 100.0
County Sweeps	4 (R 4)	

	PV %	EV
1856-1900	R 54.9, D 32.2, other 12.9	R 49, D 10, oth 10
1904-1928	R 56.3, D 34.0, other 9.7	R 50, D 20
1932-1956	R 56.6, D 42.4, other 1.0	R 41, D 18
1960-1984	R 58.0, D 38.1, other 3.8	R 43, D 7

Kansas (continued)

Top PV %, one year	Abraham Lincoln (R-1864), 79.2
Top PV %, Democrat	Lyndon Johnson (1964), 54.1
Top PV %, Republican	Abraham Lincoln (1864), 79.2
Top PV %, third party	James Weaver (POP-1892), 50.3
Home-State Candidates	2 individuals, 2 qualified
Results	1 nominee, 0 winners, 8 EV

Kentucky

Winners	D 23, DR 9, R 9, W 5, F 1, NR 1, CU 1
General Match	30-19 61.2
Convention Match	D 25-14 64.1 R 24-9 72.7
Primary Match	D 2-0 100.0 R 2-0 100.0
County Sweeps	0

	PV %	EV
1789-1816	----	DR 47, F 4
1820-1852	NR/W 52.6, DR/D 47.3	W 66, DR 40, NR 15
1856-1900	D 52.8, R 38.8, other 8.3	D 123, R 12, ot 12
1904-1928	R 48.2, D 47.3, other 4.4	D 65, R 26
1932-1956	D 54.3, R 45.0, other 0.8	D 65, R 10
1960-1984	R 50.5, D 45.9, other 3.6	R 46, D 18

Top PV %, one year	Horatio Seymour (D-1868), 74.6
Top PV %, Democrat	Horatio Seymour (1868), 74.6
Top PV %, Republican	Richard Nixon (1972), 63.4
Top PV %, third party	Millard Fillmore (A-W-1856), 47.5
Home-State Candidates	7 individuals, 11 qualified
Results	3 nominees, 0 winners, 263 EV

Louisiana

Winners	D 26, R 6, DR 5, W 2, SD 1, SRD 1, AI 1
General Match	26-16 61.9
Convention Match	D 25-13 65.8 R 23-8 74.2
Primary Match	D 1-1 50.0 R 2-0 100.0
Parish Sweeps	7 (D 7)

	PV %	EV
1789-1816	----	DR 6
1820-1852	NR/W 50.9, DR/D 49.1	D 22, DR 13, W 11
1856-1900	D 61.1, R 32.8, other 6.1	D 61, R 8, oth 6
1904-1928	D 78.0, R 18.1, other 3.8	D 68
1932-1956	D 62.2, R 29.4, other 8.4	D 50, R 10, oth 10
1960-1984	R 49.0, D 40.9, other 10.2	R 40, D 20, oth 10

Top PV %, one year	Franklin Roosevelt (D-1932), 92.8
Top PV %, Democrat	Franklin Roosevelt (1932), 92.8
Top PV %, Republican	Richard Nixon (1972), 66.0
Top PV %, third party	Strom Thurmond (SRD-1948), 49.1
Home-State Candidates	1 individual, 1 qualified
Results	1 nominee, 1 winner, 163 EV

Maine

Winners	R 30, D 8, DR 2, NR 1, W 1
General Match	28-14 66.7
Convention Match	D 31-8 79.5 R 23-10 69.7
Primary Match	never had primaries
County Sweeps	18 (R 17, D 1)

Maine (continued)

	PV %	EV
1820-1852	DR/D 51.8, NR/W 42.7, other 5.5	D 46, DR 19, W 10, NR 8
1856-1900	R 59.4, D 37.8, other 2.9	R 81
1904-1928	R 60.4, D 32.7, other 6.9	R 36, D 6
1932-1956	R 58.8, D 40.5, other 0.7	R 35
1960-1984	R 50.3, D 46.9, other 2.7	R 21, D 8

Top PV %, one year	John Quincy Adams (DR-1824), 81.5
Top PV %, Democrat	Lyndon Johnson (1964), 68.8
Top PV %, Republican	Calvin Coolidge (1924), 72.0
Top PV %, third party	Theodore Roosevelt (P-1912), 37.4
Home-State Candidates	3 individuals, 7 qualified
Results	1 nominee, 0 winners, 182 EV

Maryland

Winners	D 21, R 11, DR 6, W 4, F 3, NR 2, A-W 1, SD 1, tie (F and DR) 1	
General Match	32-17-1 65.0	
Convention Match	D 23-16 59.0	R 26-7 78.8
Primary Match	D 4-6 40.0	R 8-5 61.5
County Sweeps	1 (R 1)	

	PV %	EV
1789-1816	----	DR 41, F 35
1820-1852	DR/D 52.6, NR/W 47.4	W 36, DR 27, D 11, NR 11
1856-1900	D 48.3, R 43.4, other 8.3	D 55, R 23, oth 16
1904-1928	R 48.3, D 45.3, other 6.4	D 29, R 27
1932-1956	D 50.8, R 48.2, other 1.0	D 32, R 26
1960-1984	D 49.0, R 47.3, other 3.7	D 49, R 20

Maryland (continued)

Top PV %, one year	Horatio Seymour (D-1868), 67.2
Top PV %, Democrat	Horatio Seymour (1868), 67.2
Top PV %, Republican	Richard Nixon (1972), 61.3
Top PV %, third party	Millard Fillmore (A-W-1856), 54.6
Home-State Candidates	3 individuals, 3 qualified
Results	0 nominees, 0 winners, 7 EV

Massachusetts

Winners	R 21, D 12, F 7, W 5, DR 3, NR 2	
General Match	34-16 68.0	
Convention Match	D 22-17 56.4	R 22-11 66.7
Primary Match	D 6-13 31.6	R 10-9 52.6
County Sweeps	10 (R 9, D 1)	

	PV %	EV
1789-1816	----	F 121, DR 19
1820-1852	NR/W 47.9, DR/D 36.2, other 15.9	W 65, DR 30, NR 29
1856-1900	R 59.9, D 35.6, other 4.5	R 162
1904-1928	R 55.3, D 37.2, other 7.5	R 86, D 36
1932-1956	D 49.4, R 48.9, other 1.7	D 83, R 32
1960-1984	D 56.8, R 39.5, other 3.7	D 72, R 27

Top PV %, one year	John Quincy Adams (NR-1828), 76.4
Top PV %, Democrat	Lyndon Johnson (1964), 76.2
Top PV %, Republican	Abraham Lincoln (1864), 72.2
Top PV %, third party	Theodore Roosevelt (P-1912), 29.1
Home-State Candidates	9 individuals, 13 qualified
Results	7 nominees, 4 winners, 1,003 EV

Michigan

Winners	R 26, D 10, W 1, P 1		
General Match	28-10 73.7		
Convention Match	D 28-9 75.7	R 22-11	66.7
Primary Match	D 3-4 42.9	R 4-3	57.1
County Sweeps	4 (R 4)		

	PV %	EV
1820-1852	DR/D 49.3, NR/W 42.5, other 8.2	D 19, W 3
1856-1900	R 53.3, D 41.4, other 5.3	R 124, D 5
1904-1928	R 64.9, D 26.2, other 8.9	R 88, other 15
1932-1956	R 50.0, D 48.4, other 1.6	R 78, D 57
1960-1984	R 48.9, D 47.7, other 3.4	R 83, D 62

Top PV %, one year	Calvin Coolidge (R-1924), 75.4
Top PV %, Democrat	Lyndon Johnson (1964), 66.7
Top PV %, Republican	Calvin Coolidge (1924), 75.4
Top PV %, third party	Theodore Roosevelt (P-1912), 38.9
Home-State Candidates	6 individuals, 9 qualified
Results	2 nominees, 0 winners, 367 EV

Minnesota

Winners	R 20, D 11, P 1		
General Match	25-7 78.1		
Convention Match	D 24-8 75.0	R 19-14	57.6
Primary Match	D 1-2 33.3	R 1-2	33.3
County Sweeps	2 (R 2)		

Minnesota (continued)

	PV %	EV
1856-1900	R 56.7, D 38.1, other 5.1	R 68
1904-1928	R 55.7, D 27.0, other 17.3	R 70, other 12
1932-1956	D 52.7, R 45.1, other 2.2	D 55, R 22
1960-1984	D 51.9, R 44.8, other 3.4	D 61, R 10

Top PV %, one year	Theodore Roosevelt (R-1904), 74.0
Top PV %, Democrat	Lyndon Johnson (1964), 63.8
Top PV %, Republican	Theodore Roosevelt (1904), 74.0
Top PV %, third party	Robert La Follette (P-1924), 41.3
Home-State Candidates	5 individuals, 8 qualified
Results	2 nominees, 0 winners, 204 EV

Mississippi

Winners	D 27, R 5, DR 3, W 1, SD 1, SRD 1, ID 1, AI 1
General Match	21-19 52.5
Convention Match	D 22-16 57.9 R 23-7 76.7
Primary Match	D never had primaries R 1-0 100.0
County Sweeps	14 (D 12, R 1, SRD 1)

	PV %	EV
1820-1852	DR/D 57.0, NR/W 43.0	D 27, DR 8, W 4
1856-1900	D 61.8, R 26.6, other 11.6	D 68, R 8, oth 7
1904-1928	D 87.6, R 9.6, other 2.8	D 70
1932-1956	D 69.8, other 15.2, R 14.9	D 52, other 9
1960-1984	R 52.4, D 34.7, other 12.9	R 28, oth 15, D 7

Mississippi (continued)

Top PV %, one year	Andrew Jackson (D-1832), 100.0
Top PV %, Democrat	Andrew Jackson (1832), 100.0
Top PV %, Republican	Barry Goldwater (1964), 87.1
Top PV %, third party	Strom Thurmond (SRD-1948), 87.2
Home-State Candidates	0
Results	0 nominees, 0 winners, 0 EV

Missouri

Winners	D 27, R 12, DR 3
General Match	31-11 73.8
Convention Match	D 23-15 60.5 R 23-9 71.9
Primary Match	never had primaries
County Sweeps	0

	PV %	EV
1820-1852	DR/D 58.2, NR/W 41.7	D 35, DR 9
1856-1900	D 51.2, R 42.6, other 6.2	D 146, R 22
1904-1928	R 49.5, D 45.5, other 5.0	R 90, D 36
1932-1956	D 54.9, R 44.6, other 0.5	D 88, R 13
1960-1984	R 50.5, D 47.1, other 2.4	R 47, D 37

Top PV %, one year	Andrew Jackson (D-1832), 100.0
Top PV %, Democrat	Andrew Jackson (1832), 100.0
Top PV %, Republican	Abraham Lincoln (1864), 69.7
Top PV %, third party	Millard Fillmore (A-W-1856), 45.6
Home-State Candidates	8 individuals, 8 qualified
Results	1 nominee, 1 winner, 321 EV

Montana

Winners	R 14, D 10		
General Match	19-5 79.2		
Convention Match	D 19-7 73.1	R 22-8 73.3
Primary Match	D 2-5 28.6	R 3-4 42.9
County Sweeps	1 (D 1)		

	PV %	EV
1856-1900	D 60.4, R 33.9, other 5.7	D 6, R 3
1904-1928	R 47.8, D 37.3, other 14.8	R 18, D 8
1932-1956	D 53.3, R 44.7, other 2.0	D 20, R 8
1960-1984	R 53.5, D 42.6, other 3.9	R 24, D 4

Top PV %, one year	William Jennings Bryan (D-POP-1896), 79.9
Top PV %, Democrat	William Jennings Bryan (1896), 79.9
Top PV %, Republican	Warren Harding (1920), 61.0
Top PV %, third party	Robert La Follette (P-1924), 37.8
Home-State Candidates	1 individual, 2 qualified
Results	0 nominees, 0 winners, 0 EV

Nebraska

Winners	R 23, D 7	
General Match	21-9 70.0	
Convention Match	D 22-8 73.3	R 21-11 65.6
Primary Match	D 10-9 52.6	R 8-11 42.1
County Sweeps	6 (R 6)	

Nebraska (continued)

	PV %	EV
1856-1900	R 51.9, D 38.0, other 10.1	R 38, D 8
1904-1928	R 51.6, D 37.4, other 11.0	R 32, D 24
1932-1956	R 54.4, D 45.0, other 0.6	R 31, D 14
1960-1984	R 62.3, D 34.9, other 2.8	R 31, D 5

Top PV %, one year	Ulysses Grant (R-1872), 70.7
Top PV %, Democrat	Franklin Roosevelt (1932), 63.0
Top PV %, Republican	Ulysses Grant (1872), 70.7
Top PV %, third party	James Weaver (POP-1892), 41.5
Home-State Candidates	2 individuals, 4 qualified
Results	3 nominees, 0 winners, 493 EV

Nevada

Winners	R 17, D 13, POP 1		
General Match	24-7 77.4		
Convention Match	D 16-14 53.3	R 25-6	80.6
Primary Match	D 1-1 50.0	R 1-1	50.0
County Sweeps	8 (D 4, R 4)		

	PV %	EV
1856-1900	R 48.6, D 46.0, other 5.4	R 17, D 9, oth 3
1904-1928	R 44.2, D 40.1, other 15.7	R 12, D 9
1932-1956	D 52.1, R 47.6, other 0.3	D 15, R 6
1960-1984	R 56.5, D 38.9, other 4.6	R 16, D 6

Top PV %, one year	
William Jennings Bryan (D-POP-1896), 81.2	
Top PV %, Democrat	William Jennings Bryan (1896), 81.2
Top PV %, Republican	Ronald Reagan (1984), 65.8
Top PV %, third party	James Weaver (POP-1892), 66.8
Home-State Candidates	0
Results	0 nominees, 0 winners, 0 EV

New Hampshire

Winners	R 27, D 12, F 6, DR 4, NR 1	
General Match	37-13 74.0	
Convention Match	D 28-11 71.8	R 24-9 72.7
Primary Match	D 5-13 27.8	R 9-9 50.0
County Sweeps	14 (R 11, D 3)	

	PV %	EV
1789-1816	----	F 38, DR 15
1820-1852	DR/D 57.1, NR/W 37.1, other 5.8	D 38, DR 15, NR 8, other 1
1856-1900	R 54.7, D 43.6, other 1.7	R 55
1904-1928	R 56.2, D 39.5, other 4.3	R 20, D 8
1932-1956	R 53.8, D 45.7, other 0.5	R 16, D 12
1960-1984	R 56.1, D 40.6, other 3.3	R 24, D 4

Top PV %, one year	John Quincy Adams (DR-1824), 93.6
Top PV %, Democrat	Martin Van Buren (1836), 75.0
Top PV %, Republican	Ronald Reagan (1984), 68.7
Top PV %, third party	Theodore Roosevelt (P-1912), 20.2
Home-State Candidates	4 individuals, 5 qualified
Results	1 nominee, 1 winner, 254 EV

New Jersey

Winners	R 18, D 17, F 5, DR 5, W 4, NR 1	
General Match	36-14 72.0	
Convention Match	D 24-15 61.5	R 25-8 75.8
Primary Match	D 9-10 47.4	R 11-8 57.9
County Sweeps	4 (R 3, D 1)	

New Jersey (continued)

	PV %	EV
1789-1816	----	F 35, DR 24
1820-1852	DR/D 51.6, NR/W 47.9, other 0.6	W 30, DR 16, D 15, NR 8
1856-1900	R 50.0, D 47.0, other 3.1	D 70, R 33
1904-1928	R 57.4, D 35.6, other 7.0	R 80, D 14
1932-1956	R 51.7, D 46.7, other 1.5	D 64, R 48
1960-1984	R 50.7, D 45.8, other 3.6	R 84, D 33

Top PV %, one year	Warren Harding (R-1920), 67.7
Top PV %, Democrat	Lyndon Johnson (1964), 65.6
Top PV %, Republican	Warren Harding (1920), 67.7
Top PV %, third party	Theodore Roosevelt (P-1912), 33.6
Home-State Candidates	5 individuals, 8 qualified
Results	3 nominees, 2 winners, 754 EV

New Mexico

Winners	R 10, D 9	
General Match	18-1 94.7	
Convention Match	D 19-7 73.1	R 21-8 72.4
Primary Match	D 1-2 33.3	R 3-0 100.0
County Sweeps	0	

	PV %	EV
1904-1928	R 51.0, D 43.7, other 5.3	R 9, D 6
1932-1956	D 52.6, R 46.8, other 0.5	D 17, R 8
1960-1984	R 53.3, D 43.5, other 3.3	R 21, D 8

New Mexico (continued)

Top PV %, one year	Franklin Roosevelt (D-1932), 62.8
Top PV %, Democrat	Franklin Roosevelt (1932), 62.8
Top PV %, Republican	Richard Nixon (1972), 61.1
Top PV %, third party	Theodore Roosevelt (P-1912), 17.1
Home-State Candidates	0
Results	0 nominees, 0 winners, 0 EV

New York

Winners	R 20, D 17, DR 7, F 3, W 2		
General Match	42-7 85.7		
Convention Match	D 24-15 61.5	R 20-13 60.6	
Primary Match	D 2-2 50.0	R 0-2 0.0	
County Sweeps	3 (R 2, D 1)		

	PV %	EV
1789-1816	----	DR 73, F 53, oth 6
1820-1852	NR/W 47.7, DR/D 46.4, other 6.0	D 155, DR 85, W 78, NR 16
1856-1900	R 50.6, D 46.3, other 3.1	R 281, D 140
1904-1928	R 52.3, D 38.5, other 9.2	R 258, D 45
1932-1956	R 49.1, D 48.5, other 2.3	D 188, R 137
1960-1984	D 50.7, R 47.0, other 2.3	D 172, R 118

Top PV %, one year	Lyndon Johnson (D-1964), 68.6
Top PV %, Democrat	Lyndon Johnson (1964), 68.6
Top PV %, Republican	Warren Harding (1920), 64.6
Top PV %, third party	Martin Van Buren (FS-1848), 26.4
Home-State Candidates	38 individuals, 59 qualified
Results	24 nominees, 10 winners, 5,210 EV

North Carolina

Winners	D 27, DR 9, R 7, W 3, F 1, SD 1	
General Match	33-15 68.8	
Convention Match	D 23-15 60.5	R 21-9 70.0
Primary Match	D 3-1 75.0	R 2-2 50.0
County Sweeps	0	

	PV %	EV
1789-1816	----	DR 74, F 20
1820-1852	DR/D 56.1, NR/W 43.9, other 0.1	DR 45, D 40, W 37
1856-1900	D 49.2, R 43.2, other 7.6	D 85, R 19, oth 10
1904-1928	D 54.7, R 42.3, other 3.0	D 72, R 12
1932-1956	D 62.4, R 36.3, other 1.3	D 95
1960-1984	R 51.4, D 43.4, other 5.2	R 51, D 40, oth 1

Top PV %, one year	Andrew Jackson (D-1832), 84.8
Top PV %, Democrat	Andrew Jackson (1832), 84.8
Top PV %, Republican	Richard Nixon (1972), 69.5
Top PV %, third party	John Breckinridge (SD-1860), 50.5
Home-State Candidates	1 individual, 1 qualified
Results	0 nominees, 0 winners, 11 EV

North Dakota

Winners	R 18, D 5, tie (D, R, and POP) 1	
General Match	18-5-1 77.1	
Convention Match	D 21-5 80.8	R 19-11 63.3
Primary Match	D 3-4 42.9	R 2-5 28.6
County Sweeps	7 (R 5, D 2)	

North Dakota (continued)

	PV %	EV
1856-1900	R 56.4, D 29.2, other 14.4	R 7, D 1, oth 1
1904-1928	R 56.6, D 28.7, other 14.7	R 23, D 10
1932-1956	R 49.6, D 47.0, other 3.4	R 20, D 8
1960-1984	R 56.9, D 40.0, other 3.1	R 20, D 4

Top PV %, one year	Warren Harding (R-1920), 77.7
Top PV %, Democrat	Franklin Roosevelt (1932), 69.6
Top PV %, Republican	Warren Harding (1920), 77.7
Top PV %, third party	James Weaver (POP-1892), 49.0
Home-State Candidates	1 individual, 1 qualified
Results	0 nominees, 0 winners, 0 EV

Ohio

Winners	R 25, D 11, DR 7, W 3
General Match	37-9 80.4
Convention Match	D 26-13 66.7 R 23-10 69.7
Primary Match	D 6-13 31.6 R 8-11 42.1
County Sweeps	0

	PV %	EV
1789-1816	----	DR 21
1820-1852	DR/D 49.4, NR/W 46.4, other 4.2	D 67, W 65, DR 40
1856-1900	R 51.4, D 46.4, other 2.3	R 268, D 1
1904-1928	R 54.7, D 36.8, other 8.5	R 118, D 48
1932-1956	R 50.5, D 48.3, other 1.1	D 103, R 75
1960-1984	R 50.8, D 45.6, other 3.6	R 124, D 51

Ohio (continued)

Top PV %, one year	Herbert Hoover (R-1928), 64.9
Top PV %, Democrat	Lyndon Johnson (1964), 62.9
Top PV %, Republican	Herbert Hoover (1928), 64.9
Top PV %, third party	Theodore Roosevelt (P-1912), 22.2
Home-State Candidates	22 individuals, 31 qualified
Results	10 nominees, 7 winners, 2,129 EV

Oklahoma

Winners	D 10, R 10
General Match	16-4 80.0
Convention Match	D 15-9 62.5 R 19-5 79.2
Primary Match	never had primaries
County Sweeps	2 (D 1, R 1)

	PV %	EV
1904-1928	R 47.8, D 44.4, other 7.8	D 37, R 20
1932-1956	D 57.2, R 42.7, other 0.1	D 53, R 16
1960-1984	R 58.3, D 37.8, other 4.0	R 47, D 8, oth 1

Top PV %, one year	Richard Nixon (R-1972), 73.7
Top PV %, Democrat	Franklin Roosevelt (1932), 73.3
Top PV %, Republican	Richard Nixon (1972), 73.7
Top PV %, third party	George Wallace (AI-1968), 20.3
Home-State Candidates	2 individuals, 2 qualified
Results	0 nominees, 0 winners, 0 EV

Oregon

Winners	R 25, D 7	
General Match	25-7 78.1	
Convention Match	D 22-10 68.8	R 23-9 71.9
Primary Match	D 13-6 68.4	R 13-6 68.4
County Sweeps	6 (R 5, D 1)	

	PV %	EV
1856-1900	R 50.8, D 40.5, other 8.7	R 32, D 3, oth 1
1904-1928	R 54.0, D 33.3, other 12.7	R 28, D 5
1932-1956	D 49.5, R 48.4, other 2.1	D 21, R 18
1960-1984	R 49.4, D 46.0, other 4.6	R 37, D 6

Top PV %, one year	Theodore Roosevelt (R-1904), 67.3
Top PV %, Democrat	Franklin Roosevelt (1936), 64.4
Top PV %, Republican	Theodore Roosevelt (1904), 67.3
Top PV %, third party	John Breckinridge (SD-1860), 34.4
Home-State Candidates	1 individual, 1 qualified
Results	0 nominees, 0 winners, 0 EV

Pennsylvania

Winners	R 24, D 12, DR 9, F 2, W 2, P 1	
General Match	41-9 82.0	
Convention Match	D 29-10 74.4	R 21-12 63.6
Primary Match	D 12-6 66.7	R 9-9 50.0
County Sweeps	0	

Pennsylvania (continued)

	PV %	EV
1789-1816	----	DR 112, F 33
1820-1852	DR/D 53.0, NR/W 42.3, other 4.8	D 113, DR 80, W 56
1856-1900	R 53.9, D 41.3, other 4.8	R 322, D 27
1904-1928	R 59.5, D 30.3, other 10.2	R 220, other 38
1932-1956	R 49.6, D 49.1, other 1.3	R 135, D 107
1960-1984	D 48.9, R 48.1, other 3.0	D 117, R 79

Top PV %, one year	Andrew Jackson (DR-1824), 75.9
Top PV %, Democrat	Lyndon Johnson (1964), 64.9
Top PV %, Republican	Theodore Roosevelt (1904), 68.0
Top PV %, third party	William Wirt (AM-1832), 42.3
Home-State Candidates	14 individuals, 18 qualified
Results	3 nominees, 2 winners, 786 EV

Rhode Island

Winners	R 21, D 14, F 5, DR 4, W 3, NR 2
General Match	36-13 73.5
Convention Match	D 27-12 69.2 R 23-10 69.7
Primary Match	D 1-3 25.0 R 4-0 100.0
County Sweeps	25 (R 19, W 3, D 3)

	PV %	EV
1789-1816	----	F 20, DR 8
1820-1852	NR/W 53.2, DR/D 43.0, other 3.9	W 12, D 8, DR 8, NR 8
1856-1900	R 60.2, D 36.7, other 3.1	R 48
1904-1928	R 55.1, D 40.2, other 4.6	R 23, D 10
1932-1956	D 52.5, R 46.2, other 1.3	D 20, R 8
1960-1984	D 57.8, R 39.2, other 2.9	D 20, R 8

Rhode Island (continued)

Top PV %, one year	John Quincy Adams (DR-1824), 91.5
Top PV %, Democrat	Lyndon Johnson (1964), 80.9
Top PV %, Republican	Ulysses Grant (1872), 71.9
Top PV %, third party	Theodore Roosevelt (P-1912), 21.7
Home-State Candidates	0
Results	0 nominees, 0 winners, 0 EV

South Carolina

Winners	D 26, DR 9, R 8, F 2, SD 1, SRD 1, ID 1, IW 1
General Match	29-20 59.2
Convention Match	D 17-17 50.0 R 21-9 70.0
Primary Match	D never had primaries R 1-0 100.0
County Sweeps	12 (D 11, R 1)

	PV %	EV
1789-1816	----	DR 58, F 15
1820-1852	----	D 37, DR 33, ot 22
1856-1900	D 61.7, R 37.7, other 0.7	D 60, R 20, oth 8
1904-1928	D 95.0, R 4.2, other 0.8	D 63
1932-1956	D 61.8, R 21.7, other 16.5	D 48, other 8
1960-1984	R 53.5, D 41.2, other 5.3	R 40, D 16

Top PV %, one year	Franklin Roosevelt (D-1936), 98.6
Top PV %, Democrat	Franklin Roosevelt (1936), 98.6
Top PV %, Republican	Ulysses Grant (1872), 75.7
Top PV %, third party	Strom Thurmond (SRD-1948), 72.0
Home-State Candidates	2 individuals, 3 qualified
Results	2 nominees, 0 winners, 100 EV

South Dakota

Winners	R 19, D 4, P 1		
General Match	15-9 62.5		
Convention Match	D 18-8 69.2	R 19-11	63.3
Primary Match	D 7-12 36.8	R 3-15	16.7
County Sweeps	3 (R 3)		

	PV %	EV
1856-1900	R 52.3, D 36.0, other 11.7	R 8, D 4
1904-1928	R 51.7, D 30.3, other 18.0	R 28, other 5
1932-1956	R 53.1, D 45.9, other 1.0	R 20, D 8
1960-1984	R 55.0, D 42.9, other 2.0	R 23, D 4

Top PV %, one year	Theodore Roosevelt (R-1904), 71.1
Top PV %, Democrat	Franklin Roosevelt (1932), 63.6
Top PV %, Republican	Theodore Roosevelt (1904), 71.1
Top PV %, third party	Theodore Roosevelt (P-1912), 50.6
Home-State Candidates	1 individual, 2 qualified
Results	1 nominee, 0 winners, 17 EV

Tennessee

Winners	D 22, R 10, DR 9, W 5, CU 1		
General Match	31-16 66.0		
Convention Match	D 24-14 63.2	R 23-8	74.2
Primary Match	D 3-1 75.0	R 4-0	100.0
County Sweeps	0		

Tennessee (continued)

	PV %	EV
1789-1816	----	DR 32
1820-1852	DR/D 54.8, NR/W 45.2	W 68, DR 29, D 15
1856-1900	D 49.5, R 40.1, other 10.4	D 108, ot 12, R 10
1904-1928	D 51.1, R 44.9, other 4.0	D 60, R 24
1932-1956	D 56.5, R 41.0, other 2.6	D 56, R 22, oth 1
1960-1984	R 50.4, D 43.9, other 5.7	R 53, D 21

Top PV %, one year	Andrew Jackson (DR-1824), 97.5
Top PV %, Democrat	Andrew Jackson (1832), 95.4
Top PV %, Republican	Ulysses Grant (1868), 68.4
Top PV %, third party	Millard Fillmore (A-W-1856), 47.8
Home-State Candidates	7 individuals, 10 qualified
Results	5 nominees, 3 winners, 731 EV

Texas

Winners	D 26, R 6, SD 1	
General Match	20-13 60.6	
Convention Match	D 20-14 58.8	R 22-9 71.0
Primary Match	D 1-0 100.0	R 2-0 100.0
County Sweeps	2 (D 2)	

	PV %	EV
1820-1852	DR/D 71.2, NR/W 28.6, other 0.2	D 8
1856-1900	D 63.6, R 25.9, other 10.6	D 99, other 4
1904-1928	D 65.6, R 26.9, other 7.4	D 116, R 20
1932-1956	D 63.3, R 33.6, other 3.1	D 115, R 48
1960-1984	R 53.0, D 43.8, other 3.3	D 100, R 81

Texas (continued)

Top PV %, one year	Franklin Roosevelt (D-1932), 88.2
Top PV %, Democrat	Franklin Roosevelt (1932), 88.2
Top PV %, Republican	Richard Nixon (1972), 66.2
Top PV %, third party	John Breckinridge (SD-1860), 75.5
Home-State Candidates	3 individuals, 7 qualified
Results	1 nominee, 1 winner, 486 EV

Utah

Winners	R 15, D 8
General Match	19-4 82.6
Convention Match	D 20-6 76.9 R 21-8 72.4
Primary Match	never had primaries
County Sweeps	7 (R 6, D 1)

	PV %	EV
1856-1900	D 64.0, R 35.4, other 0.6	D 3, R 3
1904-1928	R 50.1, D 40.3, other 9.6	R 22, D 4
1932-1956	D 52.4, R 47.0, other 0.6	D 20, R 8
1960-1984	R 63.6, D 32.8, other 3.5	R 25, D 4

Top PV %, one year	William Jennings Bryan (D-POP-1896), 82.7
Top PV %, Democrat	William Jennings Bryan (1896), 82.7
Top PV %, Republican	Ronald Reagan (1984), 74.5
Top PV %, third party	Theodore Roosevelt (P-1912), 21.5
Home-State Candidates	0
Results	0 nominees, 0 winners, 0 EV

Vermont

Winners	R 32, DR 6, W 5, F 3, NR 1, AM 1, D 1
General Match	31-18 63.3
Convention Match	D 30-9 76.9	R 27-6 81.8
Primary Match	D 3-2 60.0	R 4-1 80.0
County Sweeps	23 (R 21, W 1, D 1)

	PV %	EV
1789-1816	----	DR 28, F 11
1820-1852	NR/W 55.2, DR/D 31.0, other 13.8	W 31, DR 15, NR 7, other 7
1856-1900	R 73.8, D 24.4, other 1.8	R 55
1904-1928	R 68.3, D 25.2, other 6.5	R 28
1932-1956	R 61.9, D 37.6, other 0.5	R 21
1960-1984	R 52.4, D 43.7, other 3.9	R 18, D 3

Top PV %, one year	William McKinley (R-1896), 80.1
Top PV %, Democrat	Lyndon Johnson (1964), 66.3
Top PV %, Republican	William McKinley (1896), 80.1
Top PV %, third party	William Wirt (AM-1832), 40.5
Home-State Candidates	1 individual, 2 qualified
Results	0 nominees, 0 winners, 0 EV

Virginia

Winners	D 26, R 10, DR 9, F 2, CU 1
General Match	32-16 66.7
Convention Match	D 20-17 54.1	R 23-8 74.2
Primary Match	never had primaries
County/City Sweeps	0

Virginia (continued)

	PV %	EV
1789-1816	----	DR 139, F 32
1820-1852	DR/D 57.5, NR/W 42.5	D 118, DR 73
1856-1900	D 51.4, R 38.8, other 9.7	D 97, oth 15, R 11
1904-1928	D 59.0, R 37.8, other 3.1	D 72, R 12
1932-1956	D 53.3, R 43.5, other 3.2	D 55, R 24
1960-1984	R 54.4, D 40.3, other 5.3	R 71, D 12, oth 1

Top PV %, one year	Andrew Jackson (D-1832), 75.0
Top PV %, Democrat	Andrew Jackson (1832), 75.0
Top PV %, Republican	Richard Nixon (1972), 67.8
Top PV %, third party	John Bell (CU-1860), 44.6
Home-State Candidates	7 individuals, 13 qualified
Results	9 nominees, 8 winners, 1,194 EV

Washington

Winners	R 14, D 9, P 1	
General Match	18-6 75.0	
Convention Match	D 19-7 73.1	R 21-8 72.4
Primary Match	never had primaries	
County Sweeps	5 (R 3, D 2)	

	PV %	EV
1856-1900	R 46.0, D 44.3, other 9.7	R 8, D 4
1904-1928	R 52.0, D 27.2, other 20.7	R 31, D 7, oth 7
1932-1956	D 53.2, R 44.2, other 2.6	D 40, R 18
1960-1984	R 50.0, D 45.3, other 4.8	R 45, D 18, oth 1

Washington (continued)

Top PV %, one year	Theodore Roosevelt (R-1904), 70.0
Top PV %, Democrat	Franklin Roosevelt (1936), 66.4
Top PV %, Republican	Theodore Roosevelt (1904), 70.0
Top PV %, third party	Robert La Follette (P-1924), 35.8
Home-State Candidates	1 individual, 2 qualified
Results	0 nominees, 0 winners, 0 EV

West Virginia

Winners	D 17, R 14		
General Match	24-7 77.4		
Convention Match	D 23-7 76.7	R 22-9 71.0
Primary Match	D 7-9 43.8	R 4-14 22.2
County Sweeps	0		

	PV %	EV
1856-1900	R 49.8, D 48.1, other 2.0	D 28, R 27
1904-1928	R 50.7, D 43.2, other 6.0	R 45, D 9
1932-1956	D 54.5, R 45.2, other 0.2	D 48, R 8
1960-1984	D 51.4, R 46.5, other 2.1	D 34, R 12

Top PV %, one year	Abraham Lincoln (R-1864), 68.2
Top PV %, Democrat	Lyndon Johnson (1964), 67.9
Top PV %, Republican	Abraham Lincoln (1864), 68.2
Top PV %, third party	Theodore Roosevelt (P-1912), 29.4
Home-State Candidates	1 individual, 2 qualified
Results	1 nominee, 0 winners, 136 EV

Wisconsin

Winners	R 24, D 10, P 1		
General Match	28-7 80.0		
Convention Match	D 27-8 77.1	R 19-14	57.6
Primary Match	D 11-8 57.9	R 7-12	36.8
County Sweeps	1 (R 1)		

	PV %	EV
1820-1852	DR/D 46.8, NR/W 34.6, other 18.5	D 9
1856-1900	R 54.1, D 42.7, other 3.2	R 102, D 12
1904-1928	R 51.9, D 29.7, other 18.4	R 65, D 13, oth 13
1932-1956	D 49.4, R 48.2, other 2.3	D 48, R 36
1960-1984	R 48.9, D 47.6, other 3.5	R 57, D 23

Top PV %, one year	Warren Harding (R-1920), 71.1
Top PV %, Democrat	Franklin Roosevelt (1936), 63.8
Top PV %, Republican	Warren Harding (1920), 71.1
Top PV %, third party	Robert La Follette (P-1924), 54.0
Home-State Candidates	3 individuals, 5 qualified
Results	0 nominees, 0 winners, 13 EV

Wyoming

Winners	R 16, D 8		
General Match	19-5 79.2		
Convention Match	D 19-7 73.1	R 24-5	82.8
Primary Match	never had primaries		
County Sweeps	7 (R 7)		

Wyoming (continued)

	PV %	EV
1856-1900	R 52.8, D 33.7, other 13.5	R 6, D 3
1904-1928	R 54.6, D 33.5, other 12.0	R 15, D 6
1932-1956	R 50.3, D 48.9, other 0.9	D 12, R 9
1960-1984	R 60.0, D 37.0, other 3.0	R 18, D 3

Top PV %, one year	Ronald Reagan (R-1984), 70.5
Top PV %, Democrat	Franklin Roosevelt (1936), 60.6
Top PV %, Republican	Ronald Reagan (1984), 70.5
Top PV %, third party	James Weaver (POP-1892), 46.2
Home-State Candidates	0
Results	0 nominees, 0 winners, 0 EV

Notes

CHAPTER 1. ALL REPUBLICANS, ALL FEDERALISTS: 1789-1816

1. Arthur Schlesinger Jr. and Fred Israel, eds., History of American Presidential Elections, 1789-1968, vol. 1 (New York: Chelsea House, 1971), 89.

2. Arthur Schlesinger Jr., ed., History of U.S. Political Parties, vol. 1 (New York: Chelsea House, 1973), xxxiv.

3. William Nisbet Chambers and Walter Dean Burnham, eds., The American Party Systems (New York: Oxford University Press, 1967), 64.

4. Dumas Malone, Jefferson The President: First Term, 1801-1805 (Boston: Little, Brown, and Co., 1970), 401.

5. Douglas Southall Freeman, George Washington: Volume 6 (New York: Charles Scribner's Sons, 1954), 153.

6. Ibid., 163.

7. Ibid., 154.

8. Ibid., 368-369.

9. John Alexander Carroll and Mary Wells Ashworth, George Washington: Volume 7 (New York: Charles Scribner's Sons, 1957), 362.

10. Ibid., 403.

11. Page Smith, John Adams (Garden City, N.Y.: Doubleday and Co., 1962), 880.

12. Ibid., 899.

13. Schlesinger and Israel, Elections, 1:101.

14. Ibid., 1:118.

15. Dumas Malone, Jefferson and the Ordeal of Liberty (Boston: Little, Brown, and Co., 1962), 500.

16. Malone, First Term, 395.

17. Schlesinger and Israel, Elections, 1:168.

18. Marvin Zahniser, Charles Cotesworth Pinckney, Founding Father (Chapel Hill, N.C.: University of North Carolina Press, 1967), 253.

19. Irving Brant, The Fourth President: A Life of James Madison (Indianapolis: Bobbs-Merrill, 1970), 525.

20. Chase Mooney, <u>William H. Crawford</u> (Lexington, Ky.: University Press of Kentucky, 1974), 217-218.
21. Paul Boller, <u>Presidential Campaigns</u> (New York: Oxford University Press, 1984), 30.
22. <u>Ibid.</u>, 30.

CHAPTER 2. THE COMING OF DEMOCRACY: 1820-1852

1. Schlesinger and Israel, <u>Elections</u>, 1:4.
2. Chambers and Burnham, <u>Party Systems</u>, 109.
3. Mooney, <u>Crawford</u>, 257-258.
4. Samuel Flagg Bemis, <u>John Quincy Adams and the Union</u> (New York: Alfred A. Knopf, 1965), 28.
5. Boller, <u>Campaigns</u>, 36.
6. Robert Remini, <u>Andrew Jackson and the Course of American Freedom</u> (New York: Harper and Row, 1981), 98.
7. <u>Ibid.</u>, 89.
8. Bemis, <u>Union</u>, 144.
9. <u>Ibid.</u>, 138.
10. <u>Ibid.</u>, 141.
11. Remini, <u>Freedom</u>, 366.
12. <u>Ibid.</u>, 367.
13. Boller, <u>Campaigns</u>, 57.
14. John Niven, <u>Martin Van Buren: The Romantic Age of American Politics</u> (New York: Oxford University Press, 1983), 397.
15. <u>Ibid.</u>, 390.
16. Schlesinger and Israel, <u>Elections</u>, 1:586.
17. <u>Ibid.</u>, 1:664.
18. Robert Gunderson, <u>The Log Cabin Campaign</u> (Lexington, Ky.: University of Kentucky Press, 1957), 185.
19. <u>Ibid.</u>, 126.
20. Robert Remini, <u>Andrew Jackson and the Course of American Democracy</u> (New York: Harper and Row, 1984), 500.
21. Niven, <u>Van Buren</u>, 532.
22. Oliver Perry Chitwood, <u>John Tyler: Champion of the Old South</u> (New York: Appleton-Century, 1939), 382.
23. Clement Eaton, <u>Henry Clay and the Art of American Politics</u> (Boston: Little, Brown, and Co., 1957), 179.
24. Schlesinger and Israel, <u>Elections</u>, 2:867.
25. Frank Woodford, <u>Lewis Cass: The Last Jeffersonian</u> (New Brunswick, N.J.: Rutgers University Press, 1950), 251.
26. Brainerd Dyer, <u>Zachary Taylor</u> (Baton Rouge, La.: Louisiana State University Press, 1946), 283.
27. Woodford, <u>Cass</u>, 270.
28. Robert Rayback, <u>Millard Fillmore</u> (Buffalo: Henry Stewart Publishing, 1959), 361.

CHAPTER 3.   WAVING THE BLOODY SHIRT: 1856-1900

1. Schlesinger, <u>Parties</u>, 2:1289.
2. Schlesinger and Israel, <u>Elections</u>, 2:1400.
3. Robert Johannsen, <u>Stephen A. Douglas</u> (New York: Oxford University Press, 1973), 434.
4. Philip Klein, <u>President James Buchanan</u> (University Park, Pa.: Pennsylvania State University Press, 1962), 257.
5. Allan Nevins, <u>Fremont, Pathmarker of the West</u> (New York: Frederick Ungar Publishing Co., 1939), 437.

6. J.G. Randall and David Donald, The Civil War and Reconstruction (Lexington, Massachusetts: D.C. Heath and Co., 1969), 124.

7. Klein, Buchanan, 340.

8. Gerald Capers, Stephen A. Douglas (Boston: Little, Brown, and Co., 1959), 203.

9. Sol Barzman, Madmen and Geniuses (Chicago: Follett, 1974), 100.

10. Schlesinger and Israel, Elections, 2:1101.

11. Benjamin Thomas, Abraham Lincoln (New York: Alfred A. Knopf, 1952), 202.

12. Boller, Campaigns, 109-110.

13. Randall and Donald, Civil War, 136.

14. Ibid., 149.

15. Boller, Campaigns, 115.

16. Schlesinger and Israel, Elections, 2:1170.

17. B. Thomas, Lincoln, 442.

18. Allan Nevins, The War for the Union (New York: Charles Scribner's Sons, 1971), 102.

19. Randall and Donald, Civil War, 527.

20. Charles Coleman, The Election of 1868 (New York: Columbia University Press, 1933), 87.

21. Ibid., 160.

22. Schlesinger and Israel, Elections, 2:1268.

23. William Hesseltine, Ulysses Grant, Politician (New York: Frederick Ungar Publishing Co., 1957), 120.

24. Ibid., 261.

25. Erik Lunde, Horace Greeley (Boston: Twayne, 1981), 108.

26. Schlesinger and Israel, Elections, 2:1316.

27. Ibid., 2:1317.

28. Hesseltine, Politician, 269.

29. Boller, Campaigns, 129.

30. Hesseltine, Politician, 377-378.

31. David Muzzey, James G. Blaine: A Political Idol of Other Days (New York: Dodd, Mead, and Co., 1934). 112.

32. Leonard Lurie, Party Politics (New York: Stein and Day, 1980), 126.

33. Alexander Flick, Samuel Jones Tilden (Port Washington, N.Y.: Kennikat Press, 1939), 410.

34. Allan Nevins, Grover Cleveland: A Study in Courage (New York: Dodd, Mead, and Co., 1933), 146.

35. H. Wayne Morgan, From Hayes to McKinley: National Party Politics, 1877-1896 (Syracuse, N.Y.: Syracuse University Press, 1969), 64.

36. Ibid., 65.

37. Ibid., 94.

38. Ibid., 117.

39. Allan Peskin, Garfield (Kent, Ohio: Kent State University Press, 1978), 596.

40. Boller, Campaigns, 149.

41. Nevins, Cleveland, 153.

42. David Jordan, Roscoe Conkling of New York (Ithaca, N.Y.: Cornell University Press, 1971), 421.

43. Boller, Campaigns, 146.

44. Nevins, Cleveland, 167.

45. Schlesinger and Israel, Elections, 2:1578.

46. Ibid., 2:1581.

47. Nevins, Cleveland, 380.

48. Harry Sievers, <u>Benjamin Harrison: Hoosier Statesman</u> (New York: University Publishers, 1959), 374.
49. <u>Ibid.</u>, 426.
50. Schlesinger and Israel, <u>Elections</u>, 2:1707.
51. Harry Sievers, <u>Benjamin Harrison: Hoosier President</u> (Indianapolis: Bobbs-Merrill, 1968), 218.
52. Schlesinger and Israel, <u>Elections</u>, 2:1716.
53. Nevins, <u>Cleveland</u>, 485.
54. Sievers, <u>President</u>, 244.
55. <u>Ibid.</u>, 244.
56. Nevins, <u>Cleveland</u>, 501.
57. Sievers, <u>President</u>, 250.
58. Boller, <u>Campaigns</u>, 170.
59. Stanley Jones, <u>The Presidential Election of 1896</u> (Madison, Wis.: University of Wisconsin Press, 1964), 56.
60. Schlesinger and Israel, <u>Elections</u>, 2:1795.
61. S. Jones, <u>1896</u>, 180.
62. Schlesinger and Israel, <u>Elections</u>, 2:1810.
63. Boller, <u>Campaigns</u>, 169.
64. Schlesinger and Israel, <u>Elections</u>, 2:1816.
65. S. Jones, <u>1896</u>, 314.
66. H.W. Morgan, <u>From Hayes</u>, 486.
67. Paul Glad, <u>The Trumpet Soundeth</u> (Lincoln, Neb.: University of Nebraska Press, 1960), 146.
68. Schlesinger and Israel, <u>Elections</u>, 3:1888.
69. Boller, <u>Campaigns</u>, 179.

CHAPTER 4.   THE ROAD TO NORMALCY: 1904-1928

1. Joseph Gardner, <u>Departing Glory</u> (New York: Charles Scribner's Sons, 1973), 38-39.
2. Glad, <u>Trumpet</u>, 150.
3. <u>Ibid.</u>, 153.
4. Henry Pringle, <u>Theodore Roosevelt</u> (New York: Harcourt, Brace, and Co., 1931), 347.
5. <u>Ibid.</u>, 355.
6. Schlesinger and Israel, <u>Elections</u>, 3:1992.
7. <u>Ibid.</u>, 3:2054.
8. <u>Ibid.</u>, 3:1994.
9. Donald Anderson, <u>William Howard Taft</u> (Ithaca, N.Y.: Cornell University Press, 1968), 4.
10. Pringle, <u>Roosevelt</u>, 502.
11. Glad, <u>Trumpet</u>, 164.
12. Anderson, <u>Taft</u>, 40.
13. Gardner, <u>Glory</u>, 233.
14. Schlesinger and Israel, <u>Elections</u>, 3:2153.
15. <u>Ibid.</u>, 3:2159.
16. Boller, <u>Campaigns</u>, 195.
17. Arthur Link, <u>Wilson: The Road to the White House</u> (Princeton, N.J.: Princeton University Press, 1947), 475.
18. Schlesinger and Israel, <u>Elections</u>, 3:2246.
19. Merlo Pusey, <u>Charles Evans Hughes</u> (New York: Macmillan, 1951), 316.
20. Arthur Link, <u>Wilson: Campaigns for Progressivism and Peace</u> (Princeton, N.J.: Princeton University Press, 1965), 111.
21. Schlesinger and Israel, <u>Elections</u>, 3:2258.
22. Gardner, <u>Glory</u>, 356.
23. Pusey, <u>Hughes</u>, 360.

24. Wesley Bagby, The Road to Normalcy (Baltimore: Johns Hopkins Press, 1962), 28.

25. Francis Russell, The Shadow of Blooming Grove (New York: McGraw-Hill, 1968), 314.

26. Boller, Campaigns, 213.

27. Schlesinger and Israel, Elections, 3:2372-2373.

28. Bagby, Normalcy, 138.

29. Ibid., 158.

30. William Allen White, A Puritan in Babylon (New York: Macmillan, 1939), 241.

31. Donald Young, American Roulette (New York: Holt, Rinehart, and Winston, 1972), 148.

32. Robert Murray, The 103rd Ballot (New York: Harper and Row, 1976), 44.

33. William Harbaugh, Lawyer's Lawyer (New York: Oxford University Press, 1973), 221.

34. Schlesinger and Israel, Elections, 3:2479-2480.

35. W.A. White, Puritan, 308.

36. Ibid., 360.

37. Herbert Hoover, The Memoirs of Herbert Hoover: The Cabinet and the Presidency (New York: Macmillan, 1952), 190.

38. Ibid., 193.

39. Schlesinger and Israel, Elections, 3:2601.

40. Matthew Josephson and Hannah Josephson, Al Smith: Hero of the Cities (London: Thames and Hudson, 1969), 386.

41. Edgar Eugene Robinson and Vaughn Bornet, Herbert Hoover, President of the United States (Stanford, Cal.: Hoover Institution Press, 1975), 20.

CHAPTER 5.   RENDEZVOUS WITH DESTINY: 1932-1956

1. Herbert Hoover, The Memoirs of Herbert Hoover: The Great Depression (New York: Macmillan, 1952), 343.

2. William Manchester, The Glory and the Dream (Boston: Little, Brown, and Co., 1973), 80.

3. Donald McCoy, Landon of Kansas (Lincoln, Neb.: University of Nebraska Press, 1966), 331.

4. Schlesinger and Israel, Elections, 4:2942.

5. Ibid., 3:2829.

6. Ibid., 4:3248.

7. Hoover, Depression, 218.

8. "Dark Forebodings Uttered by France," New York Times (June 14, 1932), 14.

9. Frank Freidel, Franklin D. Roosevelt: The Triumph (Boston: Little, Brown, and Co., 1956), 269.

10. Ibid., 308.

11. Ibid., 249.

12. Ibid., 366.

13. Boller, Campaigns, 235.

14. Hoover, Depression, 218.

15. James MacGregor Burns, Roosevelt: The Lion and the Fox (New York: Harcourt, Brace, and Co., 1956), 271.

16. Ibid., 266.

17. Marian McKenna, Borah (Ann Arbor, Mich.: University of Michigan Press, 1961), 327.

18. Current Biography 5 (February 1944): 33.

19. Schlesinger and Israel, Elections, 3:2818.

20. McCoy, Landon, 319.

21. Schlesinger and Israel, Elections, 3:2839.

22. Ibid., 3:2842.

23. Herbert Parmet and Marie Hecht, Never Again: A President Runs for a Third Term (New York: Macmillan, 1968), 122.

24. Ibid., 237.

25. Schlesinger and Israel, Elections, 4:2944.

26. Parmet and Hecht, Never, 251.

27. James MacGregor Burns, Roosevelt: The Soldier of Freedom (New York: Harcourt, Brace, Jovanovich, 1970), 497.

28. Edward Schapsmeier and Frederick Schapsmeier, Prophet in Politics: Henry A. Wallace and the War Years (Ames, Iowa: Iowa State University Press, 1970), 75.

29. Burns, Soldier, 506.

30. Robert Ferrell, Truman: A Centenary Remembrance (New York: Viking Press, 1984), 109.

31. Burns, Soldier, 499-500.

32. Ibid., 529.

33. Ibid., 523.

34. Ibid., 530.

35. Manchester, Glory, 354.

36. Richard Norton Smith, Thomas E. Dewey and His Times (New York: Simon and Schuster, 1982), 452.

37. Irwin Ross, The Loneliest Campaign (New York: New American Library, 1968), 148.

38. Ibid., 41.

39. Ibid., 125.

40. R.N. Smith, Dewey, 515.

41. Boller, Campaigns, 270.

42. Ross, Loneliest, 162.

43. Boller, Campaigns, 273.

44. James Patterson, Mr. Republican (Boston: Houghton Mifflin, 1972), 530.

45. R.N. Smith, Dewey, 593.

46. Schlesinger and Israel, Elections, 4:3217.

47. Joseph Gorman, Kefauver (New York: Oxford University Press, 1971), 143.

48. John Bartlow Martin, Adlai Stevenson of Illinois (Garden City, N.Y.: Doubleday and Co., 1976), 585.

49. Ibid., 759.

50. Gorman, Kefauver, 242.

51. Boller, Campaigns, 291.

52. John Bartlow Martin, Adlai Stevenson and the World (Garden City, N.Y.: Doubleday and Co., 1977), 375.

53. Ibid., 390.

CHAPTER 6. BEYOND THE NEW FRONTIER: 1960-1984

1. Public Papers of President John F. Kennedy, 1961 (Washington: U.S. Government Printing Office, 1962), 3.

2. Jack Germond and Jules Witcover, Blue Smoke and Mirrors (New York: Viking Press, 1981), 21.

3. Boller, Campaigns, 334.

4. Theodore White, The Making of the President, 1972 (New York: Atheneum, 1973), 178.

5. Janet Hook, "Reagan Defends Social Policy in `Fairness Issue´ Debate," Congressional Quarterly Weekly Report 42 (September 29, 1984): 2381.

6. Theodore White, The Making of the President, 1960 (New York: Mentor, 1967), 135.

7. Martin, World, 526.

8. T. White, 1960, 204.

9. Ibid., 344.

10. Richard Nixon, Six Crises (Garden City, N.Y.: Doubleday and Co., 1962), 339.

11. Boller, Campaigns, 298.

12. Schlesinger and Israel, Elections, 4:3469.

13. Ibid., 4:3571.

14. Robert Novak, The Agony of the GOP, 1964 (New York: Macmillan, 1965), 243.

15. Schlesinger and Israel, Elections, 4:3569.

16. Theodore White, The Making of the President, 1964, (New York: Atheneum, 1965), 201.

17. Schlesinger and Israel, Elections, 4:3669.

18. T. White, 1964, 266.

19. Ibid., 338.

20. Ibid., 377.

21. Eric Goldman, The Tragedy of Lyndon Johnson (New York: Alfred A. Knopf, 1969), 235.

22. Schlesinger and Israel, Elections, 4:3723.

23. Jules Witcover, 85 Days: The Last Campaign of Robert F. Kennedy (New York: Ace, 1969), 87.

24. Boller, Campaigns, 321.

25. Witcover, Days, 323.

26. Schlesinger and Israel, Elections, 4:3746.

27. Ibid., 4:3746.

28. George McGovern, Grassroots (New York: Random House, 1977), 157.

29. T. White, 1972, 82.

30. Ibid., 161.

31. McGovern, Grassroots, 186.

32. Boller, Campaigns, 343.

33. Congressional Quarterly Almanac, 1976 (Washington: Congressional Quarterly, Inc., 1976), 850.

34. Jules Witcover, Marathon (New York: Viking Press, 1977), 401.

35. Ibid., 431.

36. Ibid., 597.

37. Boller, Campaigns, 347.

38. Witcover, Marathon, 631.

39. Germond and Witcover, Blue Smoke, 88.

40. Boller, Campaigns, 360.

41. Ibid., 358.

42. Germond and Witcover, Blue Smoke, 244.

43. Ibid., 21.

44. "Campaign `84: The Inside Story," Newsweek 104 (November/December 1984 special issue): 39.

45. Ibid., 45.

46. Harrison Donnelly, "Democrats Launch the Mondale-Ferraro Team," Congressional Quarterly Weekly Report 42 (July 21, 1984): 1737.

47. "Campaign `84," 86.

48. "Reagan Accepts Presidential Nomination," Congressional Quarterly Weekly Report 42 (August 25, 1984): 2124.

49. Ibid., 2124.

50. "Campaign `84,", 109.

CHAPTER 7.   THE CANDIDATES

1. Dictionary of American Biography, vol. 1 (New York: Charles Scribner's Sons, 1927-1981), 81. [henceforth DAB]
2. Ibid., 1:77.
3. P. Smith, Adams, 835.
4. Bemis, Union, 99.
5. H.W. Morgan, From Hayes, 285.
6. Reginald McGrane, William Allen: A Study in Western Democracy (Columbus, Ohio: F.J. Neer, 1925), 85.
7. DAB, 1:221.
8. Walter Shapiro, "John Anderson: The Nice Guy Syndrome," Atlantic 245 (February 1980): 8.
9. Richard Whittle, "John Anderson Still Trying to Dump His `Spoiler´ Image," Congressional Quarterly Weekly Report 38 (September 27, 1980): 2833.
10. Current Biography Yearbook, 1973 (New York: H.W. Wilson Co., 1974), 20.
11. "The Ashbrook Rebellion," Newsweek 79 (January 17, 1972): 18.
12. DAB, supp. 6:36.
13. Reinhard Luthin, The First Lincoln Campaign (Gloucester, Mass.: Peter Smith, 1964), 51.
14. Charles Tansill, The Congressional Career of Thomas Francis Bayard (Washington: Georgetown University Press, 1946), 13.
15. Ibid., 244.
16. Joseph Parks, John Bell of Tennessee (Baton Rouge, La.: Louisiana State University Press, 1950), 296.
17. Ibid., 296.
18. Frederick Davenport, "The Pre-Nomination Campaign," Outlook 112 (April 12, 1916): 867.
19. Rockwell Hunt, John Bidwell, Prince of California Pioneers (Caldwell, Idaho: Caxton Printers, 1942), 122.
20. Betty Fladeland, James Gillespie Birney: Slaveholder to Abolitionist (Ithaca, N.Y.: Cornell University Press, 1955), 124.
21. Louis Koenig, "The Election That Got Away," American Heritage 11 (October 1960): 104.
22. Jordan, Conkling, 72.
23. Ibid., 421.
24. William Byars, An American Commoner (Columbia, Mo.: E.W. Stephens, 1900), 340.
25. McKenna, Borah, 211.
26. DAB, 3:9.
27. Ross Webb, Benjamin Helm Bristow: Border State Politician (Lexington, Ky.: University Press of Kentucky, 1969), 21.
28. Norma Peterson, Freedom and Franchise (Columbia, Mo.: University of Missouri Press, 1965), 123.
29. Current Biography Yearbook, 1975 (New York: H.W. Wilson Co., 1976), 50.
30. Robert Pack, Jerry Brown: The Philosopher-Prince (New York: Stein and Day, 1978), 119.
31. Louis Koenig, Bryan (New York: G.P. Putnam's Sons, 1971), 199.
32. Ibid., 199.
33. Ibid., 426.
34. Klein, Buchanan, 31-33.

35. Forrest Crissey, Theodore Burton, American Statesman (Cleveland: World Publishing, 1956), 225.
36. Nicholas King, George Bush (New York: Dodd, Mead, and Co., 1980), 84.
37. Albert Marrin, Nicholas Murray Butler (Boston: Twayne, 1976), 32-33.
38. J. Harvie Wilkinson III, Harry Byrd and the Changing Face of Virginia Politics (Charlottesville, Va.: University Press of Virginia, 1968), 153.
39. Ibid., 85-86.
40. Erwin Bradley, Simon Cameron, Lincoln's Secretary of War (Philadelphia: University of Pennsylvania Press, 1966), 423.
41. Blair Bolles, Tyrant from Illinois (New York: W.W. Norton and Co., 1951), 96.
42. James Wooten, Dasher (New York: Summit, 1978), 293.
43. Larry Light, "Carter's Style of Campaigning Provides Tough Competition," Congressional Quarterly Weekly Report 38 (September 13, 1980): 2707.
44. Wooten, Dasher, 301.
45. Woodford, Cass, 264.
46. Ibid., 264.
47. David Donald, ed., Inside Lincoln's Cabinet (New York: Longmans, Green, and Co., 1954), 19.
48. Coleman, 1868, 80.
49. Current Biography Yearbook, 1969 (New York: H.W. Wilson Co., 1970), 94.
50. Stephan Lesher, "The Short, Unhappy Life of Black Presidential Politics, 1972," New York Times Magazine (June 25, 1972): 13.
51. Carol Payne and Margaret Carpenter, Frank Church (Washington: Grossman Publishers, 1972), 7.
52. "The Man For the Democracy," New York Times (July 8, 1868): 4.
53. Champ Clark, My Quarter-Century of American Politics (New York: Harper and Brothers, 1920), 392.
54. Eaton, Clay, 171.
55. Ibid., 171.
56. Ibid., 171.
57. Richard Hofstadter, The American Political Tradition (New York: Vintage, 1974), 235.
58. Nevins, Cleveland, 153.
59. Boller, Campaigns, 157.
60. DAB, 4:227.
61. E. Wilder Spaulding, His Excellency George Clinton (New York: Macmillan, 1938), 173.
62. Francis Cockrell II, The Senator from Missouri (New York: Exposition Press, 1962), 66.
63. Jordan, Conkling, 432.
64. DAB, 4:346.
65. Ibid., supp. 1:195.
66. W.A. White, Puritan, 241, 419.
67. Mooney, Crawford, 26.
68. Ibid., 88.
69. Marvin Ewy, Charles Curtis of Kansas (Emporia, Kan.: Emporia State Research Studies, 1961), 28.
70. Schlesinger and Israel, Elections, 2:1115.
71. Willard King, Lincoln's Manager, David Davis (Cambridge, Mass.: Harvard University Press, 1960), 231.
72. DAB, supp. 5:156.

73. Harbaugh, Lawyer, 493.

74. Nick Salvatore, Eugene V. Debs, Citizen and Socialist (Urbana, Ill.: University of Illinois Press, 1982), 161.

75. Ibid., 292.

76. DAB, 5:245.

77. R.N. Smith, Dewey, 216.

78. Ibid., 545.

79. Richard Current, The History of Wisconsin: The Civil War Era (Madison, Wis.: State Historical Society of Wisconsin, 1976), 283.

80. DAB, 5:375.

81. Current, Wisconsin, 577.

82. Johannsen, Douglas, 23.

83. Ibid., 434.

84. Walter Crockett, George Franklin Edmunds (Burlington, Vt.: The Vermonter, 1919), 31.

85. Fred Greenstein, The Hidden-Hand Presidency (New York: Basic, 1982), 98.

86. William Manchester, American Caesar (Boston: Little, Brown, and Co., 1978), 166.

87. Greenstein, Hidden-Hand, 67.

88. Albert Van Dusen, Connecticut (New York: Random House, 1961), 243.

89. Current Biography 5 (September 1944): 20.

90. Carl Swisher, Stephen Field, Craftsman of the Law (Chicago: University of Chicago Press, 1969), 302.

91. Rayback, Fillmore, 187.

92. Young, Roulette, 61.

93. DAB, 6:413.

94. Alphonso Hopkins, The Life of Clinton Bowen Fisk (New York: Negro Universities Press, 1969), 104.

95. Matthew Andrews, Virginia: The Old Dominion (Richmond, Va.: Dietz Press, 1949), 425.

96. Current Biography Yearbook, 1975, 138.

97. Ibid., 138.

98. Reynold Wik, Henry Ford and Grassroots America (Ann Arbor, Mich.: University of Michigan Press, 1972), 176.

99. DAB, supp. 4:297.

100. "Ovation For Hoover is Session's Climax," New York Times (June 17, 1932): 12.

101. Nevins, Fremont, 704.

102. William DeGregorio, The Complete Book of U.S. Presidents (New York: Dembner Books, 1984), 304.

103. Peskin, Garfield, 354.

104. DeGregorio, Presidents, 303.

105. Marquis James, Mr. Garner of Texas (Indianapolis: Bobbs-Merrill, 1939), 113.

106. George Tindall, The Emergence of the New South, 1913-1945 (Baton Rouge, La.: Louisiana State University Press, 1967), 618.

107. George Wolfskill and John Hudson, All But the People (New York: Macmillan, 1969), 288-289.

108. Barry Goldwater, With No Apologies (New York: William Morrow and Co., 1979), 98.

109. Current Biography Yearbook, 1978 (New York: H.W. Wilson Co., 1979), 168.

110. John Lambert, Arthur Pue Gorman (Baton Rouge, La.: Louisiana State University Press, 1953), 193.

111. Ibid., 228.

112. Hesseltine, _Politician_, 41.
113. _Ibid._, 416.
114. "The Claims of the Candidates," _North American Review_ 187 (June 1908): 827.
115. _DAB_, 7:530.
116. Henry Stoddard, _Horace Greeley_ (New York: G.P. Putnam´s Sons, 1946), 290.
117. Robert Barrows and Shirley McCord, eds., _Their Infinite Variety: Essays on Indiana Politicians_ (Indianapolis: Indiana Historical Bureau, 1981), 225.
118. _Ibid._, 246.
119. _Ibid._, 227.
120. _DAB_, 8:105.
121. Almira Hancock, _Reminiscences of Winfield Scott Hancock_ (New York: Charles L. Webster and Co., 1887), 127.
122. Russell, _Grove_, 314.
123. _Ibid._, 559.
124. Arthur Schlesinger Jr., "Averell Remembers His Father," _American Heritage_ 33 (June/July 1982): 82.
125. Sievers, _Statesman_, 290.
126. James Green, _William Henry Harrison, His Life and Times_ (Richmond, Va.: Garrett and Massie, 1941), 292.
127. Tom Watson, "Hart Pushes `Third Options´ in Long-Shot Presidential Bid," _Congressional Quarterly Weekly Report_ 41 (December 3, 1983): 2535.
128. _Ibid._, 2539.
129. Tom Morganthau, "Battling For a Party´s Soul," _Newsweek_ 103 (April 9, 1984): 34.
130. Richard Bain and Judith Parris, _Convention Decisions and Voting Records_ (Washington: Brookings Institution, 1973), 102.
131. _DAB_, 8:448.
132. _Ibid._, supp. 5:284.
133. W.A. Swanberg, _Citizen Hearst_ (New York: Bantam, 1963), 450.
134. Barzman, _Madmen_, 144.
135. _Ibid._, 143.
136. DeAlva Alexander, _Four Famous New Yorkers_ (New York: Henry Holt and Co., 1923), 223.
137. Boller, _Campaigns_, 169.
138. David Burner, _Herbert Hoover_ (New York: Alfred A. Knopf, 1979), 151.
139. _Ibid._, 341.
140. John Hospers, _Libertarianism_ (Los Angeles: Nash, 1971), 5.
141. Pusey, _Hughes_, 786.
142. Carl Solberg, _Hubert Humphrey_ (New York: W.W. Norton and Co., 1984), 332.
143. Harrison Donnelly, "The ´Happy Warrior´: Hubert H. Humphrey," _Congressional Quarterly Weekly Report_ 36 (January 21, 1978): 109.
144. Charles Ambler, ed., _Correspondence of Robert M.T. Hunter_ (Washington: American Historical Association, 1918), 337.
145. _Ibid._, 340.
146. Marquis James, _The Life of Andrew Jackson_ (Indianapolis: Bobbs-Merrill, 1938), 621.
147. Remini, _Freedom_, 231.

148. Harrison Donnelly, "The Jackson Mystique: Emotion, Ambition," Congressional Quarterly Weekly Report 42 (January 7, 1984): 9.

149. Burtt Evans and Samuel Botsford, "Pennsylvania After the New Deal," New Republic 102 (May 6, 1940): 601.

150. DeGregorio, Presidents, 52.

151. Malone, First Term, 22.

152. Charles Jones, The Life and Services of Charles Jones Jenkins (Atlanta: James P. Harrison and Co., 1884), 24.

153. Ibid., 45.

154. Fay Brabson, Andrew Johnson (Durham, N.C.: Seeman, 1972), 60.

155. Ibid., 185.

156. Spencer Olin, California's Prodigal Sons (Berkeley, Cal.: University of California Press, 1968), 97.

157. Winifred Helmes, John A. Johnson, the People's Governor (Minneapolis: University of Minnesota Press, 1949), 168.

158. Merle Miller, Lyndon: An Oral Biography (New York: G.P. Putnam's Sons, 1980), 38.

159. Ibid., 156.

160. Leland Meyer, The Life and Times of Colonel Richard M. Johnson of Kentucky (New York: Columbia University Press, 1932), 458.

161. Barzman, Madmen, 69.

162. "Alabama Elector Quits Stevenson," New York Times (December 18, 1956): 34.

163. DAB, supp. 7:415.

164. Gorman, Kefauver, 237.

165. Current Biography Yearbook, 1978, 226.

166. Theo Lippman Jr., Senator Ted Kennedy (New York: W.W. Norton and Co., 1976), 274.

167. DAB, supp. 7:419.

168. Public Papers of President John F. Kennedy, 1962 (Washington: U.S. Government Printing Office, 1963), 492.

169. James MacGregor Burns, John Kennedy (New York: Harcourt, Brace, and World, 1961), 153.

170. Arthur Schlesinger Jr., A Thousand Days (Boston: Houghton Mifflin, 1965), 142.

171. Witcover, Days, 161, 194.

172. Anne Hodges Morgan, Robert S. Kerr: The Senate Years (Norman, Okla.: University of Oklahoma Press, 1977), 241.

173. Ibid., 240.

174. DAB, 10:400.

175. Robert Ernst, Rufus King, American Federalist (Chapel Hill, N.C.: University of North Carolina Press, 1968), 407.

176. Richard O'Connor, "`Black Jack´ of the 10th," American Heritage 18 (February 1967): 106.

177. Lawrence Levine, "The `Diary´ of Hiram Johnson," American Heritage 20 (August 1969): 67.

178. Robert La Follette, A Personal Narrative of Political Experiences (Madison, Wis.: La Follette Co., 1913), 760.

179. McCoy, Landon, 343.

180. Schlesinger and Israel, Elections, 3:2841.

181. James Hendrickson, Joe Lane of Oregon (New Haven, Conn.: Yale University Press, 1967), 137.

182. Ibid., 243.

183. "Declaration of Independents," _Time_ 67 (May 14, 1956): 31.

184. David Bennett, _Demagogues in the Depression_ (New Brunswick, N.J.: Rutgers University Press, 1969), 85.

185. _Ibid.,_ 93.

186. B. Thomas, _Lincoln_, 153.

187. _Ibid._, 206.

188. _Ibid._, 182.

189. William Miller, _Henry Cabot Lodge_ (New York: James H. Heineman Publishers, 1967), 355.

190. Manchester, _Caesar_, 309.

191. _Ibid._, 483.

192. Brant, _Madison_, 197.

193. _Ibid._, 279.

194. Henry Shanks, ed., _The Papers of Willie Person Mangum, Volume 1_ (Raleigh, N.C.: North Carolina Department of Archives and History, 1950), xxix.

195. Ivor Spencer, _The Victor and the Spoils_ (Providence: Brown University Press, 1959), 1.

196. _Ibid._, 194.

197. Gilbert Bailey, "Field Study in American Politics," _New York Times Magazine_ (September 28, 1947): 7.

198. _DAB_, supp. 3:482.

199. Richard Stout, _People_ (New York: Harper and Row, 1970), 97.

200. _Current Biography Yearbook, 1955_ (New York: H.W. Wilson Co., 1956), 377.

201. Bruce Catton, _Mr. Lincoln's Army_ (Garden City, N.Y.: Doubleday and Co., 1951), 56.

202. _Ibid._, 53.

203. Liz Mauer, "George McGovern: Once More for the Message," _Congressional Quarterly Weekly Report_ 41 (December 24, 1983): 2743.

204. Lewis Gould, _The Presidency of William McKinley_ (Lawrence, Kan.: The Regents Press of Kansas, 1980), 6.

205. Chalmers Roberts, _The Washington Post: The First 100 Years_ (Boston: Houghton Mifflin, 1977), 84.

206. Tom Watson, "Liberal, Pragmatic Mondale Follows Careful Path to Power," _Congressional Quarterly Weekly Report_ 41 (October 8, 1983): 2077.

207. _Ibid._, 2079.

208. Bernard Weinraub, "Mondale Farewell," New York _Times_ (November 8, 1984): 24.

209. Watson, "Mondale," 2083.

210. William Cresson, _James Monroe_ (Chapel Hill, N.C.: University of North Carolina Press, 1946), 115.

211. _DAB_, 13:233.

212. H.W. Morgan, _From Hayes_, 184.

213. Schlesinger, _Parties_, 2:886.

214. Keith Bryant, _Alfalfa Bill Murray_ (Norman, Okla.: University of Oklahoma Press, 1968), 184.

215. _Current Biography Yearbook, 1968_ (New York: H.W. Wilson Co., 1969), 277.

216. John Nielsen, "The Muskie Manner," _Newsweek_ 95 (May 26, 1980): 45.

217. Manchester, _Glory_, 394-395.

218. Merle Miller, _Plain Speaking_ (New York: G.P. Putnam's Sons, 1974), 135.

219. _Current Biography Yearbook, 1969_, 306.

220. Richard Lowitt, George W. Norris: The Persistence of a Progressive (Urbana, Ill.: University of Illinois Press, 1971), 400.

221. DAB, supp. 3:561.

222. Stanley Coben, A. Mitchell Palmer: Politician (New York: Columbia University Press, 1963), 198.

223. Irving Stone, They Also Ran (Garden City, N.Y.: Doubleday, Doran, and Co., 1943), 87.

224. James Yard, Joel Parker (Trenton, N.J.: New Jersey Historical Society, 1888), 15.

225. Leon Wolff, "Battle at Homestead," American Heritage 16 (April 1965): 72.

226. Louis Koenig, "The Most Unpopular Man in the North," American Heritage 15 (February 1964): 88.

227. Roy Nichols, Franklin Pierce (Philadelphia: University of Pennsylvania Press, 1931), 106.

228. Zahniser, Pinckney, 170.

229. Charles Sellers, James K. Polk, Jacksonian (Princeton, N.J.: Princeton University Press, 1957), 277.

230. Ibid., 492.

231. James Kehl, Boss Rule in the Gilded Age (Pittsburgh: University of Pittsburgh Press, 1981), 60.

232. Ibid., 126.

233. H.W. Morgan, From Hayes, 81.

234. Ibid., 189.

235. Christopher Buchanan, "Reagan Melds Acting Ability With His Prowess in Politics," Congressional Quarterly Weekly Report 38 (September 20, 1980): 2764.

236. Bill Boyarsky, Ronald Reagan (New York: Random House, 1981), 34.

237. DAB, supp. 3:622.

238. Charles Ross, "Reed of Missouri," Scribner's 83 (February 1928): 157.

239. Barbara Tuchman, "Czar of the House," American Heritage 14 (December 1962): 33.

240. Ibid., 98.

241. Current Biography Yearbook, 1976 (New York: H.W. Wilson Co., 1977), 337.

242. David Hess, "The Decline of Ohio," Nation 210 (April 13, 1970): 430.

243. Scott Thomas, "Will A New Yorker Ever Be President Again?" Empire State Report 10 (March 1984): 26.

244. Burns, Lion, 474.

245. Freidel, Triumph, 249.

246. Manchester, Glory, 355.

247. DAB, 16:137.

248. Ibid., 16:138.

249. Richard Leopold, Elihu Root and the Conservative Tradition (Boston: Little, Brown, and Co., 1954), 186.

250. Ibid., 94.

251. Harry Truman, Memoirs: Years of Trial and Hope (Garden City, N.Y.: Doubleday and Co., 1956), 494.

252. Arthur Smith, Old Fuss and Feathers (New York: Greystone Press, 1937), 244.

253. Glyndon Van Deusen, William Henry Seward (New York: Oxford University Press, 1967), 123.

254. Ibid., 221.

255. Clarence Stern, Golden Republicanism (Ann Arbor, Mich.: Edward Brothers, 1964), 2-3.

256. Ibid., 3.

257. Josephson and Josephson, Smith, 383.
258. Ibid., 87-88.
259. Ibid., 457.
260. Bernard Weinraub, "1968 Nomination?" Esquire 68 (August 1967): 98.
261. Ibid., 97.
262. Martin, Illinois, 641-642.
263. Martin, World, 549.
264. Patterson, Republican, 614.
265. Ibid., 343.
266. Anderson, Taft, 4.
267. DeGregorio, Presidents, 398.
268. Current Biography Yearbook, 1962 (New York: H.W. Wilson Co., 1963), 417.
269. Ibid., 419.
270. Sarah McCulloh Lemmon, "The Ideology of the Dixiecrat Movement," Social Forces 30 (December 1951): 164.
271. Public Papers of President Harry S. Truman, 1950 (Washington: U.S. Government Printing Office, 1965), 485.
272. Stone, Also Ran, 209.
273. Ferrell, Truman, 80, 100.
274. Witcover, Marathon, 286.
275. Evans Johnson, Oscar W. Underwood (Baton Rouge, La.: Louisiana State University Press, 1980), 172.
276. Ibid., 399.
277. S. Thomas, "New Yorker," 28.
278. C. David Tompkins, Senator Arthur H. Vandenberg: The Evolution of a Modern Republican (East Lansing, Mich.: Michigan State University Press, 1970), 161.
279. Ibid., 171.
280. Current Biography Yearbook, 1963 (New York: H.W. Wilson Co., 1964), 454.
281. Jody Carlson, George C. Wallace and the Politics of Powerlessness (New Brunswick, N.J.: Transaction, 1981), 174.
282. Schapsmeier and Schapsmeier, War Years, 76.
283. Edward Schapsmeier and Frederick Schapsmeier, Henry A. Wallace of Iowa: The Agrarian Years (Ames, Iowa: Iowa State University Press, 1968), 264.
284. Josephine O´Keane, Thomas J. Walsh (Francestown, N.H.: Marshall Jones Co., 1955), 146.
285. Ibid., 143.
286. Manchester, Glory, 737.
287. DAB, 19:522.
288. Freeman, Washington, 27.
289. Boller, Campaigns, 255.
290. Fred Haynes, James Baird Weaver (Iowa City, Iowa: State Historical Society of Iowa, 1919), 93-94.
291. Ibid., 438.
292. Robert Dalzell, Daniel Webster and the Trial of American Nationalism (Boston: Houghton Mifflin, 1973), 18.
293. DAB, 19:589.
294. Rayback, Fillmore, 361.
295. Charles Washburn, The Life of John W. Weeks (Boston: Houghton Mifflin, 1928), 203.
296. L. Paul Gresham, The Public Career of Hugh Lawson White (Nashville, Tenn.: Joint Universities Libraries, 1945), 6.
297. Donald Johnson, The Republican Party and Wendell Willkie (Westport, Conn.: Greenwood Press, 1960), 51.
298. Link, Road, 6.

299. Ibid., 91.
300. Horace Hagan, Eight Great American Lawyers (Oklahoma City: Harlow, 1923), 74.
301. Jack Lane, Armed Progressive (San Rafael, Cal.: Presidio Press, 1978), 188.
302. DAB, 20:489.

CHAPTER 8. THE PARTIES

1. Schlesinger, Parties, 4:3432.
2. Schlesinger and Israel, Elections, 2:1082.
3. Ibid., 1:537.
4. National Party Conventions, 1831-1976 (Washington: Congressional Quarterly, Inc., 1979), 37.
5. Schlesinger, Parties, 1:557.
6. Tindall, Emergence, 611.
7. Manchester, Glory, 317-318.
8. Watson, "Hart," 2535.
9. Schlesinger, Parties, 1:285.
10. Ibid., 1:241.
11. Boller, Campaigns, 31.
12. George Dangerfield, Era of Good Feelings (New York: Harcourt, Brace, and World, 1952), 99-100.
13. Schlesinger and Israel, Elections, 1:301.
14. Ibid., 2:903.
15. Ibid., 2:1523.
16. Schlesinger, Parties, 2:1283.
17. Anne Groer, "Libertarian Lark," New Republic 189 (October 3, 1983): 16.
18. Schlesinger and Israel, Elections, 1:801.
19. Ibid., 1:415.
20. Warren Weaver Jr., "Anderson Says Goals of Campaign `Must Not and Will Not End for Me,´" New York Times (November 5, 1980): 21.
21. Schlesinger, Parties, 2:1712.
22. Schlesinger and Israel, Elections, 2:1779.
23. Ibid., 3:2543.
24. Ibid., 3:2153.
25. Ibid., 3:2220.
26. Schlesinger, Parties, 4:3313.
27. Ibid., 4:3311.
28. Ibid., 4:3321.
29. Schlesinger and Israel, Elections, 2:1523-1524.
30. Schlesinger, Parties, 2:886.
31. Ibid., 3:2121.
32. Schlesinger and Israel, Elections, 3:2239.
33. Barzman, Madmen, 100.
34. Lemmon, "Dixiecrat," 168.
35. Schlesinger, Parties, 4:3319.
36. Schlesinger and Israel, Elections, 3:2871.
37. Ibid., 1:743.
38. Ibid., 2:913.

CHAPTER 9. THE STATES

1. Sheldon Hackney, Populism to Progressivism in Alabama (Princeton, N.J.: Princeton University Press, 1969), 179.

2. Ernest Gruening, The Battle for Alaska Statehood (College, Alas.: University of Alaska Press, 1967), 40.

3. Harry Ashmore, Arkansas (New York: W.W. Norton and Co., 1978), 194.

4. Robert Glass Cleland, From Wilderness to Empire (New York: Alfred A. Knopf, 1970), 249.

5. Ibid., 250.

6. James Wright, The Politics of Populism (New Haven, Conn.: Yale University Press, 1974), 207.

7. John Jeffries, Testing the Roosevelt Coalition (Knoxville, Tenn.: University of Tennessee Press, 1979), 35.

8. James Phelan and Robert Pozen, The Company State (New York: Grossman Publishers, 1973), 308.

9. A. Wigfall Green, The Man Bilbo (Baton Rouge, La.: Louisiana State University Press, 1963), 105, 123.

10. William Belvin Jr., "The Georgia Gubernatorial Primary of 1946," Georgia Historical Quarterly 50 (March 1966): 42-44.

11. Congressional Record (86th Congress, 1st Session), 3870.

12. William Wilson, Indiana: A History (Bloomington, Ind.: Indiana University Press, 1977), 204.

13. Neal Peirce and Jerry Hagstrom, The Book of America (New York: W.W. Norton and Co., 1983), 573.

14. Ross, Loneliest, 182-183.

15. McCoy, Landon, 118.

16. T. Harry Williams, Huey Long (New York: Alfred A. Knopf, 1969), 760-762.

17. Michael Barone, Grant Ujifusa, and Douglas Matthews, The Almanac of American Politics, 1980 (New York: E.P. Dutton, 1979), 363.

18. Richard Walsh and William Lloyd Fox, Maryland: A History, 1632-1974 (Baltimore: Maryland Historical Society, 1974), 880.

19. James Banner, To the Hartford Convention (New York: Alfred A. Knopf, 1970), 42.

20. Wik, Ford, 12.

21. Theodore Blegen, Minnesota (Saint Paul: University of Minnesota Press, 1975), 288.

22. Manchester, Glory, 101-102.

23. James Silver, Mississippi: The Closed Society (New York: Harcourt, Brace, and World, 1963), 46.

24. Peirce and Hagstrom, America, 458.

25. William Blair, "Missouri's Trend to GOP Watched," New York Times (March 21, 1948): 35.

26. Michael Malone and Richard Roeder, Montana: A History of Two Centuries (Seattle: University of Washington Press, 1976), 75.

27. Schlesinger and Israel, Elections, 2:1810.

28. Charles McDowell Jr., Campaign Fever (New York: William Morrow and Co., 1965), 1.

29. Thomas Fleming, New Jersey (New York: W.W. Norton and Co., 1977), 108.

30. Warren Beck, New Mexico: A History of Four Centuries (Norman, Okla.: University of Oklahoma Press, 1962), 231.

31. David Ellis, New York: State and City (Ithaca, N.Y.: Cornell University Press, 1979), 200.

32. R.N. Smith, Dewey, 598.

33. Hugh Lefler and Albert Newsome, <u>North Carolina: The History of a Southern State</u> (Chapel Hill, N.C.: University of North Carolina Press, 1973), 314.

34. Andrew Bruce, <u>Non-Partisan League</u> (New York: Macmillan, 1921), 23-24.

35. Walter Havighurst, <u>Ohio</u> (New York: W.W. Norton and Co., 1976), 179.

36. <u>Ibid.</u>, 178.

37. H. Wayne Morgan and Anne Hodges Morgan, <u>Oklahoma</u> (New York: W.W. Norton and Co., 1977), 96.

38. <u>Ibid.</u>, 145.

39. Witcover, <u>Days</u>, 202.

40. Hofstadter, <u>Tradition</u>, 101.

41. William Guess, <u>South Carolina: Annals of Pride and Protest</u> (New York: Harper and Brothers, 1957), 266.

42. "Senator Thurmond: Now He's A Republican," <u>U.S. News and World Report</u> 57 (September 28, 1964): 83.

43. Stanley Folmsbee, Robert Corlew, and Enoch Mitchell, <u>Tennessee: A Short History</u> (Knoxville, Tenn.: University of Tennessee Press, 1969), 435.

44. Seymour Connor, <u>Texas: A History</u> (Arlington Heights, Ill.: AHM Publishing, 1971) 361-362.

45. Charles Peterson, <u>Utah</u> (New York: W.W. Norton and Co., 1977), 163.

46. Schlesinger and Israel, <u>Elections</u>, 1:304.

47. Virginius Dabney, <u>Virginia: The New Dominion</u> (Garden City, N.Y.: Doubleday and Co., 1971), 581.

48. John Gunther, <u>Inside U.S.A.</u> (New York: Harper and Brothers, 1946), 87.

49. Charles Ambler, <u>West Virginia: The Mountain State</u> (New York: Prentice-Hall, 1940), 391.

50. David Thelan, <u>Robert M. La Follette and the Insurgent Spirit</u> (Boston: Little, Brown, and Co., 1976), 39.

51. Taft Larson, <u>History of Wyoming</u> (Lincoln, Neb.: University of Nebraska Press, 1965), 540.

52. <u>Ibid.</u>, 498.

Selected Bibliography

Bain, Richard and Judith Parris. Convention Decisions and
     Voting Records. Washington: Brookings Institution, 1973.
Barzman, Sol. Madmen and Geniuses. Chicago: Follett, 1974.
Biographical Directory of the American Congress, 1774-1971.
     Washington: U.S. Government Printing Office, 1971.
Boller, Paul. Presidential Campaigns. New York: Oxford
     University Press, 1984.
Burnham, W. Dean. Presidential Ballots, 1836-1892.
     Baltimore: Johns Hopkins Press, 1955.
Chambers, William Nisbet and Walter Dean Burnham, eds. The
     American Party Systems. New York: Oxford University
     Press, 1967.
DeGregorio, William. The Complete Book of U.S. Presidents.
     New York: Dembner Books, 1984.
Dictionary of American Biography, 28 vols. New York: Charles
     Scribner's Sons, 1927-1981.
Gunther, John. Inside U.S.A. New York: Harper and Brothers,
     1946.
Hofstadter, Richard. The American Political Tradition. New
     York: Vintage, 1974.
Peirce, Neal and Jerry Hagstrom. The Book of America. New
     York: W.W. Norton and Co., 1983.
Petersen, Svend. A Statistical History of the American
     Presidential Elections. New York: Frederick Ungar
     Publishing Co., 1963.
Robinson, Edgar Eugene. The Presidential Vote, 1896-1932.
     New York: Octagon, 1970.
Runyon, John, Jennefer Verdini, and Sally Runyon. Source
     Book of American Presidential Campaign and Election
     Statistics, 1948-1968. New York: Frederick Ungar
     Publishing Co., 1971.
Russotto, Patricia, ed. National Party Conventions,
     1831-1980. Washington: Congressional Quarterly, Inc.,
     1983.
Scammon, Richard, ed. America at the Polls: A Handbook of
     American Presidential Election Statistics, 1920-1964.
     Pittsburgh: University of Pittsburgh Press, 1965.

476   SELECTED BIBLIOGRAPHY

_____ and Alice McGillivray, eds. America Votes, 16
     vols. Washington: Congressional Quarterly, Inc.,
     1956-1985.
Schlesinger, Arthur Jr., ed. History of U.S. Political
     Parties, 4 vols. New York: Chelsea House, 1973.
_____ and Fred Israel, eds. History of American
     Presidential Elections, 1789-1968, 4 vols. New
     York: Chelsea House, 1971.
Stone, Irving. They Also Ran. Garden City, N.Y.: Doubleday,
     Doran, and Co., 1943.
Thompson, Margaret, ed. Presidential Elections Since 1789.
     Washington: Congressional Quarterly, Inc., 1983.
U.S. Department of Commerce, Bureau of the Census. Historical
     Statistics of the United States, Colonial Times to
     1970. Washington: U.S. Government Printing Office, 1975.
Young, Donald. American Roulette. New York: Holt, Rinehart,
     and Winston, 1972.

Index

ABOUT THE AUTHOR

G. SCOTT THOMAS is Anchor-Producer of WEBR Newsradio in Buffalo, New York. An experienced political analyst, he is a Contributing Editor for *Empire State Report*, a New York political journal.